# THE DIE-HARDS IN THE GREAT WAR

A 2

## MILITARY HISTORIES BY EVERARD WYRALL

**THE HISTORY OF THE SECOND DIVISION, 1914–1918**
(two vols.)

**THE WEST YORKSHIRE REGT. IN THE WAR, 1914–1918**
(two vols.)

**THE HISTORY OF THE 62nd ⟨W.R.⟩ DIVISION, 1914–1919**
(two vols.)

**THE SOMERSET LIGHT INFANTRY⟨PRINCE ALBERT'S⟩ IN THE WAR, 1914–1919**
(one vol.) [*shortly*]

**THE EAST YORKSHIRE REGT. IN THE WAR, 1914–1918**
(one vol.) [*shortly*]

**The KING'S REGT.⟨LIVERPOOL⟩ IN THE WAR, 1914–1919**
(three vols.) [*shortly*]

**THE 30th ⟨HOW.⟩ BATTERY, 1914–1918**
(one vol.) [*shortly*]

# THE DIE-HARDS IN THE GREAT WAR

A HISTORY OF THE DUKE OF CAMBRIDGE'S OWN (MIDDLESEX REGIMENT), 1914–1919, COMPILED FROM THE RECORDS OF THE LINE, SPECIAL RESERVE, SERVICE, AND TERRITORIAL BATTALIONS


BY

EVERARD WYRALL

AUTHOR OF "THE HISTORY OF THE SECOND DIVISION, 1914–1918"; "THE WEST YORKSHIRE REGIMENT IN THE WAR, 1914–1918"; "THE HISTORY OF THE 62nd (W.R.) DIVISION, 1914–1919," Etc., Etc., Etc.


VOL. I. 1914–1916


LONDON:

HARRISON & SONS, LTD., 45, ST. MARTIN'S LANE, W.C.2.

Printed and bound by Antony Rowe Ltd, Eastbourne

" Mysore," " Seringapatam," " Albuhera,"
" Ciudad Rodrigo," " Badajoz," " Vittoria,"
" Pyrenees," " Nivelle," " Nive,"
" Peninsula," " Alma," " Inkerman,"
" Sevastopol," " New Zealand,"
" South Africa, 1879," " Relief
of Ladysmith," " South Africa,
1900–1902"

# AUTHOR'S ACKNOWLEDGMENTS.

I should like to offer my grateful thanks to Capt. H. E. Foster and those officers of the Middlesex Regiment forming the Reading Committee, who read the manuscript of this History before it went into print, for their invaluable assistance; also to those who have so kindly lent diaries, documents and maps; to whom also the Regiment owes a debt of gratitude.

I should also like to thank Brig.-General J. E. Edmonds, C.B., C.M.G., Director of the Historical Section (Military Branch) of the Committee of Imperial Defence and his Staff for much valuable aid, without which it would have been impossible to write a regimental History of this magnitude.

EVERARD WYRALL.

AUTHORS' CLUB.

# CONTENTS

# LIST OF MAPS

" Die hard, 57th. Die hard."

Colonel Inglis, Commanding 57th Foot, at Albuhera, 16th May, 1811. (P. 3.)

" Men, we can only die once: if we have to die, let us die like men—like Die-Hards." (P. 169.)

2/Lieut. R. P. Hallowes, V.C., 4th Bn. Middlesex Regt., killed at Bellewaarde Ridge, 30th September, 1915.

# FOREWORD.

By General Sir Ivor Maxse, K.C.B., C.V.O., D.S.O.,
Colonel of the Middlesex Regiment.

THE memorials of our wars usually take the form of a stone, granite, marble, brass or bronze erection, and make their appeal to the mind through the eyes. Probably the most effective of them all is the Artillery monument near Hyde Park Corner, because it emphasizes real gunning in a gunners' war. But solid memorials suffer from the disadvantage of being immovable, and some of them do not remind us even remotely of war. They partake rather of the nature of tombstones with their inscriptions to the fallen, and those which are placed out in the open can scarcely be expected to outlast a single generation, owing to the cheap soft stone employed by their architects.

Our own at Mill Hill Barracks is solid and enduring, but will the Regiment's Depot always be quartered there? And even if it is how many officers and men of our Territorial battalions have seen the memorial or will see it in future years ?

Such thoughts as these pass through my mind as I turn over the pages of " The Die-Hards in the Great War ", for it appears to constitute a far more lasting and far more accessible memorial than any stone edifice. It is a book to be commended to every soldier who was connected with the forty-six Middlesex battalions which served in the war, and it will be highly prized as a record by future generations of officers and men. Written in plain language, it shows a reticence very becoming to a record of four years of strenuous action and heroic endeavour by plain men who did their plain duty and are ready now to do it again, should the occasion arise. It displays the true regimental spirit, unembellished by appeals to transient sentiment or by flourishes of dramatic language. The author has wisely restricted himself to a narrative of authenticated events, but these are few in number compared with the thousands of unrecorded acts by isolated companies and by individuals who did not live to tell their tale.

During the years 1914 to 1920 the British Army was out to make history not to write it, and an author must rely upon such meagre records as actually exist for his descriptions of battles and what took place in them. For instance, the laconic entry in the war diary of the 4th Battalion at Mons on the 23rd August, 1914, reads—"Battle commenced at 10.15 a.m., retirement started 3 p.m."—and is sufficient evidence that the commanding officer and adjutant were too busily engaged to enlarge upon their first clash of arms with Germans. Moreover, for those of us who were near Mons on that day, the above entry in the war diary is probably more eloquent than additional words could make it. But, nevertheless, on occasion we do wish for description and incident, especially when we recollect how essential it is to develop regimental and battalion *esprit de corps* by means of war stories and lectures by officers who were never near Mons. Think of the countless lectures which will inevitably be given, on wet days, by company officers throughout the twentieth century, and try to visualise how deadly dull such lectures usually are when material is lacking and eloquence is absent. The unfortunate lecturer jumps through a century of dates with a notebook in his hand: amongst other names he casually mentions Marlborough, Wellington, Napoleon, Blücher: he wanders over the globe to India, Canada, South Africa, mentioning numerous places unconnected with one another and manages to get through the Peninsular War, Waterloo, the Crimea, and perhaps an Indian or

Egyptian campaign within the miserable half-hour allotted to the exercise. In future he will include reliable information culled from this volume about his own regiment, but his references to facts and incidents which are briefly recorded in regimental history will lack human touch and colour. They need to be amplified in a lecture, if it is to stimulate the imagination of young soldiers whose historical outlook is limited and whose appreciation of dates and names is vague. If the human touch is lacking the men are unresponsive and only brighten up when the lecturer completes his task and dismisses them at the end of his sermon.

But surely it might all be otherwise if the lecturer were supplied with soldier-like narratives of selected episodes which occurred in the Middlesex Regiment, and in this connection I will give my own experience of what took place in French regiments before the war.

In May, 1914, I was invited privately to accompany the French General Marquis de Castelnau and some twenty French officers, Marshal Foch amongst them, on a week's staff tour in eastern France. General (afterwards Field Marshal Sir Henry) Wilson was my companion. On the last day of the tour the Director of it had certain criticisms to make to his own officers and it was not desirable to have any foreign officer present to hear them, so I paid a surprise visit to the neighbouring battalion of Chasseurs-à-Pied (" Light Infantry "). After an inspection of their up-to-date training methods, and after seeing each company at work, the officers were assembled in the lecture hall and I was asked to pick out any one of them to give a lecture on battalion history. I selected a captain and he proceeded at once to tell a thrilling story of a bugler of the battalion who had saved a nasty situation in one of the famous battles in Algeria in the nineteenth century. This bugler was the hero of the battalion, and every recruit was told the story of the fight in detail from start to finish—names, dates, maps, pictures, all were on record—but the officer who lectured to us for twenty minutes needed no notes or book, for he was so familiar with the story and told it so clearly that even I could understand him though he spoke in rapid French. Moreover, I discovered that every officer and sergeant could give a similar *extempore* lecture to his company or platoon. All ranks knew the history of their own regiment with special emphasis upon selected episodes, and I am now wondering how many Middlesex officers could similarly explain the battle of Albuhera if suddenly called upon to do so? We have no detailed account of any company's doings on that occasion, but if by chance a detailed description of that battle were discovered and put up for sale at Christie's, and if its author were an officer of the 57th Regiment, think how we would bid for it and how carefully we would reproduce it and circulate it. Similarly, a hundred years hence when companies and platoons will fight with different weapons, think how valuable would be a plain narrative by a company officer describing how the Middlesex Regiment fought at Mons in 1914, or a story descriptive of any action in which the regiment took part in France, Belgium, Italy, Turkey, Egypt, Palestine, Mesopotamia, Greece, Russia, or Siberia—I mean a soldier's tale written for soldiers, not a war correspondent's journalese for printing in a newspaper. It would be worth some trouble to secure personal narratives of this kind, and if anyone will send me such stories I will do my best to preserve them and use them for the benefit of the whole Regiment.

Ivor Maxse

LITTLE BOGNOR,
FITTLEWORTH, SUSSEX.
*April*, 1926.

# CHAPTER I.

## Mobilisation and Embarkation of the British Expeditionary Force.

IF an analysis be made of the War efforts of the Cities, Towns and Counties, which go to form the United Kingdom, it will be found that from a military standpoint no county can claim to have done more during the years 1914–1918 than the County of Middlesex. It might be said that the County, and London, the greatest City in the World, could hardly have done otherwise. But it must not be forgotten that in pre-war days, the Shires produced the greatest number of recruits for the Army and Territorial Force, leading to the pardonable supposition that in war time London and the County of Middlesex might be expected to put forth the maximum civilian effort, leaving largely to the Shires the task of raising the bulk of whatever additional military forces were necessary to augment the standing Army. The military efforts of London and the County of Middlesex were, however, prodigious. To say nothing of the Service Battalions of the New Army raised for war purposes, the Territorial Forces grew out of all proportion to their original strength. Three Regiments, the Royal Fusiliers, the Middlesex and the London (Territorials), were extended to an altogether extraordinary number of battalions, which before the War ended reached a combined total of not less than 100 battalions.* We are, however, only concerned with the Middlesex Regiment (The Duke of Cambridge's Own), to which the name Die-Hards is now frequently given from the proud soubriquet earned by the 1st Battalion in the Peninsular War.

When war was declared between Great Britain and Germany on the 4th August, 1914, the Middlesex Regiment numbered ten

* The Middlesex Regiment alone sent 26 Battalions into the field, and these fought in ten theatres of war. The number of Battalions of the Regiment serving at home and abroad during the War was 46.

B

battalions, four of which were regular (1st, 2nd, 3rd and 4th), two Reserve (5th and 6th), and four Territorial (7th, 8th, 9th and 10th).

The 1st Battalion (the 57th Foot) was stationed at Woolwich under the command of Lieut.-Colonel B. E. Ward. The 2nd Battalion (the 77th Foot) was at Malta and formed part of the Mediterranean garrison ; Lieut.-Colonel R. H. Hayes commanded the Battalion. Of the 3rd and 4th Battalions, the former was in India—in the 8th (Lucknow) Division and stationed at Cawnpore—while the latter was quartered at Devonport, one of the four battalions which formed the 8th Infantry Brigade of the 3rd Division, then in the Southern Command. The 3rd Battalion was commanded by Lieut.-Colonel E. W. R. Stephenson and the 4th by Lieut.-Colonel C. P. A. Hull.

The Headquarters of the two Reserve Battalions—the 5th (Royal Elthorne Militia) and the 6th (Royal East Middlesex Militia)—were at Mill Hill, where also the Depot of the Regiment was situated. Lieut.-Colonel C. S. Collison commanded the 5th Battalion and Lieut.-Colonel G. E. Barker the 6th Battalion. The Depot was under the command of Major W. D. Ingle.

The four Territorial Battalions constituted the Middlesex Infantry Brigade of the Home Counties Division, then part of the Eastern Command. The 7th Battalion (Lieut.-Colonel E. J. King) had its Headquarters at Hornsey; the 8th (Lieut.-Colonel W. Garner) at Hounslow; the 9th (Lieut.-Colonel J. L. Blumfeld) at Willesden Green ; and the 10th (Lieut.-Colonel C. R. Johnson) at Ravenscourt Park. The Middlesex Infantry Brigade was commanded by Colonel W. R. Clifford, and the Home Counties Division by Major-General J. C. Young.

This fine Regiment was therefore able to put into the field, immediately war was declared and mobilisation had been ordered, at least 10,000 officers and men, well-trained, eager for battle, well-equipped and endowed by past generations with glorious traditions of *esprit de corps* and devotion to duty.

To those who do not know the derivation of The Die-Hards it may be stated that the name was given to the Regiment by its own comrades of Wellington's Army of the Peninsular Wars. It was conferred on the 57th Foot after the Battle of Albuhera, and had its origin as follows :—In the Battle of Albuhera, fought on the 16th May, 1811, Colonel Inglis, who commanded the 57th Foot, having already had his horse shot under him, lay dangerously wounded on the ridge which was the key position of Wellington's Army, then being heavily attacked and outnumbered by French troops under Soult. Refusing to be carried to the rear, he lay in front of the Regimental Colours, encouraging his men and calling out to them " Die Hard, 57th, Die Hard ! " From that day the Regiment was dubbed by its comrades of Wellington's Army The Die-Hards. And it will be seen how, over a hundred years later, in the year 1915 another gallant officer of the Regiment died with the old cry, " Dic Hard," on his lips.

The circumstances under which war was declared, and the rupture of diplomatic relations between Great Britain and Germany, are now well-known and need not be repeated, and we are immediately concerned with the issue of orders to mobilise, the mobilisation of the Army and the transfer of the British Expeditionary Force to France and Flanders.

4TH AUGUST. WAR DECLARED.

A state of war was declared to exist between Great Britain and Germany " as from 11 p.m. on the 4th August, 1914." Seven hours previously (at 4 p.m.), when it was evident that war was inevitable, the British Government had given orders for the mobilisation of the Army and the Territorial Forces ; the Naval Reserves were also called out.

4TH BATTALION.

In Devonport, mobilisation orders reached the 4th Middlesex at 5.25 p.m., and the Battalion Diary records that at 5.45 p.m. (20 minutes later) an official roll showing all officers (23) fit was despatched to the War Office.* The first day of mobilisation was the 5th August, and thereafter proceeded rapidly and smoothly until the morning of the 8th, when all companies under Company Commanders paraded for inspection. During the day the Regimental Colours were sent to Mill Hill (the Depot), and late at night (at 10.45 p.m.) mobilisation was reported complete. For the next three days the Battalion carried out training, and several long route marches were made.

13TH AUGUST.

On the morning of the 13th the Battalion (in Brigade) entrained at Devonport for Southampton, and, on reaching Southampton Docks, embarked during the afternoon and early evening on board the *Mombasa*, putting out to sea later " for an unknown destination."

The rapid and secret transfer of the British Expeditionary Force, under the command of General Sir John French, from

* The War Diary of the 1st Battalion does not begin until 23rd August, the first entry being made at Valenciennes on that date.

England to France was one of the early marvels of the War, for it was not until the British public read newspaper accounts of the arrival of British troops at Boulogne that anything was known of the silent departure of our little Army.

14TH AUGUST. It was about midday on the 14th when the *Mombasa* arrived off Boulogne and slowly nosed her way into the harbour, then crowded with craft of every description. Disembarkation proceeded almost immediately, and as the troops stepped ashore the quays were crowded with Boulannais, who for several days past had spent most of their time gaping open-mouthed at the arrival of transport after transport full of troops and munitions of war, which came into the harbour, discharged their human burdens rapidly, and quickly disappeared again in the direction of England. Then, as the troops formed up and marched off through the narrow, crowded streets to the Rest Camp on the hills above the town, the excited populace broke bounds, thrust presents of flowers and all sorts of things into the hands of the British soldiers with cries of "A bas Guillaume!" "Coupez la gorge!" and similar bloodthirsty sentiments, and begged as souvenirs buttons or cap-badges.

4TH BATTALION.

It was a coincidence that a hundred and twenty-one years previously (in 1793) the old 57th Foot landed on the Continent, also on the 14th of the month, though the month was September instead of August and the port Ostend and not Boulogne.* And it is also worthy of note, from an historical point of view, that the British Force which landed at Ostend in 1793 did so in order to uphold the signature of the British Government to the Treaty of Fontainebleau, which guaranteed the rights of the Dutch over the Scheldt, just as in 1914 the British Expeditionary Force landed at Boulogne to honour the signature of Great Britain to the Treaty of London, 1839, which guaranteed the neutrality of Belgium, and to which the Governments of France and Germany had also appended their signatures. In 1793, however, the British Forces were arrayed *against* France, whereas in 1914 they *stood by her side*, to repel the German invasion.

15TH AUGUST. Throughout the 15th, the 4th Middlesex remained in the Rest Camp above Boulogne, but at 12.15 a.m. on the 16th the Battalion again entrained for "an unknown destination."

* The 4th Battalion Middlesex Regiment was, however, raised as recently as 1900, and had not previously seen active service.

How great a space of time, how many terrible, troublous years were to pass, ere battalions of the Regiment once more set foot in a French coastal town, *en route* for England! How much precious blood had been spilled and how many brave and gallant souls had gone to their deaths ere, at " the eleventh hour of the eleventh day of the eleventh month " of the year 1918, the " Cease fire " sounded! 15TH AUGUST.

Aulnoye, a small village, south of Pont-sur-Sambre and east of the Forêt de Mormal, was the " unknown destination " of the 4th Middlesex, and here the Battalion arrived at 12 noon, detrained, and marched off at 3.30 p.m. to Taisnières, four miles south of Aulnoye. For the concentration area allotted to the British Expeditionary Force was " between Maubeuge and Le Cateau, about twenty-five miles long from north-east to south-west and averaging ten miles wide." *

In Taisnières the Middlesex billeted, and with them in the same village were the three other battalions of the 8th Infantry Brigade, *i.e.*, 2nd Royal Scots, 2nd Royal Irish Regiment, 1st Gordon Highlanders, and Brigade Headquarters.

And here, for a while, it is necessary to turn from the concentration of the Ist and IInd Corps in order to explain how it was that the British Expeditionary Force came to be on the left flank of the French Armies, then in line from approximately the Swiss Frontier to Charleroi.

Although in pre-war days no definite written agreement existed between France and Great Britain, whereby the latter was bound to send troops to assist the French in repelling an unprovoked attack by Germany, the British Government had more than once allowed France to believe that in the event of war British troops would be sent across the Channel. Proof of this may be found in " the formation of an Expeditionary Force," which had existed (at least on paper) for several years prior to 1914. The manner in which the British Government decided to employ this Expeditionary Force is thus described in the Official History (Military Operations) of the War:—

" On 5th and 6th August, two meetings, attended by the principal Ministers, including Lord Kitchener, who became Secretary of State for War on the 6th, and by the leading members of the Staffs of the Navy and Army of Britain, assembled to consider the conduct of the War. The exact state of affairs at

* " Official History of the War (Military Operations)."

the moment was that Great Britain, France, and Russia were at war with Germany; that Belgium had been wantonly attacked but was making a better defence than had been expected; that Austria was at war with Serbia only; and that Italy was neutral. The main military questions to be considered were the employment and disposition of the Expeditionary Force, questions which were complicated by the delay in mobilisation. It was determined first that the Force, less the 4th and 6th Divisions, should embark for the Continent. In order to reduce the chance of a German landing in force interfering with this move, the Secretary of State decided that the 18th Infantry Brigade of the 6th Division, then at Lichfield, should move to Edinburgh, and two infantry brigades of the 4th Division should proceed to Cromer and York, in each case accompanied by some artillery. The 11th Infantry Brigade of the 4th Division was already at Colchester. Five Cyclist battalions and eventually the Yeomanry Mounted Division were also sent to the East Coast. The rest of the 6th Division was to remain in Ireland.

"Then came the final decision as to the destination of the Expeditionary Force. In view of the attack on Belgium, had the British contingent been of a size adequate for independent operations of a substantial character, there would have been much to be said in favour of making Antwerp the base of its military operations; but as it was so small, and as Antwerp, owing to part of the Scheldt being Dutch territorial waters, would have to be reached after disembarkation at Ostend and other ports, and operations in the north might involve separation from the French, the suggestion was not followed. There remained the area already considered with the French—namely, that around Le Cateau and Avesnes. Certain military opinion, however, was against a concentration of the British Forces in any area in advance of Amiens. Finally, it was agreed to leave the decision with our Allies, the French."

The Council then broke up, having decided, amongst other things, "to embark ultimately five, but for the present only four, of the divisions and the Cavalry Division of the Expeditionary Force, to commence on the 9th."

In presenting his official report to the French Government, Marshal Joffre later stated: "The directions for concentration did not mention the place eventually reserved for the British Army. . . . In the event of its arrival, its employment was looked for at the place which should be especially reserved for it, *on the left of the line of the French Armies, which it would thus prolong.*" And that is how the B.E.F. came to concentrate in the area between Maubeuge and Le Cateau.*

Before the Expeditionary Force sailed, certain troops were sent across to France to guard the Lines of Communication,† and amongst these was the 1st Battalion Middlesex Regiment.‡ The Battalion landed at Havre, two companies on 11th and two companies on 12th August, remaining in camp for ten days until the 19th Infantry Brigade was formed and moved up to the Mons–Condé Line, arriving at Valenciennes about 3 p.m. on the 23rd August, during the Battle of Mons. For the present, however, attention is centred on the 4th Middlesex, busily engaged in company training and in route-marching at Taisnières, preparatory to moving up to the position assigned to the B.E.F. in the line of battle.

1ST BATTALION. 11TH AUGUST.

4TH BATTALION.

On the 20th August, the 8th Infantry Brigade moved from Taisnières to new billets, 2nd Royal Scots to St. Aubyn, 1st Gordon Highlanders to St. Remy and the 2nd Royal Irish Regiment and 4th Middlesex Regiment to Monceau. At 8.30 p.m. on the same date, preliminary Divisional Orders were received containing instructions for the march to Maubeuge. The concentration of the B.E.F. was virtually complete,§ and Sir John French was ready to move his force northwards in accordance with the general strategic plan.

20TH AUGUST.

The French plan of operations (or rather the modified plan) had begun to take shape about the 16th of the month. In the

* The original British Expeditionary Force consisted of Ist Corps (Lieut.-General Sir Douglas Haig), 1st and 2nd Divisions; IInd Corps (Lieut.-General Sir James Grierson, who, however, died in a train *en route* for the Concentration Area, and was succeeded by Lieut.-General Sir Horace Smith-Dorrien), 3rd and 5th Divisions; the Cavalry Division (Major-General E. Allenby). The IIIrd Corps, which for the time being was not sent overseas, was to be commanded by Lieut.-General W. P. Pulteney.

† The 1st Devonshire Regiment, 2nd Royal Welch Fusiliers, 1st Cameronians (Scottish Rifles), 1st Duke of Cambridge's Own (Middlesex Regiment), 2nd Princess Louise's (Argyll and Sutherland Highlanders). All but the first-named subsequently formed the 19th Infantry Brigade (Major-General L. G. Drummond).

‡ The 1st Battalion Middlesex Regiment was the first British Regiment to arrive in France, and was accorded a tremendous reception by the French.

§ On the morning of the 20th August, the force was disposed as follows:—

Allenby's Cavalry (Cavalry Division Headquarters at Aibes) ready to join hands with the French Fifth Army (Lanrezac) east of Maubeuge, Jeumont, Damousies and Cousolre; IInd Corps east of Landrecies (Corps Headquarters at Landrecies), 3rd Division—Marbaix, Taisnières, Noyelles; 5th Division—Maroilles, Landrecies, Ors; Ist, Corps east of Bohain (Corps Headquarters, Wassigny), 1st Division, Boué, Esqueheries, Leschelle; 2nd Division—Grougis, Mennevret, Hannappes.

20TH AUGUST. original scheme of operations* the French General Staff had laid down plans for two offensives, one between the wooded district of the Vosges and the Moselle below Toul, and the other north of the line Verdun–Metz. This plan was based on the supposition that the Germans would attack across the common frontier between France and Germany. On the other hand, the German plan (Graf Schlieffen's) provided for a sweep through Belgium with a strong right wing in an endeavour to envelop the French armies from the west and drive them up against the Swiss frontier.

The French offensive in Alsace had already begun (and was making headway) when news of the advance through Belgium of strong German forces compelled General Joffre to change his plans in order to meet the threat from the north against his left wing. He therefore stopped his offensive in Alsace, gave orders for the attack between Metz and the Vosges to be of a secondary nature, whilst the main attack was now to be made through Luxembourg and Belgian Luxembourg, striking at the flank and communications of the German forces which had crossed the Meuse between Namur and the Dutch frontier, thus hoping to break the enemy's centre, then fall on his right wing with the Fifth French Army, British Army and Belgian Army (in the order given from right to left) and roll it up towards the common frontier between Belgium and Germany. The British line of advance was to be by way of Soignies in the general direction of Nivelles, *i.e.*, first a north-easterly movement followed by a turn eastwards.

On the evening of the 20th, British G.H.Q. issued orders for the movement northwards to take place during the next three days. The 5th Cavalry Brigade to move on the 21st to the neighbourhood of Binche, the right of the British line, the Cavalry Division marching level with it, but on the left, and proceeding to Lens on the 22nd ; the IInd Corps on the 21st and to reach the line Goegniès–Bavai, and the Ist Corps the line Avesnes–Landrecies. On the 22nd the IInd Corps was to move north-westwards to a line from Mons westward to Thulin, the Ist Corps north-eastwards to the line Hautmont–Hargnies ; the wheel eastward to take place on the 23rd.†

* "Plan 17."

† These somewhat tedious details are necessary in order to understand the movements and operations in which the 4th Middlesex Regiment was actively involved.

Before dawn on the morning of the 21st the troops paraded. The Cavalry had already gone forward when the 8th Infantry Brigade, forming the advanced guard of the 3rd Division, set out at 5.30 a.m., followed by the 7th and 9th Infantry Brigades; the 5th Division was in rear of the 3rd and the Ist Corps behind the IInd Corps. 21ST AUGUST. 4TH BATTALION.

The early morning was misty, but when the atmosphere had cleared the sun poured down with merciless severity upon the marching infantrymen. The way lay through Maubeuge, where the inhabitants gave the troops a hearty welcome and provided much-needed refreshment. Five miles north of the town was the village of Bettignies and here, about 1 p.m., the 8th Brigade went into billets, having covered 15 miles since early morning. The troops had marched well, but the feet of the reservists were still tender, which, added to the fact that their boots were new and in many instances ill-fitting, was responsible for 15 men falling out of the ranks of the 4th Middlesex.

The Brigade then formed an outpost line two miles north and north-east, two platoons of "D" Company of the Middlesex with troops from other battalions being detailed for this duty. About five miles west of Bettignies lay the old battlefield of Malplaquet, now overlooked by the outposts of the 9th Infantry Brigade on the left of the 8th Brigade.

At nightfall on the 21st August, the 3rd Division (on right) occupied the line Bettignies–Feignies–La Longueville; the 5th Division (on the left) the line Houdain–St. Waast–Gommegnies; the 1st (right) and the 2nd (left) Divisions of the Ist Corps had moved up to the line Avesnes–Landrecies.

Certain intelligence had reached G.H.Q. throughout the day; hostile cavalry with some infantry and guns had been located by British airmen, south-east of Nivelles; other German cavalry divisions had been reported on the line Ghent–Audenarde and between Charleroi and Seneffe; the main German forces were said to be on line extending from Grammont, through Enghien, Nivelles, Genappes and Sombreffe to Charleroi. The Fifth French Army (Lanrezac), on the right of the B.E.F., was in contact with infantry of the Second German Army (von Bülow) along the whole line of the river Sambre, from Tamines to Pont à Celles.

Just before midnight on 21st, G.H.Q. issued orders for the next day's march: the IInd Corps was to occupy an outpost line from Givry (inclusive) through Harmignies to the Bois La Haut by 12 noon, and Nimy and the line of the Mons Canal westward as far as the bridge south of Pommerœul (inclusive) not later than 1 p.m. As soon as these outposts had been established, the cavalry (acting as a screen whilst the IInd Corps was moving forward) would withdraw, the 5th Cavalry Brigade to Binche and the Cavalry Division to the left of the IInd Corps. On completion of these moves the 3rd Division would hold the right and the 5th Division the left of the IInd Corps front.

21ST-22ND. AUGUST. 4TH BATTALION. The night of the 21st–22nd August passed without incident. At 3 a.m. the 4th Middlesex Regiment was ordered to form the advanced guard of the 3rd Division during the move northwards on the 22nd. The Battalion paraded early and marched off along the Mons road, followed by the remaining units of the 8th Brigade, to which the XL Brigade, R.F.A., had been attached. The 4th Middlesex and the 2nd Royal Irish Regiment were ordered to entrench and hold the line Nouvelles-Harveng, towards Havay, facing eastwards, whilst the remainder of the 8th Brigade and XL Brigade, R.F.A., were held in reserve, first near Asquillies, and subsequently near Belian Station, in order that the Cavalry Division might withdraw westwards through the infantry. The Middlesex had already marched five miles when a halt was called and the order given to " charge magazines with 10 rounds." All ranks by now were in a state of excitement. Mons was in sight, and as the troops marched along the road they were given eggs and eatables of all kinds by the eager population. Many of these Belgians had never seen a British soldier, for not since Waterloo had Great Britain sent troops to Flanders.

Later in the afternoon 8th Brigade Headquarters issued orders to the Middlesex and Royal Irish to hold the line, road junction at Faubourg Barthelemy (just east of Mons)–Harmignies–Givry; the former Battalion to move to the northern and the latter to the southern part of this line, which faced north-east. G.H.Q. had reported that a hostile force of all arms was advancing on Bray and was engaging the British cavalry.

Again at 5 p.m. orders were received from 3rd Divisional Headquarters to " throw the line forward and northwards thus :— left at Nimy, holding the Canal bridges (I) immediately north of Nimy, (II) at Lock No. 5, (III) near Obourg Station." (The 4th Middlesex Regiment was detailed for this) : " right at St. Symphorien and Villers–St. Ghislain " (these two places to be held by the 2nd Royal Irish Regiment) . . . . " The following orders were also given :—1st Gordon Highlanders to hold and entrench the eastern slopes of Bois La Haut from road junction at Faubourg Barthélemy to road junction 300 yards north-east of Spiennes (inclusive) : 2nd Royal Scots to continue the line to high ground near Harmignies Station." After issuing these orders 8th Brigade Headquarters and XL Brigade, R.F.A., went into billets at Mesvin. 22ND AUGUST 4TH BATTALION.

Meanwhile the Middlesex had gone forward to take up their outpost lines at the bridges. The four companies were disposed in the following positions :—" D " Company on the right at the two bridges near Obourg Station, " B " Company was on the left of " D "—in touch with the 4th Royal Fusiliers. " C " Company just east of the Convent along the Obourg–Mons road, " A " Company holding a line of houses prepared for defensive purposes, south of the railway between Obourg and Nimy. Lieut.-Col. (then Captain) G. L. Oliver said of his corps (" C ") : " " C " Company were well dug in in section and platoon trenches just behind a hedge stretching from a road to the end of the hedge-frontage about 350 yards. Next to the road on its right the hedge became a garden wall and this was loopholed and strengthened.

" A section was placed back on the road to protect the right rear of the Company as it was not in touch with any other unit.

" On the left of the Company were the Maxim Guns and on the left of these was " A " Company, occupying amongst other things some houses. There was a thick wood on " C " Company's front and in front of this in the line of the Canal was "D" Company. " B " Company was on " D " Company's left and in touch with the Royal Fusiliers.

" Behind " C " Company was a Convent surrounded by very high unclimbable railings *or wall* and in the N.W. corner were the stables." Battalion Headquarters were in a quarry north of the Obourg-Mons road.

The Battalion now set to work to throw up entrenchments, but had hardly begun when a party of Uhlans fired on " D " Company, which returned the fire. No one was hit, but the Battalion had (all unconsciously) established the fact that the 4th Battalion Middlesex Regiment was the first British infantry unit to fire on the Germans in the Great War.* A little later a

* So far as the whole B.E.F. was concerned, the first shot of the War was fired by " C " Squadron of the 4th Dragoon Guards early on the morning of 22nd August in the neighbourhood of Soignies.

22ND AUGUST. 4TH BATTALION.

German Taube was observed hovering overhead and was fired on by the troops, but flew away undamaged.

At nightfall on 22nd August the 8th Infantry Brigade held a line from Villers–St. Ghislain–St. Symphorien and Nimy, joining up on the latter flank with the 4th Royal Fusiliers of the 9th Infantry Brigade. The 7th Infantry Brigade was in reserve. The 5th Division was on the left of the 3rd along the line of the Mons–Condé Canal. The Ist Corps was even then still on the road, to take up its position on the right of the IInd Corps. The 5th Cavalry Brigade was at Binche and Allenby's Cavalry Division the western flank of the B.E.F.

Thus on the night of the 22nd August, Sir John French's Army was approximately on the line assigned to it, *i.e.*, on the left flank of the French Armies, ready to advance and attack the enemy according to General Joffre's scheme of operations.

# CHAPTER II.

## THE BATTLE OF MONS.

23rd–24th August, 1914.

AT a conference held at Le Cateau during the evening of the 22nd August, Sir John French announced that the projected British offensive would not take place; for during the late afternoon information had reached him which disclosed a somewhat alarming position on his right flank, *i.e.*, the Fifth French Army (General Lanrezac) on the line of the Sambre. 22ND AUGUST.

Air reconnaissances had discovered at least two German corps attacking Lanrezac along the Sambre, and to these reports others were added: the French centre had been driven back: the X French Corps had retired to the line St. Gérard–Biesme–Gerpinnes: the III French Corps had fallen back to a line from Gerpinnes, westward to Jamioulx: only the XVIII French Corps on the left of the Fifth Army remained in its original position, echeloned to the rear between Marbaix and Thuin: Sordet's Cavalry Corps had moved nine miles south of Binche, preparatory to marching to the left flank of the B.E.F.

What had happened? Namur, upon which the Allies had pinned their faith, *i.e.*, that it would delay and disorganise the German advance, was falling rapidly under the awful fire of the enemy's huge siege howitzers, which blew stone masonry to atoms and smashed steel cupolas with demoralising ease. The fortress had been invested by the enemy and the triangle Givet–Namur–Charleroi broken.

It must therefore have appeared to Sir John French that instead of embarking on offensive operations he would very soon be on the defensive.

About 11 p.m. on the night of the 22nd, a French Staff officer brought a request from General Lanrezac that the British should attack the flank of the German forces which were pressing the

Fifth French Army back from the Sambre. In the face of large numbers of the enemy on his front (whose strength was unknown, though vaguely guessed at) it was impossible for Sir John to agree to the suggestion, but he promised General Lanrezac that he would remain in his position along the Mons–Condé Canal for 24 hours, which action would protect the left of the Fifth French Army. Sir John French's *rôle*, therefore, was to delay the advance of the enemy, and, as will be seen later, on the 4th Middlesex of the 8th Infantry Brigade and the 4th Royal Fusiliers (9th Infantry Brigade*) fell the maintenance of what was without doubt the most dangerous and difficult part of the whole British line—the Mons–Obourg salient.

4TH BATTALION.

23RD AUGUST.

When dawn broke on Sunday, the 23rd August,† a mist hung over the battlefield-to-be, and a thin rain was falling. The British Cavalry were early astir, reconnoitring the bridges east of Mons, *i.e.*, at Binche, Bray, Havré, and Obourg. While the mist still clung to the ground, the G.O.C. 8th Infantry Brigade withdrew the 2nd Royal Irish from their exposed positions at St. Symphorien and Villers–St. Ghislain to the Faubourg Barthélemy, in reserve. This withdrawal still further accentuated the dangerous position held by the 4th Middlesex. Moreover, a brigade of Field Artillery (XLth), which, after a reconnaissance, had taken up position about the Bois La Haut, found it impossible to cover the Middlesex if the latter was attacked from the north, the only possible field of fire being N.E., E., and S.E.

4TH BATTALION.

At 6 a.m. shots were exchanged between "D" Company of the Middlesex, posted at the Obourg Bridge, and German Cavalry. The Fusiliers shot a man of a hostile patrol at Nimy, whilst further west along the Canal, near Pommerœul, the D.C.L.I. captured two German cavalrymen; these were the first encounters between British infantry and the enemy on the 23rd August.

About 7 a.m. a Field company was ordered forward to prepare the bridges over the canal along the front of the 8th Brigade for demolition, but they arrived too late to effect their purpose,

* Both Brigades belonged to the 3rd Division.

† The diary of the 4th Battalion Middlesex Regiment contains only the following story of the Battle of Mons:—

"Mons, 23–8–14. Battalion occupied line from Auberge (*i.e.*, Obourg) to Mons, about 1½ miles, entrenched as far as time would permit. Order of Companies in line, 'D,' 'C,' 'A,' and 'B,' with ½ Company 'B' in reserve. Battle commenced at 10.15 a.m., retirement started at 3 p.m. Battalion arrived at Novelle (*i.e.*, Nouvelles) after dusk and bivouacked there."

and the bridges were, unfortunately, left intact, enabling the enemy to pass his troops across. 23RD AUGUST. 4TH BATTALION.

Some time between 8 and 9 o'clock, shells began to fall along the line held by the Middlesex and Royal Fusiliers. The machine-gunners of the former battalion, observing a German battery commander unlimbering his guns in the open, about 1,500 yards away, quickly compelled him to seek other positions.

About 9 a.m. hostile infantry attacks, supported by heavy artillery fire, began, enemy movement developing from a north-easterly to a south-westerly direction. Gradually all round the salient the enemy's troops could be seen pressing forward to the attack; and, to the utter astonishment of the British "Tommy," the Germans advanced in close formation, shoulder to shoulder. Little they knew that they were advancing against troops whose marksmanship was second to none; for soon there was a roar of "rapid" rifle fire, and the machine-guns of the Middlesex and Royal Fusiliers began to tear gaps in the ranks of the intrepid enemy. They were brave fellows, those Germans, their outstanding fault being their ignorance of the prowess of the British infantryman with the rifle, and for that fault they paid dearly. Orders to the Middlesex and Royal Fusiliers holding the salient had been to maintain "a stubborn resistance," and this they proceeded to do, clinging to their positions with great tenacity. The enemy, foiled in his first attempt, now began to advance more warily, working across the front in small parties with the object of forming up under cover of the woods for a fresh attack.

Meanwhile, the whole line west of the salient was becoming involved in the battle, for the wheel of von Kluck's Army was in gradual progress, and contact with his troops all along the line of the Canal was becoming general. It was obvious, therefore, that the salient must either break his progress or else be broken.

At 11 o'clock the line still held, but the 4th Middlesex had appealed for reinforcements, and some of the 2nd Royal Irish were sent up to assist in holding the line of hastily dug trenches, whilst the machine-gunners of the Irish Battalion joined those of the Middlesex, north of the Obourg–Mons road. The possession of every inch of ground between Obourg and Nimy was stubbornly contested, but about noon the Germans were observed working round in rear of the Middlesex, and the latter were compelled to fall back to the neighbourhood of Point 62; the heavy hostile artillery, machine-gun and rifle fire, opposed only by British

23RD AUGUST.
4TH BATTALION.

rifle fire, had done its work. The Germans were now across the Canal west of Obourg, and had reached the line of the railway. From this point, having been taught by bitter experience the sheer madness of advancing in massed formation, they came on in extended order.

Another appeal from the Middlesex for reinforcements brought up the remainder of the 2nd Royal Irish to Point 62, on the left of the former battalion. From the high ground north of the canal the German gunners were able to observe the movements of these two battalions, and kept them under very heavy shell-fire. By sheer weight of numbers the enemy's infantry, covered by artillery-fire, was able to work forward, so that about 2 p.m. both the 4th Middlesex and 2nd Royal Irish were driven from Point 62 back on Mons, the 9th Infantry Brigade on the left of the Middlesex falling back at the same time.

The machine-guns of both battalions were by now in difficulties; the machine-gun officer of the Middlesex had been wounded, but pluckily " carried on." In front of " C " Company and the Machine-gun Section the Germans had brought up six machine-guns. With fine devotion, the machine-gun officer sent a message to the O.C., " C " Company, offering to cover the withdrawal of the latter if he wished. Shortly after, the former officer and one of his gunners were wounded, and he had no option but that of staying and continuing the fight. Calling for six volunteers to stay with him, and sending the remainder of the Section back, this little band of men, in the old Die-Hard spirit, prepared to sell their lives dearly.

The main body of the Royal Irish was again forced to retire (about 5 p.m.), and by that time those of the 4th Middlesex Regiment who had remained in the line had been overwhelmed; many of their rifles had been rendered useless, sand having clogged the breaches.

The turn of the gallant band of machine-gunners came next. The water in the gun-jackets was by now boiling furiously, but the last rounds were fired away before the end came.

Lieut.-Col. (then Captain) Oliver's story of the Battle of Mons, so far as it concerns " C " Company, of the 4th Middlesex (which company he commanded) is as follows :—

" The Battle opened by a German shell hitting the roof of the Convent, the next shell fell within two yards of my left trench, and after that, shelling was general in " A " Company's house,

Machine Gun's and "B" Company's area. Later Germans began coming through the wood and crossing the opening "B" and in S.E. direction also appearing at "A."

23RD AUGUST.
4TH BATTALION.

"None approached my trenches directly across the open, but great damage was done to those crossing at "B" and at point "A."

"In the meantime, men approached me from the wood and these were seen to be our own men from "D" Company. They joined me. Soon Germans were reported at "D" and I went to my right to investigate and got a Company of Royal Irish sent up from somewhere to hold my flank, but this Company retired soon after, then the Germans got well round my right. On returning to my left I found the Machine Guns had been captured and that Germans were about point "E." Shortly after this I decided to retire, but the only way was through the Convent Garden. I first attempted to get my horse from the stables, but found this occupied by Germans. I then ordered a retirement by Platoons through trees up to the Convent Gate, where my servant a gallant fellow blew in the locks of the Gates with rifle shots, getting wounded by a splinter back in doing so. On passing through the garden and emerging by another gate, I found Germans to be in occupation of the wall at "X Y," and I accordingly came under cross fire from "X Y" and "D" direction. I dashed with one Platoon to the Bank in the road and under cover of this and fire from there, the other Platoons dashed across the open hollow for safety.

"At Brigade Headquarter 2, I found the Colonel and Battalion Headquarters (who had given me up for lost) and the remainder or remnants of "A" and "B" Companys, though many of these at that time were in the town of Mons."

The remnants of the 4th Middlesex got away, passing through the Gordons, and, taking the first road to the westward, eventually reached Hyon, whence the march was continued to Nouvelles (about six miles). Here, in a stubble-field alongside the road, the 4th Battalion bivouacked. "We called the roll, as well as we could, without any lists except "C" Company. We numbered about 275 [the number being increased afterwards by stragglers coming in]; our transport was not with us, so we had to manage as best we could for grub. As far as we were concerned, the fighting finished about 4 p.m.* Our list of casualties after

* Other reports state that the action was still in progress at 5 p.m.

23RD AUGUST. the fight was 14 officers and 453 in killed, wounded and missing, but this number of N.C.Os. and men was reduced somewhat by over 100 men turning up later who got astray."*

Amongst the officers, Major W. H. Abell† (commanding " A " Company), Captains J. E. Knowles and K. J. Roy, and Lieuts. J. R. M. Wilkinson and K. P. Henstock were killed. Major W. H. C. Davy (commanding " B " Company), Capt. H. E. L. Glass (commanding " D " Company), Lieuts. L. F. Sloane-Stanley (M.G. Section), L. J. Graham-Toler, and E. R. Rushton were wounded and taken prisoner, together with Lieuts. H. A. Cartwright, G. C. Druce, L. H. O. Josephs, A. B. W. Allistone and the Battalion M.O., Capt. Terry, R.A.M.C.‡

1ST BATTALION. Further west along the Canal towards Condé, the 1st Battalion Middlesex Regiment and the 1st Cameronians (19th Infantry Brigade)§ had relieved the Cavalry Division between 2 and 3 p.m., the two Battalions extending the line of the B.E.F. to Condé.

The 1st Middlesex (Lieut.-Colonel B. E. Ward) had entrained at Havre on the 22nd and had reached Valenciennes early on the 23rd. On detraining at the latter town the Battalion marched via Quievrechain to St. Aybert, the Middlesex men having been ordered to hold a bridge over the Mons–Condé Canal and Lock 3 towards Condé. " A " Company was ordered to hold the bridge and " C " Company the lock: " B " and " D " Companies were in reserve. The left flank of the Battalion (" A " Company) was then one mile west of St. Aybert Road, and the right flank (" C " Company) at Lock 5, about two miles east of St. Aybert. " A " and " C " Companies having had dinner, proceeded to dig themselves in to make the best of their position.

About 4.30 p.m. another Company was ordered to hold a bridge over the Canal E. of St. Aybert and " B " Company was sent

* Private diary of Lieut.-Colonel H. W. E. Finch, late 4th Battalion Middlesex Regiment. Lieut. and Adjutant T. S. Wollocombe, 4th Middlesex Regiment, gave the casualties as 15 officers and 467 other ranks, the latter by Companies as follows:—A—134, B—96, C—54, D—183.

† Major Abell was the first officer of the Middlesex Regiment killed in the War.

‡ The casualties of the whole B.E.F. at Mons " amounted to just over 1,600 of all ranks, killed, wounded and missing. The whole of these, except 40, were sustained by the IInd Corps, and practically half of them by two Battalions of the 8th Infantry Brigade in the Salient." *Official History.* Of the two Battalions, one was the 4th Middlesex.

§ For composition of the 19th Infantry Brigade, see footnote to p. 7.

off, arriving just in time to cover a Squadron of the Bays retiring across the bridge under shell-fire. 23RD AUGUST. 1ST BATTALION.

But soon after 5 p.m. a heavy attack was made on "B" Company, who successfully held the enemy at bay until the Germans mounted a machine-gun in a house commanding the buildings at the bridge. The latter had been blown up by an N.C.O. of a Cavalry Regiment, just in time to deprive the enemy of the use of it. The buildings, however, on the southern side had to be abandoned, though the 1st Middlesex held the enemy in check.

Hostile rifle fire gradually died down and later, as darkness fell, ceased altogether. During the night the Germans launched another attack, but it was easily driven back. The 1st Battalion had had very few casualties—2 other ranks killed and a few wounded. Of the former a lance-corporal was the first man of the Battalion killed in the War.

At the close of the battle the British centre (the Salient, as had been expected owing to its exposed position) had been forced back, and between nightfall on 23rd August and 3 a.m. on the morning of the 24th the approximate position of the 8th Infantry Brigade was Nouvelles, with the 7th and 9th Infantry Brigades on the left and with the left flank of the 2nd Division (about Harveng) on the right. The 5th Division was on the right of the 3rd with its right on the road from Quaregnon to Pâturages, leaving a gap between the inner flanks of the two Divisions. The left flank of the 5th Division was just south of Haine. The 19th Infantry Brigade, however, stood fast, and it was not until midnight that orders were received to retire in a south-easterly direction towards Elouges; these orders reaching the 1st Middlesex about 1.30 a.m.*

The casualties sustained by the 1st Battalion Middlesex throughout the day were Major H. N. Blakeney wounded, 4 other ranks killed, and 12 wounded.

Throughout the night of 23rd–24th August the Germans made no attempt to advance. 23RD-24TH AUGUST.

As darkness fell over the battlefield, to the astonishment of the British troops, German bugles sounding the "cease fire" were

* The reason for the retirement and full description of the operations of the Fifth French Army, on the right flank of the B.E.F., which materially affected the position of the British Army, cannot here be fully dealt with, but has been placed on record in the Official History (Military Operations) now available. A regimental history can only refer to the movements of Corps and Armies in a very brief manner and touch lightly upon questions of strategy and tactics.

23RD–24TH AUGUST.

heard everywhere along the line, unit by unit. The German infantry had received a rude shock. The little Army which the enemy had been taught to regard as negligible had not only given proof of its discipline, valour and fighting qualities, but had taught the Germans what really effective rifle fire was like. That first encounter at Mons gave rise to the legend that British battalions were armed with large numbers of machine-guns, so rapid and deadly accurate had been their rifle fire. In 1914 the allotment of machine-guns per British battalion was two.

Wellington at Waterloo prayed for night or Blucher; the enemy at Mons, though in vastly superior numbers, longed for darkness, for when "the summer night settled on the blood-stained battlefield and with its shade gave a protecting curtain against the hostile fire,"* one German Regiment alone had lost "25 officers and far more than 500 N.C.Os. and men."

* From a German military history of the War.

Map I.

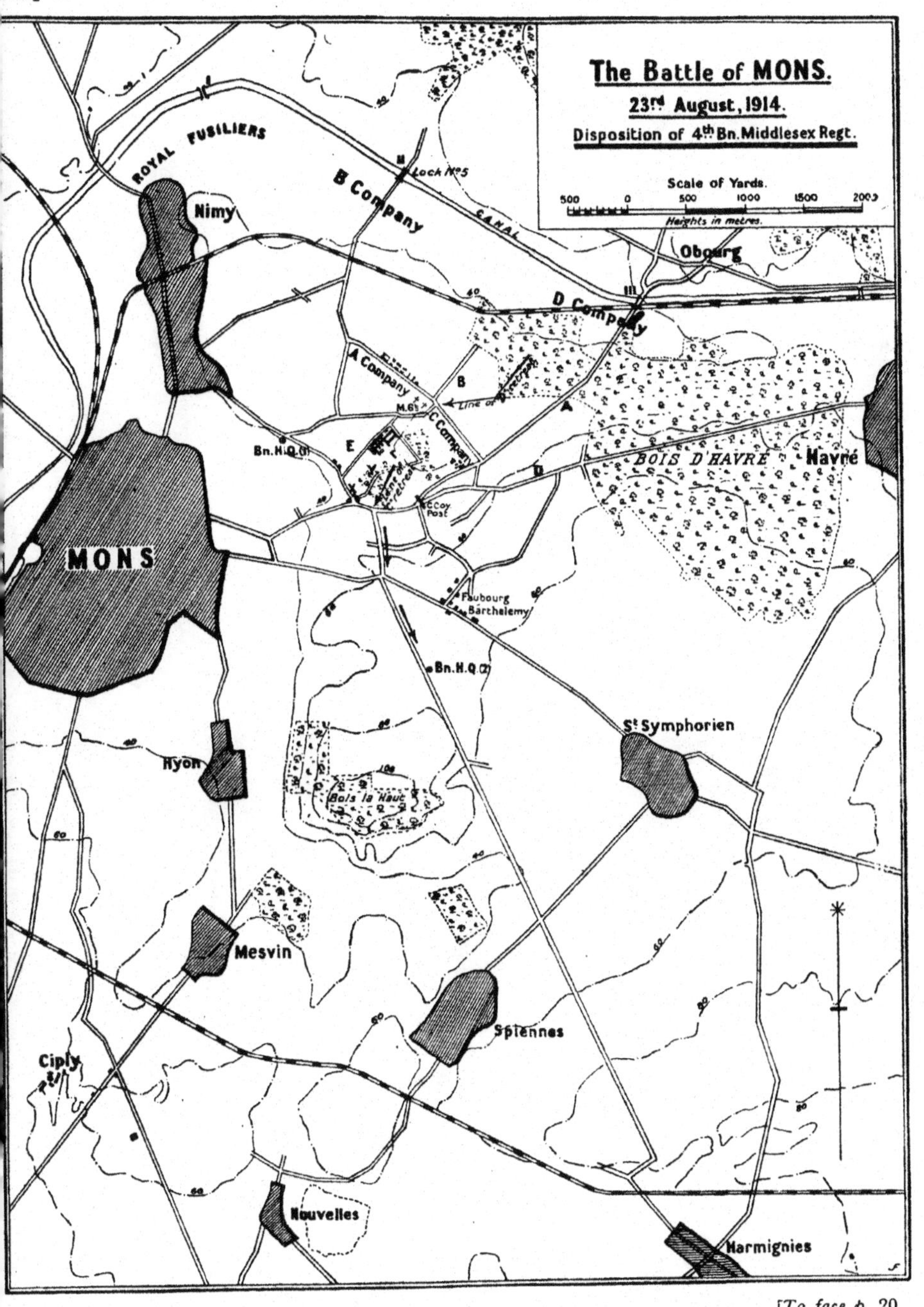
The Battle of MONS.
23rd August, 1914.
Disposition of 4th Bn. Middlesex Regt.
Scale of Yards.
500 0 500 1000 1500 2000
Heights in metres.
ROYAL FUSILIERS
Lock No 5
B Company
CANAL
Nimy
Obourg
D Company
A Company
B
Line of Retreat
A
M.G.
C Company
Bn. H.Q. (1)
E
D
C Coy Post
BOIS D'HAVRE
Havré
MONS
Faubourg Barthelemy
Bn. H.Q. (2)
St Symphorien
Hyon
Bois la Haut
Mesvin
Spiennes
Ciply
Nouvelles
Harmignies

[*To face p.* 20.

Map 1.

# CHAPTER III.

## The Retreat from Mons—I.

DISILLUSIONMENT and suffering often go hand-in-hand with the realisation of a dream. For many years before 1914 the British soldier had dreamed of the day (which he was frequently being told was surely coming) when he would find himself ranged in battle against the Germans: the enemy had similar dreams. And if the records of that first clash of arms are carefully studied—German* as well as British—it will be seen that out of that first encounter at Mons there emerged that wonderful feeling which possessed the British soldier throughout the whole war, that given equality in numbers, he was a better man than the German. And on that first night of battle, the 23rd August, 1914, confidence and a firm belief in his ability comforted him as he lay, weary from marching and fighting, fighting and marching, his poor tired body aching in every limb, as he tried to snatch a few short hours of rest before dawn. The horrors of that first day had disillusioned his mind of the "grandness of war," but in suffering he had gained strength.

23RD-24TH AUGUST.

On the night of 23rd August, the general feeling amongst regimental officers and the rank and file in the fighting line was that the Battle would be continued on the morning of the 24th. But shortly after 11 p.m. the senior staff officers of the Ist and IInd Corps and Cavalry Division were summoned to G.H.Q. at Le Cateau, and there they were told that it was the intention of Sir John French to make a general retreat southwards for about eight miles to a line running from east to west from La Longueville, through Bavai and four miles beyond the latter to La Boiserette: a front of about seven miles. The right of the new line would be

* The German Official Monograph, "Die Schlacht bei Mons," contains the following summary of the Battle:—"Well entrenched and completely hidden, the enemy opened a murderous fire . . . the casualties increased . . . the (German) rushes became shorter, and finally the whole advance stopped . . . with bloody losses, the attack gradually came to an end."

five miles west of the French fortress, Maubeuge. The Corps were to retire in mutual co-operation.

Reports of the retreat of the French on his right, of the strength of the enemy on his front and the danger of envelopment of his left, had reached Sir John and he had decided to effect a retirement to the Maubeuge position at daybreak.

24TH AUGUST.

The retirement began at dawn on the 24th,* the Ist Corps covering the movements of the IInd Corps, the cavalry simultaneously making a demonstration. The enemy had already opened fire with his artillery against the right of the IInd Corps (3rd Division), but otherwise the 8th Infantry Brigade was little troubled, and at 6 a.m. the G.O.C., 3rd Division issued orders to the Brigade to withdraw from Nouvelles. The German infantry made no advance, and at 8 a.m. the 8th Brigade† began its march in a south-westerly direction on Genly.

4TH BATTALION.

The 4th Middlesex apparently obtained but a brief respite in their stubble-field, for before it was light they marched off (or all that was left of the Battalion) towards Quévy. The Battalion numbered now about half its strength in officers and other ranks, and these were already in great need of rest, having been on the move since the morning of the 22nd.

Exactly at what hour the Battalion reached Quévy it is impossible to say,‡ but having arrived at the village the men set to work with their entrenching tools to "scrape" holes in the ground, *i.e.*, in official terms "to prepare a defensive position." Here about noon fresh orders were received to continue the march southwards, on Bavai. "Hardly had we left our 'scrapings' when the whole line we had occupied was shelled. This was to a certain extent expected, as a 'Taube' had been hovering over us,

* At dawn on the 24th August, the British Expeditionary Force held the following positions:—

Ist Corps: 1st Division, Grand Reng, Rouveroy, Givry; 5th Cavalry Brigade, Givry; 2nd Division, Harmignies, Harveng, Pâturages, Bougnies.

IInd Corps: 3rd Division, 8th Infantry Brigade, Nouvelles; 7th Infantry Brigade Ciply; 9th Infantry Brigade, Frameries.

5th Division, Pâturages, Wasmes, Hornu, Bois de Boussu, Champ des Sarts, Hornu.

19th Infantry Brigade and Cavalry Division, Thulin, Elouges, Audregnies, Quievrain.

† The diary of the 4th Battalion Middlesex Regiment and a private diary kept by an officer of that Battalion both state that the Battalion retired at 3 a.m.

‡ The 8th Brigade Diary states that the Brigade took up a position at Genly on left of 4th (Guards) Brigade of the 2nd Division (Ist Corps) at 10.30 a.m.

which was apparently signalling to a German battery by means of ' flare lights.' This somewhat hastened our retirement, but our casualties were few. From Bavai we continued the march to Amfroipret, where we bivouacked for the night. Warm day."* 24TH AUGUST.

On the left flank of the B.E.F. the 19th Infantry Brigade had retired on Jenlain via Elouges. "The retirement," the Brigade diary reports, "was carried out in good order and with little loss. Near Elouges the Brigade was placed under the orders of General Allenby, commanding the Cavalry Division. From Elouges the direction was changed S.E., and Jenlain was reached about 4 p.m., 13 miles." The village was entrenched. The 1st Battalion Middlesex had retired from St. Aybert at about 2.30 a.m., carrying away their wounded, and reached Jenlain apparently without having joined action with the enemy. For by now the IInd German Corps (First German Army) had arrived and was engaged in endeavouring to turn the left flank of the B.E.F. Very early in the morning a British aeroplane had observed this Corps moving via Peruwelz round the N.W. of Condé. 1ST BATTALION.

During the day the Cavalry and the 5th Division of the IInd Corps had been heavily engaged with the enemy,† whose efforts were bent upon holding the B.E.F. to its ground whilst the turning movement from the left developed. Von Kluck's intention was to hem the British up against the fortress of Maubeuge and, in conjunction with the Second German Army, surround it.

In an excellent summary of the operations which took place on the 24th August, the Official History states:—"Thus ended the first day of the retreat. All circumstances considered, although the casualties were considerable, the operations had been remarkably successful. The 5th Division had, indeed, been called upon not only to defend six miles of front, but also, with the help of the Cavalry and of the 19th Infantry Brigade, to parry von Kluck's enveloping attack; but it had triumphantly accomplished its tasks. The flanking battalions to the east and west, it is true, suffered much, but only one had been actually overwhelmed,

* Diary of Lieut.-Colonel H. W. E. Finch. Apparently the Battalion retired in Brigade, and the diary of the latter states that the Brigade (less 2nd Royal Scots) reached Amfroipret by 9 p.m.

† A flank guard action was fought with the enemy at Elouges.

24TH AUGUST. not a single gun had been lost, and the enemy had been very severely punished. Our troops were still confident that when on anything like equal terms they were more than a match for their opponents; the one trouble that really oppressed them was want of sleep. Long after nightfall the battalions of the 3rd Division were passing the cross-roads in Bavai, the men stumbling along more like ghosts than living soldiers, unconscious of everything about them, but still moving under the magic impulse of discipline and regimental pride. Marching, they were hardly awake; halted, whether sitting or standing, they were instantly asleep. And those men on the eastern flank of the Corps had done little fighting and endured little pressure during the day. Even worse was it on the western flank, where cavalry and infantry had had hard fighting from dawn till dusk, and many a man had been for over 24 hours without sleep or food. *And this, it must be borne in mind, was only the beginning of the retreat.*"

Despite the failure of von Kluck to wedge Sir John French up against Maubeuge, the danger of staying too long on the line taken up west of the fortress was clear. "The French were still retiring," said Sir John, "and I had no support except such as was afforded by the Fortress of Maubeuge; and the determined attempts of the enemy to get round my left flanks assured me that it was his intention to hem me up against that place and surround me."* "I felt that not a moment must be lost in retiring to another position."† Sir John's right flank was also dangerously exposed, the left of the XVIII French Corps (Fifth French Army) being already ten miles in rear of the British right.

The position to which the retreat was to be continued was some 15 miles further south, in the neighbourhood of Le Cateau, *i.e.*, roughly on the line Avesnes–Le Cateau–Caudry. The Ist Corps was to march southwards by roads east from Bavai to Montay, which meant that the Corps would retire east of the Forêt de Mormal, whilst the IInd Corps was to march west of the Forest,

* "The attack (on 24th) is to be carried out so that the enemy will be thrown back on Maubeuge, and his retreat to the west cut off."—von Kluck.

† The approximate disposition of the B.E.F. on the night 24th–25th August was as follows:—

5th Cavalry Brigade, Feignies: Ist Corps—1st Division, Feignies–La Longueville: 2nd Division Bavai. IInd Corps, 5th Division, Bavai, St. Waast: 3rd Division, St. Waast, Amfroipret–Bermeries.

Cavalry Division, St. Waast, Wargnies: 19th Infantry Brigade, Jenlain, Saultain.

mainly along the Bavai–Montay road. The IInd Corps was to be covered by two brigades of the Cavalry Division. The 19th Infantry Brigade, with the remainder of the Cavalry Division, was to act as the west flank guard.

All rear-guards were to be clear of the Bavai–Eth Road by 5.30 a.m. on the 25th.

There are, however, no records of either battalion of the Middlesex Regiment having engaged the enemy during the 25th. 25TH AUGUST.

The 7th Infantry Brigade of the 3rd Division formed its rear-guard so that the 4th Battalion was out of touch with the enemy all day. The 8th Brigade marched via Wargnies–Le Quesnoy–Beaudignies–Solesmes to Caudry, the 9th Infantry Brigade taking a road further east. The 4th Battalion Middlesex set out at 5 a.m., and, though hung up for a while before starting, owing to the crossing from east to west of long columns of French troops (Sordet's Cavalry), eventually reached Caudry, thence on to Audencourt, where very poor billets were obtained.* Just before arriving at Caudry a very severe thunderstorm broke over the troops, and when they reached Audencourt officers and men were drenched to the skin. In the few houses and barns allotted to the Battalion fires were lighted at which wet clothes were dried. The room in which the officers were accommodated was bare of furniture and dirty, and straw was the only bedding obtainable. The 2nd Royal Scots (right) and the 1st Gordon Highlanders (left) formed the outposts of the 8th Infantry Brigade for the night. 4TH BATTALION.

Meanwhile the 1st Battalion Middlesex (in Brigade) marched out of Jenlain at 4 a.m., retiring on Haussy, which was reached about midday. Here the 19th Brigade was called upon to support the Cavalry, who were in action with the enemy W. and N.W. of Haussy. Although under shell-fire, the Middlesex sustained no casualties, and the march was resumed to Solesmes, where, south of the town, the 19th Brigade passed through the outposts of the 4th Division,† thence on to Le Cateau. The latter village was reached at 10 p.m., where, tired and worn out‡ (the Brigade 1ST BATTALION.

* The march this day was just on 30 miles.

† The 4th Division had arrived from England on the 24th and had been moved out to Solesmes to assist the retirement of the IInd Corps.

‡ "Very wet, very tired, but unbroken in spirit."—Brigadier-General (then Major) F. G. M. ROWLEY.

25TH AUGUST. had marched 19 miles during the day), the battalions bivouacked in the square and goods station.

Thus, practically without incident so far as the Middlesex Regiment was concerned, closed the first stages of the Retreat from Mons. But the enemy from the front and on the left of the B.E.F. was closing in, and action could not long be delayed.

# CHAPTER IV.

## THE BATTLE OF LE CATEAU.

26th August, 1914.

WHATEVER hopes the troops of the IInd Corps (who throughout the 25th had been fighting and retiring) entertained of a night's rest on the Le Cateau–Cambrai line they were doomed to disappointment. For although a number of units had reached the new line during the evening, many others did not reach their allotted areas until late at night or in the early hours of the 26th. 25TH AUGUST.

In the battalions and lower formations another battle next day was fully expected, though at G.H.Q., and amongst the Staff generally, it was early recognised that such a battle would be fraught with the greatest danger to the B.E.F. And, indeed, the tired and weary troops were not all settled in their billets and bivouacs before orders were issued to continue the retirement at the earliest possible moment. "Although the troops had been ordered to occupy the Cambrai–Le Cateau–Landrecies position, and the ground had during the 25th* been partially prepared and entrenched, I had grave doubts, owing to the information I received, as to the accumulating strength of the enemy against me† and as to the wisdom of standing there to fight.

"Having regard to the continued retirement of the French on my right, my exposed left flank, the tendency of the enemy's Western Corps (IInd)‡ to envelop me, and more than all, the exhausted condition of the troops, I determined to make a great

* Mostly by civilian labour.

† On the morning of the 25th, the German IInd Cavalry Corps and IVth and IIIrd Corps were close enough to the British to be able to strike in force at Le Cateau in the early morning, whilst the IVth Reserve, IInd and Xth Corps were within a march of the field, with parts of the IXth and VIIth Corps, drawn from the investment of Maubeuge, available in case of need.

‡ IInd Cavalry Corps. A German Cavalry Corps at this period included troops of all arms—Cavalry, Artillery, Jäger (Rifle) Battalions, etc.

25TH AUGUST. effort to continue the retreat till I could put some substantial obstacle, such as the Somme or the Oise, between my troops and the enemy, and afford the former some opportunity of rest and reorganisation. Orders were therefore sent to the Corps Commanders to continue their retreat as soon as they possibly could towards the general line Vermand–St. Quentin–Ribemont. The Cavalry, under General Allenby, were ordered to cover the retirement."

Sir John French had, in fact, issued orders at 7.30 p.m. for the continued retirement to begin as soon as possible. There was no doubt as to the close proximity of the enemy in great force ; the Ist Corps was attacked at Maroilles and Landrecies, just as Sir Douglas Haig's troops were settling down for the night ; earlier, the IInd Corps had been struck at at Solesmes : there was no time to lose.

At 10.15 p.m. the IInd Corps Commander (Sir Horace Smith-Dorrien) had, in accordance with Sir John French's orders, issued instructions for the retreat to be continued on the following morning, the transport to start at 4 a.m., and the main bodies at 7 a.m. Later, however, as the true situation revealed itself, Sir Horace saw that such a retirement was impossible : his troops, some of which at that hour were still coming in, were too exhausted : Allenby's Cavalry was scattered and could not be collected in time to cover the retirement, and the enemy was in possession of the high ground and the ridges about it, north of Viesly, which would have to be recaptured by the cavalry in order to cover the initial stages of the retreat. There was, in fact, no
26TH AUGUST. option left him but to stand and fight and, at 3.30 a.m., a message was sent from IInd Corps Headquarters (at Bertry) to G.H.Q., then at St. Quentin, by motor car informing Sir John French of the situation, and the determination of Sir Horace Smith-Dorrien to give battle to the enemy. Sir John's reply contained the following : " If you can hold your ground, the situation appears likely to improve. 4th Division must co-operate. French troops are taking offensive on right of Ist Corps. Although you are given a free hand as to method, this telegram is not intended to convey the impression that I am not as anxious for you to carry out the retirement, and you must make every endeavour to do so."

Some units of the IInd Corps appear to have received orders to stand and fight at various times between 3.30 a.m. and 6 a.m. on 26th ; others did not receive them until they were formed up ready to move off southwards at 7 a.m. in accordance with previous instructions, not indeed until the enemy's artillery had opened fire from gun positions three miles N.N.E. of Le Cateau. With the firing of these guns—the first on that now historic day—the battle opened. The hour was just after 6 a.m., and at that period the approximate position of the B.E.F. was as follows: The right of the line, the Ist Corps, had already set out from Le Grand Fayt–Marbaix–Dammerre (1st Division) and Landrecies–Maroilles–Noyelles (2nd Division) on its retirement southwards, and was some miles east and south-east of Le Cateau when the battle opened. Of the 5th Division, IInd Corps, the 14th Infantry Brigade was split up, half lying east and half west of the town of Le Cateau, the 13th Infantry Brigade was just west of the Roman Road (*i.e.*, Montay–Reumont Road), and the 15th Infantry Brigade held Troisvilles: of the 3rd Division, the 9th Brigade held Inchy, the 8th Brigade Audencourt and the 7th Brigade Caudry. The 4th Division, on the line Fontaine au Pire–Haucourt, covered the left of the IInd Corps. The 19th Infantry Brigade was in Le Cateau. Only cavalry* operated in the very considerable gap between the Ist and IInd Corps. Portions of the 2nd, 1st and 2nd Cavalry Brigades and the 4th Cavalry Brigade were at Le Cateau, Troisvilles, Beaumont and Ligny respectively. In these positions battle was joined with the enemy. 26TH AUGUST.

When dawn of the 26th August broke—a day long to be remembered in British military history—a thick mist hung over the hills and the valleys of the battlefield-to-be. The town of Le Cateau (in which the 1st Middlesex with other units of the 19th Infantry Brigade had snatched a few hours' rest in the square and goods station) was at an early hour encumbered with a miscellaneous collection of vehicles of various formations, ambulances and G.S. wagons jostled civilian carts and battalions' transport. As a result, the 19th Infantry Brigade, which had originally received orders to be clear of the town by 5.30, had to hang on until 6.30 a.m., and the 1st Middlesex, detailed as rear-guard, came into action with the enemy. For, as already stated, very soon after 6 a.m. German artillery, hidden from view by the mist, opened fire from N.N.E. of Le Cateau. Under cover of their artillery the German infantrymen advanced, and by 6.30 a.m. had penetrated the outskirts of the town even as the British troops were withdrawing. This was the beginning of the enemy's 1ST BATTALION.

* 3rd Cavalry Brigade just east of Bazuel, with parts of the 1st and 2nd Cavalry Brigades at Catillon.

26TH AUGUST. attempt to penetrate the gap between the Ist and IInd Corps and roll up the right flank of the latter. A little street fighting took place in Le Cateau, and, as the Middlesex acted as rear-guard, it is possible that the Battalion exchanged shots with the enemy, but there are no records to that effect. The Battalion diary, however, states: "Germans had entered town before we got away: leaving town, came into action, keeping enemy back till all clear: leaving town, going S.W., passed through hastily thrown-up trenches of 5th Division and took up position in support of 5th Division by wood north of Reumont."

Meanwhile, the hostile artillery fire had greatly increased in volume, and shells were falling thick and fast upon the right flank of the IInd Corps, the high ground between Le Cateau and the Roman Road receiving special attention. The right of the British line, *i.e.*, the 14th and 13th Infantry Brigades, was caught in enfilade by German guns firing from concealed positions south of Neuvilly, and casualties became heavy.

About 9 a.m. the 1st Middlesex and 2nd Argyll and Sutherland Highlanders, still just south of the Wood N. of Reumont, were ordered out to occupy and entrench the slopes S.W. of the Roman Road, *i.e.*, the right flank of the 14th Infantry Brigade, whilst the two remaining battalions of the 19th Brigade were sent off to report to the G.O.C. of the 14th "to assist a situation described as critical, but these two battalions were scarcely engaged."

1ST BATTALION. The Middlesex and Highlanders deployed about 10 a.m. and moved eastwards, the latter Battalion occupying a position on the right of the Manchester Regiment (14th Brigade), on the high ground about the Le Cateau–Reumont road. The Middlesex dug (or rather, "scraped") entrenchments about 1,000 yards N. of Les Essarts Fme., from which position the Battalion supported the Highlanders. Both battalions were now under heavy shell fire, from which there was no shelter as their hastily dug entrenchments were but "scrapings" in the ground, for entrenching tools had been lost or thrown away during the first phase of the retreat from Mons. The time was now between noon and 1 p.m.

The intention of the Germans in the Battle of Le Cateau is perfectly clear when the nature of their attack is considered. They had fallen heavily upon the right flank (5th Division and 19th Infantry Brigade) of the IInd Corps, but until a much later hour than 6.30 a.m. the centre of the British line was not subjected to the same severity of attack, though against the left of the line

(4th Division) vigorous efforts were made by the enemy to turn that flank. The centre of the line was held by the 3rd Division, 9th Brigade (Troisvilles), 8th Brigade (Audencourt) and 7th Brigade (Caudry), in the order given from right to left. 26TH AUGUST.

At dawn the " trenches," which had been prepared by civilians under military supervision, in front of Audencourt were improved and further fresh trenches dug by troops of the 8th Infantry Brigade, who, it will be remembered, had passed the night of 25th–26th in that village. Before dawn picquets had been pushed forward to north of the main road from Le Cateau to Cambrai. Daylight found the 8th Brigade occupying the following positions: 2nd Royal Scots, right of the line; 1st Gordon Highlanders, left of the line; two companies Royal Irish Regiment prolonging and strengthening the line of the Gordon Highlanders towards Caudry, the remaining two companies in reserve in a sunken road passing from south of Audencourt through the north of the village; one company 4th Middlesex Regiment in the front line to prolong the line of the 2nd Royal Scots and connect the latter with 9th Brigade, one company on the rising ground in rear of 2nd Royal Scots, firing over the heads of the latter, and the remaining companies in reserve in the eastern corner of Audencourt. 4TH BATTALION.

About 6 a.m. the picquets fell back and, shortly after, German shells began to fall, but did so little harm that the men continued working on the trenches. Then, about two thousand yards away, the German infantry could be seen advancing in thin lines down towards the Le Cateau–Cambrai road. They were too far off to be engaged by riflemen, but the divisional artillery opened fire and the gunners burst their shrapnel beautifully amongst the enemy's troops, scattering them in all directions and strewing the ground with dead and wounded. For two or three hours the infantry of the 8th Brigade lay in their " scrapings " in the ground watching the duel between the British and German artillery, and the splendid shooting of the former whenever bodies of hostile infantry presented a favourable target. Then, about 9 a.m. the machine gunners of the 4th Middlesex and the Royal Scots found targets in small bodies of Germans who were attempting to cross the Cambrai road. But for several hours the fighting was of a desultory nature and, while the 7th Brigade in Caudry was more heavily attacked, the enemy along the whole front of the 3rd Division seemed to be husbanding his strength for a later effort.

26TH AUGUST. Indeed, an officer of the 4th Middlesex said: "Everything went merrily for us until about 4.30 p.m., when word came down the line that the Germans had broken through one of our divisions and the order was given to retire."*

1ST BATTALION. For a while it is necessary to leave the 4th Middlesex and see what was happening to the 1st Battalion on the right of the British line. Owing largely to the splendid devotion of the artillery, the right flank had maintained its position and had beaten off heavy infantry attacks: "After nearly six hours of incessant and overwhelming fire the right of the British line, which rested on Le Cateau, still stood firm. The German infantry was steadily increasing in numbers on their front and, despite all efforts, was drawing steadily nearer. Their right flank was open, they were searched with fire from right and left, and strong columns, betokening the advance of the German IIIrd Corps, were closing in upon the right flank. It mattered not: they had been ordered to stand."†

Shortly before 1 p.m. Sir Charles Fergusson (G.O.C., 5th Division), from his Headquarters at Reumont, "could see that the right of his Division was shaken and might shortly give way," and he reported the situation to IInd Corps Headquarters. A little later, observing that the enemy was making determined efforts to work round his right towards Bazuel, he suggested that unless assistance was given him he had better begin the retirement. At 1.40 p.m. the G.O.C., 5th Division, received a message from the Corps Commander asking him to hold his position "a little longer so as to allow the preliminary movements of the retirement to take effect, but to begin the withdrawal of the 5th Division as soon as he should think fit." The 3rd and 4th Divisions had been ordered to follow the withdrawal of the 5th in succession.

The route allotted to the 5th Division and 19th Infantry Brigade lay southwards along two roads (i) via Bertry–Marence, and thence the Roman Road to Vermand; (ii) via Reumont–Maurois–Busigny–Bohain–Brancourt–Joncourt–Bellenglise. The 3rd Division was to retire via Montigny–Clary–Elincourt–Malincourt–Beaurevoir–Gouy–Bony–Hargicourt–Jeancourt.

Immediately west of Le Cateau the enemy was now making desperate efforts against the British line. Splendid efforts were made by the devoted artillery to beat the enemy back, but in

* Lieut.-Colonel H. W. E. Finch.

† Official History (Military Operations) of the War.

great numbers the German infantry swarmed across the Cambrai road and, falling upon the gallant 2nd Suffolk Regiment (14th Brigade) and three platoons of the 2nd Argyll and Sutherland Highlanders (19th Infantry Brigade) were finally overwhelmed. Before the end came, however, these devoted British soldiers had taken heavy toll of the enemy, "two officers of the Highlanders, in particular, bringing down man after man, and counting their scores aloud as if at a competition." But although the Suffolks and Highlanders were overwhelmed, the enemy's advance was stayed by other troops.

26TH AUGUST.

1ST BATTALION.

It is impossible to go into all the details of that fine action, but during that tense period two companies of the 1st Middlesex, with two half-companies of the Argyll and Sutherland Highlanders, the 59th Field Company, R.E., and two companies of the 1st R. Scots Fusiliers (the latter belonging to the 9th Brigade) had moved down the western slope of the valley of the Selle to meet the threat from the right flank. Soon (towards 3 p.m.) the Germans were seen advancing from the east across the spur on the opposite side of the valley. At once the Highlanders and the machine-gun section of the Middlesex engaged them at 1,200 yards range, whereupon the enemy hesitated, and finally beat a retreat. Half an hour later the Germans again ventured to show themselves, advancing in extended order, and although it was not so easy for the machine guns to beat them back, the guns of two Horse Artillery batteries compelled them again to seek shelter. Thus the further advance of the Germans was, for the time being, held up and the retirement began.

The 1st Middlesex, on the right of the Argyll and Sutherland Highlanders, now withdrew up the valley of the Selle towards Reumont. "About 4 p.m., on all remainder of force retiring, retirement was ordered by Lieut.-Colonel Ward, commanding Battalion. Retirement was successfully carried out in good order via Reumont, where hospital was established in Church, which was shelled. Battalion, after Reumont, now became somewhat broken up owing to congestion of road. Retirement proceeded S. of Estrées, where Battalion went into bivouac about 10 p.m."* The casualty list of the 1st Battalion for 26th August gives the numbers as Capt. H. E. Spence and the Battalion M.O., Capt. McConagay, wounded, 2 other ranks killed, 36 wounded and 74 missing, with an added note "many more probably."

* Battalion Diary, 1st Middlesex Regiment.

26TH AUGUST. Meanwhile the 8th Brigade in Audencourt had, between 3.30 and 4 p.m., received orders from 3rd Divisional Headquarters to make a retirement. Almost immediately the troops on both flanks began to fall back, which left the flank of the 8th Brigade exposed and, indeed, ended in almost the whole of the battalions of 2nd Royal Irish Rifles and 1st Gordon Highlanders being cut off by the enemy.

4TH BATTALION. The 4th Middlesex appear to have withdrawn at 5 p.m. without incident to Vermand, having lost all its transport and horses, which with the Brigade Transport had been parked in a farm yard at Audencourt, and totally destroyed by the enemy's shell fire.*

* There are no further details in the Diary of the 4th Middlesex of the Battle of Le Cateau, the Battalion account numbering only 36 words. Casualties are not given.

Map II.

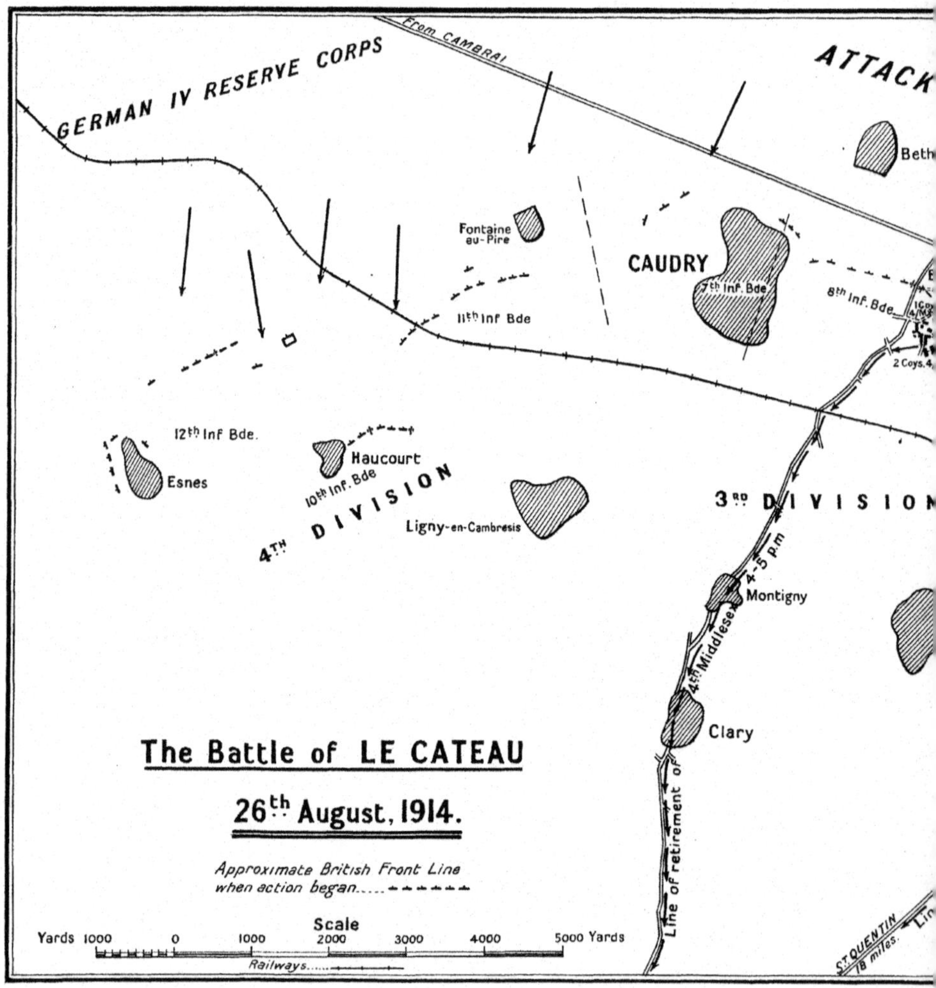
GERMAN IV RESERVE CORPS
From CAMBRAI
ATTACK
Beth
Fontaine au-Pire
CAUDRY
7th Inf. Bde
8th Inf. Bde
11th Inf Bde
2 Coys. 4
12th Inf Bde.
Esnes
Haucourt
10th Inf. Bde
4TH DIVISION
Ligny-en-Cambresis
3RD DIVISION
4-5 p.m
Montigny
4th Middlesex
Clary
Line of retirement of
ST QUENTIN 18 miles
The Battle of LE CATEAU
26th August, 1914.
Approximate British Front Line when action began
Scale
Yards 1000 0 1000 2000 3000 4000 5000 Yards
Railways

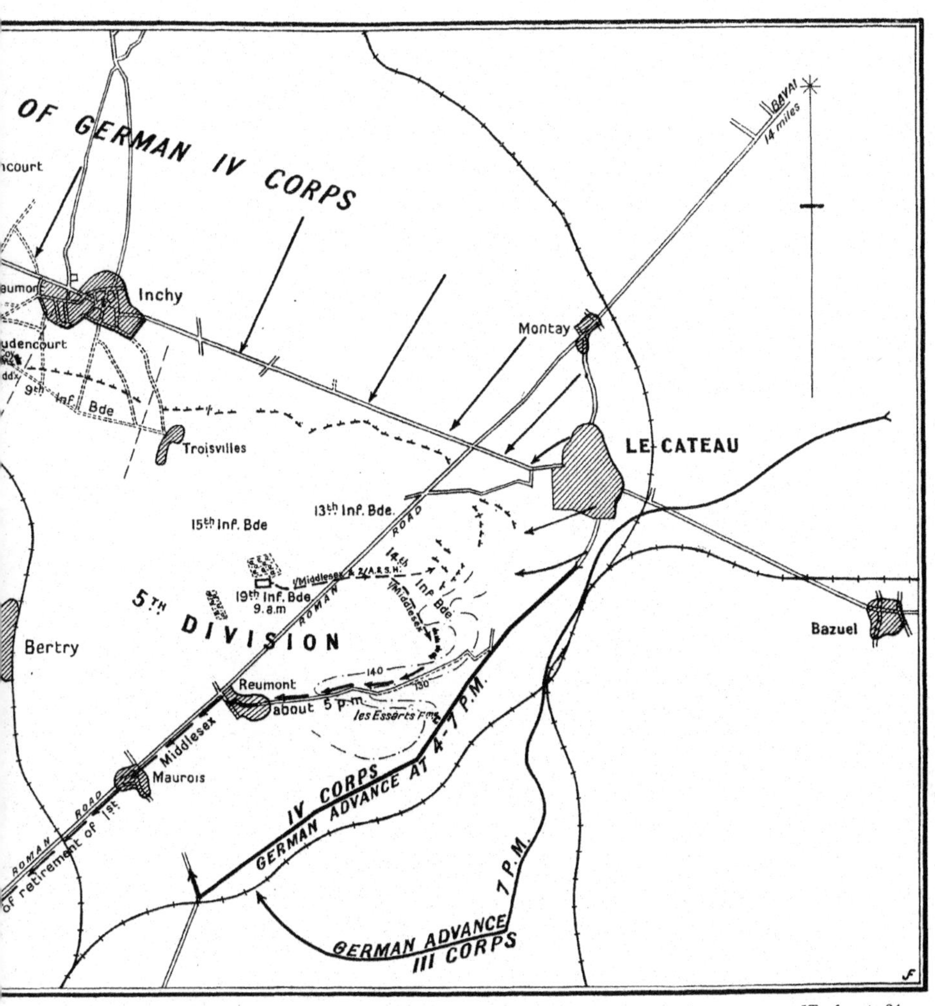
OF GERMAN IV CORPS
Inchy
Troisvilles
Montay
LE CATEAU
BAVAI 14 miles
13th Inf. Bde.
15th Inf. Bde
9th Inf. Bde
5TH DIVISION
19th Inf. Bde. 9.a.m
1/Middlesex & 2/A.&S.H.
14th Inf. Bde
1/Middlesex
ROMAN ROAD
Bertry
Reumont
about 5 p.m.
les Essarts Fme
140
130
Maurois
Middlesex
Bazuel
IV CORPS
GERMAN ADVANCE AT 4-7 P.M.
7 P.M.
GERMAN ADVANCE
III CORPS

[To face p. 34.

# CHAPTER V.

## The Retreat Resumed: II.

WHAT might have happened had the Germans closely pursued the British troops as the latter withdrew in a south-westerly direction from the battlefield of Le Cateau, it is impossible to say. But they did not. Von Kluck's Divisions were "dead beat"! Their second pitched battle with the B.E.F. had again inspired them with a wholesome fear of the deadly use to which the British soldier put his rifle, whilst the British Artilleryman had again demonstrated that, though outnumbered by about four to one, his shooting was without its equal. Heavy casualties, exhaustion and, moreover, the continual uncertainty of the exact whereabouts of Sir Horace Smith-Dorrien's troops, held up the German advance, and, indeed, von Kluck did not issue orders for the pursuit to continue until early on the 27th, by which time the B.E.F. was some miles distant, having almost lost touch with the enemy. 26TH AUGUST.

After the battle the 1st Battalion Middlesex had reached Estrées at about 10 p.m., and had gone into bivouac, a march of 15 miles. The 4th Middlesex had retired to Vermand, though it must have been very late when the Battalion arrived, for the village is between 30 and 35 miles from Audencourt, an altogether extraordinary marching feat after fighting all day.* 1ST BATTALION.

At 1.30 a.m. on the 27th the 1st Middlesex marched from Estrées on St. Quentin, the Battalion forming the rear-guard of the 19th Infantry Brigade. Strange scenes were witnessed that morning. The roads south were packed with transport and ambulances, supply wagons and countless civilian vehicles. Units were seemingly hopelessly mixed, and "confusion worse confounded" reigned. But a wonderful spirit of cheerfulness permeated the ranks of the tired, hungry and very woebegone-in-appearance battalions, as they trudged, whistling and singing, limping and 27TH AUGUST.

* This statement is authenticated both by 4th Battalion Diary and the private diary of Lieut.-Colonel H. W. E. Finch, late 4th Battalion Middlesex Regiment.

C 2

27TH AUGUST. hobbling, along the dusty roads. From St. Quentin, the 1st Middlesex (in Brigade) passed on to Ham, thence east to Ollezy, a little village about 6 miles away, where, at 4 p.m., the Battalion and the Brigade bivouacked. Colonel Ward (commanding 1st Middlesex) had assumed temporary command of the 19th Brigade, Major R. J. Ross, also of the 1st Battalion, acting temporarily as Brigade Major. Ollezy is about 50 miles from Le Cateau, and the Brigade had covered this distance since the evening of the previous day. Little wonder that the men were dead beat.

4TH BATTALION. The 4th Middlesex had also passed through Ham, having marched out of Vermand at 1.45 a.m. A halt was made at the former town, the Battalion billeting until 11 p.m., though a diarist records that "only the Colonel had a bed." From Ham, the march was continued southwards until Genvry, north of Noyon, was reached at 6 p.m., and here the Battalion put up for the night.

28TH AUGUST. 1ST BATTALION. At dawn on the 28th the troops were early astir, the 19th Brigade being ready to move off at 4.30 a.m. It was, however, 6 a.m. before the 1st Middlesex, again detailed as rearguard, relieved the outposts guarding the crossings over the Crozat Canal, and marching S.S.W. via Cugny–Noyon and Pont l'Evêque to Pontoise went into bivouac at the latter place at about 10 p.m. The day's march had been 17 miles. "Both men and horses," says the 19th Brigade Diary, "were badly in need of rest, and had it not been for the help of some empty wagons in carrying men who were 'done' there would have been many more stragglers."

Neither Battalion had been in touch with the enemy throughout the 27th and 28th.

On the night of the 28th–29th, when all movements had been completed, the Ist Corps was south of the River Oise and La Fère in the northern edge of the Forest of St. Gobain and Coucy, from Fressancourt to Amigny: the 5th Cavalry Brigade was at Sinceny (S.E. of Chauny): 1st Cavalry Brigade at Berlancourt, 2nd Cavalry Brigade at Flavy le Meldeux–Plessis and 3rd Cavalry Brigade at Jussy: the IInd Corps was north and east of Noyon, on the line Freniches–Genvry–Pontoise: the 4th Cavalry Brigade was at Cressy. The right of the B.E.F. was six miles in rear of the left of the Fifth French Army, but the left of the Force was in touch with Sordet's cavalry.

Late at night on 28th Sir John French issued orders for the B.E.F. to halt and rest on the 29th, conditionally on all formations being withdrawn "to the south of a line practically east and west through Nesle and Ham connecting with the French at Vendeuil."*

Thus it came about that on the 29th the 1st Middlesex remained in bivouac at Pontoise until 5 p.m., at which hour the Battalion placed two companies on outpost duty for the night. The 4th Middlesex, however, marched out of Genvry at 2 p.m., and crossing the Canal and the River Oise, reached Cuts about midnight, where the Battalion turned into a chateau and laid down to rest in the courtyard. 29TH AUGUST. 1ST BATTALION. 4TH BATTALION.

Nothing of importance happened on the 30th August. The 1st Battalion at Pontoise withdrew outposts at 6 a.m. after the bridges had been destroyed and then marched off southwards to Attichy (N. of Aisne River), where the Battalion arrived at 5.30 p.m. and billeted. The 4th Battalion set out from Cuts at 5 a.m. and reached Courtieux, billeting for the night in the village. Both Battalions were now only about 4 miles distant from one another. The 1st Battalion had marched approximately 15 miles and the 4th Battalion nearly 16 miles. 30TH AUGUST. 1ST BATTALION. 4TH BATTALION.

On 31st the 4th left Courtieux at 6.15 a.m., reaching Vaumoise (about 5 miles E. of Crépy-en-Valois) without incident. The 1st left Attichy at 7.30 a.m., and continued the retirement all day through the Forêt de Compiègne, thankful for the cool shade of the trees. At 6.30 p.m. the Battalion arrived in St. Sauveur (in the S.W. corner of the Forest), where outposts were posted in conjunction with 12th Infantry Brigade (4th Division). Each Battalion had marched nearly 20 miles without molestation by the enemy. 31ST AUGUST. 4TH BATTALION. 1ST BATTALION.

But the 1st September was to tell a different story. For by that date von Kluck (First German Army) had changed direction. His headlong march on Paris, hitherto in a south-westerly direction, was suddenly changed, and on the 31st his Corps were directed against the line of the Oise from Compiègne to Chauny. In view of the action which took place on the following day (1st September) the position of the B.E.F. on the night 31st August–1st September is interesting. The Ist Corps had halted for the night in the northern exits of the Forêt de Villers Cotterets (1st Division around Missy, 2nd Division in the Laversine area). The left of the Fifth French Army was 12 miles north, near Vauxaillon. The IInd Corps was in the Coyolles area, S.W. of Villers Cotterets, and at Crépy-en-Valois, 5th Division on the east, 3rd Division on the west. The IIIrd Corps had made a flank

* Official History (Military Operations) of the War.

31st August.

march through the Forêt de Compiègne to the S.W. corner of the forest about Verberie: a gap of five miles existed between the inner flanks of the IInd and IIIrd Corps, though the latter was in touch on its left with the French through part of the Cavalry Division.

Operation orders, issued at 8.30 p.m., gave the moves to be carried out on 1st September, providing that all units reached their destinations at night on 31st August: Ist Corps to the area La Ferté–Betz; IInd Corps to Betz–Nanteuil; IIIrd Corps to Nanteuil-Baron: Cavalry Division to Baron–Mont l'Evêque.

If the line of march of the First German Army and the retirement of the B.E.F. are compared, it will be seen that whereas the Germans were advancing south-easterly, the British were retiring in a south-westerly direction. Thus it came about that von Kluck's new movement to outflank the Allies was again doomed to failure; indeed, he was marching into the very net which General Joffre had spread to catch him. Nevertheless, his change of direction was responsible for the three actions which took place on 1st September—the affair of Néry, the rearguard action of Crépy-en-Valois and the rearguard actions of Villers Cotterets—his advanced troops coming into contact with Sir John French's rearguards. But in only one of these—the first—was the Middlesex Regiment concerned. In this action, however, the 1st Battalion acquitted itself splendidly.

1st Battalion.

It will be remembered that on the night of 31st August–1st September the 1st Middlesex billeted at St. Sauveur in the south-west corner of the Forêt de Compiègne. The village was about 3 miles north-east of Saintines, where 19th Brigade Headquarters had put up for the night. The Brigade Diary states that "about 4 a.m. (1st September) a few Uhlans galloping along the village street (of Saintines) created some sensation, but calm soon prevailed."

1st September.

At 5.30 a.m. the 1st Middlesex withdrew outposts and marched on Saintines, joining up with 19th Brigade Headquarters. About 6 o'clock the Brigade, having ascended the hills south of the village, was met by a messenger, who asked for assistance urgently for the 1st Cavalry Brigade and "L" Battery, R.H.A., which were in difficulties at Néry and had suffered very heavily. Major F. G. M. Rowley,* who temporarily commanded the 1st Middlesex, was ordered to march his Battalion off immediately towards Néry.

* Major F. G. M. Rowley was promoted Lieutenant-Colonel on 1st September, 1914.

1st September. 1st Battalion.

"The enemy appears to have got right round the Cavalry and had succeeded in placing some ten field guns within 800 yards of their camp. The Cavalry had a great many casualties, whilst their horses were lying dead in rows."* Taking the nearest available Company ("D") with him, Major Rowley at once set off southwards towards Néry. On arriving at the village he reported to the G.O.C. 1st Cavalry Brigade, who said that the Middlesex could best render assistance by attacking the German guns which were firing from the high ground east of the village. On reaching the eastern exits of Néry, "D" Company and the two Battalion machine-guns under Lieut. Jefferd came into action against the hostile battery. Rapid rifle fire and machine-gun fire was then opened, and after two minutes the German guns ceased firing. Major Rowley then ordered "D" Company to advance and capture the guns. With bayonets fixed and a cheer, the Middlesex men rushed across the small intervening valley and captured eight of the guns which had been firing on the 1st Cavalry Brigade and "L" Battery, R.H.A. With the exception of some 12 dead or badly wounded Germans the gun crews had fled. A few minutes later the German limbers were seen about 1,000 yards away and fire was at once opened on them, but they retired rapidly and were seen no more. The guns were found to be undamaged, two of them being loaded. No horses, however, being available the sights were removed and the elevating gear damaged.

Meanwhile the two machine-guns under Lieut. Jefferd, after assisting in silencing the hostile artillery, had moved towards the sugar factory in rear of "L" Battery. Here they were under fire from the German gun escort, Lieut. Jefferd being wounded.

About twenty minutes after the guns were captured, the German gun escort was seen retiring across the open from near the sugar factory, and on fire being opened on them about 25 surrendered.

A little later some of the captured guns were brought away by the Cavalry, who had made up teams for the purpose.

In the meantime one-and-a-half companies of the Middlesex, co-operating with a Cavalry Regiment, had captured a German field ambulance with a few prisoners, in the next village eastwards.

This small action, insignificant as it may seem, is of considerable importance to Middlesex men, as the 1st Battalion of the Regiment was the first British unit to capture German guns in the war.

* Diary 19th Infantry Brigade.

1st September. The 4th Cavalry Brigade and "I" Battery from St. Vaast, and a composite battalion of troops from the 10th Brigade (4th Division) from Verberie, had likewise responded to the call for help, which had been sent to them as well as to the 19th Infantry Brigade. The guns of "I" Battery unlimbered and came into action, but as they did so "L" Battery* ceased firing, for all of its guns had either been put out of action or the gun teams killed or wounded.

After the action the general retirement was again continued, the Middlesex forming rearguard with the remainder of the 19th Infantry Brigade. "Of the eight guns captured by Battalion at least four were brought away, remainder having to be left as not enough horses for them." The Battalion billeted that night in Fresnoy.

4th Battalion. Meanwhile the 4th Battalion had also reached Fresnoy, where Colonel Hull's Battalion took up a night outpost line, mostly in stubble fields, "with 'stucks' to repose on." The Battalion had not been engaged during the day.

2nd September. 4th Battalion. At 2.30 a.m. on 2nd September the 4th Battalion rejoined the column at Chevrelle, "where we had a very hasty apology for a breakfast in a side street, and then continued our march through Bregy, Forfry, Gesvres to Monthyon, where we again took up a night outpost line, but on this occasion a certain number of houses were just in rear of the line, so a good many of us were in billets." A long march, between 20 and 30 miles.

1st Battalion. The 1st Battalion withdrew outposts at 5.30 a.m. and marched off in a S.S.W. direction through Othis on Dammartin. The 19th Brigade formed the rearguard, and about midday a message reached the Middlesex that General Briggs, with his Cavalry Brigade, had a cavalry force of the enemy *en l'air*, and asked for the assistance of the guns of the rearguard. But the artillery could not find suitable gun positions, and nothing could be done. From Dammartin the Middlesex pushed on to Longperrier, where the whole Battalion (with the A. and S. Highlanders on the right and R.W. Fusiliers on the left) took up an outpost line, west of the village; the 1st Middlesex had also covered a distance of about 20 miles.

If the word "incident" be taken to mean action with the enemy, the final stages of the Retreat from Mons, from 3rd to 5th

* The immortal story of the gallant action of "L" Battery, R.H.A., should be read in the Official History of the War.

Map III.

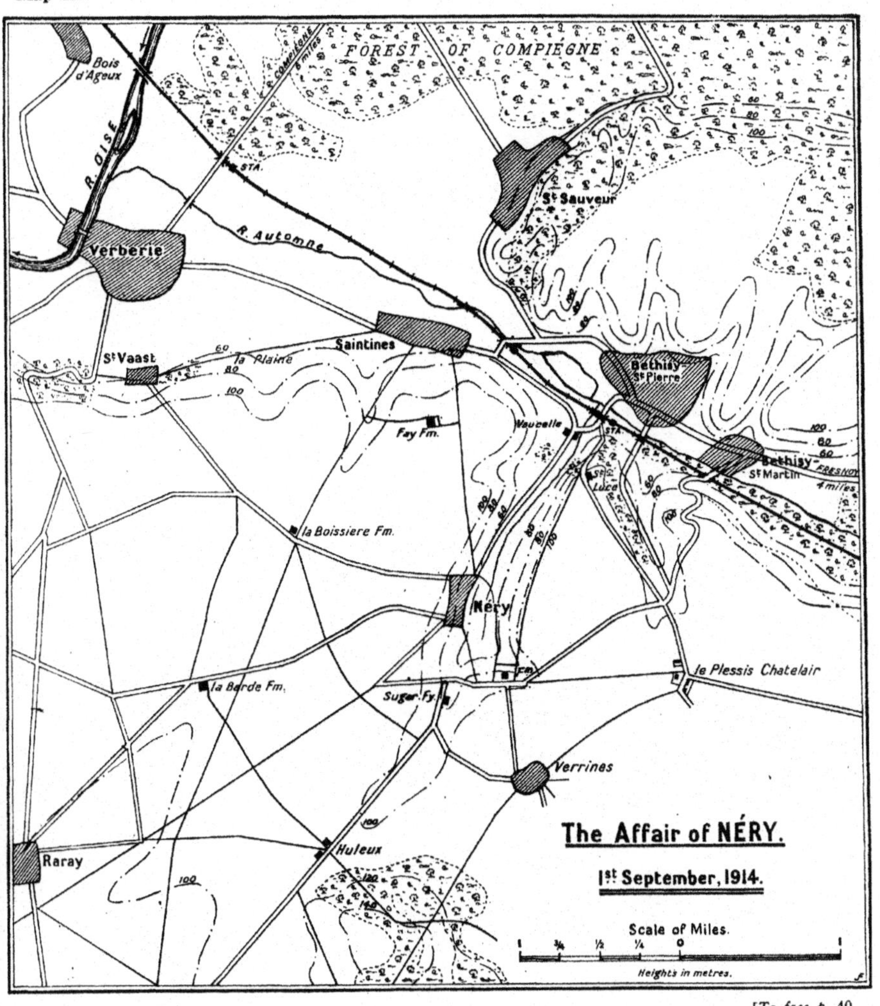


[To face p. 40.

September inclusive, were without incident. But, in common with their comrades of the B.E.F., the 1st and 4th Battalions of the Middlesex Regiment were very worn out and almost in rags. The long day marches in a merciless sun, short nights, often broken by alarms or spent on outpost duty, scanty rations picked up here and there from the roadside, where they had been " dumped " by the Army Service Corps in order that units as they passed might help themselves ; the things which kept the British soldier going were pride of regiment, his wonderful cheeriness, and extraordinary sense of humour. It came out in all directions and at all times. A civilian motor-driver, standing by the roadside and watching a squad of men go by—" a sergeant and a dozen or so Tommies, of most disreputable exterior "—asked them to which battalion they belonged. **2ND SEPTEMBER.**

" You oughter know who *we* are," said the sergeant, somewhat haughtily. " We're the lot what was first in Mons and last out, *we* are."

" That's right," piped up a squeaky voice that came from a diminutive member of the squad. " Buck, you beggar, buck. Tell 'em the tale."

A grin on half a dozen faces told that the small one might be expected to produce some comment when occasion permitted. The sergeant turned : " What's ailin' *you*, Shorty ? " he remarked.

" Tell 'em the tale," croaked the little man. " First in Mons and last out. In at three miles an hour and out at eighteen. That's us, you bet," and he snorted as the squad roared in appreciative mirth.

So they drifted on, anything but downhearted !

**3RD SEPTEMBER. 1ST BATTALION.**

At midnight on 2nd September the 1st Battalion withdrew outposts west of Longperrier and, retiring on the village, resumed its march S.S.W. on Lagny. The latter was reached by 9 a.m., but the Battalion went on to Chanteloup and bivouacked there at 1 p.m. This proved to be a long rest, for the Battalion did not move out of the village until 2 a.m. on the 5th, when, marching via Ferrières-Chevry, the last and final billets—at Grisy—of the memorable Retreat were reached at 2 a.m. Here two companies were placed on outpost duty west and north of the village ; here also Lieut.-Colonel Ward returned to his battalion, a new Brigadier—Colonel the Hon. F. Gordon—having taken over command of the 19th Infantry Brigade.*

* The 19th Infantry Brigade, with 4th Division, now formed the IIIrd Corps.

3RD SEPTEMBER. 4TH BATTALION. The 4th Middlesex marched out of Monthyon at 7 a.m. on 3rd September, and crossing the Marne at Meaux, proceeded through Nanteuil to Vancourtois, where the Battalion billeted. "This was a weary march with no fighting, only distant artillery." The 4th Battalion also had a long rest, for it was not until 6 p.m. 4TH SEPTEMBER. on 4th September that the retirement was continued to Retal 5TH SEPTEMBER. (18 miles), which village was reached at 6.30 a.m. on the 5th. But again the Battalion—"Remained all day in fair billets." A day, indeed, long to be remembered, for during the evening news came to hand that the Retreat was over and that at last the offensive was to be taken—von Kluck had walked into the spider's web.

For on the night 4th September General Joffre had issued his "Order for the Battle of the Marne," the preamble of which contained the following words:—"The time has come to profit by the adventurous position of the First German Army and concentrate against that Army all the efforts of the Allied Armies on the extreme left." The Ninth and Fifth French Armies, the British Army and the Sixth French Army, in the order given from right to left, were to take the offensive on the morning of the 6th September.

On the night of 5th September, the dispositions of the B.E.F. were as follows:—G.H.Q. was at Melun. Of the Ist Corps, the 1st Division was at Rozoy, and the 2nd Division on the line Fontenoy–Chaumes. Of the IInd Corps, the 3rd Division occupied the Chatres area, whilst the head of the 5th Division was at Tournan: the 4th Division of the IIIrd Corps held an area, triangular in appearance, from just west of Tournan to Ozoir la Ferrière, thence south-west to Brie Comte Robert: the 19th Infantry Brigade was in and about Grisy.

The right of the B.E.F. was protected by Allenby's Cavalry, whilst Conneau's Cavalry Corps filled the gap between the right of the British and the left of the Fifth French Army, then approximately on the line Courtacon–Sezanne. From Sezanne the Ninth French Army prolonged the line eastwards. On the left of the B.E.F. the Sixth French Army held the line of the Marne River (its northern banks) to Meaux, whence the line turned N.W. to south of Senlis.

The positions of the Ninth and Fifth French Armies, of the British Army and the Sixth French Army, thus formed an angle into which von Kluck was advancing headlong. For on the night of the 5th September the heads of four corps of the First German Army were across the Grand Morin, *i.e.*, IXth Corps, Esternay–Courgivaux, IIIrd Corps, Sancy, IVth Corps, Chartronges–Chevru, IInd Corps west of Coulommiers, whilst north of the Marne and west of the Ourcq only a weak flank-guard, IVth Reserve Corps, with a cavalry division, covered the right of the whole German line. 5TH SEPTEMBER.

Such, briefly, were the dispositions of the British and French Armies on the left of the Allied Line when the Retreat from Mons ended and von Kluck, having failed to envelop the Allied left, had blundered into an " adventurous position."

For thirteen days the Retreat of the British Expeditionary Force had continued, and, although the distance as the crow flies from Mons to south of the Marne was 136 miles, the men had marched at least 200 miles, to say nothing of the two days' strenuous marching in advance *to* the Mons Canal. " The Retreat from Mons," to quote from the Official History, " was in every way honourable to the Army. The troops suffered under every disadvantage. The number of reservists in the ranks was on an average over one-half of the full strength, and the units were, owing to the force of circumstances, hurried away to the area of concentration before all ranks could renew acquaintance with their officers and comrades, and re-learn their business as soldiers. Arrived there, they were hastened forward by forced marches to the battle, confronted with greatly superior numbers of the most renowned army in Europe, and condemned at the very outset to undergo the severest ordeal which can be imposed upon an army. They were short of food and sleep, when they began their retreat; they continued it, always short of food and sleep, for thirteen days, as has been told ; at the end they were still an army, and a formidable army. They were never demoralised, for they rightly judged that they had never been beaten."

By all the rules and text-books of warfare the B.E.F. should have been out of action from Le Cateau onwards—but it was not. Said a German officer (one of the German Crown Prince's Staff) to a captured British officer :—" The British Army no longer exists. It is absolutely finished ! "

That was before the Battle of the Marne.

# CHAPTER VI.

## THE BATTLE OF THE MARNE.

7th–10th September, 1914.

GENERAL JOFFRE'S "Instruction" for an offensive on the 6th did not reach Sir John French until early morning of the 5th, by which time the B.E.F. had set off on the last stages of the Retreat. The result was that on the morning of the 6th September the French attacked the enemy, whereas the British Expeditionary Force had to wheel into position before joining in the offensive. 5TH SEPTEMBER

At 5.15 p.m. on 5th Sir John French issued operation orders for the advance on the 6th, which directed the Force to wheel eastwards, pivoting on its right, so that it would come up on a line roughly parallel to, and just south of, the Grand Morin River; the Ist Corps with its right on La Chapelle Iger and left on Lumigny; IInd Corps, right on Houssaye, left in the neighbourhood of Villeneuve; IIIrd Corps, facing east in the neighbourhood of Bailly: Cavalry to cover the front and flanks and connect with the Fifth and Sixth French Armies on the right and left respectively. The Ist Corps had to complete its move by 9 a.m. and moved off early on 6th; the IInd Corps had been given until 10 a.m. and, having a greater distance to march, set out at dawn, the 8th Infantry Brigade of the 3rd Division following the 7th Brigade.

6TH SEPTEMBER
4TH BATTALION.

The 4th Middlesex (in Brigade) set out from Retal at 5 a.m. and, after marching some 15 miles via Chartres and Crevecœur, thence by the forest road to Hautefeuille, reached the latter village at 7.30 p.m. and there went into bivouacs. The 8th Brigade Diary records that this was "the first advance made since 20th August." Distant artillery fire was heard throughout the day, but no enemy was seen or encountered by the Battalion.

Similarly, the IIIrd Corps had been ordered to complete its movements by 10 a.m., the 19th Infantry Brigade marching in rear of the 4th Division. The diary of the 1st Battalion Middlesex

1st Battalion. Regiment records the day's march as follows: "Marched N. again almost over yesterday's ground via Ferrier almost to Chanteloup. After one hour's halt, midday, on to Villeneuve St. Denis, where Battalion bivouacked. In morning Lieut. Evatt and 90 men of first reinforcements joined. This sudden change of front is explained by Field-Marshal Sir John French's message to the troops, dated 6th September, 1914."*

7th September. From the British point of view the Battle of the Marne began on 7th September, the Expeditionary Force at dawn holding a line running approximately from Vaudoy–Touquin (Ist Corps)–Lumigny–Faremoutiers–Courtry (IInd Corps)–Villeneuve St. Denis–Villeneuve-le-Comte–Villiers (IIIrd Corps). Throughout the day action was chiefly confined to encounters between de Lisle's Cavalry Brigade and German Cavalry of the 2nd and 9th Guard Cavalry Division. Behind his cavalry the enemy retreated.

4th Battalion. The 4th Middlesex, 8th Infantry Brigade, furnished the advanced guard of the 3rd Division and, marching at 11.30 a.m., covered a distance of 10 miles before billeting at Chauffry on the northern banks of the Grand Morin, the Battalion supplying outposts. No incident of importance happened during the day. A party of reinforcements joined the Battalion this day.

7th September. 1st Battalion. The 1st Middlesex marched at 8 a.m. to Romain Villiers, thence via Villiers–Dainville to Le Haute Maison. On arrival just south of the latter village rifle fire was heard immediately in front and on the right flank of the Battalion, the remainder of the column having come into action with a German rearguard. At Le Haute Maison the Middlesex bivouacked, one officer (2nd Lieut. Horrocks) and 90 other ranks, reinforcements, joining the Battalion.

8th September. 4th Battalion. On the morning of the 8th, the 4th Middlesex set out for Orly at 5 a.m., the 8th Infantry Brigade again acting as the advanced guard of the 3rd Division. St. Denis and Rebais had already been passed and the Middlesex (in Brigade) were approaching the village of Gibraltar (just south of Orly) when hostile artillery opened fire on the column. Fortunately, the Battalion was in artillery formation, two companies on either side of the road. The time was about 9 a.m. The 8th Brigade then deployed for action, the 2nd Royal Scots on the right, 2nd Royal Irish Rifles in the centre, and the 2nd Gordon Highlanders on the left, with the 4th Middlesex in rear in support. As battalion in support the Middlesex halted and were shelled, but do not appear to have suffered casualties.

* See Appendix, p. 50.

"After making an unpleasant delay too near our guns to be comfortable [the German 'Jack Johnsons' were horrible], a forward move was made through the western outskirts of the village into a hollow with a wood in front of us. Arriving there the Colonel, who had been the only Colonel left in command of a battalion in our Brigade since Le Cateau, sent me back to guide the Royal Scots, who were following us. I . . . . got safely through the horrible 'Jack Johnson' swept zone, and brought the leading platoon of the Royal Scots down to the hollow with few casualties. We located the German position about 300 yards up the opposite slope (on the northern bank of the Petit Morin). They were well entrenched and took some moving. They were evidently told to hold on and they did so, and we held them in front whilst another brigade (14th Infantry Brigade) attacked their left flank. Some men who tried to get in through the wood were immediately picked off, and they added to the horrors of war by their ghastly wailings and moanings, which, I consider, is one of the most terrible things of the battlefield."* 8TH SEPTEMBER.

The 2nd Division (Ist Corps), on the right of the 3rd Division, had experienced difficulty in getting across the Petit Morin, but later succeeded in crossing and capturing Boitron village, and, with the successful attack on the left of the 3rd Division by the 14th Infantry Brigade (5th Division), the 8th Brigade was able to push on to Orly, where it halted and billeted.

On the night of the 8th both the Ist and IInd Corps crossed the Petit Morin, the IIIrd Corps remained south of the river, the head of the 4th Division at Le Corbier and the 19th Infantry Brigade at Signy-Signets. The 1st Middlesex, of the latter, had moved out of La Haute Maison at 3.30 a.m. to take up positions for an attack on the high ground about Pierre Levée; the Battalion held the centre of the line, with the Cameronians on the right and the R.W. Fusiliers on the left. The enemy had, however, withdrawn during the night, and the Brigade moved on towards Signy-Signets, the 1st Middlesex as advanced guard. 1ST BATTALION.

On reaching the high ground immediately S. of Signy-Signets, large forces of the enemy's infantry were seen retiring N.N.W., though too far off for the guns to reach them, but hostile cavalry were nearer and to the east of the general line of retirement. It was fairly evident that the enemy held the line of the Marne River. The 1st Battalion, however, moved forward in a northerly

* From private diary of Lieut.-Colonel H. W. E. Finch.

8TH SEPTEMBER. 1ST BATTALION.

direction along the road which divides Signy from Signets, until the high ground overlooking the Marne was reached. Here the Battalion deployed, but scarcely had the Middlesex got into position when heavy shell fire was opened on them, the shells falling principally on the line of the road along which the Battalion advanced. This fire caught the Battalion First-line Transport, killing nine horses and riddling a watercart with shrapnel. The Battalion must also have been under considerable shell fire, for three N.C.Os. and other ranks were killed and some thirty wounded. The Middlesex men, however, remained in possession of the high ground, and later the Royal Welsh Fusiliers moved down towards La Ferté, where skirmishes with the enemy took place. On British guns coming into action, the enemy's artillery was more or less silenced. The high ground was held by the Middlesex throughout the night of the 8th–9th without incident, but rifle and artillery fire was heard on the right flank, where the 12th Brigade (4th Division) was attacking La Ferté in order to gain the Marne crossings. The 1st Battalion apparently bivouacked on the positions taken up, Headquarters billeting in Signy-Signets.

9TH SEPTEMBER. 1ST BATTALION.

Neither on the 9th nor on the 10th September were the 1st and 4th Battalions Middlesex Regiment engaged with the enemy. On the former date at 7 a.m. the 1st Battalion was relieved in its "holding positions" by the Cameronians, and retired half a mile S. to a covered position, where all ranks rested until 7 p.m. Here 89 men, some who had been "missing" after the Battle of Le Cateau and others discharged from hospital, rejoined. A move was then made to Les Corbiers, where the Battalion bivouacked, the remainder of the 19th Brigade (less the Cameronians) going

4TH BATTALION.

on to Jouarre. The 4th Battalion left Orly at 7 a.m., the 8th Brigade having been detailed as rearguard of the 3rd Division. At Nanteuil a two hours' halt was called for lunch. The march was then continued to Crouttes, where the Battalion went into billets; distance covered during the day, 8 miles in an easy march.

10TH SEPTEMBER. 1ST BATTALION.

The 10th was equally uneventful. At 4 o'clock in the morning the 1st Middlesex rejoined the 19th Brigade, which, with artillery, formed the left flank guard to the 4th Division. The River Marne was crossed by the pontoon bridge at La Ferté sous Jouarre, the stone bridge having been destroyed by the retreating enemy. The Battalion, on reaching the high ground N. of Marcy Fme., entrenched itself and remained there for two hours, covering the main advance. The march was then resumed to Certigny, where the 1st Battalion bivouacked immediately in rear (south) of the 4th Division. The roads traversed by the Battalion on this day everywhere showed evidence of the enemy's hurried retreat; many dead horses were passed and quantities of abandoned artillery ammunition and stores were seen scattered about the roadsides. The 4th Battalion marched out of Crouttes at 5 a.m. to Chezy, a distance of 10 miles. Fighting was going on all day in front of the Battalion, but the Middlesex men were not engaged. The 8th Infantry Brigade billeted in Chezy.

10TH SEPTEMBER.

4TH BATTALION.

On the night of the 10th September the British Expeditionary Force lay just south of the River Ourcq, in the angle formed by Lizy, La Ferté Milon and Fère en Tardenois, the valley of the Ourcq and the Marne having been cleared of the enemy. Touch with the Fifth French Army, on the right, and the Sixth French Army, on the left, had been maintained.

# APPENDIX.

---

## SPECIAL ORDER OF THE DAY BY FIELD-MARSHAL SIR JOHN FRENCH, G.C.B., G.C.V.O., K.C.M.G.,

Commander-in-Chief, British Armies in the Field.

*6th September.*

After a most trying series of operations, mostly in retirement, which have been rendered necessary by the general strategic plan of the Allied Armies, the British Forces start to-day forward in line with their French comrades, ready to attack the enemy.

Foiled in their attempt to invest Paris, the Germans have been driven to move in an easterly and south-easterly direction, with the apparent intention of falling in strength on the Fifth French Army. In this operation they are exposing their right flank and their line of communication to an attack from the combined Sixth French Army and the British forces.

I call upon the British Army in France to now show the enemy its power, and to push on vigorously to the attack beside the Sixth French Army. I am sure I shall not call upon them in vain, but that, on the contrary, by another manifestation of the magnificent spirit which they have shown in the past fortnight, they will fall on the enemy's flank with all their strength, and in unison with their Allies drive them back.

J. D. P. FRENCH,

*Field-Marshal,*

Commander-in-Chief, British Armies in the Field.

## CHAPTER VII.

# THE PURSUIT TO, AND BATTLE OF, THE AISNE, 1914.*

THE official despatches state that the pursuit of the enemy began on the 11th September, but the 10th is probably a more correct date, for when night fell on the 9th, the Marne crossings were in possession of the B.E.F. and the advance was continued on the following day.

11TH SEPTEMBER.

At 7.45 a.m. on the 11th, the 8th Infantry Brigade (the rearguard of the 3rd Division) marched out of Chezy and took the road through Dammard and Neuilly to Oulchy La Ville, N. of the Ourcq. The 4th Middlesex apparently acted as rear-guard to the Brigade, as the Battalion did not leave Chezy until 8.10 a.m. The march, though only 10 miles, was made uncomfortable by heavy rain which fell about 3 p.m., and the men arrived at Oulchy drenched through, where they went into poor billets. The 1st Battalion set out from Certigny at 7 a.m., and, marching north via Coulombs, reached Marizy-Ste. Geneviève about 4.30 p.m., where the 19th Infantry Brigade billeted. En route, the cheering news was received that the Ist and IInd Corps had captured "some 1,000 prisoners, 7 guns, machine guns and much transport."

4TH BATTALION.

1ST BATTALION.

On this day Major Ross left the 1st Battalion to take over the duties of Brigade Major, 11th Infantry Brigade, 4th Division.

Heavy firing was heard between 6 and 7 p.m. by both Battalions, but they were not involved.

With the exception of the 1st Division (Ist Corps), whose bivouacs and billets stretched from Bruyères to Rocourt, the tail of the 4th Division column and the 19th Infantry Brigade (at Marizy), the B.E.F., on the night of the 11th, had crossed the Ourcq and lay in arrow-head formation with heads of columns at Beugneux (2nd Division), Gd. Rozoy (3rd Division), Hartennes

* The official date of the Battle of the Aisne, 1914, is 12th to 15th September nclusive.

(5th Division), La Loge Fme. and Noroy (4th Division), with the cavalry holding an outpost line at Loupeigne, Branges, Arcy, Droizy and Villemontoire.

12TH SEPTEMBER. Again on the 12th, the 1st and 4th Middlesex experienced none of the excitements of the pursuit, for as will be seen from the following quotations (all the information contained in both Battalions' diaries for that date) the advance was quite uneventful.

4TH BATTALION. "Marched at 6.45 a.m.," states the diary of the 4th Battalion, "about 13 miles to Braisne. Heavy fighting in neighbourhood of Soissons. Very wet day."

1ST BATTALION. "Marched at 5.30 a.m. for Chouy," records the 1st Battalion, "passed there and into billets at Buzancy. Heavy artillery action heard all day to N. and N.W. 4th Division still in front of us."

The "heavy artillery action" heard was the French driving the enemy from Mont de Paris back across the Aisne at Soissons, the guns of the 4th Division joining in the action.

The pursuit on the 12th had, however, produced one important result: it had become evident from the enemy's attitude (which had considerably hardened during the day) that he was preparing to defend the crossings over the Aisne River. Both south of Missy and of Vailly, resistance to the advance of the B.E.F. had been considerable; the enemy had apparently arrested his retreat and was determined to dispute the passage of the river.

When darkness fell on the 12th the heads of the 1st and 2nd Divisions (Ist Corps) had reached Longueval and Dhuizel respectively; the heads of the 3rd and 5th Divisions (IInd Corps) were at Brenelle and Serches; the 4th Division (IIIrd Corps) occupied Venizel and Septmonts, whilst the 19th Infantry Brigade (IIIrd Corps) was back at Buzancy. But during the night, under cover of darkness, mist and rain, the 11th Infantry Brigade of the 4th Division, acting with great boldness, pushed on and, crossing the Aisne unperceived by the enemy, reached Bucy le Long, the first British troops to get across the river—a fact not recorded in the official despatches.

13TH SEPTEMBER. Disposed as above, the British advanced against the enemy on the morning of the 13th September, and the Battle of the Aisne had begun. And here, for a while, it is useful to consider the terrain of the battlefield-to-be, seeing that it was destined not only to be the scene of a stiff struggle for the river crossings, but also the beginning of trench warfare.

"The Aisne Valley runs generally east and west, and consists of a flat-bottomed depression of width varying from half a mile to two miles, down which the river follows a winding course to the west, at some points near the southern slopes of the valley and at others near the northern. The high ground both on the north and south of the river is approximately 400 feet above the bottom of the valley, and is very similar in character, as are both slopes of the valley itself, which are broken into numerous rounded spurs and re-entrants. The most prominent of the former are the Chivres spur on the right bank and Semoise spur on the left. Near the latter place the general plateau of the south is divided by a subsidiary valley of much the same character, down which the small River Vesle flows to the main stream near Semoise. The slopes of the plateau overlooking the Aisne on the north and south are of varying steepness, and are covered with numerous patches of wood, which also stretch upwards and backwards over the edge on to the top of the high ground. There are several villages and small towns dotted about in the valley itself and along its sides, the chief of which is the town of Soissons.

13TH SEPTEMBER.

"The Aisne is a sluggish stream of some 170 feet in breadth, but, being 15 feet deep in the centre, it is unfordable. Between Soissons, on the west, and Villers, on the east (the part of the river attacked and secured by the British Forces), there are eleven wood bridges across it. On the north bank a narrow-gauge railway runs from Soissons to Vailly, where it crosses the river and continues eastward along the south bank. From Soissons to Semoise a double line of railway runs along the south bank, turning at the latter place up the Vesle Valley towards Bazoches.

"The position held by the enemy is a very strong one, either for a delaying action or for a defensive battle. One of its chief military characteristics is that from the high ground on neither side can the top of the plateau on the other side be seen except for small stretches. This is chiefly due to the woods on the edges of the slopes. Another important point is that all the bridges are under either direct or high-angle fire.

"The tract of country above described, which lies north of the Aisne, is well adapted to concealment, and was so skilfully turned to account by the enemy as to render it impossible to judge the real nature of his opposition to our passage of the river, or to accurately gauge his strength; but I have every reason to conclude

13TH SEPTEMBER.

that strong rearguards of at least three Army Corps were holding the passages on the early morning of the 13th.

"On that morning I ordered the British Forces to advance and make good the Aisne."*

The night of the 12th September was wretched in the extreme. Heavy rain fell and the roads were soon thick with mud. The advance to the river on the morning of the 13th would therefore be under great difficulties. The heads of the three British Corps were directed as follows: Ist Corps on Lierval, IInd Corps on Chavignon, IIIrd Corps on Terny. The advance was to begin at 7 a.m.

Long before 7 o'clock everyone was astir. The morning was wretchedly cold and wet, and under the worst possible conditions the troops had breakfast and then paraded. The 8th Infantry Brigade had been detailed as advanced guard of the 3rd Division, and at 6.30 a.m. the head of the column set out from Braisne, the 4th Middlesex marching at 6.45 a.m. The 8th Brigade was directed on Vailly, via Chassemy, the 9th Brigade being ordered to secure the high ground between Brenelle and Chassemy until the former Brigade had made good the latter village.

4TH BATTALION.

About 8.30 a.m. the enemy's shells began bursting in the neighbourhood of the troops, who were now advancing in artillery formation. At 9 a.m. a message was received by 8th Brigade Headquarters from 5th Divisional Headquarters, and passed round battalions, that the bridge over the Aisne at Vailly had been destroyed and the enemy was holding the northern banks. The 2nd Royal Scots then pushed on into Chassemy, the 2nd Royal Irish Rifles remaining south-east of the village in artillery formation, whilst the 4th Middlesex halted behind a wood about a mile south of Chassemy. The enemy's artillery fire was now heavy,† and a further advance was, for the time being, decided inadvisable. Shortly afterwards the 3rd Division Artillery and a Heavy Battery came into action on the ridge east of Chassemy, and, under cover of the guns, the Royal Scots advanced to the Chateau at Bois Marin.

About 1 p.m. orders to advance to Vailly were received from 3rd Divisional Headquarters. Two cavalry brigades had got across the Aisne at Bourg, whilst the IIIrd Corps, on the left of the 3rd

* Official Despatches by Sir John French.

† There are no records of casualties in the Battalion Diary.

Division, was on the high ground north and north-west of Bucy (on the northern bank of the river). 13TH SEPTEMBER.

On reaching the Aisne, the bridge at Vailly was found destroyed, but a single plank spanned the broken girders and, in single file, the troops were able to pass over. With shells bursting all round, no wonder that an officer of the 4th Middlesex in his diary records that it was "rather unpleasant crossing." Once across the river, the column pushed on through Vailly to St. Pierre, where the Middlesex men bivouacked in a farmyard, the officers spending the night in a room of the farmhouse, the wife of the farmer furnishing a "scratch meal" of baked apples and coffee. The 2nd Royal Scots were in Vauxelles Château.

Meanwhile the 1st Middlesex (in Brigade) had left Buzancy about midday, and, following in rear of the 4th Division, advanced to a position just north-east of Septmonts and there bivouacked. 1ST BATTALION. Although heavy artillery fire was heard all day immediately in front, the 19th Infantry Brigade was not engaged and passed a quiet night.

Thus, for the two battalions of the Regiment the first day of the Battle of the Aisne was comparatively uneventful.

By dawn on the 14th the British Expeditionary Force held the 14TH SEPTEMBER. following approximate positions (from right to left): The Cavalry Division; the 1st Division and the 5th Infantry Brigade of the 2nd Division were between Paissy and Verneuil, then came a gap of 5 miles; west of the gap were the 8th and 9th Infantry Brigades about Vauxelles, then another gap of 3 miles; west of the latter two battalions of the 13th Infantry Brigade held Missy, and the 14th and 15th Brigades occupied ground from Ste. Marguerite to Crouy. All these units were north of the Aisne. On the southern banks of the river were the 6th and 4th Infantry Brigades (2nd Division) at Vieil Arcy, Dhuizel and St. Mard; the 3rd and 5th Cavalry Brigades and 7th Infantry Brigade at Braisne and neighbourhood, and the two remaining battalions of the 13th Infantry Brigade south of Missy. Both flanks of the B.E.F. were in close touch with the Fifth and Sixth French Armies.

At dawn on the 14th it was discovered that the 2nd Royal Scots were not, as supposed, on the Jouy spur, and orders were issued to the Battalion to push on up the ridge towards Jouy village. Two companies of the 4th Middlesex were ordered to 4TH BATTALION. assist in making good the ridge, the remaining two companies

14TH SEPTEMBER.

4TH BATTALION.

being then between the ridge and the river. The 2nd Royal Irish Rifles also furnished two companies to assist the Royal Scots.

The advance began, but soon the Scotsmen came under fire from close range, the enemy's trenches being just on the other side of the crest of the ridge. A halt was called, as further progress, for the time being, was impossible. The Middlesex and Royal Irish were now on the left and right, respectively, of the 2nd Royal Scots. Artillery support was asked for, and although the guns did their best to give support, they could not find satisfactory positions from which to cover the advance.

Barely 1,500 strong, the three Battalions made their way slowly towards the crest of the ridge, under artillery, rifle and machine-gun fire; but it was almost impossible to gain ground against an enemy cleverly and strongly entrenched.

No details of this little affair are contained in the Battalion Diary of the 4th Middlesex, but an officer* of the regiment described it as follows:—" The enemy's artillery was fairly busy all day; in fact, we were for a short period under fire from several directions, but our casualties were luckily few.† At about 2.30 p.m. we suddenly saw all the troops hurriedly vacating the ridge; the Germans with their usual adeptness crept up on to their flanks with machine guns, which made it too hot to stay. An effort was made by some to take their machine guns, but it was a hopeless attempt, and our men got back with wonderfully few casualties. Of the officers Lieut. Tidbury was hit in the shoulder.

" Now came the moment for us to retire, and this might have been a very unpleasant experience as the enemy's guns were very busily at work on the bend of the road we had to follow before we could get on the high ground. However, we reached another ridge with, I believe, no casualties, by doubling round the bend at about 20 paces interval. The order then came that we were to hold on there (on the north side of the river) at all costs; this was about 4 p.m. Why we were not further molested that day, except by continuous artillery fire, is hard to understand, except that the Germans were still preparing a defensive position. We remained in our position, about 1 mile to the north of Vailly, and this was a portion of the line taken up for about 19 days by

* Lieut.-Colonel H. W. E. Finch.

† No details of casualties are given in the Official Diaries.

the 8th Infantry Brigade." On the night of the 14th the 4th Middlesex bivouacked just north of Vailly. 14TH SEPTEMBER.

Throughout the day the positions of the 8th and 9th Infantry Brigades had indeed been critical, for it will be remembered that a gap of 5 miles existed between the right of the 3rd Division (9th Brigade) and the left of the Ist Corps (2nd Division). The enemy's heavy counter-attacks, launched on the 14th and made for the purpose of turning both these flanks, were only frustrated after a most dogged and determined resistance. 4TH BATTALION.

At 12.30 a.m. on 14th the 1st Middlesex had marched out of Buzancy and proceeded to bivouac behind a wood 1 mile S.S.E. of Venizel. From this position the Battalion, from dawn until 9 a.m., watched the three Infantry Brigades of the 4th Division in action on the high ground on the northern banks of the river. At the latter hour a position was reconnoitred by the Battalion on the southern banks of the Aisne, along the line and in rear of the railway. Here the 1st Middlesex entrenched and remained sheltered from the enemy's shell fire, which all day long searched both banks of the river. 1ST BATTALION.

The 15th September appears to have been a comparatively quiet day for both Battalions. 15TH SEPTEMBER.

Throughout the night 14th–15th all units of the 8th Brigade collected their companies and reorganised, for during the operations of 14th they had become considerably intermingled. They then entrenched in the following positions:—2nd Royal Irish Regiment astride the Vailly–Jouy road, in touch with the 9th Brigade on their right; the 2nd Royal Scots facing N.W. were on the left of the 2nd Royal Irish Regiment; the 4th Middlesex were on the left of the Royal Scots, facing N.W. and W., with a post in the Sucrerie on the main Vailly-Condé road, watching the latter and the ground intervening between it and the River Aisne. As soon as dawn broke, the enemy's guns again became active, and the high ground on which the 8th Brigade was entrenched came in for a good deal of intermittent shelling all day long. At noon a message had been received from 3rd Division Headquarters stating that there was "no immediate intention of an advance," and, so far as hostile shell and rifle fire permitted, all ranks set to work to improve trenches. The trenches held by the Royal Scots and 4th Middlesex overlooked open ground, with a good field of fire and view across Spur 169 (which ran northwards to Jouy) and also across the Spur to the N. and W. of Celles. The high ground immediately north 4TH BATTALION.

15TH SEPTEMBER.

of the Sucrerie, and immediately east of St. Pierre, was steep and wooded. The approaches through this position were guarded by a few small posts, the positions having been selected under the personal supervision of the G.O.C., 8th Brigade. In front of the Sucrerie the ground was open.

During the afternoon, Colonel Hull received orders to move his Battalion, at 7 p.m., to the Bois Marin, in order to watch the Condé Bridge. The 4th Middlesex came down off the hill after dark and crossed the Aisne by a bridge constructed by the Sappers. The enemy had a big gun trained on this bridge, and about every 15 minutes a huge shell crashed dangerously near, but as Colonel Finch said, " Again Providence looked after us," from which it is assumed that the Battalion had no casualties.

About 1 a.m. on 16th the Battalion arrived at the Bois Marin, very tired, and the men lay down on the road and slept soundly.

1ST BATTALION.

The 1st Middlesex, under orders, vacated their position along the Aisne at 1.30 a.m. on 15th and retired to bivouacs south of the wood, one mile S. of Venizel. Here the Battalion remained all day in support of other Brigades N. of the River Aisne.

Thus closed the Battle of the Aisne, and so far as the 1st and 4th Middlesex Regiments were concerned, neither Battalion had much of the excitement of battle; the enemy's shell fire causing most of the casualties, of which, however, there are no records in the official diaries.

The close of the battle saw the beginning of trench warfare.

Map IV.

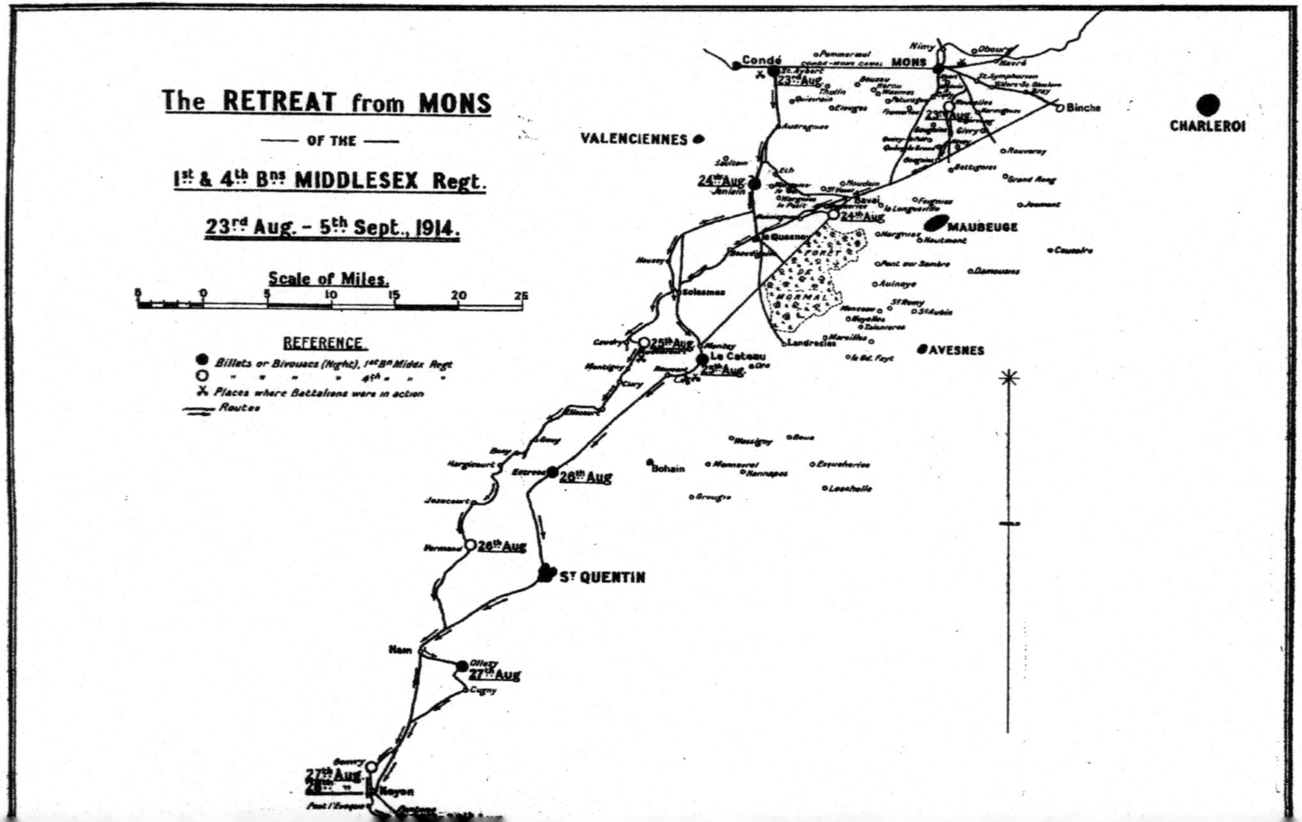

# The RETREAT from MONS

— OF THE —

1st & 4th Bns MIDDLESEX Regt.

23rd Aug. – 5th Sept., 1914.

Scale of Miles.

5 0 5 10 15 20 25

REFERENCE.

● Billets or Bivouacs (Night), 1st Bn Middx Regt

○ " " " " 4th " " "

✕ Places where Battalions were in action

═ Routes

# ADVANCE TO THE AISNE.

**1st & 4th Bns MIDDLESEX Regt.**

**6th – 13th September, 1914.**

Scale of Miles

5 0 5 10 15 20

REFERENCE.

● Billets or Bivouacs, 1st Battalion

○ " " " 4th "

Battalion in action

Routes

Advance of 1st Middx. to the Marne & Aisne.

Advance of 4th Middx. to the Marne & Aisne

6th September a.m.

5th Sept.
Here ended the Retreat of 1st Bn Middlesex Regt.

5th Sept. a.m.
Here ended the Retreat of the 4th Bn Middx. Regt.

DISTANCE MARCHED, APPROXIMATELY
200 MILES IN 13 DAYS

PARIS

MELUN

Compiègne

Soissons

Senlis

Meaux

Lagny

Coulommiers

Chateau-Thierry

Lizy

RIVER AISNE

RIVER OISE

R. MARNE

R. OURCQ

R. VESLE

R. PETIT MORIN

R. Gd MORIN

FORÊT DE COMPIÈGNE

Crépy-en-Valois

29th Aug.

30th Aug.

31st Aug.

1st Sept.

2nd Sept.

3rd–4th Sept. p.m.

3rd–5th Sept.

7th Sept.

8th Sept.

10th Sept.

12th Sept.

[To face p. 58.

# CHAPTER VIII.

## Trench Warfare on the Aisne, 1914.

TWO small actions, both of which were fought by the Ist Corps on the right of the B.E.F., are the only incidents officially recorded in the report of the Battles Nomenclature Committee, between the Battle of the Aisne and the transfer of Sir John French's Army to the left of the Allied Line, north of the La Bassée Canal. And yet those few intervening weeks cannot be dismissed without some reference to the position which, after the 13th September, confronted the Allies; and more particularly the new kind of warfare which gradually developed once the British Expeditionary Force had crossed the Aisne.

For a period short of a month Sir John French's Army clung tenaciously to the somewhat insecure and precarious positions it had won on the northern banks of the river, living and fighting under conditions such as no living soldier had hitherto experienced.

Almost entirely unequipped for trench warfare, it was natural that at the outset the British Army was forced largely to improvise the necessary "engines of war" with which to carry on against an enemy who, with perhaps greater foresight, had already armed himself with trench mortars, hand-grenades, flares and light balls, rifle-grenades and search-lights, illuminating pistols, periscopes and high-angle guns of different calibres. It is true that the Germans had designed these principally for use in the reduction of fortresses, but they were available at once on the Aisne for trench warfare. Both in artillery and machine guns, the enemy was infinitely superior so far as numbers were concerned. But poorly equipped, relatively, as were the Artillery and Infantry units of the British Army with guns and machine guns, their marksmanship was second to none.

It is interesting to note that, on 15th September, the whole of the 8th Infantry Brigade (in which the 4th Middlesex Regiment was contained) possessed only two machine guns, and these belonged to the 1st Devon Regiment, which had joined the Brigade at

15TH SEPTEMBER.

4TH BATTALION.

15TH SEPTEMBER.

4 a.m. that morning. Machine guns belonging to other units had either been lost or smashed (and not replaced) during the operations from Mons to the Marne.

Thus it will be seen that the British infantry had chiefly to rely upon their prowess with the rifle, and so successful were they that long before the Aisne was reached, the German soldier had become inspired with a wholesome dread of his opponent's rifle fire. The Germans certainly mistook the latter (seeing that at this period the British soldier was firing 15 aimed shots a minute) for machine-gun fire, which gave rise to the myth that Sir John French's Army was armed with thousands of machine guns; the allotment then was two guns per battalion, the majority of which (as already instanced) had either been lost or smashed ere ever the Aisne was reached.

With practically only his rifle, in which, however, he trusted implicitly, and in the use of which he had no equal, the British soldier settled down on the northern banks of the river to trench warfare with an enemy whose trenches were cleverly sited, and often admirably concealed, armed with mortars and howitzers with which he could pound the positions of his opponents without much fear of retaliation; hand and rifle grenades which he could hurl or fire into the British trenches when the opposing lines were close enough, as they often were.

At the close of the Battle of the Aisne (the night of 15th September) the British line, from right to left, ran as follows: The right of the Ist Corps lay along the line of the Chemin des Dames, as far as the Beaulne Spur, whence it dropped back in a south-westerly direction (taking in the Cœur de Soupir Farm) to just north of and between the villages of Soupir and Chavonne; the 3rd Division of the IInd Corps lay all around Vailly—east, north and west—upon whatever high ground could be conveniently entrenched, without being too much exposed to the enemy's shell fire; the 5th Division of the IInd Corps held Missy, connecting up on its left with the right brigade of the 4th Division, IIIrd Corps, who still held a line on the high ground north of Bucy le Long; the 19th Infantry Brigade held, and was in, the neighbourhood of Venizel.

16TH SEPTEMBER.

4TH BATTALION.

At dawn on the 16th the 4th Middlesex, having snatched a few hours' sleep on the road at Bois Marin, took up positions in the wood with instructions to watch Condé Bridge, at the same time escaping observation by the enemy. This entailed the formation of posts by day and lining the edge of the wood by night. No fires were allowed and the troops were forced to content themselves with cold rations and cold tea. Men with whistles were posted on the various roads to watch German aircraft and, on the whistle sounding, everyone "had to go to ground like rabbits." 16TH SEPTEMBER. 4TH BATTALION.

The First-Line Transport was back at Braisne, the horses at Chassemy. The Battalion, however, possessed that precious person on active service, a good quartermaster, who, an officer records, was an "A1 fellow."* Anything this quartermaster could buy, which would add to the comfort of officers and men, he bought and sent up to the front line.

The 17th, 18th and 19th September were spent by the 4th Middlesex, as was the 16th, the Battalion withdrawing at dawn, within the depths of the wood and taking up outpost lines on the edge of the wood at dusk.

In the meantime the 1st Middlesex passed the daylight hours of the 16th in bivouacs one mile south of Venizel, improving cover against hostile shell fire. The enemy tried to find the Battalion with 9-inch guns, but fortunately the shells all passed overhead and no casualties were suffered. At 9.30 p.m., however, the Battalion paraded and, crossing the Aisne by pontoon bridge, took over bivouacs previously occupied by the A. and S. Highlanders, 1,000 yards north of the bridge, the latter Battalion being ordered to Bucy in support of the 10th and 11th Brigades of the 4th Division. 1ST BATTALION.

The left flank of the 1st Middlesex was now in touch with French troops (right of the Sixth French Army) west of Bucy. The 17th, 18th and 19th were passed in the same bivouacs with no more excitement than the constant booming of artillery and the sound of rifle fire, which, like wind in the trees, rose and fell according as targets presented themselves to the opposing forces. The diary of the 1st Middlesex contains the words: "Engagement still proceeds all along our front," and for several successive days but little or no advance by British or Germans was made. Each side had assumed a defensive attitude and, with the exception of attempts made by the enemy against the Ist Corps on the dates already given (attempts quite unsuccessful), Sir John French stated in his despatches that: "The same futile attempts were made all along our front up to the evening of the 28th, when they died away and have not since been renewed."

* Lieut. and Quartermaster M. W. Farrow.

20TH SEPTEMBER. 1ST BATTALION.

On the 20th September at 9 p.m. the 1st Middlesex (in Brigade) marched back to Septmonts and there billeted, and for the remainder of the month the Battalion remained in the village, furnishing parties for work under the 4th Division and digging trenches, mainly on the slopes from Billy down towards the River Aisne.

4TH BATTALION.

On the 20th the 4th Middlesex Regiment received orders to return to its former position north of Vailly. The Battalion left the Bois Marin at 11 p.m., and after again going through the unpleasant experience of crossing the river by the footbridge at Vailly under shell fire, marched up the hill and relieved the 1st Battalion Northumberland Fusiliers at dawn on the 21st. By this date snipers of the opposing forces had become extremely active, and exposure of the head or any part of the body was almost certainly followed by the sharp crack of a rifle, and lucky the careless offender if he escaped. The enemy's shell fire was, however, slackening; his guns had been more accurately located by the British gunners, who, always at a disadvantage owing to the nature of the terrain, nevertheless again and again succeeded in silencing the enemy's artillery. In the evening (about 7.30 p.m.) the enemy made a half-hearted attack on the 4th Middlesex and the Buffs, but it was easily broken up, and the Germans retired discomfited.

After a somewhat cheerless night spent in wet trenches and "funk holes" partially filled with water, the Battalion "stood to" at dawn on the 22nd. Throughout the day intermittent shell fire continued, and in the evening sharp rifle fire rang out from the Battalion's trenches. From constant watching and waiting all day the troops gradually became "nervy," and if one man fired his rifle at a foe, real or imaginary, the whole line blazed away until orders were given to "cease fire." Hot dinners and teas were again started, the meals being cooked at Vailly, whence they were brought up to the front line trenches.

26TH SEPTEMBER. 4TH BATTALION.

On the 26th the enemy's artillery fire increased and sniping became more incessant, but the 4th Middlesex was relieved during the evening by the 1st Northumberland Fusiliers, and the Battalion quitted the ridge by companies without casualties.

The march back to Courcelles, where billets and hot meals had been prepared by the Battalion Quartermaster, was only 8 miles, but the enervating life led by the troops since the Aisne crossings had been won, had left its mark upon the men, who (many suffering from rheumatism) found the march very wearying, and all ranks were thankful when billets were reached between 12 midnight and 1 a.m. on the 27th. 4TH BATTALION.

The 27th September was spent by the 4th Middlesex in cleaning up rifles and equipment; the men's feet were also examined and treatment applied where necessary.

The 28th still found the Battalion at Courcelles, and here, late in the day, an interesting item is recorded in the 8th Brigade Diary. Fifty representatives from each unit of the Brigade paraded, and were addressed by Sir Horace Smith-Dorrien, commanding the IInd Corps. "He gave them," stated the Diary, "a short and clear account of the events of the War up to date, explaining the reasons for the retirement, etc. He impressed upon them with what pride H.M. the King and all the people at home regarded the doings of the Army."

Not again were either the 1st or 4th Battalions Middlesex Regiment to move north across the Aisne River, for early in October the British Expeditionary Force began to move north-west to positions assigned to it between Béthune and Ypres—the "Race to the Coast" had begun.

The position on the Aisne had, by the beginning of October, become that of "stale-mate." The opposing forces had settled down to defensive action, their defences growing gradually stronger. An attempt to outflank the German right was made by the French, but as the latter extended their left in order to turn the German right, the former also extended his flank to meet the threat of envelopment. Thus, gradually, the line lengthened, moving ever north-west towards the coastal towns of France and Belgium, and on Sir John French pointing out to the French Commander-in-Chief that the natural position of the B.E.F. was on the left of the French Armies, Marshal Joffre agreed that the time had come when the British Army might be transferred to the left of the French Armies.

Arrangements for withdrawal and relief having been made by the French General Staff, the 2nd Cavalry Division marched from Compiègne for the new theatre of war on 3rd October.

The IInd Corps (3rd and 5th Divisions) was ordered to arrive on the line Aire–Béthune on 11th October, "to connect with the right of the X French Army, and, pivoting on its left, to attack in flank the enemy who were opposing the X French Corps in front. The Cavalry to move on the northern flank of the IInd Corps and support the attack until the IIIrd Corps, which had to detrain at St. Omer on the 12th, should come up. They were then to clear the front and to act on the northern flank of the IIIrd Corps in a similar manner, pending the arrival of the Ist Corps from the Aisne."*

30TH SEPTEMBER. 1ST BATTALION. 4TH BATTALION.

On the last day of September the 1st Battalion Middlesex was (in Brigade) at Septmonts, and the 4th Bn. Middlesex (also in Brigade) at Courcelles. The latter was apparently the first to move, leaving Courcelles at 7 p.m. on 1st October and marching to Oulchy le Château, which place was reached at 2 a.m. on the following morning. All units had been ordered to march at night in order to screen their movements from hostile aircraft, and at

2ND OCTOBER. 4TH BATTALION.

7 p.m. on the 2nd the 4th Battalion left Oulchy and marched to Silly-la-Poterie, arriving at the latter village at about 2 a.m. on the 3rd. The Battalion again marched out of billets at 7 p.m. (on the 3rd), and reached Crepy en Valois at 2 a.m. on the 4th. In this way, marching in nightly stages which varied in distance from 12 to 15 miles, the 4th Middlesex eventually reached Pont St. Maxence and entrained for Abbeville. Trench warfare had considerably affected the marching form of the men, who, after many days spent in sitting in trenches keeping a vigilant eye on the enemy, had acquired " soft feet." " Our marching powers were now somewhat inferior to what they had been, owing to trench work. The men suffered from rheumatism, but they had to make the best of it, as there were few ambulances to give them a lift."†

At 7 a.m. on the 6th October, the 4th Middlesex arrived at Abbeville; the 8th Brigade Diary stating that by 9 a.m. all units of the 8th Brigade group had detrained and had settled in billets in and around Le Titre.

5TH OCTOBER. 1ST BATTALION.

The 1st Middlesex marched out of Septmonts at 7 p.m. on the 5th October, and bivouacked in a wood (at 2 a.m. on 6th) west of the village of St. Remy. Here the 19th Brigade lay hidden all day until 7.30 p.m., when the troops again set out, Vez (via Villers-Cotterets) being their destination. Vez was reached at 3 a.m. on 7th, where the Battalion again bivouacked in woods, lying hidden throughout the day until 5.30 p.m., when a march to Bethisy St. Pierre was begun. Arriving at 10 p.m. the Middlesex men bivouacked in woods outside St. Sauveur. Eventually, on 9th, at 12 noon, the 1st Middlesex reached Estrée St. Denis, and between

* Official Despatches.
† Lieut.-Colonel H. W. E. Finch.

that hour and 2 a.m. on 10th, entrained by half-battalion for an "unknown destination." Travelling via Amiens–Abbeville–Etaples–Boulogne and Watten, the right half battalion detrained at the latter place and then had a march of 7 miles to St. Omer, where billets were obtained at Caserne d'Albert, arriving at 11 p.m. The left half battalion travelled by the same route, but detrained at St. Omer and reached billets at 1 a.m. on the 11th. The whole of the 19th Infantry Brigade was now at St. Omer.

1st Battalion.

11th October.

But before describing the operations which took place in France and Flanders after the arrival of the B.E.F. in its new theatre of war it is necessary to turn to England, where, in the meantime, the Territorial Battalions of the Middlesex Regiment had been mobilised and the first Service Battalions were being raised, in order to take their stand in the field by the side of their comrades of the Regular Army.

D

## CHAPTER IX.

# Of the Territorial Battalions of the Regiment.

IT has already been stated that at 4 p.m. on the 4th August the mobilisation of the Regular Army and Territorial Force was ordered by the British Government, and that a state of war existed between Great Britain and Germany "as from 11 p.m." on that date. 4TH AUGUST.

For the Territorial Force mobilisation came at an awkward moment. The 3rd August, 1914, was a Bank Holiday, and many battalions were then actually on the move (by road or by train) to various camps for their summer training, when orders cancelling the latter were received. The Home Counties Division, of which the Middlesex Infantry Brigade formed a part, was then on the march from Aldershot to Salisbury Plain, having left Bordon Camp on the 30th July. When these orders were received (*i.e.*, for all Territorial battalions to return to their Headquarters in readiness for mobilisation) the Brigade had reached Larkhill (Durrington). On the morning of 4th August, the 7th* and 8th Battalions Middlesex Regiment entrained at Amesbury for Headquarters, *i.e.*, Hornsey and Hounslow respectively; but it was not until 5.30 a.m. on the morning of the 5th that the 9th and 10th Battalions got away, after passing a very uncomfortable night, lying in the road in heavy rain outside Amesbury Station. A few hours later, however, both the 9th and 10th Battalions had reached Willesden and Ravenscourt Park, their respective headquarters.

During the evening of the 4th August, the 7th Battalion (Lieut.-Colonel E. J. King) received orders to mobilise, and on the following evening (5th) entrained at Enfield for its temporary war stations, Battalion Headquarters with five companies going to the Isle of Grain, and three companies to Sheerness. On the 9th the Battalion was relieved by the 5th K.R.R. and proceeded 7TH BATTALION.

* With the exception of the Territorial Battalions of the Devonshire Regiment, the 7th, 8th and 9th Battalions Middlesex Regiment are the senior Battalions of the Territorial Army.

to Sittingbourne, in which neighbourhood the Home Counties Division was concentrating for the "six months' intensive training," which the Territorial Army was supposed to receive on mobilisation.

8TH BATTALION. Similarly, the 8th Middlesex (Lieut.-Colonel W. Garner), after mobilisation at Hounslow had been completed, moved to Sheerness, the war station of the Battalion. About the end of September the 8th sailed for Gibraltar.

9TH BATTALION. The 9th had joined the three other Battalions of the Middlesex Infantry Brigade on 26th July at Bordon, and as one officer said, when the War was over, "the most imaginative man in the Battalion had no idea when he said good-bye to his family for 15 days, that it would be four, in some cases, five years, before he returned home as a civilian, or that in many cases he would never return."

In the 9th Battalion (Lieut.-Colonel J. L. Blumfeld) it was first realised that war was a practical proposition when, on the evening of July 28th, the Commanding Officer was ordered by the Brigadier to send immediately his two special service sections to their war stations on the coast. These sections consisted each of a subaltern and twenty-five specially-enlisted other ranks, whose duty it was to look after the safety of the Cable Station at Burling Gap and Cuckmere Haven. Both officers were well acquainted with their respective areas, and all arrangements for defence had been made in advance. In one hour from the order being given the two detachments entrained at Bordon for Willesden, where, on arrival, they drew their ammunition and at 9 a.m. next morning were on their ground.

On reaching Pound Lane, Willesden (Battalion Headquarters), 5TH AUGUST. at 9.30 a.m. on the morning of the 5th August, the Battalion began mobilising immediately, and at night entrained for Minster, Sheerness, its first war station, leaving the Second-in-Command—Major W. P. Hewett—behind to carry on with mobilisation of transport, etc.

Five strenuous days were spent at Minster, where the young soldiers of the 9th Battalion dug hard all day and manned the trenches at night, constantly on the alert. Then on 10th August the 5th Rifle Brigade arrived and took over the ground, the 9th Middlesex marching off to Sittingbourne, the Battalion's second war station, and arriving in camp the same evening, found its horses, wagons and stores all complete and waiting.

On the 11th August, the 9th Battalion, in common with the remainder of the Middlesex Infantry Brigade, volunteered for service overseas. 11TH AUGUST.

Only about half of the 10th Battalion (Lieut.-Colonel C. R. Johnson) was in training on Salisbury Plain when orders to return to Headquarters and mobilise were received, the remainder of the men being unable to join the summer camp. Having returned to Ravenscourt Park, the Battalion mobilised and entrained the same day to Sheerness, leaving an officer behind at Headquarters to recruit the three hundred odd men required to bring the Battalion up to War establishment. These extra men were quickly obtained, and clothed, equipped and armed, were sent off to join the Battalion, which had in the meantime moved to Sittingbourne.* 10TH BATTALION.

Thus the four First-Line Territorial Battalions of the Middlesex Regiment were mobilised, sent off to their first war stations, and afterwards were concentrated with the rest of the Home Counties Division in and around Sittingbourne, eagerly awaiting orders to embark and cross over to France.

Meanwhile, a question had arisen as to what to do with the surplus men who had rushed to the Colours when volunteers were first called for. These men had joined the Territorial Battalions, and although the War Office wanted them to transfer to the Regular Army or the New (Kitchener) Army ("K.I."), the majority elected to remain with the Territorial Battalions which had enlisted them. For several weeks matters remained stationary, until it became obvious that when the First-Line Territorial Battalions went overseas, they would require reinforcements almost at once. And at last permission was given by the War Office to raise Second-Line Territorial Battalions, and, in this way, the 2/7th, 2/8th, 2/9th and 2/10th Battalions Middlesex Regiment came into being.

The formation of the 2/7th Middlesex (first designated the 7th [Reserve] Battalion) was authorised on 31st August, on which day the 1/7th was placed under orders to embark for Gibraltar. Major J. S. Drew, an officer of the 1/7th, was selected to command the new unit, and on 3rd September he proceeded to Hornsey 2/7TH BATTALION. 31ST AUGUST.

* To the 10th Battalion Middlesex Regiment belongs the distinction, probably unique in the Territorial Force, of having three Battalions on active service overseas simultaneously. The 1st/10th served in India; the 2nd/10th in Gallipoli, Egypt and Palestine; and the 3rd/10th in France.

2/7TH BATTALION. 4TH SEPTEMBER.

in order to raise his Battalion. The 1/7th had left behind 139 men under the age of 18½ years, and these, with two officers, also of the 1/7th, formed the nucleus of the 2/7th Battalion. On 4th September recruiting began in earnest, and soon the rush to join was tremendous. "The recruits," said Lieut.-Colonel Drew, "came from all the neighbouring districts: Hornsey, Highgate, Finchley, Barnet, Enfield, Wood Green, Edmonton, each supplied large numbers. But the contingent from Tottenham was the largest of all.* . . . In the ranks were men of almost every walk of life, from professional men to labourers, while the patriotic efforts of the London Teachers' Association resulted in 115 masters of London Elementary Schools enlisting in a body. . . . Over 130 gentlemen applied for commissions, and from these the establishment was selected. Most of those chosen had served previously in the Territorial Force or Officers Training Corps. Young, full of energy and zeal, it would have been hard to find a better lot."

When the War was over, and in describing the method adopted in raising these new units, Colonel Drew, of the 2/7th, said: "The first thing was to get a good 'tone' into all ranks from the very start. We lost no opportunity of impressing upon everyone that in joining the Middlesex Regiment they belonged to the best Regiment in the Service, and it was up to each man to uphold the credit of the Battalion. We also told them that what was good enough for Territorials in time of peace was no good in war time, and that we expected them to aim at the standard of Regular troops in every respect, turn out, drill, discipline, etc. This applied still more to officers and N.C.Os."

It is safe to say that the methods adopted in raising the 2/7th Battalion did not differ materially from those followed in raising not only the 2/8th, 2/9th and 2/10th Territorial Battalions, but all the Service Battalions which were formed simultaneously with the Second-Line Territorial units, or later. Into all the "Die-Hard" spirit was inculcated.

2/8TH BATTALION. 14TH SEPTEMBER.

The 2/8th Middlesex was formed on the 14th September, 1914, at Hampton Court, Lieut.-Colonel C. Dams being the Commanding Officer. The Battalion was quartered in the Cavalry Barracks, Hampton Court House, and other houses in the neighbourhood. Training was carried out in Bushey Park, though at

* And for that reason the King's Colour of the 2/7th Battalion was deposited, after the War, in Tottenham Parish Church.

that date no uniforms or rifles were available. On the 15th November the Battalion moved to Staines.

The 2/9th Battalion came into being at Pound Lane, Willesden (the Headquarters of the 9th Battalion), on 18th September, 1914, and was commanded by Lieut.-Colonel H. J. Dixon. The 9th Battalion, before sailing for India, had sent back a number of surplus N.C.Os. and men, and these formed the nucleus of the 2/9th Battalion. "Otherwise," said an officer of the Battalion, "the new Battalion consisted of novices who were as keen as they were innocent of the military art." On the 20th November the Battalion entrained for Staines, where it was brigaded with the corresponding Second-Line Reserve Battalions of the 7th, 8th and 10th Middlesex Regiment, and formed the Middlesex (Reserve) Brigade of the Home Counties (Reserve) Division. 2/9TH BATTALION. 18TH SEPTEMBER.

The 2/10th Middlesex were formed on the 12th September, 1914, from the surplus N.C.Os. and men of the 10th Battalion at Headquarters, Stamford Brook, Chiswick. This Battalion, as will be read hereafter, served in the Dardanelles, Egypt and Palestine. The early days were strenuous, but under Lieut.-Colonel C. R. Johnson and Major C. Jarrett training proceeded rapidly, and by the end of October the 2/10th was practically at full strength. 2/10TH BATTALION. 12TH SEPTEMBER.

Third and even Fourth-Line Territorial Battalions of the Middlesex Regiment were subsequently formed. A 3/7th Battalion was raised early in 1915 to replace the 2/7th in the Home Defence Organisation when the latter went out to relieve the 1/7th at Gibraltar. The 3/7th was first commanded by Lieut.-Colonel Low, who was succeeded by Lieut.-Colonel Cranfield. 3/7TH BATTALION.

A 3/8th Battalion was raised on the 14th February, 1915. This Battalion was commanded by Lieut.-Colonel H. R. Peake, and was first quartered on Hounslow Heath until May, when a move was made to Windsor, the men being billeted in Egham. In June the Battalion went to camp on Bulmer Downs, Lewes. 3/8TH BATTALION.

Of the 3/9th little is known, with the exception that the Battalion was subsequently raised from surplus officers and men of the 2/9th. 3/9TH BATTALION.

The 3/10th Middlesex was formed of details and surplus men of the 2/10th, in May, 1915, when the latter unit was warned for service overseas. The Battalion was first stationed at Ashford, then at Staines and Reigate, but its real training was carried out at Bulmer Camp, Brighton. The 3/10th had several Commanding 3/10TH BATTALION.

Officers: first, Captain France, then Major A. E. Hart, who was succeeded by Lieut.-Colonel Eaton, and, finally, Lieut.-Colonel C. H. Cautley, who eventually took the Battalion out to France.

4/7TH BATTALION.

The 4/7th, a Depot Battalion, was formed in 1917, and was commanded by Major Dulcken.

4/8TH BATTALION.

Soon after the 3/8th was raised, the 4/8th came into being, probably in June, 1915: the Battalion was placed under the command of Major Hill-Trevor, and was quartered successively at Hounslow, Windsor Park, Purfleet, Cambridge, thence moving back to Purfleet.

4/9TH—4/10TH BATTALIONS.

The 4/9th and 4/10th were raised later.

Thus the original Territorial Battalions of the Middlesex Regiment—four in number—were expanded before the end of the War to no less than 16 Battalions—a fine record.

In the meantime all the First-Line Territorial Battalions had left England.

## CHAPTER X.

# THE BATTLE OF LA BASSÉE.

10th October*—2nd November.

"The IInd Corps to arrive on the line Aire–Béthune on the 11th October, to connect with the right of the Tenth French Army and, pivoting on its right, to attack in flank the enemy who were opposing the X French Corps in front."

Sir John French's Despatches.

ON foot, and in light French motor lorries, Smith-Dorrien's IInd Corps, after detraining at Abbeville, moved forward towards the line allotted to it, with Gough's cavalry on its left flank and the French on its right.

As stated in a previous chapter, the 8th Infantry Brigade of the 3rd Division had arrived at Abbeville on 6th October, all units of the Brigade billeting in and around Le Titre: the 4th Battalion Middlesex Regiment was at Hautvillers. The 7th and 8th October were spent by the Battalion in billets. At 1.5 a.m. on 9th the Battalion paraded, and in Brigade, marched via Forêt l'Abbaye, Crecy, Dompierre, to Raye, where an eight hours' halt was made. At 4 p.m. the march was continued to Hesdin, which place was reached about 7 p.m. It took a long time to get the men into billets, and it was 10 p.m. before they were finally settled in for the night, in what (a diarist has it) were "rotten billets."

6TH OCTOBER.

4TH BATTALION.

Early on the following morning, at 3.30 a.m., the Battalion was enbussed in motor 'buses and taken to Rermes-en-Artois, arriving at about 7 a.m. Here the day was spent in billets.

* The date adopted by the Battles Nomenclature Committee.

The Official Despatches state that:—"The great battle, which is mainly the subject of this despatch, may be said to have commenced on October 11th, on which date the 2nd Cavalry Division, under General Gough, first came into contact with the enemy's cavalry, who were holding some woods to the north of the Béthune–Aire Canal."

4TH BATTALION.

For four days the Battalion had been moving eastwards but had not fired a shot, for the enemy was gradually retiring. On the 11th, a march of some 15 miles to Mont Bernenchon took the Battalion from 8.15 in the morning to 6 p.m., where another uncomfortable night was spent in "bad billets." On this day the Battalion reached the firing line of the battle, for artillery duels were taking place as the men marched forward. The country was now flat, sprinkled with woods and small villages.

11TH OCTOBER.

By the night of the 11th October, the IInd Corps (5th Division on the right, 3rd Division on the left) had reached the line of the canal between Aire and Béthune. Sir Horace Smith-Dorrien was then ordered to continue his advance on the following day (12th). Bringing up his left in the direction of Merville, he was then to move east to the line Laventie–Lorgies, which movement would place him on the immediate left of the Tenth French Army, and threaten the German flank.

12TH OCTOBER.

At about 7 a.m. on the morning of the 12th October, the 4th Middlesex moved off towards Vieille Chapelle, in order to take up an outpost line just east of the village: the distance was about 5½ miles. The Official Diary states that the Battalion "went into action at about 11 a.m. Lieut. Coles and two men killed, and four men wounded." A private account states that: "We cleared our front, but the battalion on our left had a more difficult task, as there was a small wood immediately across their front. The 7th Brigade, on our right, we heard charging, and apparently with success." That night the 4th Middlesex billeted in Vieille Chapelle, and apparently it was whilst on patrol duty that Lieut. S. H. Coles was killed.

Little progress had been made throughout the 12th by the IInd Corps, chiefly owing to the nature of the ground upon which the 3rd and 5th Divisions were operating, *i.e.*, covered with mining works, factories, buildings, etc. The flat character of the country rendered artillery support very difficult.

13TH OCTOBER.

On the 13th the advance was continued. The 4th Middlesex moved off by half-battalion at 5.30 a.m., the right half under Lieut.-Colonel Hull, the left half under Major H. W. E. Finch, *i.e.*, on the right and left flank respectively. There was a distance of about 600 yards between the two halves of the battalion. About 9 a.m. the Battalion came under rifle fire, and, leaving the road, advanced across fields in extended order, towards the village of Croix Barbée—the objective. Progress was, however, slow, for the

Germans were well established in a wood and were cleverly posted in all the houses, "so that you could not see them." They also had a gun in the firing line to the left of the front attacked by the Middlesex. By nightfall little progress had been made, and the Battalion entrenched for the night in rear of Croix Barbée.* Casualties suffered by the 4th Middlesex during the day's fighting were: Captains G. R. Bentley and C. F. Tulloh, and 2nd Lieut. G. T. H. Morse and 10 N.C.Os. and men killed, and Major H. W. E. Finch, Captain W. J. Corcoran,† Lieut. Moore and 35 N.C.Os. and men wounded. Major Finch was hit in the head as he was making an attempt to get back in order to give the Brigadier the situation in front of the Middlesex. 4TH BATTALION.

The action was continued on 14th, but apparently no advance was made by the 4th Middlesex, who again appear to have had serious casualties, Lieut. H. A. Tagg and 2nd Lieut. M. A. P. Shawyer and 6 N.C.Os. and men being killed and Lieuts. Sneath and Sharp and 38 N.C.Os. and men wounded. The G.O.C., 3rd Division (General H. Hamilton), was also killed on this day. 14TH OCTOBER

During the afternoon of 15th a general advance was made, and after Croix Barbée had been shelled, the 4th Middlesex moved forward and entered the village. Casualties on this day were Lieut. C. D. Sneath and 6 N.C.Os. and men killed, and Captain Passy and 20 N.C.Os. and men wounded. On the night of the 15th the 3rd Division had established itself on the line Pont du Hem–Croix Barbée. 15TH OCTOBER

The 16th was a rest day for the 8th Brigade, the latter being relieved by the 9th Brigade. 16TH OCTOBER

On 17th the 8th Brigade left Croix Barbée and marched to Aubers, where the 4th Middlesex went into billets. During the day the village had been captured by the 9th Infantry Brigade. 17TH OCTOBER
On 18th the 4th Middlesex stood to arms all day awaiting orders to move, but during the afternoon, about 4 p.m., the Battalion moved to new billets in Le Plouich in consequence of the severe shelling to which the enemy was subjecting Aubers. 18TH OCTOBER

At 3 p.m. on 19th the Middlesex moved off in support of the Royal Irish, who were attacking Le Pilly, the Battalion billeting for the night in Le Riez. About 10 a.m. on the 20th, the enemy began to shell Le Riez, and the Middlesex men, who were occupying 19TH OCTOBER 20TH OCTOBER

* The Battalion record of the action is as follows:—"Action continued, pushing Germans through Croix Barbée, and Battalion entrenched for the night in rear of village."

† D. of W., 25th October. Rank in War Office list of casualties given as "Major."

4TH BATTALION. trenches in front of the village, again suffered heavy casualties: 2nd Lieut. R. Sayers and 13 N.C.Os. and men were killed, and 2nd Lieuts. Draper and Williams and 45 N.C.Os. and men were wounded.

The strength of the Battalion at this period must have been very low. No progress was made by either side on the 21st.

22ND OCTOBER. On 22nd, at 6 a.m., the 4th Middlesex, with other units of the 8th Brigade, was withdrawn to billets in the Rue d'Enfer. From the latter place, however, the Battalion marched off at 10 p.m. to a new position near Fauquissart, after withdrawing two companies which had entrenched themselves in the Rue Deleval.

On the following day the Battalion set to work to dig trenches south-west of Fauquissart, being relieved later by the 1st Gordon Highlanders, who carried on with the work. The Middlesex men then marched off to a village about 1,500 yards west of Fauquissart cross roads, and there billeted. The front of the IInd Corps at this period extended approximately from the eastern exits of Givenchy, east of Neuve Chapelle to Fauquissart.

24TH OCTOBER. Very early on the morning of the 24th October the enemy began a heavy attack all along the line. The 4th Middlesex, in billets, having been informed that the attack was expected, stood by all day, awaiting orders to go forward. Mainly owing to the splendid way in which the guns were handled and the fine shooting of the infantry in the front line, the enemy was held off, but towards evening a further heavy attack was launched against the 7th Infantry Brigade, which was, however repulsed. A little later a determined attack on the 8th Infantry Brigade drove the 1st Gordon Highlanders out of their trenches at Fauquissart, and the 4th Middlesex Regiment was ordered to retake them. Details of the formation in which the Battalion went forward, and how the attack was made, are not recorded in the Official Diary, and only the official despatches stated that the trenches "were retaken by the Middlesex Regiment, gallantly led by Lieut.-Colonel Hull." * The Battalion in this counter-attack suffered the loss of 1 officer (name not given) and 8 N.C.Os. and men killed and 9 N.C.Os. and men wounded.†

* The Official Despatches here are incorrect. The Brigade was obviously the 8th and not the 18th. The 18th Infantry Brigade belonged to the 6th Division of the IIIrd Corps, at this period engaged further north in the Battle of Armentières.

† It is worthy of record that the Military Cross was first won (on this occasion) by an officer of the Middlesex Regiment—2nd Lieut. C. N. A. Cursons, an officer only 19 years of age, and a Middlesex man.

From the 25th to the 31st October, the 4th Middlesex remained in the recaptured trenches, improving them and keeping a constant watch on the enemy, who was very alert. The strain on both officers and men was terrible. There was little rest, for the Battalion had suffered heavy losses since the beginning of October, and refitting was urgently necessary. Parties of reinforcements of officers and men arrived, one on 25th and another on 28th, and gradually the companies were sent back into reserve and refitted. 4TH BATTALION.

Relief came on the 31st, when during the night the 2nd Royal Scots marched into the trenches, and the tired and worn Middlesex men withdrew to the cross-roads about a mile in rear to form part of the 8th Infantry Brigade Reserve. The tour in the Fauquissart trenches had cost the Battalion a further 6 N.C.Os. and men killed and 49 wounded and 7 missing. 31ST OCTOBER.

There was much truth in the official despatches which stated (at this period) that:—" The IInd Corps was now becoming exhausted, owing to the constant reinforcement of the enemy, the length of line which it had to defend and the enormous losses which it had suffered."

On the 1st and 2nd November (on which date the Battle of La Bassée closed), the 4th Middlesex were in support trenches at Baquerot. On the first-mentioned date an interesting message was circulated by G.H.Q., and is given in the diary of the 8th Brigade: " The German Emperor will arrive in the field to-day to conduct operations against the British Army. I call upon all ranks once more to repeat their magnificent efforts and show H.I.M. what British soldiers really are." 2ND NOVEMBER.

# CHAPTER XI.

## THE BATTLE OF ARMENTIÈRES.

13th October—2nd November.

"By the evening of the 11th October the IIIrd Corps had practically completed its detrainment at St. Omer, and was moved east to Hazebrouck, where the Corps remained throughout the 12th."

Official Despatches.

WHILST the 4th Battalion was engaged in the Battle of La Bassée, the 1st Battalion, farther north, had, with other units of the 19th Infantry Brigade and IIIrd Corps,* forced the enemy back eastwards in the Battle of Armentières.

11TH OCTOBER. 1ST BATTALION.

The 1st Middlesex (in Brigade) marched out of St. Omer at 7 a.m. on the 11th October, and, taking the road through Arcques, reached Renescure, in which position the Battalion covered the detrainment of the 4th Division at St. Omer. In a field near the village the Middlesex men bivouacked for the night.

12TH OCTOBER.

At dawn on the 12th the Battalion set out to occupy a portion of the line Strazeele–Caestre–St. Sylvestre, the 19th Infantry Brigade having been detailed as the advanced guard of the 6th Division. The march was by way of Wallon Capel and north of Hazebrouck to Borre; at each village a halt of 4 hours was called. At 3 p.m. the 1st Middlesex moved to Pradelles, the right-half battalion taking up position in defence of Rouge Croix† and Strazeele. The left-half battalion went into billets.

Touch had been established with the enemy about Strazeele, for "A" Company of the Middlesex was shelled and two men were

* The formation of the IIIrd Corps at this period was :—4th Division (10th, 11th and 12th Infantry Brigades); 6th Division (16th, 17th, 18th and 19th Infantry Brigades).

† Should not be confused with Rouge Croix, near Neuve Chapelle.

13TH OCTOBER. 1ST BATTALION. wounded. On the morning of the 13th the 19th Infantry Brigade concentrated at Rouge Croix, the Middlesex reaching the rendezvous at 7 a.m. Here the Brigade was in Corps Reserve, and the Middlesex men remained all day in a field, moving off to billets in Rouge Croix at 6.30 p.m. On this day the IIIrd Corps attacked the enemy on the line Vieux Berquin–Meteren–Berthen, the Corps Commander having been ordered by General Headquarters to move towards the line Armentières–Wytschaete. At 12 noon on the following day the 1st Battalion (in Brigade) marched out of Rouge Croix south-east, through Strazeele, where direction was changed to east, the 19th Brigade advancing on Bailleul with the object of attacking the village. But when the Brigade arrived the enemy had already evacuated Bailleul, and the 1st Battalion marched through the village and bivouacked

15TH OCTOBER. in a meadow east of it. Late on the 15th the 19th Infantry Brigade moved to Steenwerck, as reserve to the 4th Division; it was 11 p.m. before the 1st Middlesex bivouacked in a field just west of the village and 12 midnight before the whole Brigade was settled in.

The next day's march tried the troops of the 19th Brigade to the utmost. Since the 11th they had been moving eastwards, following a retreating enemy over very difficult country, broken by ditches and dykes, but on the 16th orders were suddenly received by Brigade Headquarters to change direction completely and march *north* to Vlamertinghe, where the Brigade was to act as reserve to the IVth Corps.*

The diary of the 1st Battalion states:—"Marched east 12.45 p.m. *via* Station-Ouderdom to Vlamertinghe, and went into billets at 8 p.m.—a long march, 17 miles." "East" should undoubtedly read "north." The four Battalions forming the 19th Brigade, worn out, very much appreciated the next two days, for they were spent in billets in the village. On the 19th, however, between 1 and 2 p.m., the Brigade marched out of Vlamertinghe, with orders to move south again *via* Neuve Eglise, Steenwerck and Estaires, thence cross the River Lys to Laventie. This entailed another long march of some 27 miles, at the end of which the tired troops trudged into Estaires at about 2 a.m. on the

* The Ist Corps had not yet arrived in the Ypres area, and at this date the IVth Corps consisted of 7th Division and 3rd Cavalry Division; the 7th Division then holding a line "east of Ypres on a line extending from Zandvoorde through Gheluvelt to Zonnebeke. The 3rd Cavalry Division was on its left towards Langemarck and Poelcapelle."

20th, finding only "very bad billets." At 12 noon the whole Brigade received orders to move on Fromelles. Half-an-hour later the Middlesex marched out of Estaires, taking up a position on the left of the Royal Welch Fusiliers, then posted along the road to Pont Pierre, in support of French Cavalry. All night long the Middlesex men were engaged in digging trenches and in putting the position in a state of defence. 1ST BATTALION.

The 19th Brigade Diary gives the general situation on the 20th October as follows:—"The right of the IIIrd Corps was at Radinghem; the left of the IInd Corps about Aubers; the space between these two points being held by French Cavalry. Two Battalions, the Welch Fusiliers and Middlesex, were pushed forward to the line Fromelles–Pont de Pierre to hold a line slightly in rear of the French Cavalry. The enemy was in touch with French Cavalry along our front, and were engaged with the 6th Division at Radinghem during the afternoon. The two battalions bivouacked about a mile north-west of Fromelles for the night." 20TH OCTOBER.

During the night 20th–21st October IIIrd Corps Headquarters ordered the 19th Brigade to occupy Fromelles and Le Maisnil, and thus fill the gap which existed between the left of the IInd Corps (about Aubers) and the right of the IVth Corps (about Radinghem). To carry out this object the 2nd Argyll and Sutherland Highlanders moved at 4 a.m. to Le Maisnil, whilst the Welch Fusiliers extended their front so as to hold from the south-west corner of Fromelles to Pont de Pierre. The Cameronians and 1st Middlesex moved to a central position about Bas Maisnil at 7 a.m.

Towards 11 a.m. the enemy opened very heavy shell fire on Le Maisnil, and the Argylls began to lose heavily. Between 11 a.m. and 12 noon Headquarters and "B" and "D" Companies of the Middlesex were sent forward to support the Highlanders in Le Maisnil. On entering the village these two Companies were shelled heavily, and suffered a number of casualties. Colonel Ward then assumed command of the village, into which the enemy's artillery continued to pour shell. At 3 p.m. a heavy hostile infantry attack was launched from Radinghem, and "B" Company of the Middlesex went forward to the Argylls, who were hard pressed, for the enemy was attacking in great strength. Colonel Ward was now wounded.* Some French cyclists, holding 21ST OCTOBER.

* Died of wounds on 22nd October, on which date Lieut.-Col. F. G. M. Rowley (senior Major) assumed command of the 1st Middlesex.

22ND OCTOBER. 1ST BATTALION. ground on the left flank of the defence, gave way about 5 p.m., whereupon the position held by the Highlanders and Middlesex became untenable, and the O.C. the Highlanders ordered a retirement. "B" and "D" Companies of the Middlesex fell back from the north-east end of Le Maisnil, "D" covering the retirement of "B" and one company of the Highlanders. Severe losses were suffered by "B" Company, for although darkness intervened, the enemy continued to shell the village heavily, and when finally the two Companies reached Bas Maisnil the Battalion's casualties numbered over 100 officers and men.* Throughout the action "A" and "C" Companies of the Middlesex, under Colonel Rowley, had remained at Bas Maisnil, throwing out pickets towards Radinghem, but when darkness fell and Le Maisnil had been evacuated, "A" Company moved to Bacquart, covering the road from Le Maisnil. All that night the Battalion lay in two lines in extended order east of road Le Maisnil–La Boutillerie, about 200 yards in advance of the latter.

On the following morning the 19th Brigade took up a defensive line La Boutillerie–Rouge Bancs, in touch with the 16th Brigade on the left and French Cavalry on the right. During the day the enemy attacked the covering parties, but was driven off. From the 23rd to the 29th of the month the 1st Middlesex occupied the same positions, suffering all the while heavy casualties from shelling and sniping,† and it was not until the 30th that the enemy again launched an infantry attack against the Battalion.

Throughout the 29th, the enemy's guns had kept the Battalion front under heavy fire, and soon after midnight 29th–30th, the Germans were heard advancing to the attack: they were coming through the farm buildings opposite the Middlesex, singing as they came. The 6th Divisional Artillery was at once informed, and opened fire on the buildings and ground in rear.

30TH OCTOBER. With commendable self-restraint, the 1st Middlesex withheld their fire until the enemy reached the wire entanglements out in front of the Battalion, a distance of about 40 yards from the trenches. They then opened rapid fire and the German advance

* Wounded: 5 officers (2 missing); 13 other ranks. Wounded and missing, 19 other ranks; missing, 64 other ranks. No names are given in Battalion or Brigade diaries.

† Casualties: 23rd October. 2 other ranks wounded; 24th, 3 other ranks killed, 5 wounded; 25th, 1 officer and 11 other ranks wounded; 26th, 5 other ranks killed, 19 wounded; 27th, 2 other ranks killed, 21 wounded; 28th, 2 other ranks killed; 29th, 3 other ranks wounded; 30th, 3 officers and 26 other ranks wounded, 16 other ranks killed.

was stayed, though at one place where there was a gap in the line between " C " and " D " Companies, about 50 of the enemy got into a trench and behind the left half of " D " Company. The O.C. " B " Company reported the situation to the C.O., also stating that he had attacked the enemy but had failed to eject him. The last of the Battalion reserve—one platoon—was then sent up from Battalion Headquarters ; a second attack was launched, but this also was a failure, as the enemy clung tenaciously to his new position. Lieut.-Colonel Rowley, who then went forward to discuss the situation with the O.C. " B " Company, was severely wounded, and Captain Osborne (" A " Company) assumed command of the Battalion. This officer organised another attack, asking meanwhile for support from the Argyll and Sutherland Highlanders. This attack, in which every man was used—servants, pioneers, cooks, etc., who were carrying ammunition or fighting with " B " Company—was entirely successful. Every German who had penetrated the line was killed—37 being accounted for in this way—or captured. And on the following morning over 200 dead Germans were counted lying out in No Man's Land in front of the trenches. But " B " Company practically ceased to exist. 30TH OCTOBER. 1ST BATTALION.

In this very gallant little fight, the 1st Middlesex lost 16 other ranks killed and 25 wounded, including Lieut.-Colonel Rowley, Capt. Gibbons and 2nd Lieut. Shaw. " Where all ranks behaved so well," said Colonel Rowley, " it was hard to single out any for reward, but at any rate all had the satisfaction of worthily upholding the name of Die-Hards.

The Battle of Armentières closed on 2nd November, with the 1st Middlesex still holding the line at La Boutillerie.* 2ND NOVEMBER.

* Captain A. F. Skaife was killed by a sniper on 1st November.

## CHAPTER XII.

# Trench Warfare from 3rd November, 1914, to 9th March, 1915.

BETWEEN the Battles of La Bassée and Armentières (which closed on 2nd November), and the Battle of Neuve Chapelle (10th March, 1915), no Battalion of the Middlesex Regiment in France or Flanders made any direct attack upon the enemy. The only operation (referred to later) of any importance in which the Regiment was involved was the attack on Wytschaete, on 14th December, during which the 4th Battalion supported the attack of other battalions of the 8th Infantry Brigade, and subsequently relieved the Gordon Highlanders in the front line. 4TH BATTALION.

The intervening period—a little over four months—cannot, however, be dismissed without a brief description of that first terrible winter in the trenches: how all ranks endured it; how they "won through" is an essential part of the history of any unit which served in France or Flanders during the first year of the war. Moreover, certain items of purely Regimental interest occur in the Diaries.

Both the 1st and 4th Battalions at the close of the two battles mentioned above had begun to settle down on that line, which was gradually becoming stabilised; the former in the forward trenches in front of La Boutillerie, north-west of Le Maisnil, the latter south-west of Baquerot, where it was occupying support trenches in the Fauquissart area. The two Battalions were from 4½ to 5 miles, one from the other.

From the 3rd of November onwards until the 14th, when the Battalion was relieved in the line and marched back to billets in Sailly-sur-Oise, the Diary of the 1st Middlesex contains an almost daily roll of casualties. The Diary of the 3rd states:—"Battalion very weak, and 'B' Company send 60 to assist 'D' every night." The constant shelling by day, to which the trenches were subjected, was gradually reducing the Battalion to a mere skeleton. For it 3RD NOVEMBER. 1ST BATTALION.

1st Battalion.

must be remembered that trenches in those early days were primitive, mere excavations in the ground compared with the scientific earthworks of later periods. Often dug on soft ground, the parapets and traverses crumbled away under the heavy rains, or were blown to bits by the enemy's shell and trench-mortar fire. Terrible in the extreme was the condition of officers and men as they stood in the trenches, often knee-deep in filthy mud and slush. For many days they had not taken off their clothes, which had become caked with mud, blood-stained and verminous; indeed, it was with difficulty that many of them remembered there had been a time when they were clean and warm, when the concentrated misery of the trenches was unknown to them. But if their feet and hands were icy cold and numbed, if their clothes were soaked and clung like sodden rags about them, limbs racked with rheumatics, if they stood in three feet of water peering cautiously over the parapets across No Man's Land, dotted here and there with the rotting carcases of what had once been brave men and their "pals," there still burned within them the old "die-hard" spirit which made light of their troubles and their discomforts, for they were British soldiers.

8th November.

On the 8th November, "D" and "C" Companies suffered, so the Diary records, a "fearful shelling." Two officers were wounded; 11 other ranks were killed and 38 wounded. On the 14th, the day the Battalion was relieved, Captain G. R. K. Evatt was killed by a sniper's bullet.* At the end of three days' rest the Battalion (in Brigade) marched off to relieve the 10th Brigade in the trenches at Houplines, the 1st Middlesex remaining in Brigade Reserve, billeted in a factory. On the 25th the Battalion relieved the Royal Welch Fusiliers in the front line east and north-east of, and about 800 yards from, Houplines, all companies manning the fire trenches, which are described as "very bad."

Major Ash took over command of the Battalion on 29th November.

20th December.

Until 20th December the 1st Middlesex held the Houplines trenches, during which period there were constant casualties, and the conditions in the line became more and more terrible. On 17th, 2nd Lieut. S. C. Bosanquet was shot by a sniper and died shortly afterwards. Three days later the Battalion was relieved

* Casualties between 3rd and 14th November—1 officer killed, 2 officers wounded, 72 other ranks killed and 70 wounded.

and marched off to billets in Armentières, where the close of the year still found the men quartered.

So far as casualties were concerned, the 4th Battalion seems to have been more fortunate than the 1st, though it is obvious that the conditions under which the former lived in the trenches were not less uncomfortable. Mud was everywhere, and a footnote to the 1st Battalion Diary records:—"Great difficulty was experienced with the rifles in the trenches. They got grit into the leads and the cases stuck in the breeches, with the result that the bolts would not open. This was overcome with careful cleaning and oiling of the bolt actions and leads." 4TH BATTALION.

From the support trenches south-west of Baquerot, the Battalion marched off on 7th November to Le Touret, as reserve to the Lahore Division. On the 8th a move was made to Zelobes; on the 9th one half-battalion marched to Croix Barbée, in reserve to the Meerut Division, and the other half-battalion to Le Touret, in reserve to the Lahore Division. Several more days were spent in Zelobes, Croix Barbée and Rouge Croix. On the 14th, at 1 a.m., the Battalion moved to Pont Logy and took over trenches from the 6th Jats. When daylight dawned the enemy's guns opened fire, and all day long continued to shell the Die-Hards, who lost 10 other ranks killed and 17 wounded. The relief, which took place during the evening, was very welcome. Billets that night were in La Couture. A move next day (in Brigade) was made to Bailleul, where all units went into billets. "A bitterly cold southerly wind, with heavy rain and some sleet, made the march a very unpleasant one; but in spite of their long stay in the trenches the men completed the fourteen-mile march without undue distress. The wind being at their backs helped them considerably."* 7TH NOVEMBER. 14TH NOVEMBER.

At 2 p.m. on the 16th the 8th Brigade marched out of Bailleul, and arrived near Neuve Eglise at 4.30 p.m., where a halt was called and hot tea served out to the men. At 6 p.m. the march was continued to Wulverghem, where the 2nd Suffolk Regiment relieved a battalion of French troops near the Wulverghem–Messines road; the 2nd Royal Scots relieved the 2nd Middlesex, with their right flank near the Armentières–Messines road, and the 4th Middlesex took over the trenches of the Scottish Rifles between the French troops and the 2nd Middlesex. The Royal Scots and the 4th Middlesex suffered about a dozen casualties from shell fire whilst approaching the trenches. 16TH NOVEMBER. 2ND BATTALION. 4TH BATTALION.

* 8th Brigade Diary.

4TH BATTALION. On this day also the 4th Battalion lost its gallant C.O., Lieut.-Colonel C. P. A. Hull having been appointed Brigadier-General and to command the 10th Infantry Brigade. The command of the 4th Middlesex Regiment was then taken over by Major H. Storr.

1ST NOVEMBER. The 8th Brigade Diary of 18th November contains an interesting note of the conditions in the neighbourhood of the trenches :—" The mud in the neighbourhood of Neuve Eglise and Wulverghem was a serious impediment to movement. The tracks on the sides of the pavée roads were nothing but a morass, which was knee-deep in places. It was along bye-roads of this description that access to the 2nd Royal Scots and 4th Middlesex trenches had to be obtained, and therefore communications for orderlies, for rations, and for evacuating wounded were very difficult."

The severe weather and awful condition of the front line now began to take heavy toll of all battalions, and on the 20th " A " Company of the 4th Middlesex sent 15 men to hospital, sick. The next day charcoal braziers were started in the trenches, and were found beneficial. After several more days in the line the Battalion was relieved and marched off to Westoutre, reaching the village about 3.15 p.m. From Westoutre " A " and " B " Companies managed to get to the bath at Bailleul, but there was no time to send, or accommodation for, more. That night fur waistcoats were issued to " A " Company, and on the following day to the three remaining Companies. A few pairs of boots were also obtained. " This article," records the Battalion Diary, " was found to be impossible to get from the Ordnance, and many men's boots were worn through the soles completely." On the

30TH NOVEMBER. 30th November the Battalion moved to Locre, under orders to turn out at 10 minutes' notice to support the 7th Brigade, if required.

13TH DECEMBER. Until the 13th of December the only items of interest in the Battalion Diary are :—On 3rd the 4th Middlesex (with other units) lined the roads along which His Majesty King George drove when reviewing the troops : on the 7th the whole Battalion " managed to get a refit of boots ; they were very badly needed."

At 10.30 p.m. on 13th orders were received to move off to Kemmel at 3 a.m. on 14th and take up a position in support of the 1st Gordon Highlanders, who were going to attack the enemy. Two companies of Middlesex were moved up in close support of the Highlanders, but were not called upon to assist in the operation, which unfortunately was a failure. The Middlesex men, however, aided the Highlanders in collecting their wounded. "The Middlesex Regiment," said the C.O., 1st Gordon Highlanders, in his official report, "gave us unstinted assistance in collecting our wounded after the hours of darkness. The wounded were lying out beyond our own trenches, and could only be brought in at grave risk." The 4th Middlesex Diary, however, only records the fact that: "Stretcher bearers and others helped a number of wounded men of the Gordon Highlanders back to the village." It avoids all mentions of "grave risks."

4TH BATTALION.

During the evening of 14th the 4th Middlesex took over the front-line trenches of the Gordon Highlanders, and on the 15th suffered heavy shelling, during which 6 other ranks were killed, 11 wounded and 1 man missing. The Battalion was relieved that night and moved to Locre. On the 19th 2nd Lieut. H. D. Hilton was killed. The last tour in the trenches (which began on the 27th December and ended on the 31st) was both costly and wretched. Capt. C. W. F. Sheffield was wounded during the relief, and when the troops got into the trenches they were found to be in a terrible condition. The 8th Brigade Diary thus describes the conditions in the front line: "Heavy rain and a violent gale during the night made conditions in the trenches very bad. Several of the trenches fell in, and had to be remade as could best be done, in soil which is *of the consistency of porridge*."

19TH DECEMBER.

On the last day of the year, when the 4th Middlesex was relieved the tour had cost the Battalion 1 officer killed, 1 officer wounded, 12 other ranks killed, 21 wounded, 9 missing and 46 sent to hospital sick, with frost bite, and 10 otherwise sick. 2nd Lieut. G. W. Hughes was killed on 31st December.

31ST DECEMBER.

The 2nd Middlesex Regiment (77th Foot) was mentioned on a previous page. This Battalion when war was declared was at Malta, forming a portion of the Mediterranean Garrison; it was commanded by Lieut.-Colonel R. H. Hayes.

2ND BATTALION.

On 5th November, the 2nd Middlesex had embarked at Southampton with other units of the 23rd Infantry Brigade, 8th Division. The latter consisted of the 23rd, 24th and 25th Infantry Brigades. The 23rd Brigade was formed of the 2nd Devons, 2nd West Yorks, 2nd Scottish Rifles and 2nd Middlesex Regiments. Havre was reached on the 6th, but the battalions

5TH NOVEMBER.

2ND BATTALION. remained on board, and it was not until 8 a.m. on the 7th that disembarkation began, and on getting ashore the troops marched out to the Rest Camp, 5 miles away. At 4 p.m. on the 8th, the Battalion (in Brigade) entrained, and, after spending all night and the whole of the next day in the train, eventually detrained at Merville at 10 p.m. on the 9th and went into billets.

12TH NOVEMBER. On 12th the 23rd Brigade moved to Steenwerck, coming under the orders of the Cavalry Corps. The same night one Battalion of the Brigade went into the front-line trenches, the right flank of the Brigade resting on the " La Hutte–Warneton road at a point due south of Messines. The trenches turned thence through the 7th kilometre on Ploegsteert–Messines road to the junction along unmetalled road running southwards from River Douve, ½ mile west of 7th kilometre referred to above. Route taken to enter the trenches *via* Wulverghem and thence along south bank of River Douve."* The first sector held in France and Flanders during the war is an interesting memory to many units.

14TH NOVEMBER. On 14th the 2nd Middlesex moved from Steenwerck to Neuve Eglise, and at 5 p.m. on 15th moved off to relieve the 2nd West Yorkshires in the front line. The relief was completed by 10 p.m.

Details of that first tour in the front line are very meagre. " Subjected to shrapnel fire for about an hour 16th inst., 12 noon, while the right of our trenches held by ' C ' Company was subjected to an attack by some infantry at 6 p.m. and again at 9 p.m." And the casualties (the first reported) are given as " 1 killed, 1 wounded, 15 missing."

17TH NOVEMBER. The Battalion was relieved on 17th November and marched to billets in Estaires. From this date until the end of the year the Battalion Diary omits all details of the severe time spent in the front line before the New Year dawned, though casualties were frequent. Two officers were killed—Lieut. C. M. Harvey on 25th November and Captain A. C. Wordsworth on 6th December. In other ranks the 2nd Middlesex lost during that period 24 killed and 36 wounded. The last day of 1914 found the Battalion

31ST DECEMBER. in reserve billets in La Flinque, the 23rd Brigade then holding a sub-sector of the line just south of Chapigny.

Thus at the end of the year there were three battalions of the Regiment in France and Flanders, *i.e.*, the 1st in Armentières, the 2nd at La Flinque and the 4th at Locre.

* 23rd Brigade Diary.

On the 2nd January, 1915, the 19th Infantry Brigade marched 2ND JANUARY.
from Armentières, three miles south, to relieve the 16th Infantry Brigade in front-line trenches running between Touquet and Rue du Bois. The 1st Middlesex relieved a battalion of the Leicester- 1ST
shire Regiment, three Companies ("B," "C," and "D") in BATTALION.
the front line, "A" Company in support. The relief was completed by 9.30 p.m.

Until the 18th of the month the 1st Battalion remained in the trenches, ekeing out an existence terrible in the extreme. On the 3rd January (the day following the relief of the Leicesters) the Battalion Diary records: "Still in trenches, which are very bad, full of mud and water up to the men's knees in many places. Raining all day." And for several days the same note of misery is contained in the Diary: "Still in trenches, weather terrible, mud and water dreadful . . . Working all day to try and keep the trenches standing. Rain causes dug-outs to fall in, and parapets to disappear. Fascines and sand-bags all sink into the mud . . . Raining hard again. Trenches very bad"—and
so on! Relief came on the 18th, but only four days were spent 18TH JANUARY.
out of the line. February was spent much in the same way, no attacks were made on or by the enemy. Shelling, machine-gun and rifle fire and sniping went on day and night, though casualties
appear to be small. On 5th of the month Captain G. H. Hastings 5TH FEBRUARY.
was wounded by a sniper and died of his wounds. The 19th
Brigade Diary for the first nine days of March contains the best 9TH MARCH.
summary of trench life at that period: "The situation remains the same in our front; daily registration of our own and hostile artillery, but no organised bombardment on either side. Sniping by day active; by night little sniping except in front of our left. A great improvement in the weather makes the trenches drier, and there is more to show for work and material put into them. In addition to general strengthening of the front line, work in connection with supporting points and defence of the main second line is carried out by battalions in reserve."

Of the 2nd Battalion and its first winter in the trenches little 2ND
can be told, for all reference to trench life from the 15th November, BATTALION.
1914, until the early days of March, 1915, when the Battalion was moving up to take over trenches previous to the battle of Neuve
Chapelle (10th March), is omitted. On the 5th March, however, 5TH MARCH.
all officers of the Battalion and 8 N.C.Os. proceeded by motor 'bus to Rouge Croix and thence on foot to Rue de Tilloy (west of

Neuve Chapelle) for the purpose of reconnoitring the position.

7TH MARCH.

The Battalion spent the 7th March in billets in Estaires, and on the 9th March moved off after dark to take up its assembly positions from which the attack was to be made.

3RD BATTALION.
1914.
24TH DECEMBER.

On Christmas Eve, 1914, the 3rd Battalion Middlesex Regiment (Lieut.-Colonel E. W. R. Stephenson) arrived at Mornhill Camp, Winchester, from India, and joined the 85th Infantry Brigade of the 28th Division. The 3rd Middlesex were brigaded with 2nd Buffs, 3rd Royal Fusiliers, and 2nd East Surrey Regiment.

Mobilisation stores were drawn on 27th December, and the new pattern rifles issued. Drafts of officers and men arrived from the 5th and 6th Battalions of the Regiment, and mobilisation and training proceeded rapidly.

1915.
12TH JANUARY.

On 12th January the Battalion (in Division) paraded for inspection by H.M. the King, an event which invariably preceded a move overseas. Six days later (on 18th), the Battalion (26 officers and 991 other ranks) entrained for Southampton, and, embarking at 12.40 p.m., sailed at 4.30 in the afternoon for France. Havre was reached at 3 a.m., but it was 2 p.m. on 19th before the Middlesex disembarked and proceeded to camp. From Havre a move was made to Hazebrouck and Flêtre,

22ND JANUARY.

and in the latter village (22nd) the Battalion settled down in billets, field work, route-marching and tactical exercises occupying all ranks until the 2nd February, when the 85th Brigade moved to a new area about Ouderdom, the 3rd Middlesex billeting in Reninghelst. On the 4th and 5th the Brigade moved north to Ypres, the Middlesex being quartered with the 3rd Royal Fusiliers in the Cavalry Barracks. The march from Reninghelst had tried the troops considerably, and the Battalion Diary records: "men in good spirits but tired."

6TH FEBRUARY.

At 6 p.m. on the 6th the 3rd Middlesex, with one day's rations, sand-bags and entrenching tools, marched off to relieve the 2nd King's Own in the front line south of Ypres.

The first sub-sector held by the 3rd Middlesex in France and Flanders is difficult to describe, for the Battalion Diary contains no details, and the only information is a brief description in the 85th Brigade Diary, outlining the relief of the 83rd Brigade. The entry is as follows: "2nd East Surreys moved at 6.30 p.m.—platoons—and at Ecluse No. 8 on the Ypres–St. Eloi road were met by guides of the Leinster Regiment of the 82nd Infantry Brigade (27th Division), and were guided to their places in the trenches about 600 yards S.E. of St. Eloi, extending for 250 yards towards the canal and S.W. of Oosthoek, joining up with the 82nd Infantry Brigade of the 27th Division on their right, and with the Middlesex on their left. The relief was effected without a casualty—3 platoons in front line, two in support. At 7 p.m. the 3rd Middlesex moved by companies at a quarter of an hour's interval with guides of the Regiment to be relieved, to continue the line taken up by the East Surreys, all companies being south of the canal. At 8 p.m. the 2nd Buffs similarly followed, with one company S. of the canal, and the remainder N. of the canal, linking up with the 84th Infantry Brigade." 3RD BATTALION.

The relief was thus described :—"The night was very dark and rain fell heavily, and owing to the large amount of kit, etc., to be carried up into the trenches, the relief took several hours to complete, and the whole relief was not finished until 4 a.m. (6th), but no casualties were experienced in the actual relief. The trenches were very wet, that on the left being very bad and full of water, in many cases over 3 feet deep. The trenches had become very wide, in many places 18 feet, and parapets require strengthening. Trenches, though in communication with one another, were not continuous, and there were gaps from 150 yards downwards, making it impossible to walk round the trench line. Enemy's trenches generally on higher ground and from 200 yards to 30 yards distant." 6TH FEBRUARY.

In this unsavoury spot the 3rd Battalion Middlesex settled down to spend its first tour in the front-line trenches, from the 7th to the 10th–11th February. So bad were these trenches and so vigilant was the enemy that no reports could be sent back to Battalion Headquarters during daylight. Heavy artillery and infantry fire was frequent, and when, at 11 p.m. on the 10th, the 2nd East Surreys began to file into the trenches of the Middlesex, and the latter filed out, the tour had cost the latter Battalion 1 officer and 26 other ranks killed and 2 officers and 56 wounded.* Casualties from frost bite were 80 per cent.

Some idea of the condition of the 3rd Battalion on the 11th February may be gathered from the fact that on receipt of orders to find 250 men to carry up rations to the 2nd East Surreys, only 220 were available, many of these suffering from frost bite. 11TH FEBRUARY.

The Battalion Diary has also the following phrase: "Many rifles hopelessly damaged owing to mud, the men standing over

* Names of officers not given.

3RD BATTALION.

their knees in liquid mud practically the whole time; in one trench only 2 rifles able to fire out of 25."

After relief the Battalion billeted in Kruistraat, but respite was brief, for at 5 p.m. on the 12th the 3rd Middlesex again marched off for duty in the trenches, relieving the East Surreys in the line originally held. One officer—Lieutenant Gransmore—was wounded.

13TH FEBRUARY.

About 6.30 p.m. on the 13th a report reached Battalion Headquarters that the enemy had sapped right up to the trenches practically all along the line. An R.E. officer gave his opinion that the trenches were untenable, and suggested the construction of a line 100 yards in rear of the front line. On the G.O.C. consenting, a new line in rear of "N," "O" and "P" trenches was at once put in hand, the men working all night, and the Battalion Diary adds: "a small party [was] to be left in the old trenches until the new ones were completed." During the night Lieut.-Colonel Stephenson personally visited the trenches to see how the work was progressing.

14TH FEBRUARY.

The Battalion Diary contains a graphic account of what happened on the 14th: "8 a.m. An urgent message was received to the effect that 'O' Trench, occupied by 'B' Company under Captain Hilton, had fallen and was in possession of the enemy. This trench had been vacated in order to take up the new line. In withdrawing, Captain [H. P.] Hilton was killed, and owing to this and his orders being misunderstood, the greater part of 'B' Company withdrew beyond the new line and arrived near the Brigade Headquarters. The new trench was consequently only lightly held. This information was received by telephone from Brigade Headquarters. Immediately on receipt of the message, Lieut.-Colonel Stephenson collected all the men at Battalion Headquarters [28], and, accompanied by Major Neale and Captain and Adjutant Large, moved out with the intention of retaking the trench. This party came under very heavy fire, and eventually reinforced 'M' Trench, which was held by a party of East Surreys. During this advance Captain [H. E.] Large and 2 men were killed. Lieut.-Colonel Stephenson took command of this trench and remained there till 6 p.m. the following evening. In the afternoon the East Surreys and a party of the Middlesex Regiment attempted to regain 'O' Trench, but were unsuccessful. Lieutenant [W. J.] Ash was killed—practically the whole party who came under heavy shell and machine-gun fire were killed or wounded. All was quiet in 'M' Trench, but a very heavy artillery fire was heard on the ridge, and it was reported that the trench on the immediate right of 'M' Trench had fallen; this trench was retaken at about 4 a.m. the following morning. An attempt was made after dark by the Buffs to regain 'O' Trench, but as the ground had not been reconnoitred it was abandoned." 3RD BATTALION.

The 15th February passed quietly in the neighbourhood of "M" Trench. "B" and "C" Companies occupied the new "P" and "O" Trenches, but the Germans still held the original "O" Trench and a portion of the original "P" Trench, from which positions they kept up heavy rifle fire. Lieut. W. P. Grieve was killed during the day, and 2nd Lieut. Moller wounded. 15TH FEBRUARY.

On the night of 15th the 3rd Middlesex was relieved by a battalion of Suffolks, and filed out of the trenches with orders to proceed to Ypres. Thus ended a very costly tour, for during the three days the Battalion had been in the front line it had lost 4 officers killed,* 3 officers wounded, 44 other ranks killed and 62 wounded, and 156 other ranks missing.

The 85th Infantry Brigade was transferred to the 3rd Division a day or two later, and on 19th February moved to Locre (in the Divisional area), where all battalions billeted, including the 3rd Middlesex, which by rare good fortune found itself beside the 4th Battalion. On the night of 22nd the 85th Brigade relieved a brigade of 7th Division troops at Kemmel, the Middlesex men relieving the Wiltshires in J2, J3, J10, J11 and S4a. The remainder of the month passed without any incident of outstanding importance taking place. This comparative quietude continued through the early days of March, casualties being small. On the 7th March all battalions in the front line were ordered to show the greatest activity for the next three days, whilst the artillery was to bombard the enemy's trenches frequently. It was hoped thereby to draw the attention of the Germans from Neuve Chapelle, where the battle was to open on the 10th. 19TH FEBRUARY. 7TH MARCH.

On the 4th January the 4th Middlesex marched to Locre and took over fresh billets. On the next day, after the C.O., Adjutant and two company commanders had reconnoitred a new part of the line at Vierstraat occupied by French troops and a part of the 7th Brigade, the Battalion left Locre at 3.30 p.m. 4TH JANUARY. 4TH BATTALION.

* Names already given (p. 94).

4TH BATTALION.

and moved off to the trenches, 1½ companies occupying the firing line, 1½ companies the support trenches, and 1 company was held in reserve. A period of normal trench warfare was now before the Battalion. No attacks were made on or by the enemy, but casualties were frequent from shell and rifle fire and the enemy's snipers, whilst the conditions in the trenches were anything but enviable.

Throughout the remainder of January and February and the first week of March there is little to record but one or two items of purely Regimental interest. Only one officer lost his life during this period—Lieut. L. H. V. Fraser—who was killed on 24th February. On 26th February Major G. A. Bridgman joined the 4th Battalion and assumed command. Scherpenberg, Locre and La Clytte appear to have been the billeting areas during relief from the front line, and on the 10th March the 4th Middlesex were in the latter village, cleaning up and resting.

10TH MARCH.

## CHAPTER XIII.

# THE BATTLE OF NEUVE CHAPELLE.

10th March, 1915.

FOUR months had passed since the beginning of that first horrible winter of trench warfare; four months of most agonising conditions in the front-line trenches, now happily but a memory—and in all that time (from 2nd November to the 9th March) the Middlesex Regiment had made no direct assault upon, neither had it been involved in any large attacks by, the enemy. All four Regular Battalions (1st, 2nd, 3rd and 4th) were now in France; the 1/7th and 1/8th Territorial Battalions were due to arrive within the next few days; the 1/9th and 1/10th were in India; the 2/7th and 2/8th were at Gibraltar; the 2/9th, 2/10th and 3/10th were training in England, as were also several Service Battalions contained in Kitchener's First, Second and Third Armies. Truly a record of which the Regiment might well be proud.

The 1st and 4th Battalions had become veterans; theirs the immortal honour of having served throughout the whole War. But the 2nd Battalion was now to show its mettle, to carry high the torch of victory, and to shed yet further lustre on the imperishable glories won by the Die-Hards. For the story of the Battle of Neuve Chapelle is a tale of heroism unsurpassed by all the heroic episodes which came after.

Sir John French stated in his despatch, dated 5th April, 1915, that about the end of February he believed that "a vigorous offensive movement by the Forces under my command should be planned and carried out at the earliest possible moment." The general aspect of the Allied situation, the success of the Russians, the weakening of enemy forces on his front, the desire to assist the Russians by holding as many hostile troops as possible to the Western Front, and the need for fostering the offensive spirit of his troops "after the trying and possibly enervating experiences which they had gone through of a severe winter in the trenches," are given as other reasons.

The objective of the attack was the village of Neuve Chapelle, the enemy's positions at that point, and the establishment of the British line as far forward as possible east of the village.

The assault was to be delivered by the 25th (right) and 23rd (left) Infantry Brigades of the 8th Division of the IVth Corps on the German trenches in front of the north-western portion of the village, and by the Garhwal Brigade of the Meerut Division (Indian Corps) on the southern portion.

2ND BATTALION. The assaulting battalions of the 23rd Brigade in the first attack were the 2nd Scottish Rifles and the 2nd Middlesex Regiment. The 2nd Devons were to join in the attack on the second objective, and the 2nd West Yorkshires were in Brigade Reserve.

The first objectives of the Brigade were: 2nd Scottish Rifles, system of trenches 17–21 inclusive; 2nd Middlesex Regiment, system of trenches 21–75–77 to 20, "taking special precautions to secure trenches leading to the left."

The second objectives were: 2nd Scottish Rifles, trenches 51–22–52 and Posts 12 and 10; 2nd Devon Regiment, to co-operate with 2nd Scottish Rifles by taking Points 78 and 22; 2nd Middlesex, locality 6 and extend their left towards the "Moated Grange."

The first assault was timed to begin at 8.5 a.m. and the second at 8.35 a.m. on 10th March.

North and south of Neuve Chapelle subsidiary ("holding") attacks were to be made by the Second and First Armies respectively.

9TH MARCH. At 11 p.m. on the night of the 9th March the 2nd Middlesex marched out of Estaires—"D" Company leading—for the trenches west of Neuve Chapelle, from which the attack was to take place. At Rue du Bacquerot the Battalion halted and a hot meal was served out to the men, the officers congregating in a small house near by. All ranks were confident of success, and Lille was freely mentioned as the final resting place of the Battalion after the attack was over. The march was resumed about 2 a.m., across country to a line of shallow trenches in an apple orchard ("E") near the Rue Tilleloy, where three Companies were ordered to lie down, whilst the Company detailed to make the initial attack crept forward to the assembly trenches at Point 15.

10TH MARCH. About 4.30 a.m. Lieut.-Colonel Hayes reported to 23rd Brigade Headquarters that his Battalion was all ready in its

10TH MARCH. 2ND BATTALION.

assembly positions, all Companies on a four-platoon frontage, one Company at Point 15, three at " E." Two companies of 2nd Scottish Rifles were on the right of the 2nd Middlesex and one Company of West Yorkshires on the left. By 5.30 a.m., the Brigade Diary records, all movement had ceased and " there has apparently been no hitch. Enemy very quiet and appear to have no inkling of our preparations."

Just after dawn broke (about 5.30 a.m.) a German aeroplane, flying low down, passed from north to south over the British lines. Had the observer discerned the closely packed trenches, which were shallow and very crowded ? Time crept on, and as the hour of attack approached the enemy gave no sign that he expected an attack.

In order to give the enemy no clue to the impending battle, the guns had been ordered to continue the usual registration of the hostile trenches until 7.30 a.m. At the latter hour, however, a general bombardment of the enemy's positions (until 8.5 a.m.) and his wire entanglements (until 7.45 a.m.), especially in front of Point 15, was to begin.

At 7.30 a.m. the tremendous " boom " of a single gun, obviously of large calibre, broke upon the ears of the lines of waiting troops ; it was " Granny "—the huge 15-inch howitzer—firing (for the first time*) the signal for the artillery bombardment to open. Immediately there was an ear-splitting roar, shaking the ground and deafening the troops as they stood ready in the front-line trenches to go " over the top," or lay on the ground in their support or reserve positions. For half-an-hour the waiting troops watched the inferno across No Man's Land ; a wall of dust and smoke, from 50 to 100 feet high, had shot up from the German trenches, as the shells fell thick and fast upon the enemy's barbed wire and front line ; it seemed impossible that any living thing could emerge from the wreckage created by that awful tornado of lyddite and shrapnel ; timber and sand-bags, clods of dirt, heads, arms and legs and mangled bodies were flung about in horrible confusion ; the upper half of a German officer, with the cap thrust down over the distorted face, fell in the front-line British trenches. Only with great difficulty could the British officers restrain their men and persuade them to keep their heads down until that dread half-hour ended ; fascinated, though the

* " Granny " was situated in an apple orchard in Labourse, S. of the La Bassée Canal, *i.e.*, in G. 29.d.1.3.

10TH MARCH. 2ND BATTALION.

shells from their guns engaged in wire-cutting passed barely 6 feet above them, they could hardly turn their eyes from the frightful things happening across No Man's Land, where Germans were being driven stark, raving mad from artillery fire such as they had never before experienced.

For five and thirty minutes the 2nd Middlesex, with the Scottish Rifles on their right and one Company of 2nd West Yorkshires on their left, watched and waited for the hour of attack.

At five minutes past eight whistles sounded all along the British line and, at the same time, shells began to burst further ahead, for the guns had lengthened their range to the village itself.

As if on parade the troops forming the front line rose to their feet and dashed out into No Man's Land towards the German trenches. A sheet of flame flashed from behind the enemy's wire and a murderous machine-gun fire from Points 21 and 76 swept the ranks of the advancing men. Along the front of the Indian Corps, the 25th Brigade and the right Company ("B") of the Scottish Rifles, the terrible wire entanglement had been well cut by the British guns. But in front of "A" Company of the Scotsmen, and the sector allotted to the 2nd Middlesex, the enemy's wire was practically uncut.

"The front line advanced," said Sergeant Daws, of the 2nd Battalion, watching the advance from the third line, "and as they leave their trenches we shout 'Go on the Middlesex! Go on the Die-Hards!' They are met by terrible machine-gun fire."

Of the first wave of Middlesex men few reached the German wire, but these tore in vain at the thick entanglements until their hands were torn and bleeding and their uniforms in rags.

The second line was then ordered forward and as the men, led by their officers, sprang over the top into No Man's Land the sight which met them was appalling; a long lane of dead and dying, lying about in horrible confusion, marked the advance of the first wave right up to the German wire, where a few frantic survivors could still be seen tearing madly at the entanglements.

The second line met the same fate as the first, only a few gallant men getting to the German wire, from behind which the enemy's machine guns and rifles were spitting out death.

An order ran down the third line—"Get ready! Advance!"

"We ran as fast as the spongy ground would allow us," said Sergeant Daws, continuing his story, "and reached an old trench of ours which was full of Devons.* We then ran up the trench, and here I saw poor Lieut. MacFarlane, the tallest and most popular officer of ours, killed. He led the bomb-throwers and made too good a target.

10TH MARCH. 2ND BATTALION.

"Now we join up in the trench facing the enemy when our machine gun jams. For God's sake pass down to the Devons to bring their machine gun here quick! The lock of our gun was examined and rectified, and just as the Devons came with their gun we got ours into action. The Devons were led by a colour-sergeant, who was bowled over as soon as he sighted the gun. All their men went down. The Germans could not find ours, and we had found out where they were situated. Then they got a peppering!"

Apparently up to this time the third line had remained in the old front line, but soon these men also received orders to go forward.

"A whistle sounds, and over the parapet we go. Go on Die-Hards! . . . The sight which met our eyes almost staggered us, our poor first and second lines lying in all positions. Then we saw red: we reached the barbed wire, trampled on it, cut and hacked it, the barbs cutting us in all places. We were beaten back."

Thus three attempts, made unflinchingly in the face of a murderous fire, had failed—and why? The preliminary bombardment had failed to cut the barbed wire in front of the left sector of trenches from which the attack was made. A further bombardment was necessary, and Colonel Hayes was fortunate in getting a message back asking for additional artillery bombardment.

At 11.45 a.m. the guns again plastered the enemy's wire entanglements and forward trenches. This was followed by another attempt by the Middlesex to secure the German trenches:

"This time we won—the trenches were ours!"

Bombing parties immediately moved along the trench in the direction of Point 60. At the cross roads, just before reaching Point 60, a party of Germans who had been sniping signified their desire to surrender. But on seeing that the foremost party of Middlesex bombers numbered only one officer and six men, the Germans ducked down in the trench again and re-opened fire. Without hesitation the Middlesex bombers pushed on, pelting the enemy with bombs, eventually driving the Germans out into the open, where they were caught by a machine gun and shot down.

* The 2nd Devons were on the right of the third Company of 2nd Middlesex at E.

2ND BATTALION.

The Middlesex men pressed forward to their objective—a large orchard north of the village (Point 6), where serious resistance was anticipated. But the Devons had already secured the position. With the Devonshire men the remnants of the 2nd Middlesex consolidated Point 6, helping the Royal Engineers to put the place in a state of defence. The time was now about 5 p.m.

The whole of Neuve Chapelle had fallen, but at what a cost! Eight officers killed* and eight wounded,† of whom one died of his wounds three days later; 70 other ranks killed, 299 wounded and 89 missing were the losses of the 2nd Middlesex. "A," "B" and "C" Companies were almost entirely wiped out.

The Battalion diary states that Point 6 (the Orchard) was held throughout the night 10/11 March and till 12.15 a.m. on the

13TH MARCH.

13th, when the remnants of the 2nd Die-Hards moved forward to a position of readiness in front of Points 88 and 87, in order to take part in a projected attack on the enemy. But whether the Middlesex took part in the attack is not clear, for there are no details in the diary, and the Brigade diary has only the following reference to the operations: "1.30 a.m. 2nd Devons *and a few others*, including 2nd Scottish Rifles, made an attack, but could not get at enemy, who were in strength and covered by blackthorn hedge and wire." A second attack was prepared, but at 1.50 a.m. orders were received from 8th Divisional Headquarters to stop the assault.

At 3 p.m. the 2nd Middlesex took over trenches occupied by

14TH MARCH.

the Northampton Regiment, but on 14th, at 7.30 p.m., the Battalion was relieved and marched back to billets at Rouge Croix.

A few days later, addressing the 2nd Battalion, Sir John French said: "I am proud of you, 2nd Middlesex! No regiment has upheld its traditions better than you, and I know that if called upon to repeat what you have done you would not hesitate."

* Captains A. H. Cooper and H. L. Homan, Captain and Adjutant J. Dixon, Lieut. J. D. Waucope, 2nd Lieuts. G. A. Cook, W. B. MacFarlane, E. A. A. Hare.

† Captain F. A. H. Castberg.

Map V.

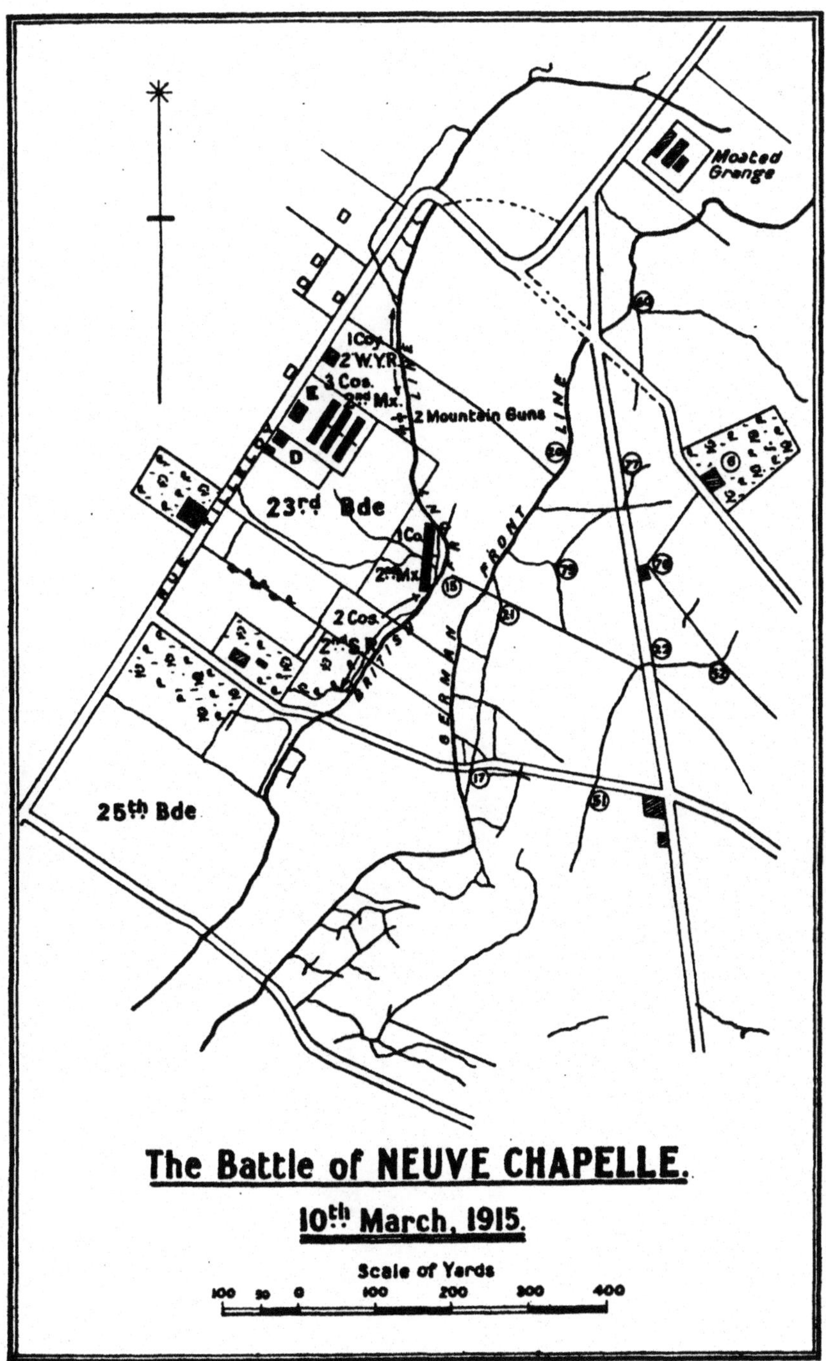


The Battle of NEUVE CHAPELLE.

10th March, 1915.

[To face p. 102.

CHAPTER XIV.

# THE BATTLES OF YPRES, 1915.

## (I.) THE BATTLE OF GRAVENSTAFEL RIDGE: THE GAS ATTACK.

22nd–23rd April.

THE evening of the 22nd April, 1915, will long be remembered by those who were serving in the Ypres Salient at that period, and are amongst the survivors of the Great War. Spring had come and the severe frosts of winter, the snow and seas of mud, had given way to better conditions, though in places the trenches were still somewhat water-logged. 22ND APRIL.

On this particular evening a steady light wind was blowing from the north-east, though the calm, pleasant weather conditions were made horrible by the roar of the great 42 cm. shells which the enemy was then raining upon Ypres. For several days the almost ruined City and the Salient as far south as Hill 60 had been plastered by the enemy with shell of every calibre, obviously heralding an attack, though none knew where it would fall.

The Salient (from the Ypres–Comines Canal to Steenstraate) on the 22nd April was held by British, Canadian and French troops in the following order, from right to left: 5th Division, from the Canal to Hill 60; 27th Division, from the left of the 5th Division, through Veldhoek to a point just west of Becelaere (east of the Polygon Wood), where it joined up with the right of the 28th Division, which continued the line to east of Zonnebeke. At the latter point the left of the 28th Division was in touch with the right of the Canadian Division, the Canadians extending their line to the Poelcapelle–St. Julien Road, whence French troops carried their front through Langemarck to Steenstraate.

22ND APRIL.
3RD BATTALION.
8TH BATTALION.

In the 28th Division were the 3rd* and 1/8th† (Territorial) Battalions of the Middlesex Regiment.

Between 5 and 6 o'clock in the evening artillery and aeroplane observers saw with astonishment a dense green cloud floating from east to west across No Man's Land towards the trenches held by French troops, and they reported what they had seen. A little later, as darkness was falling over the Salient, the significance of that green cloud became terribly apparent, for out of the gloom of the evening there suddenly appeared upon the Poelcapelle-Langemarck Road a terrified crowd of French Turco troops, coughing, gasping, tearing at their throats, stumbling blindly, but moving as quickly as their tortured bodies would allow them, back towards the Yser Canal. "The effect of these poisonous gases," said Sir John French, "was so virulent as to render the whole of the line held by the French Divisions . . . incapable of any action at all. It was at first impossible for anyone to

* From the 10th, and throughout the remainder of March, the 3rd Battalion had spent a strenuous three weeks. On 13th 2nd Lieut. H. Strong (East Surrey Regiment, attached 3rd Middlesex) was killed by a shell, and 2nd Lieut. Parriss was reported killed on 14th. The Battalion was then at Rosignol, holding the line, with hourly expectations of being involved in the operations round St. Eloi. But the Middlesex men were not called upon, and on the 16th the Battalion was relieved by the Suffolks, marching back to billets in La Clytte, whence a move was made on the 17th to Locre. On the 20th, the Battalion moved back again to La Clytte, until the 23rd, then marching off to Dickebusch, moving forward to Trenches 21, 22, 23A, 23B, 23C and S. 15, which were taken over from the Canadians. Strenuous efforts, in order to keep the defences standing, were necessary, and every officer and man was hard at work until relief came on 28th, when the Battalion was again marched back to Dickebusch. Since the 19th February the 85th Brigade had been working and fighting with the 3rd Division, but early in April it was returned to its own Division—the 28th—and on the evening of 5th the whole Brigade was in huts at Vlamertinghe. From the latter place the Brigade moved forward and on 10th April was at Zonnebeke, the 3rd Middlesex, Buffs and East Surreys in the line and the Royal Fusiliers and 1/8th Middlesex at St. Jean. On the night of 21st April the 3rd Middlesex were in billets at St. Jean and the 1/8th Battalion at Zonnebeke.

† The 1/8th Middlesex (strength, 27 officers and 851 rank and file), commanded by Lieut.-Colonel Garner, had left Hounslow on 8th March, and, embarking at Southampton, reached Havre on 9th. The Battalion moved to Bailleul, where it was posted to 85th Infantry Brigade, 28th Division. On 26th it was temporarily attached to the 7th Infantry Brigade (3rd Division), and on the following day two companies went into the trenches for instruction in trench warfare. The 1/8th Battalion suffered its first casualty on 27th—one man being wounded. Until the 1st April the Battalion was employed in digging communication trenches and generally gaining knowledge of active service conditions, but on the 2nd "A" and "B" Companies marched to billets in Kruisstraat, rejoining the 85th Brigade; "C" and "D" Companies arrived on 4th April. On 5th and 6th the Battalion left Kruisstraat for Vlamertinghe. On 9th the Battalion moved to St. Jean, and three days later relieved the 3rd Middlesex in the front line east of Zonnebeke. When the gas attack opened on 22nd April, "A" and "B" Companies were at work at Zonnebeke, supplying carrying parties, and "C" and "D" Companies were at Brandhoek.

realise what had actually happened. The smoke and fumes hid everything from sight, and hundreds of men were thrown into a comatose or dying condition, and within an hour the whole position (held by the French from the Poelcapelle Road to Steenstraate) had to be abandoned, together with about 50 guns."

Between nightfall on the 21st and dawn on 22nd April several alterations in the disposition of the 85th Brigade* had taken place, but at 5 p.m. on the latter date the Brigade Diary gives the positions of all units as follows: The 2nd East Surreys were holding Trenches 23, 24 and 25, south of the Ypres-Roulers Railway,† with "A" and "B" Companies of the 1/8th Middlesex in support; the East Surreys were due to be relieved by the 3rd Middlesex, then billeted in St. Jean; the 3rd Royal Fusiliers were holding the left sector of the Brigade front north of the railway to the wood in D.10c; 2nd Buffs were bivouacked at St. Jean, having been shelled out of Ypres; "C" and "D" Companies and Battalion Headquarters (1/8th Middlesex) were in Divisional Reserve in huts at Vlamertinghe.

1/8th Battalion.

3rd Battalion.

22nd April.

By 6.45 p.m. the tide of French Turcos, intermingled with teams and wagons of French field artillery, had swept back upon the Canadians and 28th Division, and orders were at once issued by the latter to cancel all reliefs. The 2nd Buffs and 3rd Middlesex (in St. Jean) were ordered out to take up a position astride St. Jean cross roads facing north, and entrench themselves. Colonel Stephenson (3rd Middlesex) ordered his men to dig a line of trenches facing N. and N.E. by N. about 300 yards north of the village; the Buffs were on the right of the Middlesex. At this period all units in St. Jean were placed under the command of Colonel Geddes (The Buffs). About 9.30 p.m. Colonel Stephenson received orders to send two companies of his Battalion to guard the pontoon bridge over the Canal, one and a quarter miles north of Ypres. "B" and "D" Companies (under Major Neale) were detailed for this duty. The remaining two Companies ("A" and "C") then extended and carried the line from La Brique to the Canal, the movement being completed by 3.30 a.m. (23rd April). "A" and "C" Companies, however, had barely arrived on their new line, and had begun entrenching it, when they were ordered to advance to C.20 and endeavour to gain touch with the French

3rd Battalion.

* Commanded by Brig.-Gen. C. E. Pereira.

† The 28th Divisional Diary places the 2nd East Surreys astride the railway.

23RD APRIL.

3RD BATTALION.

right. This advance was made in Artillery formation, and in the breaking dawn the Middlesex men came up, not with the French, but Canadian troops, who, with splendid gallantry, had held their line though suffering torture from the effects of the poisonous gas. The two Companies of Middlesex then pushed out an advanced guard to see if the ridge in front* was occupied, but the troops had hardly moved forward when the enemy opened fire and several casualties were incurred. "A" and "C" Companies then took up a line extending to the right of the Canadians, touch being obtained on the left with the 5th K.O.R., who prolonged the line to the right. Colonel Stephenson then arranged with the C.Os. of the Canadians and K.O.R. to work together in co-operation, as no trace could be found either of the Buffs or the French. But very shortly afterwards the 5th K.O.R. were ordered "to move elsewhere,"† leaving the right of the two Companies of 3rd Middlesex entirely in the air. Nothing daunted, however, though under heavy rifle fire, "A" and "C" Companies, together with the Canadians, advanced at 6.20 a.m. on the enemy and reached a bank some 600–800 yards from his trenches, where, utilising all available cover, they entrenched themselves until 9 a.m. Further advance, without artillery support, was impossible, for the ground in front was flat and open right up to the enemy's trenches.

And now began such a day of torture as will long be remembered by those who survived it. Heavily shelled for four hours and at times almost suffocated by gas fumes, the Canadians and Middlesex men clung to their scanty trenches with splendid tenacity. In the afternoon Canadian reinforcements, advancing with fine gallantry through murderous shell fire and across gas-drenched ground, arrived on the left of the Middlesex, and a little later another advance was ordered. The results of this attack (so far as "A" and "C" Companies of the 3rd Middlesex were concerned) were disastrous.

The attack took place, according to the Battalion Diary, "somewhere about 4.30 p.m." Major Neale, with the greater part of "C" Company, formed the front line, and Colonel Stephenson followed with one platoon of "A" Company as a

* It is impossible to obtain any information from the Diaries as to the name or the exact location of this ridge.

† Owing to a mistake of a signaller, the 5th King's Own received and acted on a message sent to the York and Lancs. to move across to near Wieltje, there being temporarily a gap in the middle of the line. But apparently the Battalion moved back again.

second line, about 150 yards in rear of Major Neale. The advance was carried out, for about 250 yards, by " rushes " over absolutely open country. The first line suffered very heavy losses. From the right front the Germans raked the line of the Middlesex men with five machine guns; two or three more guns swept the advance from the left front, where within three minutes practically everyone in that portion of the firing line was killed or wounded. Colonel Stephenson had by now reinforced the first line with his platoon of " A " Company, and almost every officer and man had been hit. Major P. M. Large, Lieut. J. S. E. G. Fergusson and 2nd Lieuts. C. L. A. Sharpe and F. A. H. Whitfield were killed.* Colonel Stephenson fell mortally wounded and, with the help of a few survivors, the Adjutant (Captain Kitchin) carried him back to a shell hole, about 150 yards from where he was hit. Here he died. A very great loss to the Regiment.

23RD APRIL.

3RD BATTALION.

By the time dusk began to fall " A " and " C " Companies of the 3rd Middlesex had practically ceased to exist. Picking his way back carefully across the bloody battlefield the Adjutant, accompanied by a Sergeant-Major and one man, tried to find Colonel Geddes in order to report the situation. But the latter could not be found, and on ringing up the 85th Brigade Headquarters was told that the Battalion was under the orders of the Canadian Division. He therefore returned and reported to Major Neale.

About 40 N.C.Os. and men remained of " A " and " C " Companies, and these dug themselves in amongst the Canadians, returning two days later to their Battalion. With the men who had formed the advanced guard and " the remnants " and a draft of 60 men, just arrived from England, the 40 who remained were formed into a third company and joined " B " and " D " Companies at St. Jean, to which place the two companies who had remained at the pontoon bridge over the Canal returned on the evening of the 24th.

Such is the story of the 3rd Battalion in the Battle of Gravenstafel.

1/8TH BATTALION.

Meanwhile, what had happened to the 1/8th Middlesex?

The Divisional Diary has very little indeed to say concerning this Territorial Battalion on 22nd and 23rd April. All that can be gathered is that on the latter date Battalion Headquarters

* The Divisional report gives the total casualties as follows:—4 officers killed, 3 wounded, 1 missing. Other ranks about 200.

1/8TH BATTALION. with "C" and "D" Companies were in huts in "Square B.5.d," "D" Company moving out to outpost duty N.W. of Ypres; "A" and "B" Companies were attached to the 2nd East Surrey Regiment, then holding the line east of Zonnebeke, "A" being billeted in the village and "B" remaining in the support trenches. A private diary* thus records the doings of these two Companies on 22nd and 23rd April:

22ND APRIL. "April 22nd: Shelling continually during the day. Front-line trenches mined. Men slept during the day and kept quiet. 'B' Company relieved during night, and 'A' Company went back into cellars at Zonnebeke. Guns going all night and much rifle fire.

23RD APRIL. "April 23rd: Fairly quiet morning. Shelling commenced afternoon and continued for some hours, intermittent all night. A great many 'non-stops.' Carried for East Surreys, 'B' Company making two journeys. Several men wounded and one killed on railway line. Shelling and rifle fire all night."

## (II.) THE BATTLE OF ST. JULIEN.

24th April–4th May.

24TH APRIL. 1/8TH BATTALION. At 7 a.m. on the morning of 24th April the Germans attacked and captured St. Julien, surrounding some Canadian troops and one company of Buffs, who held the village, and taking prisoner the survivors. Following this attack Battalion Headquarters, with "C" and "D" Companies of 1/8th Middlesex, were moved from Vlamertinghe and took up a position covering Verlorenhoek from the north.

From 4 a.m. the enemy had maintained a continuous fire on Trenches 23, 24 and 25, which lasted throughout the day, at the end of which these defences were in a sorry condition. "A" and "B" Companies of the 1/8th Middlesex (the former in cellars in Zonnebeke and the latter in close support of the East Surreys in rear of that Battalion) were not called upon during the morning, but in the early afternoon the East Surreys were seriously affected by gas fumes, and parties of "B" Company of the Middlesex were sent forward to replace casualties. In turn, these parties

* Kept by Captain Woodbridge.

were relieved, until two platoons of "B" were in the firing line; the remaining platoons of the Company were then moved up into old trenches some 50 yards behind the firing line, and "A" Company was brought up from Zonnebeke to the support trench.

The 3rd Middlesex, in reserve at St. Jean, were so heavily shelled during the 24th that the Battalion had to move out into the fields and "dig in," where a most uncomfortable existence was passed until the evening. **3RD BATTALION.**

At 10 a.m. on the 25th the enemy again opened fire on the trenches of the 85th Brigade, and after an hour "B" Company of the 1/8th Middlesex, in the close support trenches, began to suffer from shrapnel fumes, though the men were able to get some relief from cold-water douches, which had been recommended in a General Order circulated on the previous day. About 11.30 a.m. a shrapnel shell fell plumb in the trench and practically wiped out No. 6 Platoon of "B" Company. The trench now resembled a shambles. As rapidly as possible the wounded were attended to and the defences repaired, and all ranks were still busily engaged when about noon a message was received stating that the enemy had penetrated the front-line trenches, where breaches had been blown in them by the hostile trench mortars, and where the East Surreys had been stupefied by shrapnel fumes. "B" Company was immediately ordered forward along the communication trenches and word was sent back to "A" Company to come up, whilst the C.O. of the hard-tried East Surreys (whose Headquarters were in a dug-out) was informed that assistance was close at hand. On the arrival of "B" at the end of the communication trench the whole of the left section (Trench 25) was found in the hands of the Germans, who immediately emerged into the open and advanced with the evident intention of enveloping the left of "B." More Germans were then descried on the right, and it appeared as if "B" Company was surrounded. **25TH APRIL. 1/8TH BATTALION.**

Desperate, indeed, was the situation when, as if by a miracle, "A" Company, advancing across the open in full view of the enemy, arrived and reinforced the right flank of "B." A consultation now took place between Captain Isaacson (1/8th Middlesex) and Captain Hewitt (East Surreys), with the result that a counter-attack was decided upon as the only means of saving the line. Owing to the formation of the trenches the charging party, consisting of "B," half a company of "A,"

25TH APRIL. 1/8TH BATTALION.

led by Captain Cuthbert and 2nd Lieut. Stead, and the survivors of a company of East Surreys which had lost all its officers, had to pivot on its right during the charge.

And now began a fight such as the British soldier loves. With a cheer the Die-Hard Territorials and East Surrey men went at the enemy. Machine-gun and rifle bullets tore their ranks as they raced towards the Germans, and 2nd Lieut. L. Harvey of "B" Company (1/8th Middlesex) was killed, whilst three other officers fell wounded. Many other ranks were also killed and wounded during this charge, but the survivors still kept on as back across the open they chased the enemy, greatly assisted by a machine gun worked by a sergeant of the East Surreys. Then ensued a regular running fight, for directly the charging party arrived in the trenches into which they had chased the enemy, a turn was taken to the left, and up the trench, bayoneting and shooting down all Germans who refused to surrender, the Die-Hards and East Surreys forced their way, driving the enemy back at least 150 yards. But two more officers had fallen —Captain G. Cuthbert and 2nd Lieut. C. H. Stead—both killed in the hand-to-hand fighting which had taken place in the trench. At this juncture Lieut. Woods, of the East Surreys, with a company of his battalion arrived and led the trench party, capturing more prisoners.

"By then," says the Battalion narrative, "owing to the fact that the parapet had to be lined as the trench was recaptured, there were no more men left, and on reinforcements being asked for to enable Lieut. Woods to complete the recapture of the trench, it was found that every available man of the Surreys and Middlesex were in the fire trench and lining the parapet. It was then about 2.15 p.m., and it was realised that nothing more could be done with the troops present. The troops had become very mixed, and the Middlesex had lost six of their ten officers and well over 100 men out of the 240 taken into the trench. In the early evening a detachment of Cheshires unexpectedly arrived, and their presence was much appreciated. About 7 p.m. the Shropshires arrived and made two assaults on the portion of the trench not recaptured." Both of these assaults were unsuccessful.

The survivors of "A" and "B" Companies of the 1/8th Middlesex were by now disorganised, being intermingled in small parties with the East Surreys. The position in the front trench was also dangerous: "The Germans still held a small section of trench on left, cutting off one company of East Surreys from rest of line, and owing to bend in line, enabling them to snipe across the rear of (our) trench." 25TH APRIL. 1/8TH BATTALION.

Meanwhile, "D" Company, with two platoons of "C" Company, had similarly passed through a day of excitement. A narrative of "D" Company states that on 24th* "'D' Company received orders to proceed to join 3rd Royal Fusiliers as a digging party. Two platoons of 'D' Company, having already been sent to carry ammunition up to firing line for Suffolk Regiment, two platoons under Lieut. Mytton were taken from 'C' Company to make ('D') up to full strength . . . The Company proceeded to Zonnebeke Dumping Ground and was met by a guide and taken N.E. (to) Headquarters, 3rd Fusiliers, where they stayed until 4.30 p.m."

On the 25th "D" Company (with two platoons of "C") was ordered to take up a defensive position (where it is not stated) as the enemy had broken through the line held by Canadians and men of the Cheshires. "At about 10.11 p.m.," the narrative continues, "the troops on the right, Canadians and Cheshires, retired, leaving a gap of about a quarter of a mile on Company's right. O.C. Company sent a report back to 3rd Royal Fusiliers Headquarters and continued to dig in. Answer was received from 3rd Royal Fusiliers that Company would be relieved by Hampshire Regiment. Just before it was light O.C. Company retired to a trench about 100 yards behind crest line. No reinforcements arrived, and as it was getting light O.C. Company decided to advance again to his forward line of trenches. On reaching the trenches the Germans were seen advancing and the Company opened fire on them, holding the Germans up for about half-an-hour. The Germans then outflanked the Company and advanced through the gap on the right. The Company retired to position 500 yards in rear and took up a fresh position with the Durham Light Infantry. Shortly after this a further retirement was made, and in the early morning mist touch was lost between different parties of Company, and it is believed Major Ruston and a party were surrounded and captured, the remainder of Company making its way back to Battalion Headquarters at Verlorenhoek."

The officers killed in this affair were Major A. C. Ruston, Captain C. R. Dumsday and Lieuts. P. Mytton and Brough;

* Apparently after moving up from Vlamertinghe to Verlorenhoek.

1/8th Battalion

2nd Lieut. Kellard was reported missing. Of "other ranks" casualties no figures are given.

Thus ended a day at once glorious and disastrous to the 8th Territorial Battalion.

26th April.

So far as the 1/8th Battalion was concerned, the situation for the next three days (26th, 27th and 28th) was summed up by Lieut.-Colonel Garner (O.C. Battalion) in the following words: "Enemy's sniping and bombing, which now enfiladed us from both flanks, increased daily and became very nerve shaking, making many casualties. Owing to absence of trench mortars and the condition of the parapets as left by the French,* hardly any reply was possible on our part."

3rd Battalion.

28th April.

During the evening of 26th the 3rd Middlesex moved to G.H.Q. lines as reserve to the Lahore Division, sent up to Ypres to help stem the tide of the German attacks. The 27th was without incident, but at dawn on the 28th the Battalion proceeded to Verlorenhoek and there "dug in" under artillery fire all day. At nightfall the Middlesex took over a portion of the trenches held by the East Surreys, occupying the right sector of the 85th Brigade front, which from a map with the Divisional Diary was held as follows: "2nd East Surreys, 3rd Middlesex, 8th Middlesex (less two companies), 3rd Royal Fusiliers, 2nd Buffs"; the two remaining companies of the 1/8th Middlesex were in reserve. The Buffs held the apex of the salient, the line (which previously had run N.W. of Passchendaele and Poelcapelle) now bending back sharply and following almost the line of the Poelcapelle–Wieltje road to Fortuin, thence N.W. to the Yser Canal banks just east of Boesinghe. Indeed, unless further progress could be made towards the recapture of the original line north of this salient, the latter would have to be evacuated.

3rd Battalion.

1/8th Battalion.

29th April.

Sir John French therefore sent instructions to Sir Herbert Plumer to take all preliminary measures for a withdrawal to a new line which had been prepared, and on the morning of 29th April Sir John had another interview with General Foch. The latter urged the British C.-in-C. to postpone his retirement until the results of a French attack, to be made with strong reinforcements at daybreak on the 30th, should be known.

1/8th Battalion.

3rd May.

On the 29th April "A" and "B" Companies of the 1/8th Middlesex, who were in the fire trenches with the 3rd Middlesex,

* Previous to the 85th Brigade (28th Division) taking over this part of the line, it was held by French troops.

were relieved by the Machine-Gun Section, details of all companies and drafts, and returned to Battalion Headquarters at Verlorenhoek, where they remained until 1st. On 2nd May Companies were engaged in digging trenches at Frezenberg under R.E. On the 3rd the 1/8th Middlesex was relieved and marched back to billets near Poperinghe.

From 29th April to 3rd May the 3rd Middlesex occupied the fire trenches of right sector of the Brigade line. During these days the Battalion was under close artillery fire, trench-mortar fire, and constant bombing by the enemy, as well as being harassed by hostile mining operations and reverse fire into most of the trenches. The Germans had a trench in between the fire and the support trenches of the Middlesex, and from this trench kept up constant machine-gun fire, at night being particularly active. There was no rest for the men, whose nerves were tried to the utmost by continual vigilance. Every man, excepting sentries, was worked all night and every night and as much as possible during the day, in addition to constant long spells of standing to arms. As the whole Battalion was in the fire trenches, no relief was possible, and there was a great shortage of water. But on the night of 3rd May these intolerable conditions ended, for the Battalion, in conformity with the general scheme under which the salient was evacuated, withdrew and billeted near Poperinghe, for the French attack on 30th April had not achieved what had been hoped for. 3RD MAY. 3RD BATTALION.

The Battle of St. Julien was over.

Both the 3rd and 1/8th Middlesex had lost heavily during the operations between 22nd April and 4th May. The former lost 5 officers killed, 5 wounded and 1 officer missing—2nd Lieut. A. J. Jackson—who was afterwards reported killed. In other ranks the 3rd Battalion lost 325 killed, wounded and missing. Of the 1/8th Middlesex, 6 officers were killed, 6 wounded and 2 missing, and in other ranks the losses were 49 killed, 125 wounded and 152 missing.

## (III.) THE BATTLE OF FREZENBERG RIDGE.

8th–13th May.

On the morning of 8th May a violent bombardment of nearly the whole of the Vth Corps front broke out at 7 a.m., which 8TH MAY.

8TH MAY. gradually concentrated on the front held by the 28th Division, north and south of Frezenberg. The artillery bombardment was shortly afterwards followed by a heavy infantry attack, before which the line of the 83rd Brigade gave way, *i.e.*, the right at about 10.15 a.m., then the centre and then part of the left of the Brigade in the next sector to the south.

1/8TH BATTALION. At 11.30 a.m. the 3rd and 1/8th Middlesex and the 2nd East Surreys of the 85th Brigade were sent forward to reinforce the 83rd Brigade, which had been driven from the Frezenberg Ridge. During the night of the 8th–9th May the 85th Brigade Diary states that these three battalions established themselves on a new line west of Velorenhoek. The two remaining Battalions of the 85th Brigade moved to G.H.Q. line. Brigade Headquarters were later established at Potijze. Headquarters of the 83rd and 84th Brigades were also in Potijze.

3RD BATTALION. From the Diary of the 3rd Middlesex, however, it is apparent that the Battalion was involved in the attempt, on 8th, to retake the lost trenches.

The 3rd Battalion had received orders to move up via 84th Brigade Headquarters at Potijze, where information was to be obtained of the situation in the front line. On reaching the village the C.O. (Major Neale) sent back the following message (at 1.50 p.m.) to 85th Brigade Headquarters: "I have been ordered to go and retake lost trenches stretching from Arret (south of Frezenberg) in J.1.a. to wood in J.1.c., and if another attack more to the north fails, to occupy some half-dozen French trenches somewhere in that direction. I am moving from 1.3.c.7.8 now. I have nobody in support of me. I have my four Companies now." No account of what followed this message is recorded, but at 5 p.m. the O.C. "A" Company (3rd Middlesex) reported to Battalion Headquarters as follows: "The trenches we hold contain 'A' Company with about one and a half platoons 250 yards up the line. Two companies K.S.L.I. in touch on either side of railway. York and Lancs in touch on left of line. The shell fire too great to advance yet. 'C' Company are partly in trench and partly lining railway. The casualties are heavy." This message apparently followed an attempt to retake the trenches, for another message sent off later states: "Have attacked as far as 1.6.d, but am now held up by machine guns and much artillery fire." At 5.30 p.m. Major Neale despatched a message to the O.C. "A" Company:

"Hold on where you are and make as good cover as possible. Keep in touch with Y. and L. on your left, and if possible co-operate on their right and make a further attack or further advance. If situation alters, or if you want support, let me know." Yet another message followed at 5.55 p.m., this time to 83rd Brigade Headquarters, in which the C.O. 3rd Middlesex states that, "It is not possible to advance further without more artillery support directed against enemy guns. Casualties are heavy." 8TH MAY.

Again the Battalion was ordered by 83rd Brigade Headquarters to advance: "I want to ensure that you push on and occupy our old trenches." 3RD BATTALION.

There is then another gap of some hours, but at 10.30 p.m. the following message was sent to 83rd Brigade Headquarters: "Have advanced on south side of railway until I am further east than the Germans on north side of railway, where they are entrenching. It appears to me that the attack on north side of railway has not got far enough forward to enable me to push on further. As my position will be impossible by daylight, I shall have to withdraw to the support trench and the railway level crossing in I.11.b. as most of support trench is occupied by Shropshires. There are a great number of wounded, and assistance of bearer company will be necessary to evacuate my aid post, which is situated near level crossing."

The C.O. was then ordered by 83rd Brigade to withdraw his Battalion "to line of trenches running N.E. and S.W. from the railway to the Verlorenhoek road. Your right will be about I.11.b.3.4."

On moving back to occupy the line ordered, Major Neale found it already full of troops, and the 3rd Middlesex occupied the road at level crossing I.11.b. and some dug-outs near the railway. In this position the Battalion remained throughout the 9th, being subjected to a very heavy bombardment. On this date also the Battalion Diary gives the casualties "during the last 24 hours": Lieut. H. W. Tigar, killed; Lieuts. Brodie, Herbert, Foudronnier, Welsford, Power* and Dubois wounded. In other ranks the losses were 338 N.C.Os. and men killed, wounded and missing. The trench strength of the Battalion, after these casualties were reported, was only 289. The losses amongst senior N.C.Os. were specially 9TH MAY.

* Lieut. G. H. F. Power died of wounds on 9th May, evidently after the entry in the Diary had been made.

severe and platoons, in some instances, were commanded by lance-corporals.

The pity is that there are no accounts in the Diaries of actual fighting, for the tenacity with which the 3rd Middlesex hung on to the ground they had retaken, though shelled and machine-gunned unmercifully, was worthy of the very highest traditions of the Die-Hards.

12TH–13TH MAY.

Throughout the 10th, 11th and 12th the 3rd Middlesex remained in reserve until relieved during the night of 12th–13th May, when the Battalion marched back to billets west of Vlamertinghe.

1/8TH BATTALION.

8TH MAY.

The Battalion Diary of the 1/8th Middlesex is even less informative. The 8th apparently moved up to trenches in the G.H.Q. line, and there remained from 8th to night of 12th–13th, marching back to billets west of Poperinghe. Lieut.-Col. W. Garner, commanding the Battalion, was wounded on 11th, and Major Gregory assumed command. Casualties incurred during the Battle are reported as 3 other ranks killed and 21 wounded.

12TH–13TH MAY.

The 85th Brigade Diary briefly summarises the Battle of Frezenberg, as follows:—" 8th May, 11.30 a.m. 3rd Middlesex, 2nd East Surreys, 1/8th Middlesex, sent reinforce 83rd Infantry Brigade, who had been heavily attacked and driven from Frezenberg Ridge. Regiments took part in counter-attack, and during night of 8th–9th established themselves on new line west of Velorenhoek. Remainder of Brigade having meanwhile moved up into G.H.Q. line with Brigade Headquarters at Potijze, with 83rd and 84th Infantry Brigades. 9th May: 2 p.m. German attack renewed and repulsed. Brigade Headquarters established on Canal Bank in dug-outs. 10th May: 85th Brigade took over from 83rd Infantry Brigade, holding line from Velorenhoek–Ypres and to a point 300 yards south of railway, where it joined 27th Division. 11th May: Very heavy shelling on our trench line, but Brigade held their ground, beating off attempts to get round our right flank through gap made in left of 27th Division. Brigade from right disposed: 3rd Royal Fusiliers, Buffs, 2nd East Surreys, 3rd and 1/8th Middlesex in G.H.Q. line. 12th May: Heavy shelling of trench line in afternoon. 13th May: 2 a.m. Brigade relieved by 3rd Cavalry Division and returned to billets west of Vlamertinghe."

4TH BATTALION.

Thus, so far as the 3rd and 1/8th Middlesex were concerned, ended the Battle of Frezenberg Ridge. But the 4th Battalion appears to have been in the Battle area.

When the Battle opened (on 8th May) the 4th Middlesex were out of the line at Rosenhill Huts having, at 2.45 p.m. on 5th, received warning orders to be ready to move at short notice to support a counter-attack on Hill 60 by the 5th Division. Movement orders came to hand at 11.30 a.m. on 6th, and at 1.30 p.m. the Battalion marched to a château about 1 mile S.W. of Ypres. Here the Middlesex men were met by guides from the 1st Norfolks (13th Brigade) and moved up after dark to the front line, the relief being completed by 11 p.m. 8TH MAY.

Early on the 7th troops on the left of the Battalion made an attack on the salient in front of Hill 60, which had been taken by the Germans on the previous night. The 4th Middlesex were not engaged in this operation, but one officer—Lieut. B. V. Sim—was killed, whilst Major Bridgman was wounded; two other ranks were killed and two wounded. Inter-battalion relief was carried out during the next few days and, when the 4th Middlesex were relieved on 20th May and marched back to Rosenhill Huts, the battle was over without the Battalion having been involved in the operations. The tour had, however, resulted in the loss of 8 other ranks killed and 38 wounded. Captain Wollocombe was wounded during the relief. 20TH MAY.

## (IV.) THE BATTLE OF BELLEWAARDE RIDGE.

### 24th–25th May.

The last of the Battles of Ypres, 1915, opened very early on the morning of the 24th May. At 2.45 a.m., before dawn had broken, a violent projection of gas against nearly the whole line in the salient was launched by the Germans. It was followed by very heavy shell fire. In the trenches many of the men were asleep, and, the darkness hiding the approach of the deadly gas fumes, no warning could be given by those who were on the "look out," with the result that many were gassed ere ever they had an opportunity of donning their respirators. 24TH MAY.

The 3rd Middlesex were not in the front line when the gas attack began, having been relieved during the night 23rd–24th by the 2nd East Surreys and "B" and "D" Companies of the 8th Middlesex; the 3rd Battalion then moved back to G.H.Q. line. 3RD BATTALION.

24TH MAY. 1/8TH BATTALION.

The 1/8th Middlesex had returned to the trenches east of Ypres on 21st, two Companies—" A " and " C "—with machine guns going into the front line with the 3rd Battalion, while " B " and " D " Companies and Battalion Headquarters were placed in reserve in G.H.Q. line. On the night of 23rd–24th " B " and " D " moved up to the front line with the East Surreys, relieving " A " and " C," who returned to G.H.Q. line.

" D " Company went into the line under the command of O.C. " D " Company, 2nd East Surreys, and " B " Company was under the command of O.C. " C " Company, East Surreys; the platoons of " B " were separated and alternated with East Surreys.

The 1/8th Battalion Diary states the relief had been completed when, about 3 a.m., a heavy attack was made by the Germans " opening with rapid fire and gas clouds. Momentary panic, during which several men left trenches . . . Germans established themselves in British trench south of railway, and thus enfiladed us later in the day, but position was secured by reinforcements after dark. Meanwhile troops of all regiments who had retired from fire trench swept over G.H.Q. line, and carried certain men with them. " A " and " C " Companies, under their officers, stood fast, and experienced a terrific shelling. The gas, moreover, rolled down into the hollow through which G.H.Q. line runs, and affected these troops considerably, the trouble being aggravated by the addition of asphyxiating shells, which the fire trenches did not have. It was during this shelling that Captain and Adjutant Anson got hit and died immediately. Roll-call, taken under difficulties that night, showed the casualties to be 2 officers killed, 4 officers missing,* 1 other rank killed, 5 wounded and 160 missing. The remains of " B " and " D " Companies were withdrawn from fire trenches and attached to " A " and " C " in G.H.Q. line, but machine guns were still left in firing line."

3RD BATTALION. 24TH MAY.

The 3rd Middlesex, in G.H.Q. line, were badly gassed and 350 men were driven out of their trenches. In the afternoon the Battalion was ordered to counter-attack the enemy, but this order was subsequently cancelled. At night, however, the 3rd Middlesex went up to the trenches to reinforce the East Surreys.

* No names are given.

On the 23rd May the 4th Middlesex (then in Rosenhill Huts) had received orders to carry out the usual relief on the night of 24th, taking over the trenches of the 2nd Suffolks in "L" and "M" trenches. But during the early hours of 24th heavy firing was heard and gas was smelt, some of the troops being partially affected by it. At 3.30 p.m. the relief of the 2nd Suffolk Regiment was cancelled, and, at 4 p.m., the Middlesex received orders to "stand to," as the whole Brigade (8th Brigade, 3rd Division) was moving northwards. At 4.15 p.m. another order was received, instructing the 8th Brigade to march at 5 p.m. to a point on the Ypres Road, between Ypres and Vlamertinghe.

4TH BATTALION.

24TH MAY.

The march was begun at the hour stated, the 4th Gordons leading, followed by the 4th Middlesex, 2nd Royal Scots and 1st Gordons, in the order given. In a field by the side of the road between Ypres and Vlamertinghe the troops halted, and shortly afterwards word was received that the 8th Brigade was Corps Reserve to the Vth Corps.

The night 24th–25th passed without incident, men sleeping out in the fields. During the afternoon of 25th the Brigade was ordered to relieve part of the 28th Division the following evening in trenches east of Ypres, near the Ypres-Menin road. Company Commanders were sent off to reconnoitre the trenches, and the Middlesex sent a party of 200 men, under Captain Hanley, to dig under orders of the Royal Engineers. The party which went up to reconnoitre the trenches returned about 11 p.m. and reported the trenches "as yet do not exist. The 28th Division had to retire owing to asphyxiating gas, and new trenches not yet dug."

25TH MAY.

Thus the 4th Middlesex, though in the area of the Battle of Bellewaarde Ridge, were not involved in the operations.

To the Battles of Ypres, 1915, belong the terrible distinction of witnessing the first use of gas by the Germans. Hitherto, the enemy, though waging war with savage ferocity, had kept within the bounds of civilised warfare, but the use of asphyxiating gas placed him "beyond the pale," and the Allies looked upon their opponents in a new light—that of loathing and disgust.

Map VI.

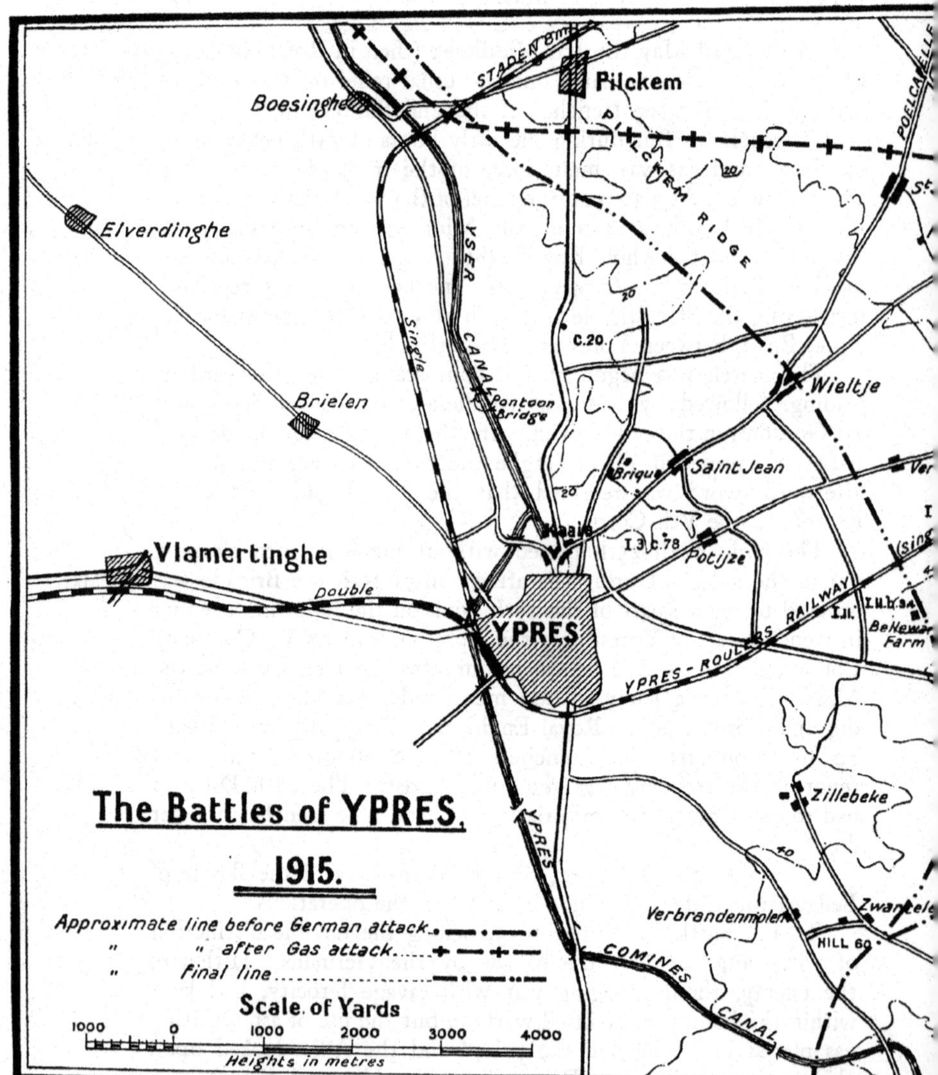

Pilckem
Boesinghe
STADEN Bᵐ
PILCKEM RIDGE
POELCAPELLE
Elverdinghe
YSER
CANAL
Single
C.20.
Wieltje
Pontoon Bridge
Brielen
le Brique
Saint Jean
20
Vlamertinghe
I.3.c.78
Potijze
Double
YPRES
YPRES - ROULERS RAILWAY
I.I.
Bellewaarde Farm
Zillebeke
YPRES
40
Verbrandenmolen
HILL 60
COMINES
CANAL
The Battles of YPRES,
1915.
Approximate line before German attack
" " after Gas attack
" Final line
Scale of Yards
1000
0
1000
2000
3000
4000
Heights in metres

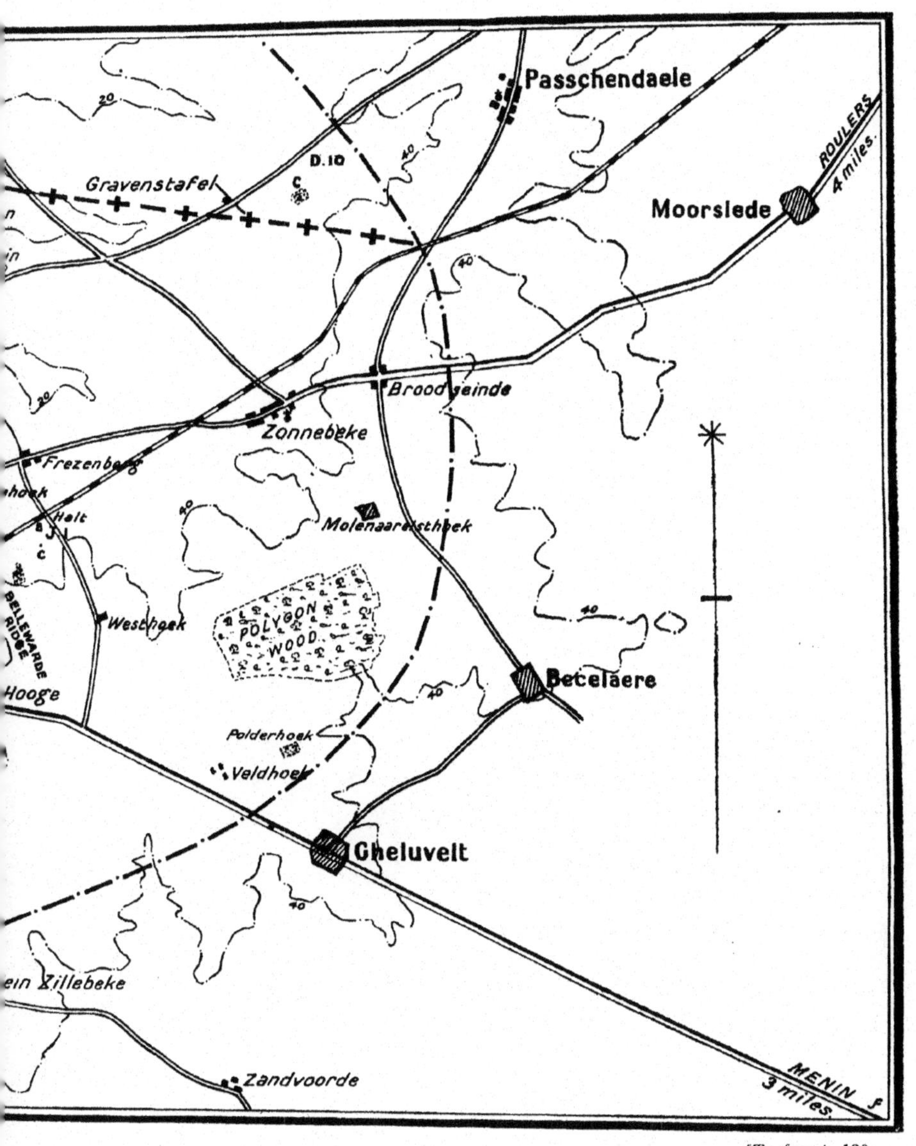

Passchendaele
ROULERS
4 miles.
Moorslede
D.10
Gravenstafel
Broodseinde
Zonnebeke
Frezenberg
Halt
Molenaarelsthoek
BELLEWARDE RIDGE
Westhoek
POLYGON WOOD
Becelaere
Hooge
Polderhoek
Veldhoek
Gheluvelt
Zillebeke
Zandvoorde
MENIN
3 miles.


[To face p. 120.

# CHAPTER XV.

## THE BATTLE OF AUBERS RIDGE.

9th May, 1915.

WHILST the Battles of Ypres, 1915, were in progress the IVth, Ist and Indian Corps had been engaged in operations against the enemy's line from the La Bassée Canal to north-west of Fromelles. The French had planned to attack the enemy between the La Bassée Canal and Arras on 9th May, and Sir John French had promised to support them by making an attack along the front held by his IVth, Ist and Indian Corps. The operations subsequently divided themselves into two parts: in the first the Battle of Aubers Ridge, fought on 9th May, and in the second the Battle of Festubert, 15th–25th May; but with the former only was the Middlesex Regiment concerned, the 8th Division of the IVth Corps attacking the enemy's line about Rouge Banc (N.W. of Fromelles).

2nd Battalion. 1/7th Battalion.

Actually, the part taken in the Battle by the 2nd and 1/7th Middlesex (both of 23rd Infantry Brigade, 8th Division) was of minor importance, as neither Battalion attacked the enemy, but its interest lies chiefly in the fact that it was the first major operation in which the Senior Territorial Battalion (1/7th) of the Regiment was involved.

The 1/7th Battalion (Lieut.-Col. E. J. King) had embarked on 4th September, 1914, for Gibraltar, and after five months spent in "eating out its heart," was at length rewarded by orders to embark for England and report for service in the field. The Battalion was relieved on 8th February, 1915, and reached Avonmouth on 13th, entraining on the following morning for Barnet. Fitting out took longer than was expected, but at length, on 12th March, the 1/7th Middlesex left Barnet for France, and disembarked at Havre on 13th. The Battalion landed with a strength of 31 officers and 904 other ranks, the four companies, "A," "B," "C"

1/7TH BATTALION.

and "D," being commanded respectively by Captain S. C. M. Smith, Captain W. J. Eales, Major S. King and Captain E. G. Frost.

On reaching La Gorgue (in the IVth Corps area) on 15th March the Battalion learned that it was posted to the 23rd Infantry Brigade of the 8th Division, which (to the delight of all ranks) included the 2nd Middlesex, and of the latter, Lieut.-Col. King (commanding 1/7th Battalion) said: "The 1/7th can never be sufficiently grateful to the 2nd for its valuable advice and guidance, which so materially assisted its Territorial Battalion to adapt itself to the novel conditions of trench warfare."

For the first ten days at the front the 1/7th Middlesex remained in reserve, sending parties to the 2nd Battalion for instructional purposes, providing working parties and gradually accustoming itself to life in the trenches. On the 18th March the Battalion billets at La Flinque, near Laventie, were shelled. On 20th March the 1/7th suffered its first casualty, Private J. E. Phillips, who was killed.

On 25th March the 1/7th Middlesex relieved Canadians in the La Boutillerie sector of the front covering Fleurbaix. This was the first sector in France for which the Battalion was responsible. Six days in the front line, six in close support, was the rule at this period, so that on 31st March the Battalion was relieved and marched back to Fleurbaix, little the worse for its first tour in the front line. April was a quiet month, without incident, the Battalion on the last day of the month being in billets at La Cruseubeau.

On 1st May the 1/7th received orders to move to Estaires and La Gorgue on the following day, preparatory to taking over a portion of the front line. At La Gorgue the Battalion went into billets, and it was not until the 4th that a move was made to Rue du Bois, where "A" and "B" Companies were placed in support of No. 1 Section and "C" and "D" Companies in support of No. 2 Section, relieving the 2nd Scottish Rifles in front of La Cordonnerie Farm, and it was in this portion of the line that on the night of the 7th May an incident took place which attracted considerable notice at that time.

In front of the section held by the 1/7th Middlesex there was a small detached post on the holding of which great stress was always laid. This post, occupied by 15 Highgate men under Lieut. A. G. Groser, and the attack made upon it, was the subject of an account by "Eye-Witness," an Army officer who at that period wrote reports under orders of G.H.Q. for publication in the press:— 7TH MAY. 1/7TH BATTALION.

"The outpost referred to was a disused trench about 40 yards long and equidistant from the English and German trenches, being 70 yards from each. A sap ran out from the trenches to the disused trench, and at times it was necessary to post a picquet in the latter to protect working parties engaged on the entanglements in the rear. At 8.30 p.m. on 7th May Lieut. Groser and seventeen men of No. 3 Platoon, 'A' Company, proceeded down the sap and into the trench and relieved the day guard posted there. It was then quite dark. While the sentries were being posted a party of Germans who had crept up and cut their way through the entanglements 'rose' out of the ground in front, on both flanks, and even in rear of the trench, fired at the picquet and then made an attempt to rush the trench, using clubbed rifles and knives. The party of the 'Highgate Boys' were quite equal to the occasion, and, after a hand-to-hand fight lasting about three minutes, the Huns were driven off under a very rapid fire turned on to them. On the extreme right of the trench Lance-Sergeant Hocking, with Lance-Corporal Willis and five men, withstood the attack of twelve Huns, who, firing on them from front, flank and rear at a distance of five yards, attempted to rush their post.

"In the meantime the left end of the trench was attacked by eight Huns, who rushed in and jumped into the trench, using clubbed rifles. One German, armed with a knife, attacked Lance-Corporal Hutchings, who, lunging forward with his bayonet, and missing, was quite exposed. Lieut. Groser, however, slipped in between them and, after a fierce struggle on the ground, during which his left hand was wounded by the knife, succeeded in drawing his revolver and shooting the German in the chest. No sooner had Lieut. Groser got up than he found himself covered by the rifle of a German standing on the parapet. The man with whom Lieut. Groser had the fight was found to be decorated with the Iron Cross." Colonel King also reported of Lieut. Groser that "he fought splendidly, killing the leader with his own hands after a sharp struggle in which he was wounded."

The result of this incident was that the enemy was beaten off, leaving five dead behind him, while the losses of the

1/7th Middlesex were 1 other rank killed and 7 wounded, including Lieut. Groser.

The 8th May was uneventful, but final preparations were made for the attack on the Aubers Ridge, which had been definitely fixed for 5.40 a.m. on the 9th.

9TH MAY.

2ND BATTALION.

1/7TH BATTALION.

On the morning of the 9th, the 2nd and 1/7th Middlesex held Nos. 1 and 2 Sections (respectively) of trenches as Divisional Reserve. The attack of the 8th Division was launched by the 24th (Right) and 25th (Left) Infantry Brigades. The remaining Battalions of the 23rd Brigade were in support of the left attack. The point attacked was the enemy's trench system on each side of the Sailly–Fromelles road, the attack issuing from the 23rd Brigade front between Nos. 1 and 2 Sections. A forty-minute bombardment preceded the assault. The attack was unsuccessful, for, although troops of the 25th Brigade succeeded in reaching the enemy's trenches, the 24th Brigade was unable to advance, and, after two attempts, abandoned the attack. The 25th Brigade thereupon fell back to its original trenches.

2ND BATTALION.

So far as the 2nd Middlesex was concerned, the Battle is described in the Battalion Diary in very few words: "During the whole of the 9th May, and at intervals during the 10th May, the enemy's artillery heavily shelled our trenches and the approaches to them." Two companies of the 2nd Middlesex, however, appear to have held the front line of No. 1 Section, covering the attack by rifle fire, and again the withdrawal when the assaulting troops were drawn back to their original trenches. The shell fire cost the Battalion 14 other ranks killed, 65 wounded and 2 missing.

1/7TH BATTALION.

The 1/7th Middlesex took similar action to that of the 2nd Battalion. Two companies—"B" and "C"—held the left half of No. 2 Section, with "A" and "D" Companies in support. Throughout the day, with the exception of covering fire maintained by the Machine Gun Section and "B" and "C" Companies, the 1/7th Battalion was in reserve. In the evening, the Battalion was ordered to take over the Brigade frontage in order to cover the withdrawal of the Brigade and the shattered remnants of the assaulting battalions. The 1/7th was not withdrawn from the front line until the night of 11th May.

11TH MAY.

"During this period," said Colonel King, "the casualties were extraordinarily slight; whilst the battalions of the 23rd Brigade were losing men by the hundred, the 1/7th Middlesex had only 15 killed and 37 wounded, and it was from this time that it began to be known as 'the lucky 7th,' a soubriquet which it retained until the tragic days on the Somme."

The casualties amongst senior officers during the period of the Battle were, however, somewhat disproportionate: Captains Frost, Eales and Tully were wounded on 9th, and Captain Moody on 11th. The first officer killed, belonging to the 1/7th, was Lieut. C. N. Stacey, who was shot through the head by a Bavarian sniper early on the morning of 10th, and died the same day of his wound.

# CHAPTER XVI.

## Trench Warfare and Items of Interest.

Between the Battle of Aubers Ridge, 9th May, and the beginning of the Actions of Hooge on 19th July, no one Battalion of the Middlesex Regiment was engaged in active operations other than the usual round of trench warfare.

ON the 13th March, the 1st Middlesex relieved the Leicestershire Regiment in the front line in Rue du Bois. It was a quiet part of the line and the activities of the opposing sides were turned mostly to sniping, the firing of rifle grenades and occasional bomb throwing. Shelling was intermittent, but rarely severe, and only a very few casualties are recorded in the Battalion Diaries. Colonel Ingle, commanding the 11th (S) Battalion of the Regiment, then in England, but soon to cross the water to France, paid a visit to the 1st Battalion on 17th March, staying 24 hours. He had a good look round the trenches, and on his return was, no doubt, able to give his officers and men a much clearer vision of what was before them. Quiet days in the trenches or routine work and drill in billets, occupied the Battalion during the remainder of March and the months of April and May, though some excitement prevailed in the front line on the 16th of the latter month, the Middlesex men having received orders to maintain heavy rifle fire on the enemy's trenches with a view to holding him to his ground: the Battle of Festubert was in progress. On this day, the anniversary of the greatest Battle Honour of the Regiment—Albuhera—the Brigadier sent the Die-Hards a "most inspiriting message."*

1ST BATTALION.

16TH MAY.

On the 28th May, the 19th Infantry Brigade (in which the 1st Middlesex was contained), which from October, 1914, had served with the 6th Division, was transferred to the 27th Division. The change is not referred to in the Battalion Diary, but at this

24TH MAY.

* Quotation from the 1st Battalion Diary, but the message is not given.

1st Battalion. period Brigades, and indeed Battalions of the old Regular Army, were transferred from their original formation to Divisions of the New Armies, which had begun to arrive in France and Flanders. It was thought necessary to " stiffen " the ranks of the New Army Divisions by introducing units from the original Expeditionary Force, which were now looked upon as veteran soldiers, as, indeed, they were. Not only officers, but N.C.Os. and men who had weathered the storm from August, 1914, to the Spring of 1915, were of priceless value in the training of the New Armies. Thus it came about that the 1st Battalion of the Die-Hards, with other units of the 19th Infantry Brigade, was transferred to the 27th Division; the 1st Middlesex, however, still remained in the same sector of the line, either in the Rue du Bois trenches or in billets in Gris Pot throughout June.

2nd Battalion. 30th June. The remainder of May (from the Battle of Aubers Ridge) and the whole of June were uneventful, and casualties were small. One officer was killed—2nd Lieut. W. W. Hardwick—who was shot and died of wounds on 11th June. On the last day of the latter month, the 2nd Middlesex were in Divisional Reserve, occupying billets one mile west of Sailly on the Estaires Road.

3rd Battalion. From the night of 24th–25th May, when the 3rd Middlesex went up to the front line trenches to reinforce the East Surreys, until the night of 28th, the Battalion had a quiet time: the enemy's activities after the Battle of Bellewaarde Ridge slackened considerably; indeed, he had suffered very heavy losses, so that for him also reorganisation and " rest " were necessary. On 28th the 3rd Battalion was relieved, and went into billets near Poperinghe, where on the 30th the G.O.C. Division addressed the Battalion, thanking and praising all ranks for the splendid tenacity and determination with which they had met the enemy's attacks. June was also a quiet month without incident, the Battalion spending only one tour—from the 3rd to 8th—in the front line at Vierstraat, with the remnants of the 8th Middlesex attached. Then followed a welcome " rest " out of the line from the 9th to 30th May. the night of 29th–30th, when front-line trenches in the St. Eloi sector were taken over from the 3rd Royal Fusiliers; these trenches were O 3 to P 46 S.W. of St. Eloi.

1/7th Battalion. About the middle of May, the 23rd Brigade, in which the 1/7th Middlesex were contained, side-stepped to the right from the lines in front of Fleurbaix to those covering Laventie, and on the 21st the Battalion relieved the 2nd Middlesex in the trenches running through Fauquissart, officially known at that time as "E" Lines. 1/7TH BATTALION.

In all France and Flanders at that period there was not a more peaceful part of the line than that about Laventie, and as the C.O. of the 1/7th Battalion said: "The time spent there was always looked back upon as a kind of golden age. These were certainly the happiest days that the Battalion spent in France." All men spoke in terms of comparison in those days. In ideal weather the days and weeks passed, the ordinary routine and incidents of trench warfare remaining unbroken until 14th June, when the 23rd Brigade was ordered to make a noisy demonstration likely to give the impression of unusual activity in order to draw attention from the line farther south, where the Second Action of Givenchy was to open on the following day. That night the whole of the transport under Major Hudson clattered along the road running parallel with and close to the trench line. The wagons and limbers were loaded with tins filled with stones, and the noise could be heard for miles. The enemy opened fire with his guns, but the transport had passed and was beyond reach when the shells fell upon the road.

One small incident illustrates the "mettle" of these Middlesex Territorials during that quiet time, and how they kept themselves free from that inertia often the result of inaction. The Germans had planted a flag about 20 yards in front of a sap-head they held across No Man's Land. The presence of this flag annoyed the Middlesex, and during the morning of 19th June, and in broad daylight, Sergeant Spencer, of "D" Company, crawled out through the long grass to the sap-head, removed the flag and returned with it in safety amidst the cheers of his comrades. A little later, down came a message from the Brigadier:—"Well done, Sergeant Spencer!" When dawn broke three days later (on 22nd) it was discovered that the Germans had replaced their lost flag by two more flags. But, nothing daunted, a private of "A" Company (Private Stinson), ran out, under fire, and triumphantly brought in the flags. The name of another intrepid N.C.O.—Sergeant E. J. King—is several times mentioned in the Battalion Diary for his patrol work. 19TH JUNE.

The terrible fighting through which their comrades of the 1/8th Battalion had passed at Ypres was brought home to all ranks of the 1/7th Middlesex when, on 21st June, the remnants of the former arrived at Sailly Station, under Major E. D. W. Gregory. 21ST JUNE.

The remnants of the 1/8th Battalion—6 officers and 394 other ranks—had received orders to be temporarily amalgamated with the 1/7th Battalion, owing to the difficulty in obtaining drafts. The
23RD JUNE. amalgamation took place on 23rd, the 7th Battalion being then in billets in the neighbourhood of Wangerie. On the last day of June the 1/7th Middlesex were in Divisional Reserve in Bac St. Maur.

8TH BATTALION. 28TH MAY. The 1/8th Middlesex were relieved in the G.H.Q. line on 28th May by the Scottish Rifles and returned to bivouacs at A.30.a (the woods north of Brandhoek). The following day a Brigade Order stated that "for tactical purposes, 1/8th Battalion will be attached to 3rd Battalion, and will form an integral part of that Battalion in the trenches." On the 30th the nominal roll of the 1/8th Battalion was 13 officers and 361 other ranks.

7TH JUNE. Only one tour—from 3rd to 7th—was served by the Battalion in the fire trenches during June, and, on the latter date, the 85th Brigade (in Division) was relieved and moved back to Busseboom and then to Houtkerque. Drill and route-marching occupied
20TH JUNE. the Battalion until the 20th, when the 85th Brigade and the Division returned to the trenches. The 1/8th Middlesex did not accompany the Brigade, for during the time the 28th Division was out of the line it had been decided to amalgamate the 1/8th with the 1/7th Battalion of the 23rd Brigade, 8th Division. The Battle of Ypres had so weakened the former Battalion that it had fallen below the strength (400) of a Territorial Battalion. And, therefore, when its former Brigade and Division moved back into the line, the 8th was notified that motor 'buses would arrive to convey the remnants of the Battalion to Sailly.

As the temporary amalgamation of these two Territorial Battalions of the Middlesex Regiment is of historical interest, the story, as contained in the War Diary of the 1/8th Battalion, is given in full:—

"21st June: Seventeen 'buses arrived at 9.15 a.m. and conveyed the Battalion to Sailly. The remainder of the transport, under Lieut. White, journeyed by road.

21ST JUNE. "On arrival at Sailly, the Battalion was met by General Pinney, G.O.C. 23rd Brigade, and acting G.O.C. 8th Division. With him were Lieut.-Colonel King, of the 7th Middlesex, and the General's staff. The Battalion was given a cordial reception by these officers, and it was learned that the 8th was to be amalgamated with the 7th. Billets had been arranged and the Battalion then marched to them . . .

"22nd June: At 10 a.m. the Battalion was officially inspected by G.O.C. Brigade, who again welcomed them. Major Gregory, C.O. of the Battalion, lunched with the General. **22ND JUNE.**

"At 6 p.m. the General paid an unofficial visit and explained the idea and reasons for amalgamation with the 7th. He mentioned that when a Territorial Battalion fell below 400 in strength it was to be amalgamated with another battalion, and, although the 8th was now just over 400, at the time the order was given it had been considerably below. He then invited questions from anyone present with a view to assisting the men to overcome their feelings at losing their unit. To the questions put to him, he gave the following replies:—(1) That the new Battalion would be known as the 7th and 8th Composite Battalion; (2) that leave would be given to N.C.Os. and men who could put in a plea of 'Urgent Private Affairs.' On leaving, he assured the men that the records of the 8th would be kept quite separate from those of the 7th, and that as soon as efficient drafts could be raised the Battalion would again be set up, and those who were with the 7th would return.

"23rd June: Lieut.-Colonel King, C.O. 7th Middlesex, visited the Battalion at 11 a.m. He welcomed them to the 7th, and expressed his admiration of the name that the Battalion had won. He sympathised with them in their lot, but assured them that everything would be done to respect their feelings until the time came when they could again be restored to their position as an independent unit. The system of amalgamation, he explained, was to be that each platoon of the 8th would be attached to the corresponding platoon of the 7th, thereby retaining the elements of organisation. All details, however, must return to duty. **23RD JUNE.**

"At the officers' meeting afterwards, Lieut.-Colonel King had the officers presented to him, and personally welcomed each one. As far as possible each officer was to go to his corresponding platoon of 7th. Lieut. White, the machine-gun officer, becoming No. 1 Platoon Commander; Captain Chipp was the only officer to be transferred and was to be the senior Captain of the amalgamated Battalion. The remaining officers and staff sergeants were to be returned to the base.

"At 3 p.m. the amalgamation took place, the following officers and 394 other ranks going into the 7th Battalion: Captain Chipp, Lieut. White, 2nd Lieuts. Dark, Hugleman, Levy, Peat.

"The remainder of the Battalion was left behind pending their return to the base. They consisted of: Major Gregory, Captain Woodbridge, Lieut. Dobbie, R.A.M.C. (attached), Lieut. and Quartermaster Louch, 13 warrant and non-commissioned officers, three officers' servants and the Interpreter—M. de Failly. (Lieut. Dobbie returned to the 84th Field Ambulance and the Interpreter to his Headquarters.) The remainder of the transport was handed over to the A.S.C., and all stores, including M.O.'s, to the Quartermaster of the 7th Battalion.

"The amalgamation was completed by evening."

The Diary is signed by Captain and Acting Adjutant F. F. Chipp and by the C.O.—Major E. D. A. Gregory.

Thus for a little while (and it *was* only a little while) the 1/8th Battalion, through the ravages of war, lost its identity.

# CHAPTER XVII.

## The 4th Battalion and Hooge.

AT 7.30 p.m. on 26th May, the 4th Middlesex, who had passed the night of 25th–26th in a field near Vlamertinghe, paraded under orders to move up to the front line with the remaining units of the 8th Brigade. At 7.45 p.m. the Brigade marched, the 4th Middlesex (in the following order of Companies—" A," " B," " C," " D ") leading, followed by 4th Gordons and 1st Gordons: the 2nd Royal Scots had gone to the trenches the night before. The route lay through Ypres, *via* the Lille Gate, and through the railway cutting to the level crossing on the Roulers Railway, thence to the trenches. The latter lay between Hooge and the Ypres-Roulers railway, and at this period were very " sketchy "; indeed, the line had yet to be properly dug. " A " and " C " Companies had been detailed for the front line and the former succeeded in occupying the shallow trenches allotted to it. But " C " Company found the 2nd Royal Scots in possession of the trenches the Company was to occupy, and the Scotsmen refused to move out; " C " Company, therefore, had to dig themselves in, in rear of the front-line trenches. " B " and " D " Companies (in reserve) found very inadequate room in G.H.Q. line. Two or three hours passed before the Battalion was properly fitted in, and then the men got to work at once on the trenches. Before daylight on 27th a new line of fire-support trenches, with the necessary communication trenches, had been begun, whilst the R.E. had also put out wire entanglements in front of the line. The 2nd Cavalry Division held the line on the right and the 85th Brigade (28th Division) the line on the left of the 8th Brigade; the latter was attached to the 27th Division.

26TH MAY.

4TH BATTALION.

27TH MAY.

The 27th was a noisy day, the enemy's shell fire was severe and the British gunners could make but little reply, owing to lack of ammunition. The Germans, however, were quiet and

3rd June. 4th Battalion.

were as much engaged in work and the reinforcement of their trenches as were their opponents. The month closed quietly, though hard work on the defences was continual. On 3rd June, 2nd Lieut. C. H. R. West was shot dead by a sniper. For thirteen days the 4th Battalion held the front line, but during the night 15th–16th June the 8th Brigade was relieved, the front line being taken over by the 7th and 9th Brigades of the 3rd Division in order to carry out an attack on Bellewaarde on 16th. The 8th

16th June.

Brigade moved back behind Ypres, the 4th Middlesex occupying a farm. The machine guns and signallers of the 4th Battalion were, however, left at their posts. The attack was successful, and the 8th Brigade was not called upon, though on the night of the 17th the 4th Middlesex furnished large fatigue parties to clear the Menin Road and fill in shell holes, bury dead in the neighbourhood of the trenches and salve derelict equipment. Several days were spent on the ramparts in Ypres, and then the 4th Middlesex moved back to rest and train. Rain fell heavily

25th June.

on 25th, and the diarist of the Battalion thus records the inclement weather: "It rained, unhappy spot when wet."

The remainder of June and the early part of July were spent

12th July.

in camp near Vlamertinghe, but at 7.45 p.m., on 12th, the Battalion paraded, and, with other units of the 8th Brigade, moved forward to the trenches. Two battalions took over the front line and two were placed in reserve, and the 4th Middlesex, being of the latter, occupied dug-outs in H.11.d. Five days were spent in reserve, the Companies working, some by day and others by

18th July.

night, on the defences. But during the night of the 18th the Middlesex men relieved the 1st Gordons in the trenches near Hooge. During daylight the C.O., the Bombing Officer and his bombers, the Sniping and Machine-Gun Officers went in advance to the trenches, the Battalion moving up from its reserve position at 8 p.m. Shortly after 10 p.m. the front line was reached, where "A" and "C" Companies were put into the fire trenches, "C" Company and one platoon of "A" occupying the left sector under Captain Rowley, the three remaining platoons of "A" Company taking over the right sector under Captain Williams. "B" and "D" Companies were in support.

For some days previously work had been carried out on a mine which had been dug and prepared under a German redoubt between the western end of Hooge and the Bellewaarde Lake. The mine was to be fired at 7 p.m. on the 19th, and the 8th Brigade had taken over the front line with orders to seize the opportunity of improving its position by occupying the mine crater and trenches on either side of it. 19TH JULY. 4TH BATTALION.

Two Companies of the 4th Middlesex Regiment with two parties of bombers from that Battalion and one party from the 1st Gordon Highlanders had been ordered to make the attack following the explosion of the mine. There was to be no artillery bombardment previous to the firing of the mine, but immediately the explosion occurred all howitzer batteries were to open fire, special attention being paid to the junction of the German communication trenches, up which their bombers would probably advance for the purpose of making a counter-attack.

Preparations for the attack continued throughout the 19th, three separate stores of bombs, ammunition and Véry lights being established in the front line of the Middlesex. As the attack was to be made by three columns, each column made itself acquainted with the position of these stores, and men were told off to superintend issue.

The O.C. 4th Middlesex Regiment (then Major C. A. Bridgman), who had been given charge of the operations, finally had at his disposal for the attack: two sections of 56th Company R.E., 4th Middlesex Regiment, two companies 2nd Suffolk Regiment in Sanctuary Wood, 10 bombers, snipers, and machine-guns of the 1st Gordon Highlanders, the snipers and machine-guns of the 2nd Suffolk Regiment and No. 24 Trench Mortar Battery.

Owing to the trace of the trenches and the probability that the glacis would be altered and covered with debris after the explosion, affording only a few narrow paths, the left Company was disposed as follows: The left platoon in C.10 to remain in position and cover the left of the assault; the other three platoons, who were to make the assault, were drawn up with their heads in the front trench south of the road. These were the three columns. The order of each column was four men carrying bill-hooks and wire-cutters, bombers, reserve bombers, and the rest of the platoon, which was to advance by successive sections as the space in the hostile trench became available and the O.C. Platoon should direct. Some of the men carried shovels, others a bundle of sand-bags.

Owing to the probability of the explosion altering the appearance of the crater, each column was ordered to move first of all on the crater, which was previously fixed by distant trees. The

19TH JULY. 4TH BATTALION.

columns were then to work along to their final positions. The left column was to make good as far as point "H," the centre column was to occupy the far side of the crater, and the right column to form the right face of the intended addition to the Middlesex position. The work of the Sappers was to link up either end of the new position, and the Trench Mortar Battery, owing to the shortage of ammunition, was only to fire at any promising target which presented itself.

The right Company in the trenches was to maintain its position and cover the right of the assault. The third Company from Zouave Wood was to move up and replace the assaulting platoons in the original line, the fourth Company being held in reserve in Zouave Wood. The two Companies of 2nd Suffolks were to remain in Sanctuary Wood until called upon.

The time selected for the attack was finally fixed for 7 o'clock in the evening, "which," the records state, "would allow time to see the captured ground before darkness set in, and yet not give the enemy sufficient time to locate the extent of the attack and position of affairs and so 'register' before darkness set in."

At 7 p.m. a solitary big gun—9.2—boomed out, and with a scream the shell passed over the heads of the troops (assembled and waiting for the order to attack) and fell, bursting near the German trenches. It was the signal for firing the mine. Almost immediately the ground trembled, and there was a terrific roar, as earth, debris and bodies of men shot up into the air amidst a cloud of smoke and dust. Three distinct shocks were felt, the ground heaving and rocking in a sickening manner; then clods of earth, bricks, wood and the mangled remains of Germans began to fall. The intensity of, and danger from, this cloud of debris may be gathered from the fact that ten men of the 4th Middlesex were killed by falling objects and two of the dumps of stores were completely buried.

Forty seconds after the first shock the order was given to the Middlesex men to advance on the crater. When the leaders of the columns had climbed the parapet and got out into No Man's Land they found themselves in dense clouds of dust, but without hesitation they advanced direct on their objectives. Almost at once the enemy's howitzers opened a wild fire, which continued for several hours. The British "Heavies" bombarded selected points for twenty minutes and then switched off, leaving to the field guns the work of assisting the attack when called upon.

*The Left Column.*—For several minutes there was anxiety as to the initial results of the attack, but just before darkness fell men were seen signalling from the crater. Major Greenway, on going forward to ascertain the cause, joined the left column about the crater, and finding that the signal had been for more men, sent back for reinforcements. He then proceeded along the German trench to the left. Near the sap he found Lieut. Erskine, of the 1st Gordon Highlanders, who was in charge of the bombers of the left column, lying mortally wounded. Major Greenway then took charge of the bombers and led the men forward. But the advance was slow. Checks were frequent, for there was a lack of bombs, and casualties were becoming alarmingly frequent. But at last "Y.20" was reached, the position being determined by the fact that hostile bombs, coming from two directions, were falling thereabouts. At "Y.20" a block was begun, but so persistent were the German bombers, and so little had Major Greenway and his party with which to reply, that a withdrawal to Point "H" became necessary. The work of forming the block was, however, still carried on though desperate fighting went on the whole time. Eventually it was finished. The formation of blocks in a trench during bombing attacks was always a desperate and dangerous task, but never was one formed more gallantly or thoroughly than this. It was 7 feet high from the bottom of the trench, eight layers thick from front to rear, and in width from 4 to 8 feet, being built near a traverse. By sparing use a small reserve of bombs was formed, but it was not to last long. From about 3 a.m. the Germans made a vigorous bombing attack, and the scanty supply of bombs was expended. Still more desperate became the situation of Major Greenway's party, and the little party of bombers was in danger of being wiped out entirely, when, with splendid presence of mind, one of the Die-Hard bombers picked up a burning "potato" bomb and hurled it among the enemy's bombers. This man's action saved the Middlesex bombers from further casualties, for it successfully checked for the time being the advance of the Germans. With rifle fire the Middlesex men then maintained themselves, until another rush of the enemy's bombers drove the party back to the next bay. Very slowly Major Greenway's party fell back until about 4 a.m., when rapid rifle fire was opened by the garrison of C.10 on the enemy, whose confidence had led him to throw from outside the trench, a confidence which cost

19TH JULY. 4TH BATTALION.

20TH JULY.

20TH JULY. 4TH BATTALION.

him dearly. In spite of his casualties, however, he continued to advance, but presently the timely arrival of a small but continuous supply of bombs put an end to his progress. The extraordinarily long and accurate throwing of a 4th Middlesex man—Private Matthews—and a lance-corporal of the 1st Gordon Highlanders was the outstanding feature of the enemy's repulse at this point. The throwing of Matthews was marvellous. He was said to have hurled bombs fully 70 yards from the fire step of the trench. Whenever the enemy presented a good mark, a bomb hurtled through the air, and Matthews very seldom missed. Entirely disconcerted, the enemy left the trench and ran back suffering loss, but soon returned with bayonets fixed. Under cover of rifle and machine-gun fire from craters (which caused several casualties amongst the Middlesex) he again advanced, but was checked at bombing distance. Major Greenway's party was now left with only one bomb, and when this had been thrown the men prepared to meet the enemy with the bayonet. Determined to sell their lives dearly, the Die-Hards waited; but the enemy had apparently had enough of the fight, for he checked his advance, his bombers ceased throwing and he withdrew to a safer position.

At 6.15 a.m. another supply of bombs arrived, but they were accompanied by the intimation that few more would be forthcoming. In view of the shortage, therefore, Major Greenway decided not to advance again to Point "H," but to make a stop out of bombing distance of the sap. The party, therefore, advanced 30 yards and formed the stop. It consisted of filling in a solid 30 yards of trench to and beyond the sap; this work was carried out under a brisk rifle fire. The trench was 7 feet deep and from 8 to 9 feet wide.

The work completed, the party awaited a further counter-attack, but none came. Consolidation then proceeded until 5 p.m. on 20th, when the left column was relieved by the 1st Gordon Highlanders. Four machine guns had been captured and passed back along the trench.

*The Centre Column.*—The centre column reached the far side of the crater and immediately opened fire on the distant German trenches. Second Lieut. Curzons, with the bombers, proceeded some 75 yards along the trench, the first 50 of which had been filled up by debris. Here he temporarily maintained his position, but on retiring, several casualties were suffered, the men being exposed while following the line of the filled-in trench. Part of the column engaged in a rifle duel with the enemy, the remainder consolidating the lip of the crater. But the work went slowly; men carrying up sand-bags were shot down and had to be replaced. Other sand-bags intended for consolidating purposes had been buried in the debris. The men, therefore, were not properly "dug in" when the enemy launched his counter-attacks. 20TH JULY. 4TH BATTALION.

The first attack took place about 9 p.m., when a bombing duel took place between the enemy and the Die-Hards; this attack was repulsed. About midnight, a more determined attack, also with bombs supported by rifle fire, was made. The enemy advanced across open ground and pressed hard, but again he was bloodily repulsed, the Middlesex bombers being assisted by machine-gun fire. Still, a third counter-attack was launched—about 2.30 a.m.—the Germans advancing in extended order from the north, their bombers working along the trench. This attack shared the same fate as the first and second attempts; not an inch of ground was gained by the enemy. After this occasional German bombers advanced, but they threw at too great a distance, and their bombs exploded harmlessly short of the Middlesex.

From dawn onwards and throughout the 20th July no further counter-attacks were made, but the enemy's snipers were busy, their marksmanship being very good. One large trench-mortar bomb fell in the crater, causing some casualties, otherwise no incident occurred during the day, and at 5 p.m. these positions of the line were also taken over by the Gordon Highlanders.

*The Right Column.*—The right column was fortunate. The debris from the explosion had obliterated the enemy's trenches on the eastern side of the crater, so that when the column advanced to consolidate the eastern lip, as ordered, no opposition was encountered and no counter-attacks were launched by the enemy. The position was handed over to the Gordons at 5 p.m. At an early hour the Middlesex reserves, with the exception of one platoon, had been used up for carrying and digging purposes, repairs to the original line and to the trenches and communication trenches held by the right Company. There was a possibility that the enemy's counter-stroke would take the form of blowing up the Stables and Bull Farm, and rushing the crest of the rise from the N.E. One company of 4th Gordons was therefore sent up to strengthen the line.

4TH BATTALION. The right Company, whose task had been to maintain the original line against a counter-attack from the N.E., and cover the right of the attack, had removed all men from buildings and exposed places when the mine explosion took place at 6.45 p.m. But, unfortunately, four men were caught in the storm of debris and were killed, a quantity of sand-bags from the parados falling on them. The dust from the debris necessitated the immediate cleaning of rifles, and when this had been done, rapid fire was opened on the enemy's parapet.

The 20th July, though a day of uncertainty and anxiety, was without incident excepting artillery (field gun and howitzer) duels between the opposing forces, and during the night the 4th Middlesex were relieved and marched back to the Ramparts, Ypres, moving back during the evening of 21st to Brandhoek. (21ST JULY.) Heavy losses had been sustained by the Battalion during the operations—300 all ranks killed, wounded and missing. Two German officers and 20 men were captured and severe casualties inflicted on the enemy.

Thus ended the first of the actions of Hooge (19th July), during which the Die-Hards had acquitted themselves splendidly; so much so that on 24th, after the Battalion had settled down in Brandhoek, all ranks were paraded and congratulated by the Brigadier on their fine fighting during the recent operations. (24TH JULY.)

7TH AUGUST. Until 7th August the 4th Middlesex remained out of the line, but on that date relieved the 2nd Royal Scots in Trenches 34 to 31 inclusive. "B" and "D" Companies went into the front line, occupying the trenches immediately on the right of those held by the Battalion in May.* "A" and "C" Companies were in support in dug-outs in the wood in rear. The relief was completed by 11.15 p.m. without casualties.

30TH JULY. Meanwhile, on 30th July, the Germans had regained from the 14th Division all the positions won at such great cost by the 3rd Division, and although the 6th Division was successful in another attack on 9th August in recapturing all the lost ground, not all of it could be held, part of the trenches having to be evacuated. The 8th Brigade (3rd Division) assisted in the operations by fire attacks, in which the 4th Middlesex took part. Casualties on the 9th were 1 other rank killed and 8 wounded.

* The line held by the 8th Brigade in the latter part of May lay between Hooge and the Ypres–Roulers railway. Owing to lack of maps, it is impossible to give the exact position of Trenches 34–31.

# CHAPTER XVIII.

## THE BATTLE OF LOOS.

25th September—8th October, 1915.

1st Battalion. 2nd Battalion. 3rd Battalion. 4th Battalion. 1/7th Battalion. 1/8th Battalion. 11th Battalion. 13th Battalion.

FOR several reasons the Battle of Loos and the subsidiary operations connected therewith will always remain of special interest to the Middlesex Regiment. The first Victoria Cross awarded to the Regiment in the Great War was won by a gallant young officer—2nd Lieut. R. P. Hallowes, of the 4th Battalion—during the Second Attack on Bellewaarde (25th–26th September); two "Service" Battalions (11th and 13th) for the first time took part in a set battle, therefore all Battalions of the Regiment then in France or Flanders (1st, 2nd, 3rd, 4th, 1/7th, 1/8th, 11th and 13th) were engaged in the main or subsidiary operations, and lastly the 1/8th Battalion, having resumed independent formation in August, once again held a portion of the front line.

The official despatches may be searched in vain for the intentions of the Allied Commanders, which British and French troops, with the utmost gallantry, attempted to carry out with only partial success. Without going into a lengthy discussion of the general situation along the Western Front, which gave rise to the operations which began on 25th September and continued until the third week in October, the intentions of the Allies were briefly as follows:—(1) to break the enemy's front; (2) prevent him re-establishing his line; (3) to defeat decisively his divided forces.

The British attack was to be carried out by the First and Second Armies operating practically along the whole front from just west of Loos to east of Ypres. The main attack was to take place from just east of the mining village of Grenay to Givenchy, north of the La Bassée Canal. In this attack two Corps, the IVth (3rd Cavalry, 1st, 15th and 47th Divisions), and Ist (2nd, 7th, 9th and 28th Divisions) (from right to left) were to take part, whilst the XIth Corps (Guards, 21st and 24th Divisions) was held in reserve. There were to be three subsidiary attacks: (1) on the Moulin du Pietre by the Meerut Division of the Indian Corps (First Army); (2) at Bois Grenier by the 8th Division, IIIrd Corps (First Army); (3) on Bellewaarde Farm by the 3rd Division (Vth Corps) and 14th Division (VIth Corps) of the Second Army. In the subsequent "Action of the Hohenzollern Redoubt," the 1st and 42nd Divisions (IVth Corps) and Guards, 2nd, 12th and 46th Divisions—all First Army troops—were engaged.

As already stated, every Battalion of the Middlesex Regiment then in France and Flanders fought in the Battle, *i.e.*, either in the main or the subsidiary operations. The 1st Battalion (2nd Division), 3rd Battalion (28th Division), and 13th Battalion (24th Division) were engaged in the main operations. The 4th Battalion (3rd Division) attacked the enemy east of Ypres—at Bellewaarde—with the idea of holding him to his ground, whilst the 2nd, 1/7th and 1/8th Battalions of the 8th Division were similarly engaged at Bois Grenier; these were the subsidiary operations. The 11th Battalion (12th Division) was engaged in the subsequent Action of the Hohenzollern Redoubt.

The main attack was to be made after asphyxiating gas had been discharged over the enemy's trenches. Massed artillery, numbering about 1,000 guns, were to bombard the enemy's lines from Loos to La Bassée.

Sir John French thus described the terrain of the battlefield-to-be: "The country over which the advance took place is open and overgrown with long grass and self-sown crops. From the Canal southward our trenches and those of the enemy ran roughly parallel, up an almost imperceptible rise to the south-west. From the Vermelles–Hulluch road southward the advantage of height is on the enemy's side as far as the Bethune–Loos road. There the two lines of trenches cross a spur in which the rise culminates, and thence the command lies on the side of the British trenches. Due east of the intersection of spur and trenches, and a short mile away, stands Loos. Less than a mile further south-east is Hill 70, which is the summit of the gentle rise in the ground." Other tactical features in the line were "Fosse 8"—a coal mine with a high and strongly-defended slag heap; the Hohenzollern Redoubt, a strong work thrust out nearly 500 yards in front of the German line, so that it came within a short distance of the

British trenches, the "Quarries," situated west of Cité St. Elie, Hill 70, east of Loos and "Puits 14 Bis," another coal mine possessing great possibilities of defence, north of Hill 70. Between Loos and La Bassée, and situated well behind the German front line, were the villages of Cité St. Auguste, Hulluch, Cité St. Elie and Haisnes.

The hour of attack for the Ist and IVth Corps was 6.30 a.m. on 25th September. Of the three Battalions of the Middlesex Regiment (1st, 3rd and 13th) engaged in the main operations, only the 1st attacked the enemy on the morning of "Z" day; the 3rd and 13th Battalions came into the line later.

The 1st Middlesex since the last day of June had spent a comparatively quiet existence, either in billets in Grispot, near Steenwerck, or Laventie, or in the front line. Casualties were few, though in officers 2nd Lieut. B. O. Dewes was killed on 30th July, whilst out in front of the parapet. On the 15th August the 1st Middlesex were relieved by the 11th K.R.R. in the Laventie sector and moved back to billets. This was the last tour in the trenches in that part of the line, for on the 14th the 19th Infantry Brigade had issued orders to all units of the Brigade that after relief the troops would billet in the area Vieux Berquin–Neuf Berquin–Doulieu until 19th August, when the Brigade was to march to the Ist Corps area to replace the 4th (Guards) Brigade in the 2nd Division. Thus, once again, was the 19th Brigade transferred to another Division.

1ST BATTALION.

15TH AUGUST.

19TH AUGUST.

At 8.30 a.m. all units of the Brigade set out on their march southwards to the new area. *En route* they passed the Windmill at Hinges, where Lord Kitchener and his staff were waiting by the roadside to see them go by, and from the congratulatory messages which subsequently reached all C.Os. it was evident that the march discipline, smartness and general turn-out of the Battalions pleased the Secretary of State for War.

Between 2 and 3 p.m. the 19th Brigade marched into Bethune, where billets were speedily allotted to the Battalions. Inspection by the G.O.C. 2nd Division, on 20th, was followed by three days in billets, and then, on 24th, the Brigade took over the front-line trenches in the Cuinchy sector, the Middlesex being billeted in Annequin, with one company holding support points behind the trenches. The Battalion's first tour in the front line began on 27th August, but it only lasted three days, and on relief by the 2nd Royal Welch Fusiliers on 30th, the Middlesex returned to

1ST BATTALION.

27TH AUGUST.

billets in Annequin, though holding posts at Annequin, Tourbières and Carter's and Braddell Redoubt.

The early days of September were very quiet, and from the 6th to 11th special training was carried out in view of the coming operations. On the 23rd the 1st Battalion relieved the 2nd Royal Welch Fusiliers in the right sub-sector of the Cambrin sector.* The latter was the right of the three sub-sectors held by the 2nd Division. On the right of the 1st Middlesex were troops of the 9th Division, and on the left the 2nd Argyll and Sutherland Highlanders. "Relieved the 2nd R.W.F. in Cambrin trenches at 5.30 p.m." records the Battalion Diary, and that is all; no description of the trenches, nothing (in view of the coming operations) of the preparations for the attack—no names, positions, or even co-ordinates. The trenches of the 1st Middlesex were apparently situated between the Vermelles–La Bassée railway and the Vermelles–La Bassée road. Behind the front-line trenches were support and reserve trenches, and in rear of the latter (in Lewis Alley) there was a fortified post named Sims Keep; a similar post, some distance further back, called Lewis Keep, gave its name to Lewis Alley—a communication trench connecting Cambrin village (or ruins) with the front-line system. Sims Keep, Lewis Keep and Lewis Alley were, however, all inclusive to 9th Division, and therefore outside the 19th Brigade area.

23RD SEPT.

24TH SEPT. 1ST BATTALION.

Final orders for the attack were issued on 24th September, so far as the 19th Infantry Brigade was concerned. The following are the principal points: the objectives of the Brigade were (1st) Les Briques Farm and Vermelles railway line as far N. as road crossing A.22.b.1.2 inclusive; (2nd) Auchy-lez-La Bassée and Triangle Alley from A.29.b.4.8 to A.23.a.6.2 (both inclusive); (3rd or main objective) railway line from B.25.b.7.7 (inclusive) to A.24.b.4.2 (exclusive).† The 1st Middlesex, on the right of the Brigade front, was to assault Railway Trench from A.27.b.9.5. to the Vermelles–La Bassée road. The 2nd A. and S. Highlanders, on the left of the Middlesex, were to capture Mine Trench from A.21.d.6.4 to A.21.d.7.7. As soon as the attacking Battalions had vacated their trenches, the 2nd Royal Welch

* The Cambrin sector apparently ran from a point R.1 almost on the Vermelles–La Bassée railway north to Gun Street, which was just south of the Cambrin–La Bassée road. In co-ordinates the front line of the Brigade is expressed as from A.27.b.8.0. to A. 21.d.4.9.

† The objectives for the whole Brigade are given in order that the action of the 1st Middlesex might be more clearly understood: co-ordinates are unavoidable.

Fusiliers were to occupy those previously held by the Middlesex, and the 1st Cameronians those lately occupied by the Highlanders.

In spite of the preliminary bombardment, which for several days had kept the enemy's trenches and wire under a continual hail of shell, the reports show that the wholesale destruction of the trenches to be assaulted and the wrecking of the thick wire entanglements in front of them had not been accomplished. For, on 24th, Lieut.-Colonel Rowley, commanding 1st Middlesex, reported to Brigade Headquarters that one of his patrol parties had been out in No Man's Land and had found that the wire behind the hostile craters was little damaged and was about 25 *yards thick.* The craters referred to in this report were great holes in No Man's Land, and often so close together that only a narrow path existed between them. The heavy rain had made these paths greasy and thick in mud, whilst the " going " generally across the dread space between the opposing lines was difficult. Thus the attacking troops were confronted not only by formidable positions, but would have to make their assault across ground deep in mud and broken by shell and mine craters.

Throughout the night of 24th–25th September, final preparations were made, and, at 3.30 a.m. on the latter date, the Brigade reported that all units were in positions of assembly in the trenches south of the La Bassée road from Gun Street to R.1 ; the Middlesex on the right holding from R.1 to D crater, and the Highlanders from the latter to Gun Street.

" Zero " hour had been postponed to the last possible moment, but during the night it had been definitely fixed for 5.50 a.m., when the gas projection was to take place and smoke candles burned.

When dawn broke on the morning of 25th it seemed as if the elements had again conspired to make the attack abortive, for heavy rain fell and the wind, what there was of it, shifted almost continually ; it was a bad day for the projection of gas. Indeed, one Brigade of the 2nd Division (6th) notified Divisional Headquarters that the wind was unfavourable, but was ordered to proceed with the projection. So, at 5.50 a.m., the cylinders were opened and great clouds of asphyxiating gas were projected into the air, whilst the smoke candles were lighted. But instead of the gas floating across No Man's Land and settling down over the German trenches, it hung lifeless in the air or blew back upon

25TH SEPT. 1ST BATTALION.

25TH SEPT. 1ST BATTALION.

the British trenches from which it had been projected, in many places with disastrous effects.

The left Battalion (the Highlanders) of the 19th Brigade fared worse than the right—the Middlesex—for the ground in front of the former was much cut up by craters, and in these the gas hung about with exasperating stillness.

Across No Man's Land the Germans could be seen donning gas masks and using sprays—in order to dispel the gas—whilst all along their parapets, at intervals of about 20–30 yards, they lighted fires for the same purpose, and by their activities they appeared quite unaffected by the noxious fumes. For forty minutes the gas projection lasted and then, at 6.30 a.m., the signal was given for the assault.

"A," "B" and "C" Companies of the 1st Middlesex, awaiting the order to go forward, at once began their advance; "D" Company was in reserve. But the men had not gone more than a few yards ere a storm of rifle and machine-gun bullets tore their ranks to shreds and No Man's Land was soon littered with killed and wounded. Undeterred by the gas fumes the Germans stood up in their trenches, in many places upon the parapets, and poured a deadly accurate fire upon the advancing British troops. For not alone from in front of the gallant Die-Hards did fierce resistance take place, but all up and down the line. Unable to make further progress, the Middlesex men laid down. By this time the German trenches, which when the advance began had been lightly held, were packed with men and the volume of fire increased. With orders to reinforce the three forward companies, "D" Company now "went over the top," only to share a similar fate, and survivors lay close to the ground with a rain of bullets pouring overhead. The Battalion Diary records the action in the following and all too brief words: "At 5.50 a.m. a gas attack was opened on the German trenches for 40 minutes. This was not, however, very successful, and did not have much effect. At 6.30 the Battalion attacked with three Companies in the front line and one Company ('D') in reserve. The Battalion was all flung into the line, but failed to get further forward than 100 yards and were then hung up. Gunners again shelled the hostile line, but no further advance was made. At 12 noon the Battalion was ordered to withdraw into Brigade Reserve, having lost very heavily in both officers and men. A large proportion of N.C.Os. were casualties."

25TH SEPT. 1ST BATTALION.

The 19th Brigade Diary throws but little further light on the action, though the position of the Brigade at 7.30 a.m. is given thus: "1st Middlesex about 100 yards in front of our front-line trenches; 2nd A. and S. Highlanders being under cover of the German parapet by the wire" (a terrible position). Then a little later the narrative states: "2nd A. and S. Highlanders withdrawn to their original trenches, leaving many men behind, including two complete platoons who reached the German front trenches. 1st Middlesex, trying to get on, are a hundred yards in front. Artillery shell the German front line very heavily. A bombardment under 2nd Divisional orders was arranged to start at 9 a.m., after which infantry were to advance. 2nd Royal Welch Fusiliers now put out two companies to support the Middlesex, but they were met with fierce opposition and lose heavily. Bombers of 1st Middlesex reach the craters at 'D,' but are heavily fired on by our own artillery." At 9.45 a.m. orders were received at Brigade Headquarters stating that as the attack on the right of the 2nd Division was progressing favourably, no further attack was to be made for the present by the 19th Brigade and the 6th Brigade (the latter was on the left of the former).

Amongst the appendices to the Diary of the 19th Infantry Brigade, however, are several field messages of special interest to the Middlesex Regiment, and although there are gaps in the story it is possible to follow the course of the Battle from a battalion point of view.

The first message, timed 6.57 a.m., is from Brigade Headquarters to Battalion Headquarters Middlesex and reads: "Any news aaa How far have you advanced aaa Is gas returning you aaa Keep me well informed so that artillery barrage may be altered to suit if you want it." In reply to this message there follow several, one after the other, from the O.C. Middlesex, and they are given in their correct order, though the first was evidently despatched while the Brigade message was on its way to Battalion Headquarters: (i) "6.50 a.m. Much opposition to our front. Please ask guns to shell Les Briques trench." (ii) "7 a.m. Reserve company has got on, but we are being very heavily fired at." (iii) "7.16 a.m. Line held up. Very heavy fire aaa Have" (here the message is overwritten and is unreadable." (iv) "7.20 a.m. Ask guns to shell German front-line trench aaa Railway trench I mean." (v) "7.26 a.m. Don't think gas is affecting us or Germans. They are holding their front-line trench aaa Our Battalion is all out in area

25TH SEPT. 1ST BATTALION.

between their front trench and ours aaa 2nd Royal Welch Fusiliers are now up aaa It is essential to now shell hostile front trench." (vi) "7.30 a.m. Reported casualties probably 400, but impossible to tell aaa Have observed an enormous number fall." (vii) "7.55 a.m. Must shell German first line aaa Our men are all out in front aaa Almost all must be killed or wounded aaa Please shell first line aaa Welch Fusiliers are now advancing." And, at 8 a.m. the Commanding Officer asks for men for the attack on his left: "Is there any news *re* Argylls and Sutherlands?"

It is apparent from the last message that no news had reached the Commanding Officer of the Middlesex from his own front line of the situation on his left flank. About 8 a.m., however, Colonel Rowley received the following message from Lieut. A. D. Hill (commanding "C" Company): "Enemy very strong in front with machine-guns and rifles. 'C' Company strength only about 30 or 35 men. Impossible to advance on account of machine guns. Mr. Henry and 3 men alone remain out of two platoons. Can we have reinforcements? We are in Square 27B in crater S.E. of road and about 60 yards south Point 79." To which, at 8.12 a.m., Colonel Rowley replied: "Hang on where you are until reinforced." The next message is written on a small muddy and blood-stained piece of paper: "8.30 a.m. 'B' Company attack held up 100 yards out of own trench. Major Swainson wounded. 'B' Company knocked out, few men stand fast." It is signed "P. Choate, 2nd Lieutenant."

The only other information received by Colonel Rowley from No Man's Land was a second message from Lieut. Choate, timed 10.50 a.m.: "So far as can ascertain 'B' Company nearly wiped out. A few men are lying near me 100 yards in front of our front trench to left of wrecked aeroplane and facing Les Briques Farm. I have not enough men to advance further. Can you reinforce or give orders?" There is no reply in the Diaries to this message.

The one bright spot in the attack was an assault from the left flank carried out by the Grenade Reserve platoon, assisted by a platoon of the Reserve Company ("D"). These gallant fellows attacked a large crater (at D) and actually captured it.

There is little more to tell! At 1.15 p.m. the Battalion—all that was left of it—was ordered into reserve at Siding No. 3 and Braddell Trench. When this movement had been carried out, but a handful of men—84 other ranks—were mustered, though when darkness had fallen over the battlefield on the night of 25th other men, who had been lying out all day in No Man's Land, were able to withdraw. The little party of "D" Company who had hung on to the crater they had captured were also withdrawn. During the day they had actually pushed beyond the crater, but were held up by very thick hostile wire entanglements, and the grenade officer was killed whilst trying to force a way through. A machine gun had also been pushed forward into the crater and did great execution, but the machine-gun officer being wounded, the gun had to be withdrawn. Throughout the morning the Battalion stretcher-bearers performed many gallant deeds and worked heroically. 25TH SEPT. 1ST BATTALION.

Ten officers killed* and 7 wounded; 73 other ranks killed, 285 wounded, 66 missing, 7 gassed and 2 suffering from shell concussion—a total of 455—were the casualties suffered by the 1st Middlesex throughout the day. Well indeed might the Brigadier-General (P. R. Robertson) commanding 19th Brigade write in a letter to Colonel Rowley, dated 26th September: "Please convey to all ranks my very high appreciation of the splendid behaviour of all ranks in yesterday's action. They did all that it was possible to do under such circumstances; their conduct was most gallant and fully upheld the fine reputation of the Die-Hards.

From the 26th to the 30th September the 1st Battalion remained in Brigade Reserve in dug-outs behind the front line, and here for a while it is necessary to leave them and relate what befell the other Battalions of the Regiment on the first day of the Battle. 26TH SEPT. 1ST BATTALION.

From the official despatches it is clear that whereas the southern portion of the initial attack from Loos, northwards to the neighbourhood of Fosse 8, had gained ground, north of the latter point to the La Bassée Canal and just beyond it from the Givenchy front, no progress had been made. This was the position about 9.30 a.m., when Sir John French placed the 21st and 24th Divisions at the disposal of the G.O.C. First Army, who ordered them up in support of the attacking troops. Between 11 a.m. and 12 noon the central brigades of these Divisions filed past Sir John at Bethune and Nœux-les-Mines respectively. At 11.30 a.m. the heads of both divisions were within three miles of the original 25TH SEPT.

* Captains N. Y. L. Welman, F. V. A. Dyer, L. G. Coward and R. J. Deighton; 2nd Lieuts. C. A. J. Mackinnon, C. Pery, B. U. Hare, A. L. Hill, R. C. Mellish, J. H. Linsell; Lieut. A. W. R. Carless died of wounds on 27th September.

British front line. The Guards Division was also ordered up to Nœux-les-Mines, while the 28th Division was moved from Bailleul in a southerly direction and was soon to become involved in the Battle. The 28th Division contained the 3rd Battalion Middlesex Regiment and the 24th Division the 13th (Service) Battalion—the first service Battalion of the Regiment to be engaged in major operations in France or Flanders. Of these two battalions the 13th was the first to enter into the Battle.

13TH BATTALION.

The 13th Middlesex, one of the earliest of the " Service " Battalions of the Regiment, had had practically a year of soldiering in England ere it crossed the water to France. Throughout its period of training, before proceeding overseas, it had remained with the 73rd Infantry Brigade of the 24th Division, to which it was originally posted soon after its formation. Several months were spent by the Division at Shoreham, Sussex, and then for the winter months—December, 1914, to April, 1915—the various units went into billets at Hove, moving back again to Shoreham in the spring. A two-day march to Reigate in May for two weeks' practice in trench construction, a move from Shoreham to Aldershot in July for musketry and field training and then inspections, first by Lord Kitchener and then by H.M. the King in August, sums up the activities of the 24th Division, and incidentally, the 13th Middlesex, during the first eight months of the year 1915.

21ST AUGUST.

On 21st August the 13th Middlesex received notification that it would probably embark for France about 29th with other units of the 24th Division. It was, however, the 31st before the advanced party of the Battalion marched to Woking, and there entrained for Southampton. On the following day, 1st September, the Battalion in two trains entrained at Brookwood for Folkestone, and about 10 p.m. the same night in a heavy rain the " Die-Hards " went aboard the *Duchess of Argyll*, which soon after put out to sea. The strength of the Battalion on embarkation (including the advance party) was 30 officers and 952 other ranks. Lieut.-Colonel L. G. Oliver was in command, Major J. H. R. Cox was second-in-command and also O.C. " D " Company, the other three Company Commanders being: Captain C. E. Hill (" A "), Captain A. C. Fraser (" C "), and Captain L. H. Dawson (" B "). The Adjutant was Captain J. O. Dicker. Boulogne was reached about midnight. Disembarkation began almost immediately, and the Battalion marched through the town out to the rest camp about one and a-half miles away, where it remained throughout

1ST SEPTEMBER.

the 2nd September. Very early on the morning of the 3rd the Battalion was astir, marching to the railway station and, entraining at 5 a.m. for Maresquel, arrived shortly after 8 a.m. Here it was joined by the advanced party and the transport, and in a heavy rain the Battalion (in Brigade) set out on a 10 to 12 mile march to the Remboval–Embry–Créquy area. The 13th Middlesex reached their destination—Créquy—about 3.30 p.m., and were billeted in farms and sheds in the village, Battalion Headquarters being established in an empty house—" La Villa Marguerette " ; Brigade Headquarters were at Torcy and 24th Divisional Headquarters at Royon. 13TH BATTALION.

From the 3rd to 21st September the Battalion remained in this area, training, marching and in other ways making final preparations for the next move, which all knew would be to some sector of the front line. It should be remembered, however, that during this period of training the units of the 24th Division were given no opportunity of putting in a period of instruction in the front-line trenches, and that when they were called upon to enter into battle they had had no actual experience of hostile rifle, machine-gun or shell fire. 3RD/21ST SEPTEMBER.

Sudden orders to march came to hand on 21st September, and at 8 p.m. that night the 24th Division set out on its long and weary march southwards, the 13th Middlesex forming the advanced guard. The first stage of the march was 11 miles through hilly country, and was carried out in brilliant moonlight. At about 1 a.m. on 22nd the Middlesex men marched into Laires, their destination, and spent the remainder of the night in farms and barns in the village. The march was resumed at night at the same hour, 8 p.m., and although the moon was bright, the distance (14 miles), owing to the numerous checks along the route, tired the men considerably, and when L'Eclême was reached about 3 a.m. (23rd) the Battalion lost little time in taking over the farms and barns allotted to it. Another rest during the day, followed by another march, and soon after 11 p.m. on the night of 24th September the Battalion billeted in Beuvry. 24TH SEPT.

That night as the Battalion lay in billets with activity all around (for Beuvry was only a short distance from the firing line) all ranks knew that a grim battle was to begin on the morrow, and that they also would probably be included in it.

Early next morning ear-splitting roars awoke officers and men, the farm houses and sheds in which the Battalion was billeted

25TH SEPT.
13TH BATTALION.

literally shaking and rocking from the thundering of a thousand guns. The great 15-inch howitzer (" Granny ") at Sailly La Bourse had added " her " voice to the roaring of other " Heavies," and pandemonium reigned.

At 10 a.m. the Battalion received orders to march out of Beuvry in an easterly direction along the Vermelles road. These orders read as follows: " The Brigade (73rd) will march in the order already given (12th Royal Fusiliers, 9th Royal Scots, 7th Northamptons, 13th Middlesex) aaa Starting point cross roads *Y* of Beuvry at 11.5 a.m. aaa Advanced Guard one company 12th Royal Fusiliers aaa Only 20 officers to go into action, not including transport officers, and one officer to collect stragglers aaa Remainder, to include one Captain and one Lieutenant, will join Reserve Brigade on arrival at rendezvous." The 73rd Brigade had been placed at the disposal of the 9th (Scottish) Division, then engaged in a desperate struggle with the enemy for the possession of the Hohenzollern Redoubt and Fosse 8. On the right of the 9th Division the 26th Brigade had secured the latter place after heavy fighting, but the 28th Brigade of the same Division, having captured the German trenches east of the Vermelles railway, was eventually driven back to its own trenches, having suffered considerable losses. It was the 26th Brigade that the 73rd Brigade of the 24th Division was destined to relieve.

The 13th Middlesex had not gone far along the Vermelles road before they met the first evidence of real warfare. For down the roadway there came, in ones and twos and sometimes in small batches, wounded men with all the signs of a bloody struggle fresh upon them, limbs bandaged with " first-aid " dressings, tunics torn open, or stained with mud through which dark-red patches had begun to make their appearance, some limping and stumbling, others with that curious, upright, nonchalant air, which often covered a ghastly wound. And then behind the wounded British soldiers, herded together under strong escorts, came a crowd of German prisoners, their faces depicting every emotion from that of a man snatched from a horrible death and happy in his release though a prisoner of war, to that of loathing and hatred of their captors, discernible in the sullen expressions and the smouldering fires glowing in the eyes of some of the captured Teutons.

About 12 noon the Battalion arrived west of Sailly La Bourse, where it was directed to the left, and formed up west of a small stream west of Vermelles. Here the Middlesex men were joined by the 71st and 72nd Infantry Brigades of the Division, the remainder of the 73rd Brigade having proceeded further east towards the firing line. 25TH SEPT. 13TH BATTALION.

Soon after 4 p.m. instructions were received by Colonel Oliver to move his Battalion forward to east of Vermelles, and in the gathering darkness this movement was carried out. The Middlesex men were now assembled near the railway at the western end of a long communication trench (Barts Alley), which led from the old British front line about three-quarters of a mile in front. The Battalion Diary states that it was in this position that "the Battalion for the first time came under fire (shell and rifle fire)," but it is presumed that no casualties were suffered as none are mentioned in the records.

At nightfall on 25th September the official despatches give the British line roughly as follows: "From the Double Crassier, south of Loos, by the western part of Hill 70 to the western exits of Hulluch, thence by the Quarries and western end of Cité St. Elie, east of Fosse 8, back to our original front line."

At 5.25 p.m. 9th Divisional Advanced Headquarters sent a message to the G.O.C. 73rd Infantry Brigade, "the 73rd Infantry Brigade will relieve the 26th Infantry Brigade and will form a defensive flank on the line junction of Slag and Fosse Alleys–3 Cabarets–Corons de Pekin–Corons de Maron-Mad Point back to our own trenches. Actual line to be selected by Brigadier. Present artillery barrage Pekin Alley–Madagascar Houses–Mad Point–Madagascar Trench."*

Although the 73rd Brigade Diary states that the Brigade moved up at 8 p.m. to relieve the 26th Brigade, the records of the 13th Middlesex state that it was 11 p.m. before that Battalion advanced. The move forward took place in artillery formation, over open ground, to trenches which had been the old British support line. In many places these trenches were knee deep in water and the men had a most uncomfortable time. From these trenches it was vividly evident that fighting was still going on all up and down the line. In front of them the desperate struggle for the Quarries was proceeding; machine guns "barked" and there were loud reports from trench bombs and hand-grenades, punctuated by the steady rattle of rifle fire. On the left front were the Hohenzollern Redoubt and Fosse 8. Burning buildings

* G. 942 Adv. 9th Division.

26TH SEPT.
13TH BATTALION.

threw a lurid glare over the battlefield as hour after hour passed, and still no orders to go forward reached the Middlesex men. At last, about 3 o'clock on the morning of 26th, under instructions from the Brigadier, Colonel Oliver with his Adjutant and "A" and "D" Companies proceeded across the open to the left front towards the "Slag Heap" of No. 8 Fosse; one platoon of "B" Company accompanied the Brigadier-General as escort. The position taken up by Colonel Oliver and his two Companies is thus described in the Battalion Diary: "The trenches occupied by these two Companies were German support trenches south-west of the Hohenzollern Redoubt, to the west of two German communication trenches leading from that Redoubt to the German support trenches; 'A' Company (Captain Hill) was on the left and occupied a portion of the trench going to the left facing the Slag Heap and a portion of Slag Alley (a communication trench on the south-west side of the Slag Heap, No. 8 Fosse); 'D' Company was on the right joining up with the 2nd Queen's Regiment facing Haisnes Church. (The Commanding Officer was with this Company.)" What *is* more certain, however, is the desperate situation in which they found themselves once they had taken up their position. For they were now exposed to heavy shell and rifle fire and repeated attacks by the Germans, who made savage efforts to wrest the trenches from the Die-Hards, all to no purpose. By the skilful use of their machine guns, and even counter-attacks by bombers, these two Companies of Middlesex men successfully held their own and beat off all attacks. They suffered casualties, but no one thought of giving way. They suffered also from want of food and water, for none had been issued to them. Owing to the hurried departure from Beuvry on the morning of 25th the Battalion had marched before rations for that day were received, and owing to the isolated position of the men in the front trenches it was impossible to pass up supplies excepting by night. On the night of 26th and 27th a small quantity of water, biscuits and ammunition was sent up from the Companies in the support trenches to those in front, but the forward Companies would have suffered much more severely if it had not been for the kindness of the 2nd Queen's Regiment, who generously shared with the Die-Hards what rations they had.

About the Hohenzollern Redoubt and Fosse 8 the struggle continued, rendering, almost hourly, the position of the 13th Middlesex more precarious. With splendid fortitude, however, they clung to their desperate situation, though suffering severe casualties, until at last, on the morning of 29th, relief came and the little party (all that was left of the two Companies), numbering 170 all ranks, marched back to Beuvry and thence by train to Lillers, whence they marched to Lambres and rejoined the remainder of the Battalion (in billets) about 11 a.m. on 30th September. 13TH BATTALION.

The story now turns back to the morning of 26th (Sunday). After " A " and " D " Companies, led by Colonel Oliver and his Adjutant, had crossed the open ground to the left front towards the " Slag Heap of No. 8 Fosse," " B " and " C " Companies were extended to occupy the length of trenches previously occupied by the whole Battalion. About 2 p.m. most of these two Companies were moved forward about 100 yards, as the enemy's guns had found the exact range of the original trenches. Of what happened to these two Companies between 2 p.m. on Sunday and Monday afternoon (when it became necessary to move forward again for the same reason) there are no records, but the Battalion Diary states that about 5 p.m. on the latter day the enemy made a determined attack on the left flank, which was repulsed by men of various Regiments—Royal Scots, Black Watch and Argyll and Sutherland Highlanders, assisted by Northants and Middlesex—who were moved down to meet the attack. Throughout the night these attacks were constantly repeated, but in every instance they were beaten off and the enemy retired, leaving the ground littered with dead and wounded.

" B " and " C " Companies were relieved about 8 a.m. on 28th and moved back *via* Bart's Alley, whence, after a short rest, the march was continued through Vermelles to Sailly-la-Bourse. In the latter place the two Companies were visited by the Divisional Commander, " who," the narrative states, " warmly congratulated the Battalion on the work it had done." The Brigadier also visited the Companies, and expressed his pleasure at their fine and soldierly conduct. 28TH SEPT.

Whilst in bivouacs at Sailly-la-Bourse a draft of 40 N.C.Os. and men from the 15th Battalion arrived, and these with the two Companies paraded at 8.30 p.m. and, in heavy rain, marched to Nœux-les-Mines, entraining at the latter place about midnight. At 2 a.m. the half-battalion reached Berguette Station, and, after wandering about in the dark, eventually (at about 5 a.m.) reached billets at Fontes, where all ranks settled down for a few hours' rest. At 5 p.m. another move was made to a small village

—Rombly—about two miles away, where the Battalion transport joined. Finally, at 10 a.m. on the 30th September, the Middlesex men marched to Lambres, a distance of some three and a-half miles, being joined later by Colonel Oliver and his party, and the Battalion was enabled for the first time to render a casualty return. One officer (Captain C. E. Hill) had been killed; eight officers (Major J. H. R. Cox, Captains A. C. Fraser and B. Wells, Lieut. C. K. Allen and 2nd Lieuts. W. L. King, S. Smith, P. Worthington and F. A. Bailey) wounded, and another officer (Lieut. C. E. Harman) was reported wounded and a prisoner of war. In other ranks the Battalion had lost 13 killed, 77 wounded and 70 missing.

30th Sept.
13th Battalion.

The first Service Battalion of the Regiment engaged in major operations had worthily upheld the best traditions of the Die-Hards. The conduct of the men under every sort of discouragement was splendid. They had had no previous experience of trenches or shell fire, they had not even had the advantage of an instructional tour in a quiet sector. But unflinchingly they stood their ground and made isolated counter-attacks on their own initiative. The Battalion had been specially trained for open warfare, and on the march back from Loos one of the privates remarked:

"Well! if that's what they call open fighting, we'll 'ave to take our tunics off if we are to 'ave any room for close fighting!"

28th Sept.
3rd Battalion.

Meanwhile, before daylight on 28th September, the 3rd Middlesex had been moved up into the battle front opposite the Hohenzollern Redoubt.

The 28th Division, to which the 3rd Battalion belonged, had arrived at Bethune on 26th, having been drawn back to Bailleul out of the line with orders (the official despatches record) to hold itself in readiness to meet "unexpected eventualities," and when on the morning of 27th it was placed at the disposal of the G.O.C. First Army, the Division was already "standing to" ready to march off. Orders to move were received at 8.45 a.m., and at 10 a.m. the march to Vermelles was begun.

In order to give a better understanding of the action of the 3rd Middlesex it is necessary for a brief space to refer to the orders received by, and movements of, the 85th Brigade generally.

The Brigade, after arrival at Vermelles, was to take over the front-line trenches "in a general line, the Quarries and Fosse 8, the left resting on the Vermelles–Auchy road." On arrival at

Vermelles these orders seem to have been amplified, for at 1 p.m. the Brigade Diary states that the Brigade was to "take over from 26th and 27th Brigades (9th Division) the line New Trench–Fosse Trench–Corons de Maron to junction of Slag Alley and Fosse Alley, thence to the Quarries." Fifteen minutes later this line was reported as "lost," and verbal orders were issued to the Brigade to move at once and hold the Hohenzollern Redoubt. The 2nd East Surreys were to make good "Little Willie," the Royal Fusiliers the line from where Central Boyeau cut the Redoubt to the junction of West Face and South Face. An attack on Fosse Trench and Dump Trench was to be made by the 2nd East Surreys on the left and Royal Fusiliers on the right. Already the Brigade had fallen in to comply with these orders when a message was received that help was urgently needed. In consequence, two Companies of the Buffs and the 3rd Royal Fusiliers, who were ready, moved off, the Brigadier (Brigadier-General C. E. Pereira) and his Staff leading the way. Colonel Roberts, the C.O. of the Royal Fusiliers, having been ordered to report on the situation in front, made his way up to the Hohenzollern Redoubt and there met Brigadier-General Jelf (commanding 73rd Brigade, 24th Division), who told him things were in a critical state. Meanwhile the two Companies of Buffs had arrived at the Redoubt and found it choked with men of the 26th, 27th and 73rd Brigades. Quickly grasping the situation, the C.O. of the Royal Fusiliers asked General Jelf to remove the remnants of the three Brigades and returned to bring up his own Battalion—the 3rd Royal Fusiliers. He brought two Companies up first, but on returning for the remaining Companies, found that General Pereira had been wounded and the Brigade-Major (Captain Flower) was missing, though it was afterwards discovered that the latter had also been wounded. Handing over command of his Battalion to Major Baker with instructions to take up the two remaining Companies to the Redoubt, Colonel Roberts assumed command of the Brigade. It was now 6 p.m., and at 7.30 p.m., having had a terrible march up communication trenches blocked with wounded, which delayed their progress, the 2nd East Surreys arrived at Brigade Headquarters, then situated in a dug-out about 500 yards S.W. of the Hohenzollern Redoubt. The East Surreys were ordered to take up the line New Trench–Old Line British Trench, "and a Company with their right at the junction where Central Boyeau runs into redoubt and left into Little Willie." This was done.

27TH SEPT. 3RD BATTALION.

27TH SEPT. 3RD BATTALION. About 9 p.m. the acting Brigadier received orders from 28th Divisional Headquarters that the position lost during the day—*i.e.*, Caron Alley–Caron Maron—had to be retaken, and immediately sent off for Colonel Worthington and Colonel Neale, the C.Os. of the 2nd Buffs and 3rd Middlesex respectively. On arrival at Brigade Headquarters, these two officers had the situation explained to them and they hurried off, the C.O. of the Buffs to bring up his two remaining companies and Colonel Neale to bring up his Battalion.

From the time of their arrival (1 p.m.) on 27th at Vermelles the 3rd Middlesex remained in the open, where they had halted, until 2 a.m. on the morning of 28th. They were by now comparatively old campaigners, and knew from past experience how to look after themselves, whilst waiting to go into the line; in this they were different from the newly-arrived 13th Battalion, which had been forced to spend days in the trenches almost without food and water.

28TH SEPT. But at 2 a.m. the Battalion moved off *via* Central Boyeau up to the old British front line opposite the Hohenzollern Redoubt. In this position orders were received to support the Buffs, who were to attack immediately towards the Dump, clearing all trenches and communication trenches on the left of the Dump. But again, owing to the difficulty of assembling the troops in crowded trenches, the attack was delayed, and it was not until 9.30 a.m., after the guns had heavily bombarded the German positions, that the advance took place.

The Buffs attacked across the open, but the 3rd Middlesex, first moving along South Face Trench until Point 35 (Dump Trench) was reached, made a bombing attack against the left face of the trench. Fine progress had been made when the supply of bombs gave out and urgent appeals were made for more. Before a fresh supply could be brought up the Germans launched a violent bombing attack and the Middlesex men began to suffer heavy casualties. The narrow trench in which the Battalion was fighting soon became congested with wounded and men of other units who had been relieved and were on their way out of the trench. On the right of the Middlesex the Buffs had also to give way. The C.O. of the Middlesex, realising the danger of his position, gave orders to withdraw slowly. This operation was most difficult, the trench being narrow and 7 feet deep. From both flanks the Battalion was now under heavy enfilade machine-gun fire, and it was impossible to show a head above the parapet. "About this time," records the Diary of the 3rd Middlesex, "the C.O. (Colonel Neale) was killed"—a great loss to his Battalion and the Regiment. 3RD BATTALION.

The Battalion having been withdrawn down South Face, orders were received to hold Big Willie, and all four Companies were distributed along that trench, whilst the Royal Fusiliers were ordered to hold South Face. During the day the Germans heavily attacked the latter trench, but were held by the Middlesex bombers.

On 29th South Face was again heavily attacked by the enemy's bombers, but were once more held. About 5 a.m. two Companies of the 1st York and Lancs. Regiment passed through Big Willie to relieve the 2nd Buffs, who were then on the right of the Middlesex holding Dump Trench. On withdrawal the Buffs filled the gap between the left of the Middlesex and right of the 3rd Royal Fusiliers. 29TH SEPT.

The 85th Brigade Diary gives the positions at 8 a.m. on the 29th thus: "2nd East Surrey occupied New Trench and small portions of Little Willie, north and south; their supports were in Old First-Line British Trench. 3rd Royal Fusiliers occupied whole of Hohenzollern Redoubt, and had bombed up a portion of North Face and South Face. 2nd Buffs had withdrawn and had been placed in Big Willie on right of Royal Fusiliers. 3rd Middlesex continued line in Big Willie to Quarry Trench and was in touch at that place with 7th Division."

About 11 a.m. the German attack was pressed more vigorously, and in a little while the Die-Hards were again short of bombs, and it became clear that another withdrawal would have to take place. The C.Os. of the Buffs and Middlesex then held a consultation, and it was decided that if South Face had to be evacuated the Buffs would have to withdraw also on account of the narrowness of the trench and to give room for the Middlesex; the left flank of Big Willie would also be left in the air.

All day long the struggle continued, the British troops contesting every inch of ground. But about 5 p.m., as the garrison of South Face was steadily being bombed back, orders were issued for one company to remain in Big Willie, one to reinforce the right of the Royal Fusiliers in West Face and two in the communication trench from West Face to the Old British Front Line. These orders were carried out. But later West Face was taken by the

3RD BATTALION.

Germans and all Companies of the Middlesex re-organised in the Old First-Line Trench, where they remained until they were relieved at midnight, 30th September–1st October. On relief the 3rd Middlesex marched back to billets in Annequin, moving at 4 p.m. on 1st October to Beuvry, where all units of the 85th Brigade were billeted.

1ST OCTOBER.

From 27th September to 1st October (inclusive) the 3rd Middlesex suffered in casualties 6 officers killed* and 2 wounded; in other ranks 42 killed, 189 wounded, 88 missing.

Two days in billets in Beuvry and two in Annequin, followed by a sudden order to move up into the Reserve Trenches, and then billets in Bas Rieux, sum up the movements of the 3rd Middlesex during the first six days of October. Then followed several days of digging trenches in the neighbourhood of Gonnehem for instructional purposes in the attack and bomb throwing. On the 19th the Battalion moved into the Givenchy sector, taking over Givenchy Redoubt, Marie Keep and Gunners Siding, but relief came on the morning of 20th and the Middlesex moved back to Hingette. By this time the 28th Division had received orders to move to Salonika, and on the 22nd the 3rd Middlesex (in Brigade) entrained at Touqereuil for Marseilles, arriving at the latter place at 7.30 p.m. on 24th. Early on the morning of 25th October the Battalion embarked on H.T. *Transylvania*.

19TH OCTOBER.

25TH OCTOBER.

The main operations of the Battle of Loos ended on 8th October, but meanwhile subsidiary attacks had been made by the Vth Corps on the Bellewaarde Ridge, east of Ypres, and by the IIIrd and Indian Corps north of the La Bassée Canal and along the whole front of the Second Army.

* No names are given, these figures being taken from the 83rd Brigade Diary; the Battalion Diary of the 3rd Middlesex does not mention casualties other than that of the C.O.

# CHAPTER XIX.

## THE BATTLE OF LOOS: SUBSIDIARY OPERATIONS.

### The Second Attack on Bellewaarde.

THE object of the secondary attack of the Second Army was to distract the enemy's attention from the main operations and hold his troops to their ground, and the official despatches speak of these intentions as having been "most effectively achieved."

25TH SEPT. 4TH BATTALION.

The most important of these subsidiary operations began on 25th September and ended on the following day, and although the 4th Middlesex (of the 8th Infantry Brigade, 3rd Division) were not in the front line which attacked the enemy but were held first in reserve and then in support, the action is of considerable interest to Middlesex men, for it was during the operations between 25th September and 1st October that 2nd Lieut. Rupert Price Hallowes,* of the 4th Battalion, won the first Victoria Cross awarded to the Regiment since the outbreak of war.

Between the 9th and the 23rd August the 4th Middlesex had spent a very uncomfortable period in the line in Trenches 34 to 31. Heavy artillery bombardments, persistent bomb-throwing with trench mortars, sniping, rifle fire and machine gunning characterised those fourteen days in the forward trenches, and when the Battalion reached Dickebusch all ranks were worn out. The constant vigilance necessary had been a great strain on officers and men, for the Ypres Salient at this period was a noisome, terrible place, and rarely are "quiet days" recorded in the Diaries.

On 11th September the 8th Brigade received orders to take over the Hooge sector on the 12th; the 4th Middlesex were to go to Ypres ramparts. These moves duly took place, and the Battalion spent several days in supplying working and carrying

* 2nd Lieut. Hallowes had previously won the Military Cross for gallantry during the actions at Hooge on 19th–20th July.

25TH SEPT. 4TH BATTALION.

parties. On the 18th, however, the Battalion vacated the ramparts and moved forward into Sanctuary Wood. On the 19th, during the afternoon, the Germans very heavily shelled the Wood with both high and low-bursting shrapnel, and the Battalion was extraordinarily lucky in having only one man hit by a splinter.

The enemy's snipers were also extremely active, one of these pests, who could not be located, shooting three men. Just after dawn on 20th three more men were killed and two wounded by the same sniper, and shortly afterwards an English bullet fired by the same man was found. Apparently he was using a new rifle, as the Battalion Diary records that the grooves were exceedingly well-marked on the bullet. The story of this persistent German's efforts continues thus: "Our snipers went up to find him and succeeded. He was about 30 feet up a tree with a hole bored through the tree to snipe through. To-morrow we are getting the Regiment occupying the front trenches to turn a machine gun on him from both sides as soon as he starts sniping. 21st. . . The sniper did not start until 9.30 a.m., when our sniping officer went up to deal with him in conjunction with the Northumberland Fusiliers. . . . The sniper's tree was hit by shrapnel but he was not silenced. . . . 24th, Major Greenway and four men wounded by the sniper who got thirteen men of various units during the day." Here the story ends, and as no further mention of the sniper's activities occurs in the Diary, the sequel may be assumed.

Orders for the attack on the Bellewaarde Ridge, subsidiary to the main operations at Loos on 25th September, had been received at 8th Brigade Headquarters on 21st. The 14th Division of the VIth Corps was to attack Bellewaarde Farm and the trenches to the south of it with three Battalions; two Battalions of the 7th Infantry Brigade (3rd Division) were to attack about Hooge Château and the 8th Infantry Brigade from the Ypres–Menin road (inclusive) to a point opposite Stirling Castle; one Company of the 1st Royal Scots Fusiliers of the 9th Brigade was to attack on the right of the 8th Brigade in order to straighten out the line opposite the 9th Brigade front.

The frontage of attack allotted to the 8th Brigade was 1,500 yards, and the assault was to be made by the 2nd Royal Scots and 1st and 4th Gordon Highlanders, the 2nd Suffolk Regiment and the 4th Middlesex Regiment being held in reserve. The artillery bombardment was to take place from 3.30 to 4.20 a.m., and the infantry assault at the latter hour.

The Diary of the 8th Infantry Brigade during the preparations for, and the attack on, Hooge is very interesting, for there are many comments contained in it which throw considerable light on the operations, comments which are entirely lacking in the Battalion Diaries. "It was thought that the number of guns and the ammunition allotted to them was inadequate for the attack," is one comment, and this is followed up by another of equal importance: "Three trench-mortar batteries are also to take part in the bombardment, but the ammunition for these is also very limited." In 1915 the question of ammunition supply was acute and the guns were strictly rationed. This shortage of ammunition is reflected in the statement that "it is doubtful if much damage has been done to his (the enemy's) wire entanglements." And yet the enemy must have suffered severely, for on 19th September (as one instance) the "usual bombardment" of the enemy's trenches at Hooge was carried out by 21 batteries of guns of all calibres, *i.e.*, 8-inch Howitzers, 60-pounders, 4.7-inch guns, 6-inch, 5-inch and 4.5-inch Howitzers and 18 and 15-pounders. To these bombardments the enemy replied vigorously, and on the 23rd he is reported as bombarding the 3rd Divisional trenches very heavily, shells falling at the rate of quite 100 per minute, though the astonishing thing is that in recording this bombardment the Brigade Diary reports: "Little damage reported to have been done."

25TH SEPT. 4TH BATTALION.

The 8th Brigade moved up into the trenches on the night of 23rd September, and on the same night reports that the total number of bombs of all kinds (15,000) available for the operation was considered inadequate for the purpose. But the Brigadier, after appealing for more, was told that no more were available. Another trenchant paragraph appears in the Brigade Diary on 24th September: "The Brigade was ordered to hand over 90 pairs of wire cutters to 7th and 9th Brigades, as none were available in Ordnance Stores for them, it being thus seen that after 14 months of war even a sufficiency of wire cutters cannot be obtained before an action."

At 3.50 on the morning of the 25th September the final bombardment of the enemy's trenches began. In all, about 112 guns poured shell on to the German positions opposite the 8th Brigade front. A comment in the Brigade Diary that many of these guns, being 18-pdrs., they were unsuitable for wire cutting, being too light, is not quite correct, for the field gun with its low trajectory

25TH SEPT.

4TH BATTALION.

and firing shrapnel was found most suitable for destroying the enemy's entanglements.

Three minutes after the British guns opened fire, a red rocket, followed by a white rocket, which burst into white stars, soared up into the sky from the German lines; this was the enemy's signal that he was being attacked. The German guns opened almost immediately. At 4.19 a.m. two mines were exploded under the German trenches opposite the Royal Scots. Half-a-minute later two more mines were fired in the same place. In these explosions a whole company of Germans (about 180 men) of the 122nd Regiment was destroyed.

At 4.20 a.m. the assault took place. Rain was falling, and owing to the mist the morning was darker than usual. Until just past 5 a.m. there was no news from the attacking Battalions. Then, at 5.5 a.m., a message was received at Brigade Headquarters from the O.C. Royal Scots stating that his Battalion had got into the German trenches, but it was still too dark to determine the exact situation.

The 4th Middlesex recorded that about 6.30 a.m. prisoners and wounded began to dribble back from the German lines and continued to do so for the next two hours.

At 10 a.m. the Battalion learned that, partly on account of a heavy hostile bombardment and lack of bombs, the line was giving way. The Middlesex bombers were hard at work detonating the Brigade supply of bombs when a message was received, ordering a party of bombers, with two platoons to support them, to bomb up the communication trenches leading to the Fort which the 4th Gordons had taken in their assault, and from which they had been driven out again. The remaining two platoons of this Company ("D" Company) were also sent up to relieve the remnants of the 4th Gordons. The gallant Highlanders had reported the capture of "Fort 13" at 8 a.m., but soon after their supply of bombs, and, indeed, their reserve of bombers, ran out, and at 10.40 a.m. a message was received from their Colonel stating that the situation on his front was very serious. The Germans had broken in between his left flank and the right of the 1st Gordons and had cut off many of his men in the Fort, though some of his Battalion had retired to the original line. Throughout these early reports constant reference is made to the shortage of bombs and bombers.

Somewhere between 11 a.m. and 12 noon, "B" Company of the 4th Middlesex was sent up to garrison B. 8 and B. 8 support

25TH SEPT. 4TH BATTALION.

trenches (at the northern edge of Sanctuary Wood). The communication trenches had all been blown in by trench-mortar bombs, heavy and field-gun shells, but although both "D" and "B" Companies of the Middlesex were heavily shelled they clung to their trenches and were lucky in escaping without serious casualties.

By 2.20 p.m. the Brigade supply of bombs was nearly exhausted. Counter-attacks, made with great gallantry at first with a certain amount of success, had finally to be abandoned, for there were no bombs with which to keep the enemy off.

At about 3 p.m. "C" Company of the 4th Middlesex was sent up to reinforce the 2nd Royal Scots, who were in a precarious position, owing to the fact that the enemy had got between them and the 4th Gordons. This Company was also heavily shelled, but casualties were few.

At 4.30 p.m. the Royal Scots were forced to retire from the position they had captured and throughout the day had clung to with splendid tenacity, and thus the last of the trenches captured in the early morning were regained by the enemy.

An hour later the 4th Middlesex was ordered to relieve the Royal Scots in B. 3, B. 4 and 1/2 B. 7. "A" Company was sent up to 1/2 B. 7, and "B" Company relieved "C" Company in 1/2 B. 4 and 1/2 B. 3. Casualties in the Battalion throughout the day were 5 men killed, 2nd Lieut. C. A. B. Cook and 40 men wounded.

26TH SEPT.

All night long the Middlesex men were hard at work repairing and rebuilding the trenches which, when dawn broke on the 26th September, had been made once more continuous. But there was still much to be done, and so the Battalion worked all day in the firing line and communication trenches, though one point in the line—the "B. 4 Salient," as it was called—had to be left, as it had been too badly damaged by the previous day's bombardment and was too near the enemy's front-line trenches to admit of repair in daylight. When darkness had fallen, however, the working party crept out and started work on this salient, which was in the north-east corner of Sanctuary Wood, jutting out towards Stirling Castle.

Towards midnight, 26th–27th, the Middlesex bombers saw a party of Germans in front of them, and 2nd Lieut. Farr and Sergeant Remnant, with three men, engaged the enemy and drove him back to his own lines. Lieut. Farr was badly wounded in the leg by a shell splinter on getting back to the Middlesex trenches

26TH SEPT. 4TH BATTALION. after the bombing attack was over. This enterprise unfortunately started a regular artillery duel between the British and German gunners, for 8th Brigade Headquarters, under the impression that the Middlesex men were being attacked, sent the "S.O.S." signal round the field batteries, who immediately opened rapid fire, which spread to the "Heavies." Soon every gun in the sector was plastering the German trenches with shell, which drew retaliation from the enemy. Working parties in rear of the firing line and ration parties at the dump were thrown into confusion and another working party out in front of the line, at work making an old sap into a fire trench, had to be withdrawn. In several places the firing line was blown in by hostile shells, but was subsequently repaired before dawn. The duel lasted about three-quarters of an hour and then died down, but not before further casualties had been suffered by the Middlesex. 2nd Lieut. H. P. Ochs and two men were killed, another officer and several other ranks were wounded. The Battalion M.O.—Captain A. E. Bulloch—who had been continuously with the 4th Middlesex since 14th September, 1914, was killed by a stray bullet at the "dumping ground."

27TH SEPT. When dawn broke on 27th it was seen that the bombardment had knocked the German trenches about very badly, and a lot of dead bodies were in front of the enemy's lines. Work all day on the trenches again occupied the Middlesex, and at night the nose of the "B. 4 Salient" was finished and occupied. Two more officer casualties were suffered during the day: 2nd Lieut. C. M. Talbot was killed and 2nd Lieut. A. D. Herbert wounded; one other rank was also killed.

28TH SEPT. The 28th was similarly a quiet day, but at night the party working at B. 4 Salient encountered another German party, and bombing and rifle fire broke out, which again started a heavy artillery bombardment by both sides, and when dawn broke on the 29th the dead ground in front of the German trenches was again littered with many corpses; the guns had caught hostile working parties out in front of their trenches.

29TH SEPT. About 4.30 p.m. on the 29th, the enemy sprung a mine on the left of the Middlesex front, and shortly afterwards German bombers rushed across from the northern side of the crater into the back of "B. 4" (the Battalion's left trench), clearing the trench before the Middlesex bombers could get into action. A gruesome sight was seen by an officer who rushed up to the front line after the alarm had been given. He saw that the garrison of B. 4 were all in the trench, but they were dead. Not one had left the trench, but, faithful to their duty, they had stood their ground until every man had been killed by the enemy's bombers. Eventually the German bombers were stopped and a line was adjusted across the B. 4 Salient from Pollock Street to the middle of B. 7 (the right trench of the Suffolks on the left of the Middlesex men), but leaving a gap between the two Battalions.

29TH SEPT. 4TH BATTALION.

At the moment that the mine was fired the enemy opened very heavy fire with guns and trench mortars all along the 8th Brigade front, and some of the Germans who rushed across No Man's Land were dressed in the uniforms of the 2nd Royal Scots, doubtless taken from men of that Battalion captured on 25th September.

Again a shortage of bombs* hampered the Middlesex men, and after working all night detonating bombs which were sent up only in small driblets, it was decided to attack at 2 p.m. on the 30th.

The ground lost, though only a few hundred yards in extent, nevertheless deprived the Brigade of a good observation station and gave the enemy a valuable piece of high ground.

30TH SEPT.

Zero hour on the 30th had subsequently to be altered until 3.15 p.m., as the attack could not be organised by 2 p.m. The guns were to bombard the enemy's trenches for a quarter of an hour, beginning at 3 p.m., and at the close of the bombardment the assault was to be made by one company of the 4th Middlesex on the right, a company of 2nd Royal Scots in the centre and a company of 2nd Suffolks on the left, all companies being preceded by bombers, who would work up the communication trenches.

Bombers of the Honourable Artillery Company and the 10th Liverpool Scottish were also to take part in the attack, whilst the Honourable Artillery Company was to be in close support.

Throughout the night 29th–30th the Middlesex men awaited the arrival of an adequate supply of bombs, but unfortunately they were not forthcoming, and as the Battalion Diary records: " It was decided to attack at 2 p.m. with an inadequate supply by higher authority." The Honourable Artillery Company could not

* " Attention has repeatedly been called to the lack of bombs which had hampered every operation in which the Brigade had taken part for some months past, and which has been responsible for many lives."—Extract from 8th Brigade Diary, 29th September, 1915.

30th Sept. 4th Battalion.

get up into the line in time and (as already stated) zero hour was subsequently put off until 3 p.m. At 3 p.m. the guns opened on the German trenches and continued for 15 minutes. The enemy's position lay along commanding ground, and he had put out wire entanglements of considerable thickness and strength. His machine guns were well placed, sweeping the whole terrain in front of his defences, and in addition he was evidently armed with an unlimited supply of bombs.

The bombardment was very effective so far as the enemy's trenches were concerned, and in many places the German lines were breached and tumbled by British shells; but after the advance began it was apparent that the hostile wire entanglements had not been sufficiently cut to allow the passage of troops. At 3.15 p.m. the bombing columns advanced to the attack. Along B. 4 the 4th Middlesex, on the right of the attack, made good progress, and the Suffolks on the left also succeeded in working to the north of the Salient. But in the centre the Royal Scots were held up by wire blocks in the trenches and could not get further. It was now that the shortage of bombs made itself felt. Checks were constant, as the men waited for supplies to be passed up, and presently the position became so precarious that finally the bombing columns were ordered to dig in at the most advanced position they had won and conserve what bombs remained to repel hostile bombing attacks which would almost certainly be made. The time was about 4.30 p.m. when the men started to dig themselves in. The line then ran from 25 yards from the crater in B. 7 through B.S.4, B.2.S, Pollock Street and Cranston Terrace; this line was consolidated and held. The eastern lip of the crater was held by the Germans, whose machine guns took heavy toll of the attacking troops. A 60-pounder trench mortar, which had been specially detailed to deal with the crater, broke down after firing one round, otherwise the whole of the crater might have been captured by the Middlesex men, but the real cause why the attack was only partially successful was the shortage of bombs: "Had we had an adequate supply of bombs in the first instance," records the Battalion Diary, somewhat bitterly, "the whole of the lost trenches would have been quickly and easily recaptured." During the night 30th September–1st October two lines of trenches were dug by the Middlesex, assisted by Royal Engineers and the 4th South Lancs, but as the Sappers were late in arriving the front line could not be wired.

Many brave and gallant men gave their lives for their country on that day of hard fighting under great disadvantages and difficulties, but none met death more bravely or gallantly than a young second lieutenant whose name will for all time live in the memory of Middlesex men, for he gained for the 4th Battalion that most coveted honour to which a soldier aspires—the Victoria Cross,* the first awarded to the Regiment in the Great War. 30TH SEPT. 4TH BATTALION.

The Battalion Diary states that " the conduct of 2nd Lieut. R. P. Hallowes was an example to all; he showed great coolness and resolution on this and on previous occasions." Indeed, throughout all the fierce fighting which took place at Hooge from 25th to 30th September the magnificent bravery and untiring energy of this officer was the constant admiration of all who witnessed his unforgetable cheerfulness and disregard of danger. His example to the men of his Battalion was most inspiring. On four separate occasions the trenches held by him and his men were subjected to prolonged and powerful bombardments which struck terror into the hearts of the timid, but, regardless of danger, this young Lieutenant clambered up on to the parapet amidst the bursting shells and the battered, crumbling trenches, calming the fears of his men by his reckless bravery. Again, when the attack was made and his men were out of bombs, he went back under heavy shell fire and brought up a fresh supply. At last he was struck down (on 30th September), but still as he lay, mortally wounded and dying, he continued to cheer on his men and inspire them with fresh courage. Then the end came, which surely shows how precious a thing to him was the honour of his Regiment, and the glorious history of the Middlesex Regiment at Albuhera, for his last words were " Men, we can only die once; if we have to die, let us die like men—like Die-Hards!"

On 1st October the position remained the same, and the day was passed in comparative quietude. The mournful task of carrying away the dead and wounded from the trenches was done without interference from the enemy; the battered trenches were also repaired and gaps in the parapets and communication trenches made good. In the evening the 4th Middlesex were relieved by the Worcesters, and during the early hours of the 2nd October the Battalion reached the Rest Camp in H.13.a.1.1. There were no casualties on the way back, but the men were in a state of exhaustion, and some of them found it impossible to drag their weary bodies 1ST OCTOBER. 2ND OCTOBER.

* *London Gazette*, 18th November, 1915.

2ND OCTOBER. through the six inches of slippery mud which covered the unmetalled road.

Six officers * and 32 other ranks killed, 8 officers and 119 other ranks wounded and 117 missing—in all 16 officers and 268 other ranks—were the losses of the 4th Middlesex during this tour in the line.

## The Action of Bois Grenier.

### 25th September, 1915.

Meanwhile, south of Armentières, the 2nd, 1/7th and 1/8th Middlesex had also been engaged in the subsidiary operations.

While the Vth Corps was attacking Bellewaarde Farm, the IIIrd and Indian Corps had succeeded admirably in the task allotted them, that of holding the enemy away from the main theatre of operations at Loos, by assaulting his position at Le Bridoux † and the Moulin du Pietre respectively.‡ The official despatches state that " The 8th Division of the IIIrd Corps and the Meerut Division of the Indian Corps were principally engaged in this part of the line," but with the former only is this narrative concerned, three Battalions of the Middlesex Regiment—2nd, 1/7th and 1/8th—being in the battle area.

2ND BATTALION. From the end of June until the subsidiary operations on 25th September the Battalion Diary of the 2nd Middlesex is colourless. Tours in and out of the line are recorded briefly, casualties were small and there was apparently little to relieve the ordinary round of trench warfare. One officer was killed (2nd Lieut. W. W. Hardwick on 12th June) and 11 other ranks lost their lives during this period.

The 23rd Infantry Brigade, having been detailed as Divisional Reserve for the operations of 25th September, the 2nd Middlesex, at 7.10 p.m. on 24th, marched to assembly positions at Rouge de Bout, where the Battalion dug shelter trenches. The whole Brigade, when the operations began on the following morning, was assembled along the Rue Biache, but the Battalion Diary of the 2nd Middlesex merely states that " The Brigade occupied this position during the action 25th–26th September and was not

25TH SEPT.

* No names other than those given were obtainable from the Diaries.
† Action of Bois Grenier, 25th September.
‡ Action of Pietre, 25th September.

further engaged." On the last day of September the Middlesex were in the front-line trenches east and west of La Boutillerie. 30TH SEPT.

At the beginning of July, the 1/7th Battalion found itself back again in the original trenches at La Boutillerie, and although this sector of the line was comparatively quiet, the Middlesex men set to work by means of patrols by night and snipers by day to make the life of the enemy as unpleasant as possible. The energy of Colonel King's officers and men, indeed, caused General Pinney to describe the 1/7th Middlesex as "great hunters of the Bosche." Their enthusiasm knew no bounds. "Amongst the many gallant men who deserved well of their country," said the C.O., "no name stood out more conspicuously during this period than that of Sergeant E. J. King, of Hornsey. As a daring and successful patrol leader, he had made a considerable reputation, when a severe wound put a stop to his career, but not before he had earned a mention in despatches, and his name was in the first list of those to whom the Military Medal was awarded." Of the Battalion N.C.Os., Lance-Sergeant C. E. Reynolds, of Tottenham, had also made his name as one of the most cunning and successful of snipers. 1/7TH BATTALION.

Towards the end of July the 1/7th Middlesex shifted its front a little to the right, with Battalion Headquarters in the Rue des Moulins (better known as "Dead Dog Farm"). It was in this sector that Lieut. Ashby, the Battalion Sniping Officer, was badly wounded on 21st August. His loss was great, for he had brought the Sniping Section to a high state of efficiency.

Four days later the Battalion lost one of its most promising Subalterns—2nd Lieut. E. J. Godward. This young officer had taken out a patrol of six men with the object of intercepting a hostile patrol. The party had gone some little distance across No Man's Land, when it suddenly came upon a concealed sap-head containing a machine-gun. The Germans opened fire immediately, and Lieut. Godward and Private Gilbert were shot down. As the latter fell, he hurled a bomb into the sap which put the machine-gun and its crew out of action. The action of this gallant man saved the remainder of the party, who dropped into a ditch under cover, while Lance-Corporal A. Fuller at once went back to fetch up the stretcher bearers. In the meantime, Captain Gillett, hearing the sudden burst of fire and a cry for help from a wounded man, dashed out to the patrol and took charge. The bodies of Lieut. Godward and two wounded men were safely

1/7TH BATTALION. brought back in spite of heavy rifle fire and the efforts of a Bavarian patrol which had advanced from the German trench to intercept them. Captain Gillett personally covered the retirement.

On the afternoon of the 24th September the 1/7th Middlesex, which had been resting a few days at Sailly-sur-La-Lys, moved forward to its position of assembly—the Rouge de Bout—and

25TH SEPT. remained there throughout the attack which took place at 4.30 a.m. the following morning. Despite the gallantry of the 25th Brigade, which carried the enemy's trenches in the first rush, the attacking Battalions had to fall back to their own trenches during the evening and the Divisional Reserve never came into action. A hundred men of the 7th Middlesex, who were sent forward to work under the Royal Engineers, two machine guns, which were brigaded close up to the trenches, and the Grenadier Platoon (also brigaded at Croix Blanche) were the only actions the Battalion was called upon to take and, in spite of heavy hostile shelling, including the advanced detachments, only three other ranks were

29TH SEPT. wounded. On the 29th the Battalion moved again into its old trenches at La Boutillerie.

1/8TH BATTALION.

2ND AUGUST.

August, 1915, will always remain notable in the history of the 1/8th Middlesex, for it was on the 2nd of that month that the Battalion once more assumed independent formation as a Territorial unit. Since its amalgamation with the 1/7th Battalion in June, considerable drafts of officers and men had arrived, until, at the end of July, the amalgamated Battalions had attained the unwieldy strength of 56 officers and 1,700 other ranks. The separation of the two Battalions was then sanctioned, and the story is told thus in the first entry (on the 2nd of the month) in the Diary of the 1/8th Middlesex for August, 1915: "The members of the 1/8th Middlesex, who had been absorbed into the 1/7th Battalion on 23rd June, paraded and were inspected by Lieut.-Colonel King, commanding 1/7th Battalion, prior to departure. In wishing the men farewell, the Colonel thanked them for the way they had behaved and treated the amalgamation, and wished them good luck in their new start in life. Captain Chipp replied on behalf of the 1/8th Middlesex, and the Battalion gave three cheers for Colonel King. The Battalion then marched off. North of the River Lys they were met by Major Gregory,* who was received with hearty demonstrations, and on arrival at their billets were

* Major E. D. W. Gregory was gazetted Lieutenant-Colonel on 12th June, 1915.

welcomed by a large draft which had arrived on 31st July from Gibraltar. In the afternoon the Battalion was arranged into its original companies and the draft allotted. Fourteen junior officers recently joined remained with the 1/7th Battalion to complete their course of instruction in the Officers' Class." 1/8TH BATTALION.

On the 5th August the 1/8th Middlesex had a strength of 26 officers and 728 other ranks, but for the remainder of the month the Battalion reorganised, trained, collected transport and re-equipped, furnishing working parties and sending officers and other ranks into the front-line trenches, who had not had previous experience of trench warfare, for instructional tours. On 30th of the month an 8th Divisional Routine Order stated that: "The 1/8th Battalion Middlesex Regiment will in future belong to the 25th Infantry Brigade." 30TH AUGUST.

A new C.O.—Lieut.-Colonel P. L. Ingpen (2nd West York Regiment)—assumed command of the Battalion on 2nd September. On the evening of 4th the 1/8th Middlesex again took over front-line trenches—the first sub-sector held since the Battalion separated from the 1/7th. Several tours in and out of the line took place before the actions of 25th September. During one of these tours (on 14th September), 2nd Lieut. J. J. de Salis was shot through the head as he was looking over the parapet.*

The night before the operations of 25th September the Battalion left billets at 7.45 p.m. and marched to bivouacs near Croix Blanche, having been detailed as Brigade Reserve in the attack to take place the following day. At 2 a.m. on the 25th, the Battalion left bivouacs and moved to positions of assembly, *i.e.*, two companies on the River de Layes and two companies at Battalion Headquarters in the 250-yards trench from Jay Post to Tin Barn Avenue. Four machine guns and 25 grenadiers under the Brigade Machine-gun Officer were placed in the 250-yards trench from Jay Post to City Road. These machine gunners and grenadiers were the only men of the Battalion who took an active part in the operations of the 25th, though two companies were used as carrying parties to take tools and water up to the captured German trenches, and at 10.30 a.m. the two remaining companies were moved up into the front-line trench from Well Farm to Brigade advanced Headquarters. At 4 p.m. the Battalion received orders to hold the original front-line trench from east of 25TH SEPT.

* Died of wounds, 3rd October, 1915.

25TH SEPT. Well Farm Salient–Chord Line to advanced Brigade Headquarters, but at 11.30 p.m. the 1/8th Middlesex was relieved by the Worcesters and marched back to reserve billets at Elbow Farm and Post.

Thus no attack had been made by the 1/8th Battalion, but all day long heavy shell fire swept the positions held, and the carrying parties worked only in the midst of considerable danger. When on the 26th, at 2.30 p.m., the Battalion moved back to billets at Sailly cross roads, 2 officers had been wounded, 6 other ranks killed, 15 wounded and 23 were missing; the latter were afterwards accounted for. The 1/8th were still in billets at the end of September.

## Actions of the Hohenzollern Redoubt.

### 13th–19th October, 1915.

11TH BATTALION. The "subsequent" actions of the Hohenzollern Redoubt concern the 11th Battalion of the Middlesex Regiment, which, in May, 1915, arrived in France as part of the 36th Infantry Brigade of the 12th Division—one of the First New Army Divisions.

The 11th Middlesex was the first Service Battalion of the Regiment raised. On 8th August, 1914, three officers and 12 N.C.Os. were sent from the 1st Middlesex (then at Woolwich) to the Depot at Mill Hill to form the nucleus of the new 11th Battalion. Three days later, three more officers and 12 N.C.Os. arrived at Mill Hill from the 4th Middlesex, then at Devonport, while several former warrant officers and N.C.Os. re-enlisted and were appointed to their old rank; amongst these were the R.S.M. and the R.Q.M.S.

In a week the whole Battalion was recruited and training was carried on continuously. About 22nd August the 11th proceeded by train to Colchester and there joined the 12th Division of "K.I." Major W. D. Ingle was appointed to command the Battalion, Lieut. L. L. Pargiter was the Adjutant, and Lieut. English the Quartermaster. Many old men and officers joined at Colchester, and the utmost enthusiasm prevailed throughout the whole Battalion.

With experienced officers and formed of the splendid fighting material which was forthcoming in August, 1914, and the early days of the War, the Battalion soon engaged in vigorous training.

In October the 36th Brigade proceeded by train to camp at St. Martin's Plain, Shorncliffe, moving in November into a "hutted" camp at Sandling. By the end of 1914 the 36th Brigade had made another move, this time to billets in Folkestone, Battalion Headquarters of the 11th Middlesex being at the Westcliff Hotel. 11TH BATTALION.

The 11th remained at Folkestone until February, 1915, when the Battalion, in Brigade and Division, proceeded by march route to Aldershot, there to undergo the final training before going abroad for active service. The march to Aldershot occupied five days, and was by way of Ashford, Maidstone, Edenbridge, Dorking and Guildford. Three months more of strenuous work, and at last, on the morning of the 31st May, the advanced party (consisting of 3 officers, 108 other ranks, and the Regimental Transport) entrained at Farnborough for Southampton, embarking at 4 p.m. for France. The same evening the Battalion, at a strength of 27 officers and 785 other ranks, left the Government Siding at Aldershot in two trains for Folkestone, embarking in the early hours of the 1st June on the *Princess Victoria*. At 3 a.m. the boat entered Boulogne Harbour. Disembarkation took place immediately, and by 4.30 a.m. the whole Battalion was settled in, in Ostrohove Large Camp, having marched from the harbour, a distance of two miles. From this camp the Battalion (now at full strength—30 officers and 893 other ranks) moved with other units of the 36th Brigade to the Blendecques area, the Middlesex being billeted at Concardennes. 31ST MAY.

At 7 a.m. on 5th June the 36th Brigade set out on a 15-mile march for the Hazebrouck area. Although hardened as they were by months of training in England and used to long route marches, this first march along the pavé roads of France was an extremely trying experience. The hard dusty cobbles, the heat of the day and the heavy pack carried full, were a great strain on the men, many of whom fell out, and it was a great relief to all ranks when bivouacs in the fields about a mile west of Hazebrouck were reached. At 6.25 a.m. on the following morning the march was continued to Borre Merris and Noote Boom, and, although the heat was again trying, the roads were better and few men fell out, the 11th Middlesex having three only. On 10th the units of the 36th Brigade marched to Armentières for attachment to Brigades of the 27th Division for instruction in trench warfare. The 11th Middlesex were fortunate in being allotted to the 19th Infantry Brigade, which at this period contained the 1st Battalion of the

11TH BATTALION.

Regiment, and at 9 p.m. parties of officers and N.C.Os. of the 11th marched into the trenches of the 1st Middlesex and 2nd Royal Welch Fusiliers for a twenty-four hours' tour. They were relieved at 9 p.m. on 11th by two companies of the Battalion, who, in turn, were relieved by the remaining two companies at 9 p.m. on 12th. During these tours three men of "B" Company were wounded on 11th, one of whom died of his wounds, and two men of "C" Company wounded were the first casualties suffered by the 11th Middlesex in the front-line trenches. These "period" tours lasted until the 15th, when the Battalion, after relief, marched to billets at School, Noote Boom, for several days' instruction out of the front line. On 25th, however, at 5 a.m. the Battalion (in Brigade) left Noote Boom, as the 12th Division had taken over a sector of the line, and the 36th Infantry Brigade had been allotted to the Ploegsteert Wood sub-sector. The 11th Middlesex had been detailed to relieve the 8th Worcesters, and at 8.30 a.m. reached the Wood, where the Battalion laid up all day until the evening. Rain had fallen heavily during the day, and when at 6 p.m. the relief began the "going" was difficult, the ground being sodden and muddy. Ploegsteert Wood at the best of times was not a very delectable spot, and after rain it was always in an appalling condition, so that it is not unusual to find an entry in the Battalion Diary stating that the trenches were "very muddy and dirty." Lieut.-Col. Ingle had his Headquarters at Ash House. But the tour lasted only until the night of 27th June, when the Middlesex men were relieved by Canadians and marched to billets at Oosthove Farm; the tour had cost the Battalion one man died of wounds, one wounded and one accidentally injured.

25TH JUNE.

The first six-day tour in the front line began on the night of 3rd–4th July, when the 11th Middlesex relieved the 9th Royal Fusiliers in Trenches 95 and 101, Battalion Headquarters being at Despierre Farm. Casualties during this tour were 6 other ranks killed and 15 wounded. The first officer casualty was also reported —Captain H. A. Hill being wounded on 8th.

It is of interest to read what the Battalion Diary records of this first prolonged tour in the front-line trenches, written after the Middlesex had been relieved by the 6th Buffs during the night 9th–10th June: "During the above tour of duty in trenches the Battalion obtained a marked superiority over Germans in trenches opposite. In all ten enemy snipers are known to have been hit, and two of their men on working parties and one of their stretcher-bearers. One of the above snipers, a red-haired man nicknamed 'Rudolf,' who had been very active for some months past, was shot by No. 5350 C.S.M. Bentley, 'C' Company. Another was shot by No. 233 Lance-Corporal Hazley, 'B' Company. All our casualties were caused by snipers and H.E. shell, of which the enemy made great use. Battalion Headquarters was shelled on 5th, but had no casualties. Good work was done by all ranks, and there was never any lack of volunteers for working parties in front of our lines, patrols, &c." 11TH BATTALION.

Thereafter tours in and out of the line occupied the Battalion for some weeks. During one of these, on 27th July, 2nd Lieut. H. G. Hawkins was shot in the head and died later in a Field Ambulance. He was the first officer of the 11th Middlesex to lose his life. On the 4th August (the Battalion was then in the Houplines sector) Capt. T. L. Mills was also shot in the head whilst looking over the parapet, and died the following day. 4TH AUGUST.

Demonstrations were carried out by the 11th Middlesex on 25th September, while the main operations at Loos were in progress, but there is nothing abnormal to record, and on 26th the Battalion was relieved and proceeded to billets near Armentières Station. 25TH SEPT.

On 27th the Battalion (in Brigade) marched to Bailleul, entraining at the latter place on 28th at 9 a.m. The 12th Division was now under orders for the Loos area, and the Middlesex men (in Brigade), having reached Chocques at 11.30 a.m., marched to La Vallée, continuing the march on 29th at 10 a.m. to Verquigneul, arriving at 3.30 p.m. On the morning of 30th September, at 10 a.m., Colonel Ingle and the Adjutant (Captain Pargiter) set out to inspect the trenches about Lone Tree, west-south-west of Hulluch, and at 4.30 p.m. the Battalion, marching *via* Vermelles, took over the line (the old German front line) from the 2nd Coldstream Guards, the 12th Division having orders to relieve the Guards Division; the relief was completed at 1 a.m. on 1st October, rain falling heavily during the time the Middlesex men were "taking over." The disposition of Companies was: "C" in the front line, "D" in support, then "B" Company, "A" Company and Battalion Headquarters in the old German fire trench. The exact position given in the Battalion Diary is "G.17.d. and north part of G.23.b. and G.24.a." 27TH SEPT.

It is apparent from the official records that the 11th Middlesex (as a whole) neither attacked the enemy, nor did the latter attack

11TH BATTALION. the Battalion during the Actions of the Hohenzollern Redoubt, 13th–19th October. Nevertheless the Middlesex men played an important part in the operations, for the bombers were always more or less engaged, and on several occasions with splendid tenacity and courage discomfited the enemy and beat him back to his own trenches, on one occasion, indeed, recapturing trenches which he had taken by a surprise attack from another Battalion. The casualties suffered by the Battalion for the month of October, viz., 3 officers wounded, 36 other ranks killed and 114 wounded, also show how it was possible for battalions to suffer heavy losses though not engaged in any direct attack.

The sector taken over by the 36th Infantry Brigade on the night 30th September–1st October lay due west of Hulluch and just south of the Hulluch road. The 12th Division had relieved the Guards Division. On the left of the 36th Brigade lay the Hohenzollern Redoubt, one of the most fiercely contested points in the whole line from Hill 70 to the La Bassèe Canal.

1ST OCTOBER. The morning of 1st October was comparatively quiet, but about 2 p.m. the enemy opened fire with H.E. and shrapnel, and shelled the trenches of the 11th Middlesex and both flanks incessantly until dusk. The fire then slackened off, but about 7.30 p.m. very heavy firing broke out on the left of the Battalion, apparently about the Hohenzollern. The 3rd and 4th October were days of considerable anxiety—heavy shelling characterised this period—though casualties were fortunately small there was little rest for those in the front line. On the night of 5th the London Scottish filed into the trenches, relieving "C" and "D" Companies of the Middlesex, the former moving back to the old British support trenches immediately north of Le Rutoire, while "D" Company

7TH OCTOBER. went back into the second line. On the 7th the 1st Division took over the front line from the 12th Division and the latter moved back into reserve. The 11th Middlesex were relieved by the 2nd Black Watch and marched back to bivouacs in the Château grounds at Vaudricourt, where in great discomfort the Battalion arrived about 1.30 a.m. on 8th and had to pass the remainder of the night in swampy woods. On the 12th the Battalion marched into houses and trenches on the southern side of Vermelles, everyone being settled in by 6 p.m. The operations known as the Actions of the Hohenzollern Redoubt were to begin on the following day.

In his despatch dated 31st July, 1916, Sir John French thus refers to the confused fighting which took place between 13th and 19th

October, 1915: "Up to the end of October the most important operation was an attack, which commenced about noon of the 13th, by troops of the XIth and IVth Corps against Fosse No. 8, the Quarries, and the German trenches on the Lens–La Bassée road. The Divisions chiefly engaged were the 1st Division (IVth Corps) and the 12th and 46th Divisions (XIth Corps). Speaking generally, the objective of the 1st Division was the enemy's trenches on the Lens–La Bassée road; that of the 12th Division was the Quarries; whilst the troops of the 46th Division attacked the Hohenzollern Redoubt and Fosse No. 8." 13TH OCTOBER.

Of the 12th Division, the 37th Brigade on the right and the 35th Brigade on the left were to attack the Quarries and secure a line beyond, the 36th Brigade was in reserve at Noyelles and Vermelles and therefore did not take part in the initial attack, which began at 12 noon under cover of a heavy artillery bombardment and a smoke screen. But from the regimental point of view the chief interest in the whole of the operations is centred in the action of the Battalion bombers of the 11th Middlesex, of whom a party of 50 men, under 2nd Lieut. Leach, were sent up to assist the 35th Infantry Brigade. Unfortunately none of the official diaries (Battalion, Brigade or Divisional) contain detailed narratives of the operations, and all that can be gathered from them is the fact that the gallant Middlesex men acquitted themselves splendidly, and that they were still fighting side by side with troops of the 35th Brigade when their own Brigade (36th) moved up to relieve the 37th Brigade in the front line on 14th October. The 11th Middlesex (less the bombers) took over the trenches of the 6th Royal West Kent and East Surreys, which, the Battalion Diary states, "extended from G.12.d. central (road exclusive) to G.12.a.54." The Battalion Diary also adds: "Staff arrangements for relief very poor; we were not told which units we were relieving, and had to find our own ration dump during night. No arrangements for water." Good staff work was rare during the whole of the operations at Loos in 1915; the absence of it was one of the most potent reasons that greater results were not obtained from the splendid efforts made by the troops of all divisions. 11TH BATTALION. 14TH OCTOBER.

The centre of the line taken over by the 11th Middlesex was still held by one company of the 8th Royal Fusiliers, whose bombers were of great value to the Middlesex, for, as stated by the latter: "Our own bombers not returned though asked for

11TH BATTALION.

urgently, as the middle of our line can be held only by bombers, about Point 22."*

15TH OCTOBER.

By 12.30 a.m. on the 15th the relief of the Royal Welch Fusiliers and East Surreys had been completed and the 11th Middlesex awaited the breaking of dawn, which was certain to witness a continuation of the struggle which had begun on the 13th. The sun had hardly risen when the Germans began to throw bombs at the Middlesex men, who could make no effective reply, owing to the Battalion bombers being still engaged at the Quarries. All day long the bombing continued, varied occasionally by violent bursts of shelling with H.E. and aerial torpedoes; in two places for a distance of 50 yards the parapet had been levelled. About 6 p.m., tired out and almost exhausted, the bombers at last returned. And what a story they had to tell! They had been engaged in continuous bombing operations at the south-east corner of the Quarries, where they practically held the line themselves. Six other ranks killed, 1 died of wounds, and 8 other ranks wounded were the losses of the 11th Battalion on this day.

16TH OCTOBER.

On the 16th the trenches again came in for a heavy shelling, and in many places the parapet was levelled; the men of "D" Company in particular had a most trying time, as their trenches appeared to be specially marked down by the enemy's guns, with the result that the defences were much knocked about. At night time, however, helped by a platoon of 5th Northamptons, the trenches were repaired.

On this day the Battalion bombers, having rested, took over Points 22 and 39 from the 8th Royal Fusilier Bombers. Casualties during the day were 1 officer (2nd Lieut. C. D. Brodie) wounded, 6 other ranks killed and 11 wounded.

The trenches were again shelled heavily on the 17th and the parapet was once more levelled. Continuous bomb fights day and night kept the bombers busy; they stuck to their grim work with extraordinary tenacity and flung their missiles with great effect.

18TH OCTOBER.

The 18th was a day of prolonged torture. From early morning the enemy's guns poured H.E. and shrapnel on to the trenches of the 11th Middlesex, "A" and "C" Companies having a particularly bad time. Men were blown up or buried in the debris, numbers of them suffering from concussion. Again the parapet

* No maps exist either in Battalion, Brigade or Divisional Diaries.

was levelled, though promptly repaired as soon as merciful darkness hid the men from the enemy's observers. To make matters worse, the British shells were bursting short over the position held by the Middlesex men. One officer (Captain H. G. Money) was wounded, 15 other ranks were killed, 1 died of wounds and 35 were wounded. 18TH OCTOBER. 11TH BATTALION.

At last, about 4 p.m. on 19th, a Battalion of Argyll and Sutherland Highlanders began to file into the trenches of the Middlesex men, but not before another officer (2nd Lieut. A. A. Allan) had been wounded, 1 other rank killed, and 14 more wounded from the enemy's shell fire.

In those early days of the War, reliefs of Battalions in the front line were not the carefully-organised operations they were during the latter years, and this particular relief took many hours to complete. For about 5.30 p.m. the enemy probably observing that a relief was in progress, attacked the Battalion on the left of the Middlesex, but was bloodily repulsed. During this attack the trenches of the Middlesex were heavily shelled, and everyone had to take cover. Moreover, the enemy's riflemen and machine gunners poured a constant stream of bullets on to the trenches of their opponents. About 7.30 p.m. the fire slackened sufficiently to allow the relief to proceed, but it was 12.30 a.m. on 20th before it was completed, and at that hour "A," "B," and "C" Companies of the 11th Middlesex were in reserve trenches in the old British front line, and "D" Company was in the old German front line in support. The Battalion bombers, still under 2nd Lieut. Leach, were moved up to "D" Company and fitted out with a fresh supply of bombs ready for instant action.

And here the action of the Hohenzollern Redoubt officially ends. But it is not the end of the story so far as the Middlesex Regiment is concerned, for before the Battalion was finally relieved on the 21st October and reached Noyelles, the Battalion bombers and "D" Company had again come into action and had greatly distinguished themselves.

21ST OCTOBER

On the night of 20th–21st October the enemy had made a surprise attack on the bombers of the 7th Royal Sussex Regiment, attached to 9th Essex Regiment (to which the 11th Middlesex were in support) and had captured a portion of their trenches about G. 5.d.9.0. At once Lieut. Leach took his bombers forward (the Battalion Diary stating that "our bombers went from trenches"), and finding the utmost confusion prevailing in the

21st October. 11th Battalion.

front line, took command and recaptured the lost position, killing many Germans and driving the remainder out in confusion. Captain Brown (commanding " D " Company) moved his Company up to the captured spot and supported Lieut. Leach in his attack, the former lining the parapet with his men as soon as the bombers were at work.

The C.O. of the 9th Essex Regiment wrote to the C.O. of the 11th Middlesex acknowledging the assistance lent by the latter Battalion, concluding his letter with these words : " I am awfully glad to be able to report so well, and am most grateful to you and the Middlesex Regiment for their help."

For the remainder of October the 11th Middlesex remained in billets in Fouquières, Noyelles and Sailly La Bourse.

Such, so far as the Middlesex Regiment is concerned, is the story of the main and subsidiary actions of the Battle of Loos, 1915, and the subsequent actions of the Hohenzollern Redoubt, and it is a record of which the Regiment has every reason to be proud, for Regular, Territorial and Service Battalions had fought most gallantly.

Map VII.

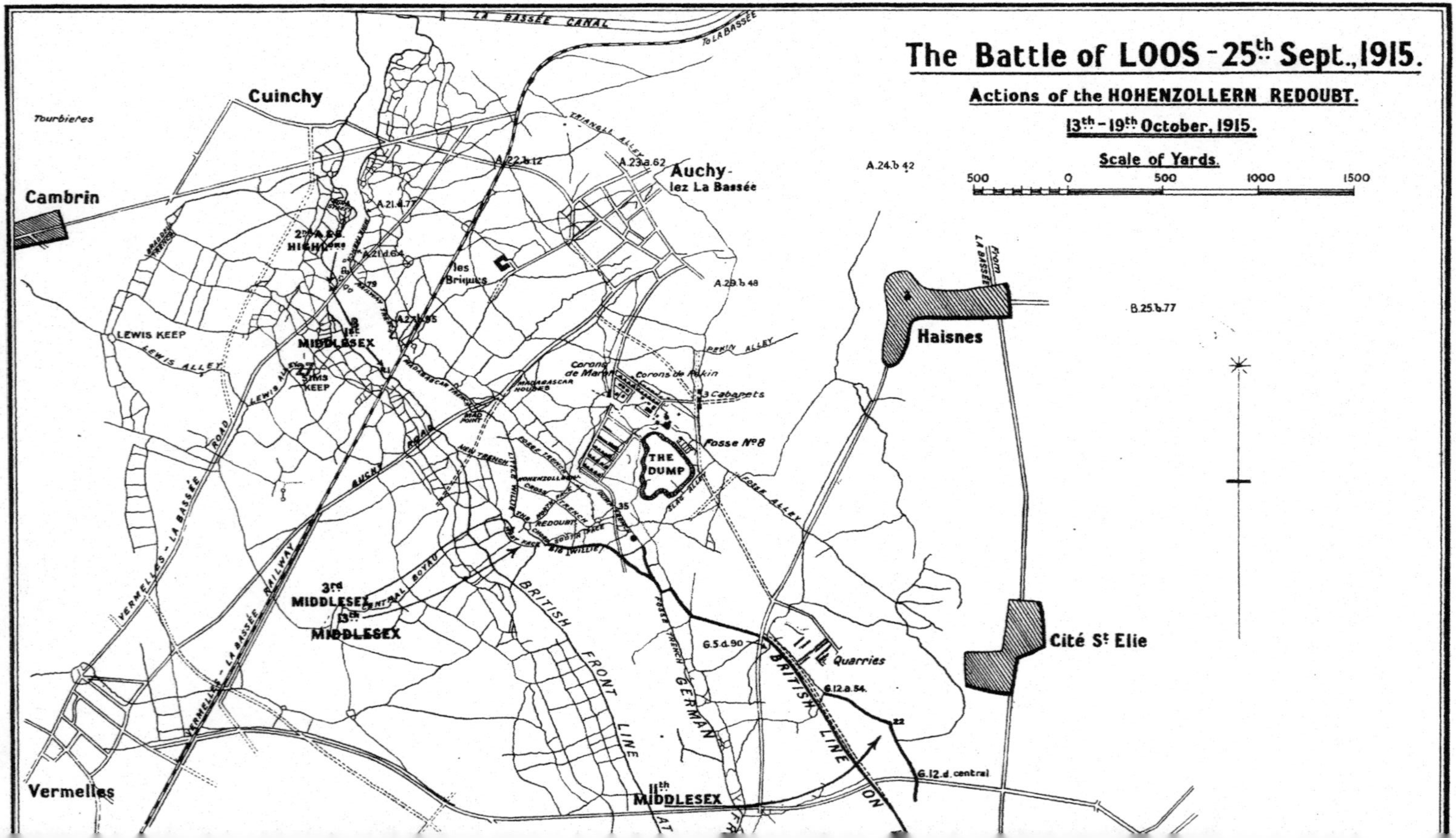

# The Battle of LOOS - 25th Sept., 1915.

## Actions of the HOHENZOLLERN REDOUBT.

13th - 19th October, 1915.

Scale of Yards.

500 0 500 1000 1500

LA BASSÉE CANAL
To LA BASSÉE
Cuinchy
Tourbieres
Cambrin
A.22.b.12
A.23.a.62
Auchy-
lez La Bassée
A.24.b 42
TRIANGLE ALLEY
A.21.d.77
2nd A.&S. HIGHLdrs
A.21.d.64
les Briques
A.29.b 48
From LA BASSÉE
Haisnes
B.25.b.77
A.27.b.55
LEWIS KEEP
1st MIDDLESEX
LEWIS ALLEY
SIMS KEEP
PEKIN ALLEY
Corons de Maron
Corons de Pekin
MADAGASCAR HOUSES
MADAGASCAR TRENCH
3 Cabarets
Fosse No 8
THE DUMP
NEW TRENCH
LITTLE WILLIE
HOHENZOLLERN
THE REDOUBT
SOUTH FACE
BIG WILLIE
35
FOSSE ALLEY
SLAG ALLEY
AUCHY ROAD
VERMELLES - LA BASSÉE ROAD
VERMELLES - LA BASSÉE RAILWAY
CENTRAL BOYAU
3rd MIDDLESEX
13th MIDDLESEX
BRITISH FRONT LINE
FOSSE TRENCH
GERMAN
G.5.d.90
Quarries
G.12.a.54.
BRITISH LINE ON
22
G.12.d. central
Cité St Elie
Vermelles
11th MIDDLESEX

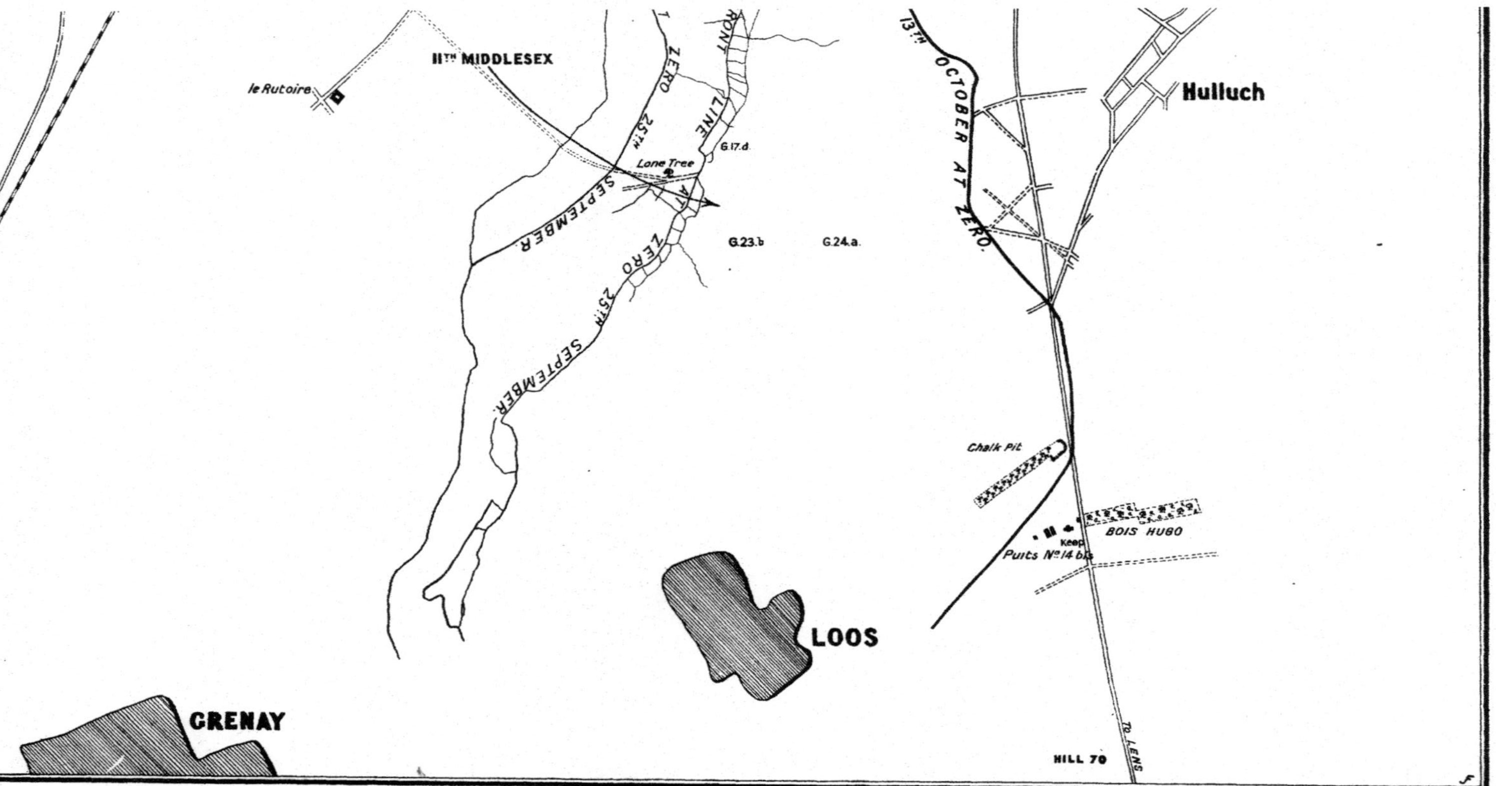

11TH MIDDLESEX
le Rutoire
Hulluch
13TH OCTOBER AT ZERO.
ZERO 25TH SEPTEMBER.
LINE AT ZERO 25TH SEPTEMBER.
G.17.d.
Lone Tree
G.23.b
G.24.a.
Chalk Pit
Keep
BOIS HUGO
Puits No. 14 bis
LOOS
GRENAY
HILL 70
To LENS


[To face p. 18].

## CHAPTER XX.

# THE DARDANELLES CAMPAIGN.

## THE BATTLES OF SUVLA.

### 6th–21st August, 1915.

FROM the blood-soaked battlefield of Loos and the subsidiary actions thereto, the story of the Middlesex Regiment turns back to that epic of the War—the Gallipoli Campaign—where on the sandy shore of Suvla Bay, the 2/10th (Lieut.-Colonel C. H. Pank) Battalion had landed about midnight on 8th August. 2/10TH BATTALION.

About Christmas, 1914, Lieut.-Colonel Johnson had been obliged, for medical reasons, to relinquish command of the 2/10th Battalion, and for several weeks Major Jarrett was in charge until Major Pank, of the 7th Middlesex, who was to succeed Colonel Johnson, could be brought back from Gibraltar, where at that time the 7th Battalion was quartered.

The winter of 1914–1915 was devoted to hard training, and, at last, in April, welcome orders reached the 2/10th that the Battalion had been selected for service overseas. Orders were next received to join a Brigade then being formed of troops from a Second Line Home Counties Division; this Brigade (subsequently the 160th) joined a Welch Division (afterwards the 53rd). At the end of April the 2/10th Middlesex left Ashford and joined its new formation at Cambridge; the Battalion was brigaded with 2/4th Royal West Surrey Regiment, 2/4th Royal West Kent Regiment, and 1/4th Royal West Sussex Regiment. As soon as the 53rd Division was complete it moved to Bedford, and training was continued for nearly two months.

Early in July the 53rd Division was ordered to equip for tropical service. On a miserably wet night—the 17th/18th July—the 2/10th Middlesex (in Brigade) entrained for Devonport, and the Middlesex men, with the 5th Welch Regiment, embarked

18TH JULY. 2/10TH BATTALION. on the morning of 18th on the *Huntsgreen*, sailing later for an "unknown destination." On 1st August, after an uneventful voyage, the transport reached Alexandria, where for the first time the troops began to suspect their destination. On the 3rd August the Battalion reached Port Said, and, after a conference held aboard the vessel containing the G.O.C. Division, word went round that the 53rd was to take part in operations at Suvla Bay, on the northern coast of the Gallipoli Peninsula. Other Divisions were already on the way. On the 7th the 2/10th arrived
8TH AUGUST. off the Island of Lemnos, and on the 8th at Imbros, by which time the die had been cast and the landing at Suvla had already begun.

Without going into all the details of the plan of operations carefully worked out by General Sir Ian Hamilton (the Commander-in-Chief, Mediterranean Expeditionary Force) and his Staff, it may be said that the scheme provided for a vigorous offensive from Anzac combined with a surprise landing to the north of it, *i.e.*, Suvla Bay. The intention was to try and win through to Maidos, leaving behind a well-protected line of communication starting from the bay at Suvla. More clearly defined, the official despatches give Sir Ian's intentions in the following words :—

"(i) To break out with a rush from Anzac and cut off the bulk of the Turkish Army from land communication with Constantinople.

(ii) To gain such a command for my artillery as to cut off the bulk of the Turkish Army from sea traffic, whether with Constantinople or with Asia.

(iii) Incidentally, to secure Suvla Bay as a winter base for Anzac and all troops operating in the northern theatre."*

The night of the 6th August had been selected for the landing at Suvla, after attacks had been begun during the afternoon of the same date from Anzac and Helles. Throughout the 7th and 8th the battle waged fiercely, but the Turkish resistance was hardening, especially at Suvla, where the enemy's reinforcements were arriving in considerable numbers, and although his troops had been driven off the beaches they were contesting vigorously the possession of the heights above the sandy stretches which sloped down to the

* Sir Ian Hamilton's despatch, dated 11th December, 1915, should be read in conjunction with this Chapter.

waters of the Bay. Such was the position of affairs when the vessels carrying the 53rd Division steamed into the Bay at midnight on 8th August.

" During the night of the 8th-9th and early morning of the 9th," stated Sir Ian Hamilton in his despatches, " the whole of the 53rd (Territorial) Division (my general reserve) had arrived and disembarked. I had ordered it up to Suvla, hoping that by adding its strength to the IXth Corps, General Stopford (the Corps Commander) might still be enabled to secure the commanding ground round the Bay. The infantry brigades of the 53rd Division (no artillery had accompanied it from England) reinforced the 11th Division." 8TH—9TH AUG. 2/10TH BATTALION.

As the vessels carrying the 53rd Division dropped anchor in Suvla Bay motor lighters drew up alongside and the troops were quickly transferred to them—500 men being packed in each lighter. The night was perfect, a glorious moon shone down on the waters of the Bay, the sea was dead calm. In silence the lighters neared the shore and soon the troops were tumbling out on to the beach. The 2/10th Middlesex, with other units of the 160th Brigade, had been ordered to land on " C " Beach, from which the Turks had already been driven.

Without mishap the Middlesex men landed, at about 2 a.m., and awaited the coming of dawn. They sat or lay about the beach, with the grim silence of the hills above them, broken occasionally by the sharp crack of a rifle. Few knew what was happening in the front line, then about 1,000 yards away. There was to be another attack by the 11th Division at dawn * in a final attempt to gain possession of the heights above the Bay, but success was doubtful. It was known that the Turkish reinforcements were moving up rapidly, and at any moment might sweep down from the hills in a desperate effort to drive the invaders back into the sea. For beyond a small advance " by a part of the 11th Division between the Chocolate Hill and Ismail Oglu Tepe, and some further progress along the Kiretch Tepe Sirt ridge by the 10th Division, the day of the 8th had been lost." 9TH AUGUST.

With the breaking of dawn came the rattle of musketry and the boom of guns: the attack had begun. The 2/10th Middlesex

* On the night of 8th, under the impression that the troops of the 32nd Infantry Brigade (11th Division) were concentrated, Sir Ian Hamilton had ordered another attack to be made at the " earliest possible moment," but on further investigation it was found that the units of the 32nd Brigade were scattered and the attack could not be made until 4 a.m. on 9th.

9TH AUGUST. 2/10TH BATTALION.

were not, however, destined to take part in the operations of that day. The Battalion had been detailed for the unloading of stores and ammunition, and also for the pumping of water from barge tanks into canvas troughs on the beach. The beach was in full view of the Turks and their guns searched the whole area where the Middlesex men were working—a trying experience for raw troops under fire for the first time. Apparently the Battalion suffered its first casualties on this day, for although there is no mention of losses in the Battalion Diary, Major C. Jarrett, writing in The Die-Hards for August, 1922, stated that "the casualties were not heavy."

All day long, shelled heavily, the 2/10th carried on their work, exasperated at being fired at though unable to fire a shot in reply. Rumours drifted back from the firing line and information was gathered from wounded men that the advance was hung up a few thousand yards away. At last night fell, mercifully shielding the men on the beach from the enemy's artillery observers: the Middlesex then moved to the western slopes of Lala Baba.

When darkness had fallen the 2/10th were ordered to join the 158th Brigade (53rd Division) in an attempt to drive home an attack on Chocolate Hill (or Yilghin Burnu) on the morning of 10th.

The following Operation Order, issued from 53rd Divisional Headquarters at 11 p.m. on the night of 9th, not only gives the position as then known, but also outlines the orders given to the 2/10th Middlesex for the attack which was to take place on 10th:

"(i) The 11th and 53rd Divisions are holding the line Yilghin Burnu–Hill 50–*I* of Sulaj*i*k-last *A* of Anafart*a* Ova. The 10th Division holds the line Bench Mark 200 on Kiretch Tepe Sirt—about Sq. 135 Y.6—about Sq. 118 a.7.

(ii) Enemy have shown strength on ridges Ismail Oglu Tepe–Anafarta Sagir, and have opposed steadily 10th Division advance to-day.

(iii) The 158th Brigade,* with the addition of 10th (2/10th) Middlesex from the 160th Brigade, and the 159th Brigade will carry out an attack to-morrow against the

* The 158th Brigade was less one Battalion—the 2/10th Middlesex was ordered to join the Brigade in place of it.

ridge from the points where the road cuts contour 100 about 105 P.5 to the point where the road cuts contour 100 about 106 G. half-way between points 3 and 6. The 159th Brigade will commence the attack at 6 a.m. and advance from Sulajik with its left to the south of the Kanli Keupru Dere, and its right on the track through 105 I.3 to 105 J.8, its first objective is the line 105 I.3–Knoll at 105 D.8–first *E* of Kanli Keupru Dere. After making good this position it will act as reserve to the 158th Brigade which will pass through it, and attack the ridge from 105 P.5 to 106 G.,* half-way between points 3 and 6. All troops must keep south of the Kanli Keupru Dere which will be shelled by our artillery." 9TH AUGUST. 2/10TH BATTALION.

Dawn was breaking on 10th when the 2/10th Middlesex joined the 158th Brigade at about 4 a.m. The attack was to begin at 6 o'clock. 10TH AUGUST.

The 159th Brigade, which had been detailed to capture the first objective, had been fighting hard the whole of the previous day, and at nightfall its units were much scattered, and the work of collecting and reorganising the Battalions went on through the night. By the morning of 10th, however, all battalions but one (7th Cheshire Regiment, a large part of which had not rejoined the Brigade) had been assembled in their jumping-off positions ready for Zero hour.

At 6 a.m. the guns of the 11th Division and aboard the naval boats off Suvla opened fire on the Turkish position and the advance began.

The country over which the troops were advancing was flat, covered with scrub, trees and hedges, but afforded little cover. There were few landmarks, and in the absence of previous reconnaissance and from the poor nature of the maps supplied, it was extremely difficult if not impossible for Battalion Commanders to locate their exact positions or those of the enemy. Roughly, the objectives of the attack lay between Scimitar Hill on the right and Baka Baba on the left, the jumping-off line of the 159th Brigade being about Sulajik.

From the meagre reports concerning the actions of the 2/10th Middlesex it is impossible to give an adequate idea of the part

* The Brigade O.O. says "105 G.," but 106 G. is obviously meant.

10TH AUGUST. 2/10TH BATTALION.

taken in the operations by the Battalion. The Battalion Diary describes the happenings of the 10th August in the following brief words: "Battalion took part in an advance on Salt Lake in an easterly direction, being the reserve Battalion in the Brigade (158th). During progress across Salt Lake came under shrapnel fire. Men absolutely steady. Came into action later in the day and held a line of trenches until the afternoon of Wednesday 11th, when the Battalion was allotted another part of the line." It will be seen that no casualties are mentioned.

Writing in the Die-Hards' Journal of August and November, 1922, however, Major C. Jarrett thus describes the action of the 2/10th Middlesex:—

"Accordingly at dawn on the 10th August, we advanced across the intervening plain. This was named on the map 'Salt Lake,' but at this time of the year it was a dry plain with marshy edges. We ploughed across the stinking mud on to the hard bed of the lake, and for the next thousand yards of the advance there was no scrap of cover. The shelling was terrific, and towards the far side of the plain the Battalion came into the zone of machine-gun and rifle fire. Once among the foothills there was more chance of cover in the scrub, but the advance was much hampered by the volume of fire. Advancing up the slopes of Chocolate Hill the various Companies got out of touch and near the top they became merged into a firing line made up of many units. Thenceforward anything like control by Battalion Commanders was out of the question. The hill was already a shambles, and, to add to the distress of the troops, the want of water became a very serious matter. The heat was awful, and the men had used the water they carried in their bottles and no more was to be had yet."

"The firing line was quite unable to push on. Isolated attempts were bravely made by officers to lead on parties of their men, but all were doomed to failure, and night came down without any progress being possible."*

"Perhaps the most terrible incident that evening was the fire which started in the dry bush. Many wounded men were unable to get away from the flames and their moans were heart-rending. Superhuman efforts were made to rescue some of them,

* This is a little misleading. The Brigade Narrative states that "By about noon the attack had almost succeeded in taking the first objective."

and foremost in this work was our Medical Officer, Major Paull, and his orderlies. 10TH AUGUST. 2/10TH BATTALION.

"Meanwhile the Turks were doing their utmost to drive us off the position, but they, too, were beaten to a standstill, and so the two forces were in a state of stale-mate. The order came from the Corps Commander that we were to dig in on the line held and prepare for trench warfare. It was a bitter disappointment to us all, but it seemed to be the only alternative to being driven off the Peninsula.

"The Battalion was so dispersed in the line that it was impossible to ascertain the casualties that night, but we knew that Captains E. W. Britten and M. J. A. Foley and Lieuts. Pope and J. G. Hollingsworth had been killed; also that Lieuts. Snowden and Reid Todd had been badly wounded.

"All that night the men did their best with their entrenching implements to scratch some sort of cover, for no picks or shovels had come up to the line yet. During the night our tireless Quartermaster Wallis had been toiling to bring us up food and water. He had gallantly attempted this several times during the day, but it had been impossible to bring his mules across the deadly Salt Lake.

"The next day, the 11th August, having collected the Companies more or less during the night, the Battalion was ordered to take over another sector of the line a few hundred yards to the left of our first position, and this was done by noon under great difficulties, and from then on till the late night of the 13th/14th we dug ourselves in, suffering many more casualties,* but keeping the line intact. That night we were relieved by the 2/4th Battalion Royal West Kent Regiment, and went back to Beach 'A' for duty, unloading lighters, &c. Here we were reinforced by the party which had been left behind at Alexandria, and we had a very trying period on this work till the 4th September." 11TH AUGUST. 4TH SEPT.

From the 14th to the 31st August the Battalion Diary has only the following entry: "Employed on beach duty 'A' Beach. Continually shelled during day."

Thereafter there is little of interest in the Diaries of the 2/10th Battalion until December, when the evacuation of Gallipoli and Suvla began: the story of the Middlesex next turns to Egypt.

* It is impossible to obtain any figures as to the numbers.

Map VIII.

GULF
OF
SAROS
KIRETCH TEPE SIRT
Anafarta Ova
Beach A
SUVLA
BAY
Salt Lake
Lala Baba
Nibrunesi Point
2/10th Middlesex Regt
Beach C
Sand hills
Beach B
Yilghin Burnu
CHOCOLATE HILL
2/10th Middlesex Regt.
SCIMITAR HILL
Sulajik
Baka Baba
Anafarta Sagir
TEKKE TEPE
HILL
Ismail Oglu Tepe
THE DARDANELLES CAMPAIGN.
The Battle of SUVLA.
6th - 21st August, 1915.
Scale of Yards.
1000
500
0
1000
2000

[*To face p.* 190.

# CHAPTER XXI.

## Western Egypt:

## Operations against the Senussi.*

VERY few regiments of the British Army saw service in as many theatres of war from 1914 to 1919 as did the Middlesex. In 1914 and 1915 in Flanders and France and Gallipoli, battalions of the regiment had already crossed bayonets with the enemy, and the story now turns to Western Egypt, where, at the close of 1915, the 2/7th and 2/8th Battalions first became involved in operations against the Senussi. The beginning of the rupture between Great Britain and the Senussi—a powerful desert tribe—is thus described in the official despatches: "As early as May, 1915, signs were apparent that the steadily increasing pressure brought to bear upon the Senussi by the Turkish party in Tripoli, under the leadership of Nuri Bey, a half-brother of Enver Pasha, was beginning to take effect. For some time, even after the outbreak of hostilities between Great Britain and Turkey in 1914, the anti-British influence of this party was not strongly felt and the attitude of the Senussi towards Egypt remained friendly. It was not until the advent of Gaafer, a Germanised Turk of considerable ability, who arrived in Tripoli in April, 1915, with a considerable supply of arms and money, that this attitude underwent a change."

**2/7TH—2/8TH BATTALIONS.**

For several months it was evident that the Turkish influence was gaining ground, and on the 16th August, 1915, the first hostile incident of any importance occurred. Two British submarines, sheltering from the weather near Ras Lick on the coast of Cyrenaica, were treacherously fired on by Arabs, commanded by a white officer, and casualties were suffered on both sides. For this incident, however, the Senussi apologised profusely, but in

**16TH AUGUST.**

* The term used in the official despatches, but more correctly "THE SENNUSIA" as "THE SENUSSI" means the head of the tribe, who at the time of these operations was AHMED ES SHERIF ES SENUSSI.

November, other incidents occurred which placed beyond doubt the hostile intentions of this Arab tribe. The crews of two British boats, H.M.S. *Tara* and H.M.T. *Moorina*—torpedoed by enemy submarines on the 5th and 6th of the month—landed in Cyrenaica and were captured and held prisoners by the Senussi, who, in reply to strong representations for their immediate release, feigned ignorance. On the night of the 14th–15th, Muhafizia (Senussi regulars) rushed two Egyptian sentries at Sollum and carried off their rifles and bayonets: the following night the company at Sollum was sniped. Again on the 17th, at Sidi Barrani (fifty miles east of Sollum), the Zawia was occupied by some three hundred Muhafizia, and on the 18th, during the night, the Coastguard Barracks at that place were twice attacked, one coastguard being killed. On the 20th a similar attack was made on a coastguard outpost at Sabil, a small post about thirty miles S.E. of Sollum, though, as at Barrani, the attack failed.

There was now no alternative but to recognise a state of war and to take action accordingly. The Western Frontier posts were ordered to withdraw to Mersa Matruh, and it was decided to concentrate in the latter place a force sufficient to deal swiftly with the situation. The Alexandria–Dabaa Railway was to be secured as a secondary line of communication by land with the railhead at Dabaa: the Wadi Natrun and the Fayum were to be occupied as measures of precaution, while the Oasis of Moghara was to be kept under constant observation and reconnaissance.

Orders for the assembly of two composite brigades (one mounted and the other infantry) were issued on the 20th November, after news had been received of the enemy's attack at Barrani. The Mounted Brigade consisted chiefly of Yeomanry and Australian Light Horse, with a battery of horse artillery. The infantry brigade was made up of 1/6th Royal Scots (T.F.), 1/7th and 2/8th Battalions Middlesex Regiment (T.F.), 15th Sikhs, and some auxiliary troops. The whole force was commanded by Major-General A. Wallace, and the Infantry Brigade by Brigadier-General the Earl of Lucan.

Both the 2/7th and 2/8th Middlesex had disembarked at Alexandria from Gibraltar on the 1st September.

**2/7th Battalion.**

A year had passed since the formation of the 2/7th Middlesex was authorised by the War Office, and during that period the Battalion had passed through varied experiences. After several busy weeks spent in recruiting the men and preliminary training, the 2/7th had left Hornsey on the 24th September, 1914, for Barnet, where officers and men were billeted. On the last day of the month the first consignment of uniforms was received and, by the end of October, the whole unit was in service dress. Another move, this time to Egham, took place on the 20th November, the Battalion joining the Middlesex Brigade of the Home Counties Division. In Windsor Great Park hard training was continued, though as only fifty rifles were in possession of the Battalion, instruction in musketry presented the greatest difficulties. " All through these weeks of hard work," said Lieut.-Colonel J. S. Drew, who commanded the 2/7th, " the discipline and soldierly spirit of the Battalion steadily improved." On the 27th January, 1915, orders were received to embark for Gibraltar at an early date. " This was a great shock, for high hopes had been entertained that the Battalion would be sent to France." However, the Battalion swallowed its disappointment and, on the 1st February, entrained for Southampton, embarking on arrival at the docks aboard the *Grantully Castle*, being joined later in the day by the 2/8th Middlesex, who were also bound for " Gib."

2/7TH BATTALION

27TH JAN.

After a rough voyage lasting several days, the two Battalions reached Gibraltar on the 7th February, though they did not disembark until the following day. On the way up the Rock the 2/7th met the 1/7th marching down to embark for France. This was the only occasion on which the two Battalions met throughout the whole course of the War.

For the next six months the Battalion continued its training, especially in musketry, for which special facilities were available. On the 3rd July orders were received to send a draft of 3 officers and 260 other ranks to the 1/7th Battalion in France. Their departure was a heavy blow to the Battalion, which, by this time, had attained a high degree of efficiency. The draft, however, was replaced the same day by the arrival of a similar number of men from England.

On the 12th August the Battalion was ordered to prepare for Egypt, and, with the 2/8th Middlesex, embarked on H.M.T. *Minnewaska*. Out at sea the destination of the ship was changed, and a few days later the vessel steamed into Mudros Harbour, the greatest excitement prevailing on board, as everyone expected to land on the Gallipoli Peninsula. At Mudros, however, it was made evident that the move to that Island was due to a Staff misunderstanding, and that the proper destination of the

12TH AUGUST.

2/7TH—2/8TH BATTALIONS.

2/7TH BATTALION. vessel was Alexandria. So, again choking down their disappointment, the Middlesex men saw their hopes of immediate active service dashed, and the boat put out to sea once more, for Egypt. Alexandria was reached on the 31st August, and on the following day the Battalion disembarked and entrained for Cairo, taking over the Citadel from Australian troops, a strong detachment of the Middlesex being sent off to guard prisoners of war at Maadi.

Ten pleasant weeks were spent at Cairo, and then, early in November, there were rumours of trouble brewing with the Senussi tribes of Western Egypt. (20TH NOV.) On the 20th November the Composite Cavalry and Infantry Brigades were formed, and on the 22nd the 2/7th Middlesex was ordered to join the latter Brigade at once at Alexandria. The Brigade went into camp at Qamaria and refitted.

With the exception of its formation the history of the 2/8th Middlesex is largely that of the 2/7th Battalion.

2/8TH BATTALION. 14TH SEPT. The 2/8th Middlesex was formed at Hampton Court on the 14th September, 1914, its first C.O. being Lieut.-Colonel L. C. Dams. The Battalion was quartered in the Cavalry Barracks, Hampton Court, Hampton Court House, and other houses in the neighbourhood. Training was carried out in Bushey Park, though no uniforms or rifles were then available. On the 15th November, 1914, the Battalion moved to Staines, becoming (like the 2/7th Battalion) part of the Middlesex Brigade of the Home Counties Division. From this period onwards there is little in the early history of the 2/8th which differs from that of the 2/7th, though on the day of the departure of the two Battalions from Southampton, great was the excitement aboard the *Grantully Castle* when, at the last moment, a draft of three officers and a small number of men joined the 2/8th: the men wore scarlet tunics! Like the 2/7th, the 2/8th also sent a large draft of officers and men to France, but to the 1/8th Battalion. When the Battalion left Gibraltar and arrived at Alexandria on the 31st August, the 2/8th was likewise quartered in Cairo, moving back to Alexandria on the 22nd November to join the Composite Infantry Brigade.

23RD NOV. 2/7TH—2/8TH BATTALIONS. By the 23rd November the concentration of the Force under General Wallace was completed, and the troops began to move to Mersa Matruh. It was not, however, until several days later that the two Middlesex Battalions received their orders. The 2/8th* was the first to leave Alexandria, the Battalion embarking

* There are no Diaries of the 2/8th Battalion in existence.

on trawlers—two platoons per trawler—for Mersa Matruh on 4TH DEC. the 4th December. The trawlers reached their destination on the 5th, and the Middlesex men were landed and pitched camp close to the village. On the 6th December Battalion Headquarters and " A " and " B " Companies of the 2/7th Middlesex embarked on trawlers and aboard H.M.S. '*Clematis*' for Mersa Matruh, " C " and " D " Companies remaining at Alexandria.

Concentration of the Force at Matruh was completed on the 7th December, and the village was prepared as a fortified base 7TH DEC. from which the Senussi could be attacked.

With the 2/8th, the 2/7th Middlesex was allotted a sector of the defences, and at once began digging operations. An insufficient supply of water was only one of the many difficulties. Wells were dug in the beach, but only brackish water was obtainable, and this had to be drunk in the form of tea: even then it was most unpleasant.

The first encounter with the Senussi took place on the 11th December, but neither of the Middlesex Battalions were 11TH DEC. engaged in the operations, which were carried out by other troops.

At midnight on the 14th December, Colonel Dams was 14TH DEC. ordered to take his Battalion out to Old Matruh to assist the 15th Sikhs and 6th Royal Scots (under Colonel Gordon), who had gone out in the morning and had been heavily engaged with the enemy. After marching through the night, the 2/8th Middlesex, at dawn, took up a defensive position, through 2/8TH BATTALION. which Colonel Gordon's force retired. Colonel Dams then threw forward two companies of his Battalion on the flank of the retiring column and engaged the enemy, H.M.S. '*Clematis*' firing her 6-inch guns over the heads of the Middlesex men into the enemy, who were massed in the hills on the Battalion's flank. The 2/8th finally formed a rearguard to the force retiring, until the latter reached camp at Matruh. "The whole thing," said Colonel Dams, "worked like an Aldershot field-day—the Battalion carried out the various movements with drill-book precision."

For the first fortnight the 2/7th Middlesex, without seeing 2/7TH BATTALION. anything of the fighting, had a strenuous existence. Three times the line of defence was changed, each change necessitating the digging and wiring of several miles of trenches; many stone sangars were also constructed.

18/19TH DEC. On the night of the 18th–19th December the camps of both Battalions, which occupied somewhat exposed positions, were heavily sniped by the Senussi. An advanced post of the 2/7th was also attacked, but beat off its assailants without difficulty. This was the first occasion on which the 2/7th and 2/8th Middlesex during the War came under rifle fire from the enemy.

2/7TH—2/8TH BATTALIONS.

2/8TH BATTALION. The 2/8th Battalion each night mounted picquets round the camp, most of the picquets being situated on a line of hills running parallel with the sea and about half a mile from it. During the night of the 19th December a detached picquet (known as Pinnacle Picquet) was sniped by a small body of Senussi. The Middlesex men returned the fire, but so far as could be seen no casualties were inflicted on the enemy.

From the 15th to the 23rd December no operation of importance was undertaken against the enemy, but in the meantime it was known that he was concentrating in the neighbourhood of Gebel Medwa, about eight miles south-west of Matruh, his forces being estimated at about 5,000, with four guns and some machine guns, commanded by Gaafer.

25TH DEC. On the 25th December (Xmas Day) General Wallace attacked these forces. He divided his Command into two columns—the Right and the Left. The former consisted mostly of infantry, which included the 2/8th Middlesex; the latter column was a mobile force of cavalry.

Before dawn on the 25th both columns left camp, and by 7.30 a.m. the cavalry had cleared the Wadi Toweiwa, about seven miles south of Matruh. The Right Column moved westwards, and at 6.30 a.m. the advanced guard came under fire from artillery and machine guns from the south-west. But the enemy was soon driven off, and by 7.15 a.m. the main body of General Wallace's Force had crossed the Wadi Raml, and could see the enemy in occupation of an encampment about a mile south of Gebel Medwa.

At 7.30 a.m. the 15th Sikhs were ordered to attack the enemy's right flank, the Bucks Hussars and 2/8th Middlesex to co-operate by making a containing attack along his front, to be launched simultaneously with the attack of the Sikhs. Deploying west of the road and despatching one Company to occupy Gebel Medwa in order to secure their right, the Sikhs advanced. At the same time the Bucks Hussars moved forward, while the Middlesex, keeping to the north-east of Gebel Medwa, sent a Company to

relieve a company of 15th Sikhs occupying the hill, which thereupon 25TH DEC.
rejoined the Battalion. This Company of Middlesex men was apparently the only one of the Battalion which saw fighting on the 25th December, the action being thus described by an officer* then serving with the Battalion: "The whole Battalion took part in a big attack on enemy forces about seven or eight miles inland from the camp. A start was made before dawn on Xmas Day, and the fighting lasted all day. The Battalion bivouacked that night in the desert, and returned to camp the following morning. Only one Company ('C' Company, under Captain Alliston) actually found themselves in the front line of the attack, and suffered casualties (three men wounded). The attack was a great success, and a considerable number of the enemy was killed or captured."

The attack by the Sikhs was successfully carried out, and by 2.15 p.m. the nullahs at the head of the Wadi Majid had been cleared, and by about 4 p.m. the Wadi itself was taken. The enemy's losses were over 100 dead, 34 prisoners, 80 camels and much livestock, also 30,000 rounds of S.A.A. and a quantity of artillery ammunition.

In this action the 2/7th Middlesex took no part, but from the 2/7TH
28th to 30th December the Battalion formed part of a mobile BATTALION.
column intended to attack a Senussi camp some twenty miles distant, at Jerawla. On the approach of the column the enemy forsook his camp and fled, leaving behind large quantities of grain, nearly 100 camels and about 500 sheep. The camp was burned, and on the 30th the column returned to Matruh.

This affair carries the narrative of operations in Western Egypt 31ST DEC.
up to the end of 1915.

* Captain Palmer, 2/8th Middlesex R.

# CHAPTER XXII.

## The Second Winter in the Trenches.

## Trench Warfare to the Battles of the Somme, 1916.

### I.—To the End of 1915.

BETWEEN the actions of the Hohenzollern Redoubt, which officially ended on the 19th October, 1915, and the Somme Battles 1916, which began on the 1st July of that year, no Battalion of the Middlesex Regiment in France or Flanders was involved in any attack of sufficient importance to be claimed as a Battle Honour. And yet the struggle was never-ceasing. By day and by night, trench warfare, with all its beastliness and ghastliness, went on, through the mud and filth of winter, to the coming of Spring and the early days of Summer. Nine months, so far as the Middlesex Regiment was concerned—nine months of watching and waiting and preparation, during which the sniper's bullet or the enemy's shells took toll of the gallant fellows who through every imaginable agony and horror maintained the line, dealing blow for blow, taking life for a life. That extraordinary period of minor activity is aptly described in Sir Douglas Haig's first despatch after he had taken over command of the British Forces in France and Flanders from Sir John French.

" Artillery and snipers," said the Commander-in-Chief, " are practically never silent, patrols are out in front of the lines every night, and heavy bombardments by the artillery of one or both sides takes place daily in various parts of the line. Below ground there is continual mining and counter-mining, which by the ever-present threat of sudden explosions and the uncertainty as to when and where it will take place, causes perhaps a more constant strain than any other form of warfare. In the air there is seldom a day, however bad the weather, when aircraft are not busy reconnoitring, photographing and observing fire. All this is taking place constantly at every hour of the day or night and in every part of the line."

By the time the fierce and bloody struggle for the possession of the Hohenzollern Redoubt in the middle of October had quieted down there were in France and Flanders no less than nine Battalions of the Middlesex Regiment, *i.e.*, 1st, 2nd, 3rd, 4th, 7th, 8th, 11th, 12th and 13th; three more Battalions—16th, 17th and 18th—were under orders to leave England, landing in France during November, whilst before the Somme Battles opened the 19th, 20th, 21st and 23rd Battalions had also arrived on the Western Front.

1ST BATTALION. The first concern of the 1st Middlesex (19th Infantry Brigade, 2nd Division) on coming out of the line after the Battle of Loos was to regain its strength, for (as already stated) the Battalion had lost no less than 17 officers and 455 other ranks during the operations. Wet and tired, but cheerful, with that wonderful cheeriness which has always been a peculiar attribute of the British soldier, the Middlesex men on relief from the trenches moved back to S. of Vermelles, where they had spent a few hours, then marched to billets in Sailly, arriving at 9.30 p.m. on the 1st October. On the 2nd the Battalion moved to fresh billets in Vendin-lez-Bethune, and here drafts (150 other ranks on 3rd, 248 on 4th and 43 on 6th) arrived, which brought the strength of the Battalion up to somewhere near the number before the Battle opened. The 16th saw the Battalion, now nearly its former strength, back in the trenches in front of Cambrin, and for the next three days the words " enemy very quiet " appear in the Diary. On the 19th October, however, the words " but massing further south " are added: the actions of the Hohenzollern were in progress. Thereafter, until the 27th November there is nothing of interest in the Battalion Diary; but on that date there is a statement that " The Battalion from to-day forms part of the 98th Brigade, 33rd Division." The 19th Infantry Brigade had again been transferred from its Division (2nd) to another, though this was to be the last occasion, for it remained with the 33rd to the close of the War. The 1st Middlesex then marched to the 33rd Division area. On the last day of 1915 the Battalion was in advanced billets, North Annequin, supplying working parties.

1ST OCTOBER.

27TH NOV.

31ST DECEMBER.

During the winter of 1915–1916 the quietest part of the Western Front was probably the line S. of Armentières, where the 2nd

Middlesex of the 8th Division passed an uneventful existence until the 19th December, when the Division was relieved and moved to the Morbecque area in G.H.Q. Reserve. **19th Dec. 2nd Battalion.**

Physical training, boat drill and lectures to officers and N.C.O's. on mountain warfare occupied the 3rd Middlesex (28th Division) aboard the *Transylvania*, until the vessel reached Alexandria about 12 noon on the 30th October. Disembarkation took place on the 31st, and by 9 p.m. that night the whole Battalion, having detrained at Ramleh Station, reached camp at Sidi Bishr (about seven miles from Alexandria). The ultimate destination of the 28th Division was Salonika, and after training and much route-marching the 3rd Middlesex embarked aboard H.T. *Hururata* on the 25th November, sailing the following day. The vessel arrived at Salonika on the 30th, the 3rd Middlesex disembarking on the 2nd December and marching to Lembet Camp, about six miles north of the town. Much hard work was now before the Battalion, for the defences around Salonika were of the flimsiest. No sooner, therefore, were the Middlesex men settled in camp than digging operations began in earnest. But the constant strain on the nerves such as life on the Western Front imposed, was absent in Macedonia, for which all ranks were devoutly thankful. On the 13th December new trenches were begun on the Turkish and Greek hills, near the top of the line of the defences of Salonika. On the 31st December the Battalion was still digging. **3rd Battalion. 30th October. 31st Dec.**

Of the four regular battalions of the Regiment the 4th was having, at this period, the most strenuous existence. After the attack at Bellewaarde the 4th Middlesex had spent several days "resting" (a quite misleading term) out of the front line, in camp at "H.B.a.1.1." But on the 8th October the Battalion again went into the front line, relieving the Worcesters. The relief was completed about 11.40 p.m. and the night passed quietly. So, indeed, did the next day until 4 p.m., when the enemy threw trench-mortar bombs into the reserve line of trenches occupied by "D" Company, killing three men and wounding three more; a man of "A" Company had also been shot dead by a German sniper. That night the enemy was reported working in front of B.7, and also in front of B.3. **4th Battalion. 8th October.**

At 10.15 a.m. on the 10th the enemy again became active with trench-mortar bombs, mortaring the junctions of Pollock Street and B.3, blowing in a considerable portion of these two trenches. **10th October**

10th October. 4th Battalion. His bombers then began an attack: they tried to bomb up B.3 and from the outside of B.3, whilst other Germans threw bombs into Pollock Street. They were, however, held by the Middlesex bombers, and for a little while the attack died down. At 12.30 p.m. a fresh outburst of bombing took place, but the enemy achieved nothing, though the Middlesex suffered casualties. That night there was a digging contest between the opposing forces as to which should occupy the blown-in portion of the trench. Both sides dug-in towards one another, the Middlesex forward and the Germans from the other end. Despite the hard work put in by the Battalion, when dawn broke the enemy had gained two bays, had built a new block and had wired it; he had advanced about thirty yards. During the day the Middlesex had lost 7 men killed and 33 wounded. Hostile shell-fire was heavy on the 11th, several portions of B.3 parapet being blown in, but promptly built up again. At night a block was made beyond the junction of B.3 and Pollock Street, three more blocks were formed in the forward communication trenches and B.3 was filled in for about twenty yards from Pollock Street junction. These bombing affrays were frequent, but they were generally inconclusive, for what was lost on one day was invariably regained either the same night or following day. On the 12th the Battalion's losses were 2 killed
13th October. and 20 wounded; on the 13th 6 killed, 22 wounded and 22 missing, and when at night the Battalion was relieved by the 4th Gordon Highlanders and marched back to Ouderdom, 34 men had also been evacuated sick during the tour (8th–13th).

At this period there was a lack of artillery ammunition, and the Diary of the 8th Infantry Brigade (3rd Division), of which the 4th Middlesex formed part, contains this entry: "Instructions were received that our field guns were on a daily allowance of *two rounds per gun per diem*. Ammunition for heavy guns only to be used in an emergency." So that whereas the Germans were able to pound the British trenches and plaster them with shell of all calibre, the British guns were practically reduced to impotence. On the 13th Lieut.-Colonel Bridgman was evacuated sick, temporary command of the 4th Middlesex being taken over by Lieut.-Colonel F. J. Duncan, 2nd Royal Scots, who, however, left the Battalion as soon as it reached bivouacs in Ouderdom.
22nd October. The Middlesex men moved to billets at Steenvoorde on the 22nd, and five days later Major H. P. F. Bicknell (from the 2nd Battalion) took over command. One officer had been killed since the

Battalion came out of the line—2nd Lieut. H. Major—who lost his life owing to an accident whilst instructing bombers. **4TH BATTALION.**

On the 11th November orders were received at Battalion Headquarters that the 4th Middlesex had been transferred to the 63rd Infantry Brigade, 21st Division, and were to leave Steenvoorde on the 13th. This was a heavy blow to the Battalion, in which the 3rd Division had been engaged; but the change was a necessity, for Battalions of the New Army were being drafted into the regular divisions in order that they might profit from the experience of seasoned warriors. On the 13th the 4th Middlesex marched out of Steenvoorde for Bailleul, and on the 14th to Armentières to join the 21st Division. **11TH NOV.**

The first trenches occupied by the 4th Middlesex were S.E. of Armentières, with their right resting on the Lille Road. It was soon evident that the Battalion had come to a quiet part of the line, for casualties were few, whilst the activities of the enemy were confined to occasional shell-fire, "whizz-banging" and sniping. The German attitude on this part of the front is best illustrated by an incident which occurred on the night of the 27th November. The sentries were suddenly surprised to hear voices from across No Man's Land shouting several times "We are fed up." A few rounds of rifle fire put an end to the shouting.

Little of interest happened until the 16th December, when the 8th Somerset Light Infantry, on the left of the 4th Middlesex, undertook a "cutting-out" enterprise against the enemy. The operation was a splendid success, but it awoke the somewhat apathetic enemy, who bombarded the line heavily, with the result that the Middlesex suffered two killed and twenty wounded, amongst the latter being Captain Harris, who was severely wounded in the head. The trenches were also much damaged. Two mines were blown by the enemy on the 19th, but he was prevented from occupying the craters. On this day also the Battalion lost a gallant young officer—2nd Lieut. C. J. Cottam—who had joined but a week previously. Mortally wounded during the enemy's bombardment, his devotion to duty was splendid, and his last words were of encouragement to his men: "Take charge, the oldest soldier, and keep a steady look-out in front." He died full of the "Die-Hard" spirit. **16TH DEC.**

On Christmas Eve there was very little activity on either side during the day, but when darkness had fallen machine guns and rifles were busy. As Christmas morning dawned, the firing died

25th Dec. down, and the Germans were heard singing carols across No Man's Land. Then, through the darkness came shouts of "We want peace," to which the Middlesex men replied with "5 rounds rapid." The Battalion was relieved on the 27th and marched back to billets in Armentières, where, on the 28th, the men's 31st Dec. Christmas dinner took place. On New Year's Eve the Battalion moved back again into the front line.

1/7th Battalion. Throughout the autumn the 1/7th Middlesex were holding the trenches at La Boutillerie (into which the Battalion had moved on the 29th September) with short intervals in Brigade Reserve. It is evident from the Battalion Diary that the enemy's snipers were extremely active, but, judging from the casualty returns, the Middlesex men had obtained almost a complete mastery over the Germans in this dangerous method of waging warfare. For 10th October. instance, on the 10th October, when the 1/7th were relieved, the Battalion had sustained during a tour of thirteen days in the front line three other ranks killed and two wounded, whilst the Middlesex sharpshooters had accounted for 21 Germans and 10 periscopes: in a previous tour the Battalion had lost 9 killed and 17 wounded, but inflicted on the enemy 40 casualties. On the 13th 2nd Lieut. R. E. E. Scott, in command of a Trench Mortar Battery, was mortally wounded, and died later in the day. The Battery had been taking part in a demonstration in co-operation with an attack further south, and was packing up ready to move out of the front line when a high-explosive shell fell into the midst of the personnel of the Battery, killing or wounding the whole.

23rd Nov. On the 23rd November the 1/7th were withdrawn from the trenches to the Rue de Bruges. The 8th Division was to be taken back into Corps Reserve and given a long period of rest. On 26th Nov. the 26th the 1/7th reached Morbecque, near Hazebrouck, where the Battalion was to remain for the next six weeks.

1/8th Battalion. The story of the 1/8th Middlesex, from the last day of September, is practically that of the 1/7th Battalion, the two being 23rd October. still in the same Division (8th), but on the 23rd October the 1/8th was transferred to the 70th Brigade in accordance with the 11th Nov. reorganisation of Divisions. On the 11th November the Battalion went into Divisional Reserve north of Sailly-sur-la-Lys, and the Battalion Diary records that: "The Battalion had been in the trenches and immediate support for 40 days. Of these the last 20 days had been spent continuously in the trenches, one-half of the Battalion relieving the other half every five days. The last two weeks it rained nearly every day and night, and the trenches were very wet. Despite this, the health of the Battalion had been good, and there were only five cases of 'trench feet' (slight)." Little wonder that Colonel Ingpen (the C.O.) and his officers and men were glad to get away from the line for the long " rest " in Corps Reserve with the 8th Division, even though the Battalion had to put up with tents and huts.

Whatever the conditions, bad as they were, under which the 1/7th and 1/8th Middlesex spent the period between the end of September and the close of the year, they were cheerful compared with the appalling state of the trenches which the 11th Battalion occupied in November.

At 1 p.m. on the 1st the 11th Middlesex relieved the 6th West Kents in the line west of the Hohenzollern Redoubt. " Sticky Trench " was the name of the trench in that part of the line, and " sticky " it was in the extreme, for the Diary states that " all trenches in an appalling condition, with mud and water *waist high* in most places." The relief was not completed until 7 p.m., *i.e.*, six hours to take over the line, and rain fell steadily the whole time and on through the night. 1ST NOV. 11TH BATTALION.

When dawn of the 2nd broke the position was more hopeless than ever. No one had slept during the night, for it was impossible to lie down, the floors of the trenches being deep in mud and filth. There were no dug-outs or shelters of any kind whatever, and both men and officers had to remain on the fire steps all night. The parapets of the trenches were continually falling in, some twenty or thirty yards at a stretch. Sand-bags were no use, and of revetting material there was none, though urgent appeals had been made for it. Cold and wet, any relief from these horrible surroundings—even death—seemed preferable to the men. Out in front of Sticky Trench the Battalion Bombers from the fire-bombing posts hurled their missiles at the enemy, who shelled the trenches of the Middlesex, knocking them about and adding to the destruction and ruin caused by the incessant rain. On the 4th conditions were much the same, though the rain stopped and the work of clearing the trenches of mud, and rebuilding the fallen parapets was hurried on. A half-company of Pioneers, specially sent up to repair the trenches, declared that it was impossible to mend the parapets, and the Pioneer Officer withdrew his party. On this day five other ranks had been 2ND NOV.

11TH BATTALION. killed and twelve wounded, but these casualties were small compared with those from sickness, for by now the Battalion was in the grip of disease. Rheumatism claimed 25, exhaustion 28, and "frost-feet" 18, most of the latter being men who had already been through the first winter in the trenches. On the 5th* the sick list totalled 63; on the 6th, 68; on the 7th, 38; on the 8th, 25; and on the 9th, 24; the majority being "frost feet," though rheumatism and bronchitis claimed a goodly number. Survivors of the 11th Middlesex will surely never forget that terrible period in the trenches in front of the Hohenzollern Redoubt.

14TH NOV. The Battalion (in Division) was relieved on 14th November, and went back to billets in Sailly Labourse, moving to Bourecq on the 18th. The 12th Division moved back into trenches about Festubert on the 10th and 11th December, but the tour was uneventful. On the 23rd December the Battalion took over trenches north of Givenchy; on the last day of the year the 11th Battalion was in billets at Les Choquaux. 31ST DEC.

In July another battalion of the Middlesex Regiment—the 12th—had arrived in France.

12TH BATTALION. The 12th Battalion Middlesex Regiment was raised at Colchester in the middle of September, 1914, and was encamped, first on the rifle range and later in huts. It formed part of the 54th Infantry Brigade (Brigadier-General H. Browse-Scaife) of the 18th Division, commanded by Major-General Ivor Maxse.† The remaining Infantry Brigades of the Division were the 53rd and 55th. The 12th Middlesex were brigaded with the 6th Northants, 10th Royal Fusiliers and 11th Royal Fusiliers. Colonel R. F. B. Glover was the first Commanding Officer.

After several months at Colchester the 54th Brigade moved to the East Coast and, on 5th May, set out on the march to Salisbury Plain, where the 12th Middlesex went into huts at Codford. On the 24th June the 18th Division was inspected by H.M. the King, near Stonehenge, before embarkation for an overseas theatre of war.

* Extract from the Battalion Diary of 5th November: "An officer from 12th Division Staff went round one trench and said of course things were bad, but that they were not anything like what had been reported by us. All ranks had now been soaked through and standing continuously in mud and water for over 100 hours with no chance of sleep or even lying down."

† Now General Sir F. Ivor Maxse, K.C.B., C.V.O., D.S.O., Colonel of the Middlesex Regiment.

The 12th embarked at Southampton on the 25th July and, reaching Le Havre early on the following day, marched to No. 1 Rest Camp, where the remainder of the 26th was spent. On the 27th, about midnight, the Battalion entrained and reached Amiens, detraining and marching to Talmas, there billeting. The 18th Division had been ordered to concentrate in the Flesselles. 25TH JULY. 12TH BATTALION.

The 18th Division was now in the Third Army. Units of the Division were first attached to the 5th and 51st Divisions for instruction in trench warfare. The 12th Middlesex marched to Laviéville on the 22nd August and was placed under the 154th Brigade of the 51st Division, eight platoons (two from each of "A," "B," "C," and "D" Companies) going into the front-line trenches for three days on the 23rd. On the following day two men were wounded—the first other rank casualties suffered by the Battalion. Three days later the first eight platoons were relieved by the remaining platoons, and on this day the first officer casualty (2nd Lieut. E. G. M. Stot, wounded) appeared in the casualty list.

On the 22nd August the 18th Division began the relief of the 5th Division near Carnoy, but it was not until early September that the Diary of the 12th Middlesex contains any item of outstanding interest. The 54th Brigade was at first in Corps Reserve, but relieved the 55th Brigade on the night of 4th–5th September in the front line. The 12th Middlesex had taken over "Sector III," and until the evening of the 6th were engaged in building up the trenches and in clearing the Tambour du Clos. At 6.30 p.m. the Germans exploded a camouflet opposite the Tambour and one of the Middlesex saps running out to it was wrecked, ten men being brought in suffering from gas. The enemy then trench-mortared and machine-gunned the trenches, evidently with the idea of keeping the Middlesex men from occupying the crater. A patrol sent out later found the crater unoccupied by the enemy. Another mine was exploded on the site of the former at 6.30 p.m. on the 9th September, part of the parapet of the Tambour being shaken down. German snipers were deadly pests and soon began to take toll of the 12th Battalion, whose marksmen were not supplied with telescopic sights, whereas the enemy seemed to have a plentiful supply. On the 14th the Battalion was relieved and marched back to billets at Dernancourt. 22ND AUGUST.

On the 20th October Major H. P. Osborne assumed command of the 12th Middlesex, vice Colonel R. F. B. Glover. 20TH OCTOBER.

21ST OCTOBER.

12TH BATTALION.

The first officer of the Battalion killed was 2nd Lieut. W. M. Wallace, who, with two other ranks, lost his life on the 21st October. The Battalion M.O.—Captain A. G. Miller, R.A.M.C.—was killed by a trench-mortar bomb or a rifle grenade on the 20th October.

Up to the end of 1915 the only incident of importance was a small "cutting-out" enterprise carried out on the night of the 14th–15th December in the "D.I." sector. No Man's Land in this sector was much broken up by mine craters and shell holes, and out in front of the trenches (opposite the Fort) there were two mine craters overlapping one another. On either side of the double crater were other craters, that on the right lying between the Quarry and the enemy's lines. The German side of the double crater was connected with the enemy's trenches by two short communication trenches which led up to and gave command to the enemy of the eastern edges of the crater.

14TH—15TH DECEMBER.

The enterprise in question was carried out by two bombing parties, each of an officer and seven men. The right party was commanded by Lieut. Ponsonby and the left by Lieut. Trevor. The former was to advance between the crater on the right of and in the double crater; the latter between the crater on the left of and in the double crater. Having reached the German front line, each party was to form a block in the enemy's trench to the right and left respectively, driving any Germans they might encounter up the communication trench to the double crater, and then clear the latter, either killing or capturing any of the enemy found therein.

On the previous night the two officers had made a reconnaissance of the enemy's trenches.

At 2.30 a.m. the two parties crept out and, unmolested by the enemy, crossed No Man's Land; Lieut. Trevor's party, on the left, got through the German wire and into the hostile trench. The block was formed on the left and the remainder of the party then moved to the right in accordance with the plan of attack. Ten yards down the trench a dug-out was found in the rear parapet. Two bombs were thrown into this dug-out and groans were heard. Two more bombs were thrown in and the groans ceased. Ten yards further on the party came to a traverse from which bombs were hurled at them. Two Germans were seen, but from the number of bombs thrown it was evident that some five or six of the enemy were present. The German trench was about six feet deep with about two feet of mud at the bottom, which made movement very difficult. No sounds were heard of the advance of the right party under Lieut. Ponsonby and, after throwing some ten or twelve bombs, Lieut. Trevor decided to retire. During the retirement Trevor and one of his men were wounded by bombs, but the whole party eventually got back to their starting point.

14TH—15TH DECEMBER.

12TH BATTALION.

The right party had failed to enter the enemy's trenches. Lieut. Ponsonby successfully led his men across No Man's Land until the German wire was reached. But the entanglements at this point were much more formidable than those which had confronted the left party. In getting through the wire one of Ponsonby's party was hit by a bullet, the enemy now being thoroughly on the alert. The officer got through the wire and for half-an-hour lay between the wire and the parapet of the trench; his men, however, were hung up and eventually he retired, bringing his men with him.

The failure of this little enterprise was thus commented upon by Lieut.-Colonel Osborne (the C.O. of the 12th Middlesex): "All Lieut. Trevor's party were men who had done this kind of work before; those under Lieut. Ponsonby, though they were volunteers, had no previous experience."

As the war progressed these raids became more and more affairs of considerable importance, and, in the later stages of the struggle, the raiding parties often numbered between one hundred and two hundred men who had practised every step of the raid over practice trenches before the actual attempt was made. Some of the most daring fighting ever carried out in France and Flanders took place during these raids on the German trenches.

1ST OCTOBER.

13TH BATTALION.

On the 1st October the 13th Middlesex (Lieut.-Colonel L. G. Oliver commanding) were in billets in Lambres, a village in the Mazinghem area, to which the 73rd Infantry Brigade (24th Division) had been withdrawn from the Battle of Loos. To the 24th and 21st Divisions belongs the distinction of having been rushed, raw and inexperienced as they were, into a great battle, without having previously held a front-line sector either in France or Flanders; they had been put into the battle almost immediately on arrival from England. Their apprenticeship had been very rough indeed, and they had suffered heavy losses as might be expected. Nevertheless, they had acquitted themselves admirably. On being withdrawn from the battle, however, they had yet to

1st October. 13th Battalion. learn the rudiments of trench warfare, and for this purpose were attached to other divisions in the line for instruction in trench fighting, bomb-throwing, sniping and the hundred and one things to be learned in the front line.

With this end in view the 24th Division began to move north to be attached to troops in the Ypres salient. On the 2nd October the 73rd Brigade moved to Herzeele and on the 7th to the Proven area, the 13th Middlesex being billeted in farms some two miles south-west of the village and two miles north of Watou. The next day saw the first party of Middesex men off to the trenches—five officers and 400 men proceeding in motor 'buses to Brielen, where they were split up into parties and attached to other battalions of the 6th Division for a forty-eight hour tour in the front line.

11th October. Early in the morning of the 11th October (at 3 a.m.) these parties returned, having suffered the loss of one other rank killed and four wounded whilst in the front line. Those officers and men who had not been sent up to the trenches were instructed in bomb-throwing and lectured generally on trench warfare by officers and N.C.Os. from the 16th and 18th Brigades (6th Division).

On the 11th the 73rd Brigade received orders to relieve the 43rd Brigade (14th Division) in trenches P.1 to U.26 in the St. Eloi sector, the 13th Middlesex to hold R.3—T. 23.

Leaving billets at 8 a.m. on the 11th, the Middlesex men marched off via Proven, Poperinghe and Reninghelst to a wood about two miles south-east of the latter town, where, until the afternoon of the 14th, the Battalion was accommodated in tents. At 3.15 p.m. on the 14th, the Battalion paraded and marched off along the Ypres road to the Café Belge, thence through Kruisstraat Hook to Voormezeele, taking over the trenches of the 1st Somerset Light Infantry in the left centre section of the St. Eloi sector.

The first front-line sector held by a battalion in France or Flanders remained always in the memory of those who fought on the Western Front. That first guarded look across "No Man's Land" towards the German trenches was not easily forgotten, nor the first night spent in a dug-out, or on the fire step, nerves on edge, waiting for something which might occur at any moment: the ping of a bullet, the thud and burst of a grenade or bomb, the roar of an exploding shell, or perhaps the rush of a party of armed Germans; these things experienced for the first time left their indelible memory on the mind.

The five days' tour which followed the relief of the Somerset men by the 13th Middlesex were, however, quiet and uneventful, and on the 19th the Battalion was relieved after dark and marched back to " C " Camp, Reninghelst, having lost one officer wounded, one other rank killed and eight wounded. A month of tours in and out of the front line followed the first, and on the 19th November the Battalion, having been relieved, marched back to the rest camp at Reninghelst, where the 24th Division concentrated on the 20th and set out on the road towards the Hellebroucq area. Several days were occupied in marching to the latter place, which was to be the training area of the Division until the end of the year. 19TH OCTOBER. 13TH BATTALION. 31ST DEC.

During November three other service battalions of the Regiment had arrived in France, *i.e.*, the 16th, 17th and 18th Middlesex. They had come as part of the 33rd Division. The first of these—16th (Public Schools) Battalion—had been raised by Lieut.-Colonel J. J. Mackay in London on the 1st September, 1914; the second —the 17th (1st Football Battalion)—was raised by the Rt. Hon. W. Joynson-Hicks, M.P., on the 12th December, 1914, also in London; the third—the 18th (1st Public Works Pioneers)—raised by Lieut.-Colonel J. Ward, M.P., in London on the 19th January, 1915. Lieut.-Colonel J. H. Hall commanded the 16th Battalion, Colonel H. T. Fenwick the 17th, and Lieut.-Colonel H. Storr the 18th Battalion. 16TH, 17TH, 18TH BATTALION.

There are no records of the early days of these three Battalions before they left England, but the war training of one battalion was very much like that of another, and real interest in their history does not begin until they landed in one of the theatres of war. It is, however, worth recording that at this period and towards the end of 1915 no less than seventeen Battalions of the Middlesex Regiment had left England for service overseas, a splendid record.

The 16th, 17th and 18th Middlesex went out to France with the 33rd Division, the first two as infantry battalions forming part of the 100th Brigade, the latter as Divisional Pioneers. The last-named Battalion arrived at Le Havre at midnight on the 14th November, the 17th Battalion at Boulogne early on the 18th November, and the 16th Battalion at the same port on the 17th November. On the 19th November the 100th Brigade was concentrated in billets in the neighbourhood of Boeseghem, moving on the 25th to a fresh area, *i.e.*, La Miquellerie, where the remainder of November was spent.

2ND DEC. The 18th Middlesex, being Pioneers, concentrated with the Divisional Troops.

On the 2nd December the 100th Brigade moved to Bethune, the 16th and 17th Middlesex with the 13th Essex Regiment billeting in the town.

First instruction in trench warfare began on the 4th for the 16th Middlesex.

17TH BATTALION. 8TH DEC. The 17th Middlesex and the 13th Essex were transferred to the 6th Infantry Brigade of the 2nd Division on the 8th December, much to the regret of the other two Middlesex Battalions in the 33rd Division. "We now (9th December) made our next move," records the Diary of the 17th Battalion, "after being exactly a week at Bethune; our orders this time were to march to Annequin Fosse on the afternoon of the 9th, this place being a distance of four kilometres. We had now arrived at the actual scene of fighting, our billets being a matter of two or two and a-half miles from the trenches. Our position was practically between La Bassée and Loos, the former being on our left."

Instruction in trench warfare began immediately, the right-half Battalion going into the front line attached to the 1st Royal Berks and 1st Herts (T.) Regiments for the tour. On the 10th the right-half Battalion was relieved by the left-half. On the 11th the Battalion suffered its first casualty, Pte. J. Macdonald of "B" Company being shot dead. He had been but seven hours in the trenches. Nothing of importance happened during the 31ST DEC. remainder of the month, the 31st finding the 17th Middlesex billeted in Busnes, having changed the area on the 27th.

16TH BATTALION. 9TH DEC. The 16th Middlesex had moved to Bourecq on the 9th December, when "A" and "C" Companies went for instructional tours into the trenches of the Royal Fusiliers; five other ranks (the first casualties recorded in the Diaries of this Battalion) were wounded on the 25th. The Battalion marched to Beuvry on the 30th, "B" and "D" Companies going into the trenches 31ST DEC. on the 31st.

18TH BATTALION. 2ND DEC. From the 1st to 10th December the 18th Middlesex (Pioneers) remained at Gorre hard at work on the water-logged trenches, re-boarding the bottoms, and in revetting. On the 2nd the 33rd Division had taken over the front line from the 7th Division. Casualties suffered by the Pioneers in this tour were: 4th December, 1 other rank wounded; 6th December, 1 other rank killed; 7th December, 2 other ranks killed, 2 wounded; 8th December,

2 other ranks killed, Captain Kennedy, 2nd Lieut. Baxter and 5 other ranks wounded. The 33rd Division was relieved on the night 10th–11th December, and the 18th Middlesex marched via Bellerive, Busnes, Busnettes, Bethune and Le Préol, where from the 29th the remainder of December was spent.

10TH—11TH DECEMBER.

31ST DEC.

# CHAPTER XXIII.

## The Second Winter in the Trenches.

### II.—To the 1st June, 1916.

SINCE the 4th August, 1914, the Middlesex Regiment, which on the declaration of War consisted of ten Battalions (Regular, Reserve and Territorial), had expanded enormously. By the 1st January, 1916 (fourteen months from the outbreak of hostilities), no less than seventeen Battalions had left England, twelve of which were fighting in France and Flanders. In England other battalions had been raised and were undergoing training, four of these (19th, 20th, 21st and 23rd Middlesex) joining the British Armies along the Western Front during the first six months of 1916.

19TH, 20TH, 21ST, 23RD BATTALIONS.

The early period of that year was spent in stupendous preparations for the Somme Battles, upon which towards the end of 1915 the Allies had decided. Hard work upon the defences, the waging of trench warfare with its incessant need for the utmost vigilance, and training when out of the front line, sum up generally the latter part of the winter and spring which preceded the struggles on the Somme.

Only four local operations (three in the Ypres salient and one on Vimy Ridge) disturbed the comparative quietude of the first half of 1916, and from the general standpoint of military history that period is uninteresting. But from a regimental point of view six months of the War cannot be dismissed lightly or without details (brief though they may be) of what was happening to Battalions during the preparations for the grim and sanguinary battles which began on the 1st July.

1ST BATTALION. 1ST JANUARY.

On the 1st January, 1916, the 1st Middlesex (Lieut.-Colonel F. Rowley) when in the front line held trenches between the La Bassée Canal and Loos, and when "resting" were billeted in Beuvry, Annequin Fosse, or other villages in the neighbourhood. The word "resting" is here used in its comparative sense, for

1ST BATTALION. often work in the back areas was just as strenuous as in the front line, though the Battalion was relieved from the constant danger and vigilance of life in the latter. Cuinchy was the sector in which the 1st Battalion spent most of its time when in the front line, and from the Diaries it is obvious that the early months of the year were quiet and without incidents of a startling nature. January and February were particularly uneventful months; March was enlivened by one or two bombing raids on the enemy. One officer—2nd Lieut. J. L. Hidding—died of wounds on the 28th. In April "A" Company carried out a very successful raid

25TH APRIL. at 10 p.m. on the night of the 25th. The point selected for the raid was the crater at Mad Point. After an artillery bombardment lasting five minutes, two parties (commanded respectively by 2nd Lieuts. Birdwood and J. Coughlan) entered the German trenches, bombed several dug-outs, bayoneted two of the enemy and took three unwounded prisoners, as well as arms and equipment. Identifications were thus secured, and as the policy of G.H.Q. just then was to know exactly how the German forces were disposed, the taking of prisoners was looked upon with great favour by the higher command. On the 10th May the C.O., Colonel Rowley, had a narrow escape. He was conducting Lieut.-Colonel C. A. Madge, of the South African Forces, round the trenches when a "Minnie" "plomped" into the trench, killing Colonel Madge but without even injuring the C.O. of the 1st Middlesex. Shell-fire on both sides was becoming more intense and regular, and by the end of the month fifty casualties in the Middlesex had been reported. On the 10th June, to the great regret of the Battalion, Colonel Rowley left to take over command of the 56th Infantry Brigade, Major Bagley assuming temporary command until Major H. Lloyd,

24TH JUNE. Welsh Regiment, arrived on the 24th June. The Battalion was then in billets in Bethune.

2ND BATTALION 11TH JANUARY. 1/7TH BATTALION. On the 11th January the 2nd Middlesex (Lieut.-Colonel R. H. Hayes) and the 1/7th Middlesex (Lieut.-Colonel E. J. King), then at Morbecque, paraded at 8.50 a.m. and marched (the 2nd as leading Battalion of the 23rd Infantry Brigade) back to the front area, billeting for the night at Estaires. The next day the march was continued to Bac St. Maur, where the 2nd Middlesex went into billets, the 23rd Brigade being in Divisional Reserve; the 1/7th Middlesex were at Rue de Quesnoy. On the 18th both Battalions went into the front line in the Fleurbaix sector.

For the 2nd Battalion the months of January and February were uneventful, but for the 1/7th those two months witnessed incidents which must be recorded. The 1/7th Middlesex, on going into the line on the 18th January, had taken over its old trenches at La Boutillerie. But in this sub-sector of the line it was not destined to remain long, for its period of duty with the 8th Division was coming to a close; the 56th (London) Division was assembling in the Abbeville area and the 1/7th had been transferred from the former to the latter, of which more later. This last tour at La Boutillerie was marked by the loss of two of the original officers. On the night of the 24th January Lieut. F. Smith, who had succeeded Lieut. Tait as Machine-Gun Officer, was laying one of his guns on a spot across "No Man's Land" where movement had been detected, when he was shot through the head. Two days later, just as the Battalion was withdrawing into Divisional Reserve at Doulieu, Major Frost, who had gone into "C" Lines between Fauquissart and Neuve Chapelle in order to place crosses on the graves of some of his men buried there, was also shot through the head by a German sniper. After the Battalion had been relieved and arrived in Doulieu news was received that all Territorial units were to be withdrawn from Regular divisions and formed into Territorial divisions. This was a bitter blow to the 1/7th. The Battalion had been with the 8th Division for nearly a year and had formed a close and intimate friendship with the 2nd Battalion, and were on cordial terms with all the other Battalions of the Division. "In the years to come," said Colonel King, "all those who had served in the 8th Division looked back upon their time with it as a sort of golden age." On the 8th February the 1/7th was inspected by the Corps Commander, and on the 9th entrained at Lestre for Abbeville, to join the 56th (London Territorial) Division.*

2ND—1/7TH BATTALIONS. 1/7TH BATTALION. 18TH JANUARY. 8TH FEBRUARY.

In March the 2nd Middlesex had a new C.O. On the 7th Lieut.-Colonel Hayes was evacuated sick, and on the 16th Major E. T. F. Sandys (4th Middlesex) arrived and assumed command of the Battalion. The 8th Division was now under orders to move south to the Somme area, and on the 26th March the 2nd Middlesex marched to Dump House, near Sailly Bridge, and billeted for the night. On the following day the Battalion again took the road to Calonne, and on arrival billeted until midnight, resuming the

2ND BATTALION. 16TH MARCH.

* The Diary of 1/8th Battalion for January, 1916, is missing and the story of its joining the 56th Division is included in the narrative of the formation of that Division.

28TH MARCH. 2ND BATTALION. march to Merville Station. At 1.30 a.m. on the 28th the 2nd Middlesex (in Brigade) entrained at Merville and shortly after midday reached Longeau (near Amiens), detraining and marching off in forty minutes for Bourdon. The latter place was reached at 9.55 p.m., but so poor was the accommodation in the village that on the following day "C" and "D" Companies moved to Hangest. The destination of the 8th Division was, however, Albert, where, east of the town, front-line trenches were to be taken over. On the 2nd April, therefore, the 2nd Middlesex were again on the march, billeting that night in St. Gratien. On the 3rd a pleasant surprise awaited the Battalion. The march from St. Gratien had been resumed at 3 p.m., the destination being Albert via Querrieu. As the Battalion entered the latter village the drums of the 4th Middlesex met the 2nd Battalion and played them through the village, to the great delight and unbounded enthusiasm of all ranks. Albert was reached at 8.30 p.m., companies marching into billets by platoons. On the following night (4th) the Battalion paraded at 7.15 p.m. and marched off by platoons for trenches and posts east of Albert, with Battalion Headquarters at Maissin.

8TH APRIL. The change from the quiet Laventie sector to the noisy Somme area was soon apparent. On the 8th ten other ranks were wounded by shell-fire and 2nd Lieut. A. H. Newton died of wounds. But the enemy's artillery was not always active, nor were his observers always on the alert, for on the 23rd April the Battalion Diary records, "the first daylight relief since the Battalion arrived in France." The relief was begun at 9.30 a.m. and was not finished until 1 p.m. The remainder of April was uneventful. Similarly, the early part of May was bare of any untoward incident, but on the 11th the Battalion raided the enemy's trenches—the first raid in the Somme area. At 2 a.m. three officers, 2nd Lieuts. G. A. T. Benson, F. V. Smith and W. Spatz, and 74 N.C.Os. and men crossed "No Man's Land" in an attempt to raid the German lines opposite "X. 77." Details of the raid are not given, but the Battalion Diary stated that "the raid, as a raid, was not a success owing to sheer bad luck and the wire being uncut. Several of the party, however, forced a way through uncut wire and inflicted heavy losses on the enemy with bombs. The object of the raid was to capture a prisoner. This was effected, and the prisoner gave one of the most important pieces of information that could have been obtained, besides furnishing an identification." It would seem that the raid, "*as a raid,*" was a distinct success. Casualties suffered in this raid were 2 officers and 19 other ranks wounded and 2 other ranks killed. On the last day of May the 2nd Middlesex 31st May. were in billets at Millencourt.

The 4th Middlesex (Lieut.-Colonel Bridgman) ushered in the 4th Battalion. New Year in an unfortunate manner. The Battalion had taken over front-line trenches in the Armentières sector on the night of 31st December–1st January, and at 1 a.m. a "cutting-out" enterprise was carried out by the 23rd Division (on the flank of the 21st Division) with the result that the trenches of the Middlesex were very heavily shelled by the enemy, the Battalion losing 5 other ranks killed and 30 wounded. Towards dawn the shelling died down, and at daybreak things were once more normal: but it was a bad beginning. On the 6th Lieut.-Colonel F. 6th January. Bicknell assumed command of the battalion, vice Lieut.-Colonel Bridgman.

Apart from the daily round of trench warfare the Diaries of the 4th Middlesex contain nothing of outstanding interest during January and February and the first two weeks of March, 1916. The Battalion remained in the Armentières sector until the 17th Division relieved the 21st on the night of 19th–20th March. From 19th—20th March. the 16th November, 1915, until it was relieved on the night of 19th–20th March, 1916, the total casualties suffered by the Battalion were 1 officer killed and 7 wounded; in other ranks the losses were 32 killed and 140 wounded.

From the Armentières sector the 21st Division moved back to "rest" in the Outtersteene–Strazeele–La Crèche area; the 63rd Brigade was billeted at Strazeele, the 4th Middlesex arriving in billets at about 2 p.m. on the 22nd March. The "rest" period was, however, destined to be of short duration, for on the 27th March Divisional Headquarters issued movement orders, as the Division had been ordered to join the XIIIth Corps, then on the Somme. The move was to take place on the 31st March–1st April. The last day of March was spent by the 4th Middlesex in packing up preparatory to the move south. At 7.30 p.m. the Battalion arrived at Godewaersvelde, entrained and twenty minutes later was on the way to the Somme area. The last entry in the Diary states: "the limited time spent in this area has not allowed of much other than work, and the weather has been bad, so there are not many regrets at moving to a new area."

Yet a little while and those months at Armentières would seem like a paradise compared with life on the Somme!

1st April.
4th Battalion.

Of all the names of towns and villages of France and Flanders imprinted indelibly upon the minds of those who saw service on the Western Front, that of Amiens holds unforgetable memories, for there were few battalions of the British Armies which did not, at some time or other, pass through the town. It was at Longpré, on the outskirts of Amiens, at about 7 a.m. on the 1st April, that the 4th Middlesex arrived and detrained. The weather was glorious, sunny and warm, and the seven-mile march through Amiens to Allonville was very pleasant. Allonville lay about twelve miles behind the firing line; it was a clean, healthy little village with the country round about well cultivated. In this delectable spot the 4th Middlesex spent a quiet week.

From the 1st to the 8th April the 21st Division had been taking over a portion of the front line which Operation Orders refer to as "F.9.a.5.6, to X.20.d.2.0," which, translated, meant just east of Bécourt, the latter village being just over one kilometre east of Albert. The 63rd Brigade received orders to move on the 7th April to the Buire–Ville area, and on the morning of that date, at 8 a.m., the 4th Middlesex marched from Allonville to Ville.

14th April.

For several days "there is nothing to report," but on the 14th the 4th Middlesex relieved the 9th K.O.Y.L.I. in the front line, and the Battalion Diary thus describes the first sub-sector held on the Somme: "This new sector of the line is a marked contrast to the trenches which the Battalion has been used to. The country is hilly and the ground chalky, and therefore, though harder to dig than Flanders mud, the revetting of trenches and the enormous quantity of sand-bags which had to be utilised for that purpose are conspicuous by their absence. The nature of the soil lends itself to mining enterprises, which fact is duly realised by both sides. Reliefs of units can be made during the day owing to the depth of C.Ts. and also the rolling nature of the ground. The relief was completed by 6 p.m. The enemy's artillery was active at night: here they are able to conceal flashes naturally, and not as in Flanders where the ground was so flat. Our artillery reply very quickly at all times and respond on principle to every annoyance from the enemy. In one sector of the line, the Tambour, rifle grenades are the chief arrivals and the cause of 80 per cent. of our casualties. Our casualties were 1 killed and 4 wounded the first night owing to this weapon."

The sub-sector of the line taken over by the 4th Middlesex was from the Cemetery, opposite Fricourt (which lay in the German lines), northwards to the Tambour. Three Companies were in the line and one in support. 14TH APRIL.

The scarcity of hostile snipers was one of the earliest things noticed by the 4th Middlesex on taking over the line, but if these pests were inactive the same could not be said of the enemy's artillery, grenades, trench mortars and aerial torpedoes. The last-named were new to the Middlesex men, but as the diarist records, they "can be seen and dodged," and their effect was extremely local. Of that first tour on the Somme there is nothing further to add, the Battalion being relieved on the night of the 22nd–23rd April and moving, by march, back to La Neuville, the Divisional rest area. 4TH BATTALION. 22ND—23RD APRIL.

At La Neuville Companies first began their training in "practising the attack" in extended formations on facsimile trenches. This was new to the men, of whom the records state: "The desire to train hard and do things well is very marked in all ranks," but lack of uncultivated ground for training purposes somewhat hampered the Battalion. On the 3rd May the Battalion moved to Ville, for work chiefly in building gun emplacements, digging cable trenches, dug-outs, etc., and in improving communication trenches. Several casualties were incurred during these days of work.

On the 12th May the 4th Middlesex relieved the 1st Yorkshire Regiment in Queen's Redoubt, Bronté Redoubt and Bécordel Defences (in the Fricourt sector), Colonel Bicknell having his Headquarters in Méaulte. The Battalion was now in support. On the 16th, the anniversary of Albuhera Day, telegrams wishing the 4th Battalion "good luck" were received from the 2nd, 6th and 13th Battalions. This tour in the line was again followed by another period of hard training at La Neuville, in which wood-fighting, practising the attack on facsimile trenches and bomb-throwing formed the chief parts. That these exercises were very beneficial is evident from the records, which state that they "are doing much to foster the offensive spirit in all ranks, which is apt to deteriorate in the trench warfare which has lasted so long." On the 1st June the Battalion moved to Méaulte. The period at La Neuville had greatly benefited all ranks, who "are appearing extraordinarily fit and are full of *esprit de corps*." 12TH MAY. 1ST JUNE.

The Diary of the 167th Infantry Brigade, 56th (London) Division, records that on the 9th February, 1916, both the 1/7th and 1/8th Middlesex Regiments, commanded respectively by 1/7TH—1/8TH BATTALIONS. 9TH FEBRUARY.

9TH FEBRUARY. 1/7TH—1/8TH BATTALIONS.

Lieut.-Colonels E. J. King and P. L. Ingpen, arrived in the Hallencourt area and were billeted, the 1/7th in Longpré and the 1/8th in Airaines. The Division to which these two Battalions had been transferred was a newly-formed Second Line (London) Territorial Division, commanded by Major-General C. P. A. Hull, an old Middlesex Officer, who at the Battle of Mons in 1914 was in command of the 4th Battalion. The 1/7th and 1/8th Middlesex were brigaded with the 1/1st and 1/3rd Battalions City of London Regiment; the two other Brigades were the 168th and 169th. On the 27th February the 56th Division moved north to a new area, the 167th Brigade being billeted in Halloy les Pernois, Pernois and Berteaucourt. The march north-eastwards was continued on the 12th March, the 167th Brigade reaching the Rebreuve area on the 14th; the 1/7th Middlesex were at Baudricourt and the 1/8th at Rebreuvrette E. Until

30TH APRIL.

the 30th April training was carried out in the Rebreuve area, but on the last day of the month the Brigadier proceeded to Sailly au Bois to inspect trenches and the sector of the line that was to be taken over by his Brigade. On the 2nd May orders were issued to move to Souastre prior to taking over part of the line to be held by the 56th Division, which orders were carried out by the 1/8th Battalion on the 3rd and 1/7th Battalion on the 4th. On the latter date the 1/8th took over trenches from the 1/5th Gloucester and the 1st Berks Regiments. The 1/7th continued its march on the 5th through Bayencourt to Sailly au Bois, where it became part of the Brigade Reserve, supporting the 1/8th Middlesex and the 1/3rd Londons, holding trenches in front of Hebuterne. On the 8th the 1/7th relieved the 1/3rd Londons in the left sector of the Hebuterne defences, while the 1/8th were relieved by the 1/1st Londons.

Seeing that nearly four months were spent by the Middlesex men in this new sector, some description of the trenches is both interesting and necessary. The first things noticed by the 1/7th and 1/8th Battalions on going into the front line were the depth of the trenches and the masses of barbed wire above men's heads. Unlike the swampy plains of Flanders, Artois is a country of rolling downland. In the former, trenches, in the proper sense of the word, were almost impossible, the opposing defences consisting rather of massive breastworks, rarely more than 250 yards apart, so that to show a head above the parapet in daylight was certain death from a sniper's bullet. But in the Hebuterne sector the trenches were deep and well dug. They were, moreover, about 700 yards or more apart, and, for a while, sniping ceased to be an important part of the day's operations. Yet the greater distance between the two lines of trenches had its drawbacks, for they were more easily (and frequently) subjected to heavy shell fire.

Towards the end of May preparations for the attack on the Gommecourt salient (a subsidiary operation to the Battles of the Somme) began to take more definite shape. The 56th (London) Division was to attack the enemy from Hebuterne, but the distance between the opposing trenches—700 yards—was obviously a great drawback, and would almost certainly result in very heavy casualties to the attacking troops. The only way out of the difficulty was to push forward the line to within easy striking distance of the enemy. After a conference it was decided to dig an entirely new line parallel with, and within 250 yards of, the German trenches. In the face of an enemy always on the alert day and night this decision to advance and dig a new line of trenches under his very nose was, to say the least of it, bold. But it was done, and the enemy, strange though it may seem, knew nothing until one morning he realised that the British trenches had suddenly become very much nearer his own. The feat accomplished was so extraordinary that it merits closer description.

The task of taping out and digging the new line was entrusted to the 167th Brigade, as the senior Brigade of the 56th Division, the first night of the operations being 25th May.

1/7TH—1/8TH BATTALIONS.

The Divisional front to be advanced had been divided into four sections, each of which was allotted to a battalion of the 167th Brigade. From right to left these sections were as follows: (A) To be dug by the 1/1st Londons; (B) by the 1/8th Middlesex; (C) by the 1/3rd Londons plus one company of 1/5th Cheshires; and (D) by the 1/7th Middlesex. The new line was to extend from the Bucquoy Road across the Gommecourt Road, round the "Z" ledge to No. 4 Sap in Y Sector. Only the work of pegging out the new line was done on the first night. Screens of patrols, each consisting of one officer, an N.C.O. and 10 men, were placed at 50 yards' interval out in "No Man's Land" in front of the pegging-out parties. These patrols were furnished by the units of each section.

25TH MAY.

At 9 p.m. on the 25th these covering parties crept out and took up their positions. At 10 p.m. the pegging-out parties followed, and the work of tracing out the new line, putting the pegs in the

25TH MAY. ground and connecting them with string was accomplished without the slightest interference from the enemy. The nights at this period were intensely dark. The next night, again at 9 p.m., the covering parties again moved out and, on this occasion, established themselves close up to the German wire, blocking every known gap in it; their orders were to rush with the bayonet any parties of Germans endeavouring to come through their wire, but on no account were shots to be fired. The covering parties having established themselves out in "No Man's Land," the four Battalions of the Brigade moved out of their trenches and advanced in extended order on the allotted frontage to the pegged-out line. They then set to work to dig hard. The digging parties were followed by wiring parties, the two working together. As an instance of the 1/8TH BATTALION. progress of the work on this (the second) night of the operation, the 1/8th Middlesex in four hours dug 800 yards of new trench. On the third night the same procedure was followed, the Battalions being employed in improving the trenches dug on the previous night, in digging communication trenches and in erecting barbed-wire entanglements. The new line was then ready for occupation. It was an altogether extraordinary programme, and no wonder that congratulations were showered on the 167th Brigade by the Divisional, Corps and Army Commanders.

1/7TH—1/8TH BATTALIONS. Examination of the Diaries of the 1/7th and 1/8th Middlesex reveals the fact that only one officer (Capt. H. E. Martin, 1/8th Battalion) was wounded during the time the new line was being prepared.

11TH BATTALION. 5TH JANUARY. An entry in the Diary of the 11th Middlesex (Lieut.-Colonel W. D. Ingle commanding), dated the 5th January, after moving back into the Festubert sector on the 4th, briefly describes the kind of existence the Battalion was eking out in the front line at the beginning of 1916: "Pumping and baling carried out almost continuously in 'A' and 'D' Companies' trenches. 'D' Company's Island Group relieved every twenty-four hours, and go back to Le Touret for twenty-four hours to get dry. Enemy quiet, a few shells on 'B' Company's right during the morning, and a few 77-mm. shells on Rue de Bois—casualties nil." Relief came on the 13th, and the Battalion moved back into billets. 11TH FEB. On 11th February the Battalion marched to Sailly Labourse, preparatory to moving into trenches near the Quarries on the morning of the 12th, the 12th Division having taken over a portion of the line between Loos and the La Bassée Canal.

The 13th February was a day of trial and heavy loss to the Battalion. As soon as it was light enough to see each other's trenches a duel with trench-mortar bombs and rifle grenades broke out between the opposing forces. About 10 a.m. the enemy's artillery joined in the combat, bombarding the trenches of the Middlesex with H.E. and (as the Battalion Diary has it) "smaller stuff." The trenches were damaged considerably and several casualties were suffered. But the Divisional Artillery and the "Heavies" retaliated, and, after some hours (about 3 p.m.), things were once more normal, although only for a little while. At 5.30 p.m. the enemy's artillery fire broke out again, and hostile shells of all calibre, up to 9-inch, fell in considerable numbers on the front line, support and communication trenches, which were blown about, and, in many places, completely wrecked. There were very few dug-outs in the line, and the Middlesex men had poor shelter from this hail of shell, with the inevitable result—heavy casualties. Just after 6 p.m. there were two enormous explosions, one from beneath the Kink and the other under Alexander trench, and clouds of earth, equipment, timber and the bodies of men shot up into the air—the enemy had exploded mines. Immediately following the explosions five groups of Germans, each of about ten men, rushed across from Bill's Bluff and tried to enter Bigger Willie. Rifle and machine-gun fire, and a storm of grenades, caused most of them to fall back; others fell dead or wounded, but six were successful in getting into the trenches of the Middlesex. Their triumph was, however, short-lived, for they were either shot down, bombed or bayoneted. They had already filled their pockets with Mills grenades when they were killed. As the Germans advanced, the enemy's artillery had lifted to the support trenches behind Bigger Willie and the Kink. At 6.25 p.m. the hostile bombardment died down, but twenty minutes later fires were lighted by the enemy in his front-line trenches, and he threw smoke bombs, though the wind carried the smoke northwards. At 7 p.m. normal conditions again reigned. The losses suffered by the Middlesex on the 13th were 2 officers wounded, 10 other ranks killed, 49 wounded and 5 missing—a costly day. The Battalion had clung to its position with great tenacity and gallantry, and a fitting acknowledgment of the steadfastness of all ranks was contained in a message from the G.O.C., First Army, which arrived during the 14th: "The G.O.C., First Army, wishes his

13TH FEB. 11TH BATTALION.

13TH FEB. 11TH BATTALION.

congratulations conveyed to the officer commanding and troops who counter-attacked and drove back the enemy who had effected a lodgment in our trenches in the neighbourhood of the Kink on the evening of 13th." Lieut.-Colonel Ingle had every reason to be proud of his officers and men.

14TH FEB.

The 14th was comparatively quiet. The 15th was similarly uneventful, though several aerial torpedoes were fired by the Germans, one of which caused six casualties. Relief came on the 16th, the 9th Royal Fusiliers taking over the line from the 11th Middlesex, and the latter moved back to Railway Reserve and Lancashire Trenches and Vermelles.

29TH FEB.

On the 29th the Battalion again took over the trenches previously occupied opposite the Quarries.

It was not long, however, before the 11th Middlesex were again involved in heavy losses, even more serious than on the 13th February, for an attack had been ordered on the Chord, a particularly strong sector of the German line opposite the left of the 36th Brigade front. The attack was to be carried out by the 8th and 9th Royal Fusiliers. Three mines were to be exploded close to the Chord and the craters formed by the explosion, as well as the Chord itself, were to be occupied. It was expected that the enemy would make a desperate resistance. As all the orders referring to this little operation concern the two Battalions (8th and 9th Royal Fusiliers) making the attack, it is unnecessary to give more than the above outline. It was in rendering assistance to the attacking force that the 11th Middlesex became involved and sustained heavy losses. The attack was to take place on the 2nd March at 5.45 p.m. On the previous evening at 6.20 p.m. a party of 11th Middlesex, consisting of one N.C.O. and 15 other ranks, was sent to Clarke's Keep to detonate grenades. Another party of one N.C.O. and 20 men followed on the morning of the 2nd at 9 a.m. to the same place and for the same purpose. Two hours later the first party returned, having been hard at work all night. That afternoon at 3.30 detailed orders for the attack reached the O.C., 11th Middlesex, and these were followed, half an hour later, by orders to detail a party of four N.C.Os. and 50 men (half from "C" Company and half from "B" Company) to be at the junction of Saville Row and Support Line under the O.C., 9th Royal Fusiliers; this party reached its destination at 5.15 p.m. Five minutes later the "Heavies" opened heavy fire on the enemy's trenches. At 5.30 p.m. all men of the Middlesex Regiment were moved out of

2ND MARCH.

their dug-outs, and when fifteen minutes later the mines were exploded, all ranks were "standing to." No less than 32,000 lbs. of explosives were used, and the explosions were deafening. Three large mines and one small mine were blown under the Chord, and the infantry advanced immediately. But instead of being taken by surprise and shaken by the explosions, the Germans lined the parapets of their trenches and opened a steady fire on the attacking Fusiliers. No word reached the O.C., 11th Middlesex, until 7.30 p.m., when orders came to hand to render all possible assistance to the 9th Royal Fusiliers, who were on the left of the Middlesex. Half an hour later, 2nd Lieut. Marcus, with 50 men from "A" Company, was sent off to the junction of Saville Row and Support Line under the O.C., 9th Royal Fusiliers. At 8.40 p.m. 2nd Lieut. Moore, 50 men of "A" Company, and two grenadier squads were similarly despatched to come under the orders of the O.C., 9th Royal Fusiliers. At 9.30 p.m. orders were received by Colonel Ingle to place two of his companies at the disposal of the 9th Royal Fusiliers, and as these left the Battalion area, "B" Company extended to the left, taking over "A" Company's front, with its left flank in Poker Street, the remainder of "A" Company moving back to Vigo Street. "D" Company also extended its left to the junction of Massa Alley with Bigger Willie. About midnight on the 2nd March the dispositions of the 11th Middlesex appear to be as follows: "B" and "D" Companies held the front line; "A" Company on the left and "C" Company on the right of Vigo Street. The Middlesex men were reinforced at 11.55 p.m. by a company of 6th Connaught Rangers: this Company was attached to "D" Company of the Middlesex. Of the desperate fighting which had taken place during the day not a word is mentioned in the Battalion Diary of the Middlesex, nothing but moves and dispositions. But from the casualty list given later, from the 2nd to 4th March, it is obvious that the Battalion was heavily engaged with the enemy during that period.

2ND MARCH. 11TH BATTALION.

At 9 a.m. on the 3rd Major Overton of the 9th Royal Fusiliers arrived at Colonel Ingle's Headquarters with orders for the Middlesex to relieve the Fusiliers, the Connaughts to relieve the Middlesex. At what time the relief began it is impossible to say, but apparently it was completed by 2.10 p.m., the dispositions of the Battalion being then: "D" Company—two platoons (right) in Kaiserin Trench from Clifford Street to Poker Street, two platoons in Vigo Street; "B" Company—two platoons

3RD MARCH.

3RD MARCH. 11TH BATTALION.

(left) in Kaiserin Trench from Poker Street to Saville Row; "A" Company—in Northampton Trench; "C" Company—15 men in No. 1 Crater, 20 men in No. 2 Crater and 30 men in "A" Crater; the remainder of the "C" Company was on the right of Northampton Trench. The Battalion Bombers, thirty in number, were in Triangle Crater. Nos. 1 and 2 Craters were just south of the Chord and "A" Crater was on the left of it. Triangle Crater was just south of No. 2.

The 36th Brigade Diary has an interesting note on the relief: "The two Battalions which delivered the attack on the night of the 2nd were relieved on the 3rd, and their place taken by the 11th Battalion Middlesex Regiment, on the right, and the 7th Royal Sussex Regiment, on the left. These two Battalions had heavier casualties than the Fusilier Battalions, which took the positions and held them during the first night. All the men of these two Battalions had been employed throughout the previous night as reinforcements and working parties."

The Middlesex and Sussex Battalions were, however, soon called upon to beat off repeated heavy and desperate counter-attacks. The position won on the 2nd March was magnificent; it commanded the whole of the German trenches as far as Fosse 8, and gave possession of practically the whole of the remainder of the Hohenzollern Redoubt, for which much bloody fighting had already taken place. Moreover, the British trenches between the Hohenzollern Redoubt and the Vermelles railway were no longer overlooked or exposed to the enemy's rifle and machine-gun fire. It was, therefore, unlikely that the enemy would allow the possession of this valuable position to remain undisputed. Nor did he, for three separate attacks were launched against the Middlesex before, at 8.15 p.m. on the night of the 3rd, the Battalion Diary records, "shells and bombing quietened down." All these attacks (launched against the Sussex also, on the left of the 11th Middlesex) were beaten off with heavy loss to the enemy, though at 10 p.m. he was reported to be in occupation of the further lip of Triangle Crater. The night was passed in comparative quietude, all ranks being engaged in strengthening the defences and in sand-bagging

4TH MARCH.

the Craters. But at 5.45 a.m. on the 4th the Germans made fresh heavy bombing attacks, and more bombs and S.A.A. were called for to resist these attacks. A German sniper had, during the night, established himself in the further lip of Triangle Crater, commanding the trench between Craters Nos. 2 and "A." This man could not be shifted and caused many casualties. The latter hours of the 4th seem to have been fairly quiet, but again, at 1 a.m. on the 5th, another heavy bombing attack was launched against the Middlesex men in Crater No. 2. It was beaten off with loss to the enemy. 4TH MARCH. 11TH BATTALION.

At 9 a.m. the 6th Buffs began to arrive in order to relieve the Middlesex men. But the relief took hours to carry out, and it was 4 p.m. before the line, with the exception of Crater "A," was taken over by the incoming Battalion. Repeated attempts to relieve the troops in Crater "A" had failed, and it was not until darkness had fallen that the exhausted garrison was replaced and marched back to Sailly Labourse.

During those three days—the 2nd to 4th March inclusive—not a single casualty is recorded in the Battalion Diary of the 11th Middlesex, but from the Diary of the 36th Brigade Headquarters the following list is taken :—"Officers killed : Capt. A. F. Henty; Lieuts. H. L. Hughes-Jones, L. A. Hughman, C. V. Dodgson; wounded, Lieut. W. E. G. Henkel; 2nd Lieuts. R. Underhill, F. A. Moore, S. W. Hedgecock, D. S. Marcus; other ranks, 35 killed, 207 wounded. Total, 9 officers and 242 other ranks."

Several days were spent in billets cleaning up and reorganising and then, on the 11th March, the 11th Middlesex again took over front-line trenches in the Quarry sector. The 12th and 13th were quiet days, but during the evening of the latter date a little incident occurred which amply demonstrated the good comradeship which existed between officers and men, even to the point of sacrificing their lives one for the other. 11TH MARCH.

In front of the trenches occupied by the Middlesex, and outside Lookout Crescent, there were a number of mine craters, in which the Tunnelling Company had received orders to set off a small mine. Colonel Ingle gave orders for the disposition of his men so that no one should be injured by the explosion or falling debris. At 5 p.m. the mine was fired, and after the explosion Lieut. Crombie (O.C., "B" Company), 2nd Lieut. C. K. Smith and a few men went along the trench and found some miners stretched out senseless in the mine shafts. The two officers led the way and tried to drag the unconscious miners out, but were themselves gassed, together with three other ranks. The second officer (2nd Lieut. Smith) was so badly gassed that he died within an hour. The fine heroism of this young officer and the "greater love" for others

11TH MARCH. 11TH BATTALION. had cost him his life. Apparently a mistake in putting only seven-foot tamping, when ten-foot tamping had been ordered, was the cause of the explosion coming back up the shafts and filling the place with gas fumes. "This gross neglect of orders," records the Battalion Diary, " caused the death of one of our best officers."

Towards the end of March (on the 24th and 25th) the enemy exploded two mines, and for several days there was much activity in bombing, trench-mortaring and the firing of rifle grenades by both sides. The Middlesex suffered a number of casualties during these operations—2 officers were wounded and 41 other ranks were killed, wounded or missing. April was uneventful, and May was spent entirely out of the front line. In June the 12th Division received orders to move south, and on the 16th the 36th Infantry Brigade entrained at Fouquereuil Station for " a new area." All units reached Longeau during the night 16th–17th, and on the latter date marched to billets in Vignacourt. The 11th Middlesex had now a new C.O.—Lieut.-Colonel G. L. Oliver (who had joined the Battalion on the 14th June), vice Lieut.-Colonel W. D. Ingle. On the 30th June the 36th Brigade proceeded to fresh billets at Fréchencourt, arriving at midnight.

16TH JUNE.

12TH BATTALION. 1ST JANUARY.

For several days from the 1st January the 12th Middlesex (Lieut.-Colonel H. P. Osborne) of the 54th Brigade, 18th Division, were billeted in Méaulte, but on the 8th moved forward to the front line, taking over trenches in " D.1 " south of Fricourt. During the month the Battalion lost 1 officer, Lieut. S. L. Ponsonby, who, after being severely wounded in the thigh during patrol work on the night of the 8th, died in hospital on the 12th. During the first month of the year there were no incidents of outstanding importance. February was spent out of the front line, and it was not until the 5th March that the Battalion, moving via Corbie and Bray, relieved the 2nd Wilts in " A.1 " sector. Colonel Osborne, having been evacuated sick, Major M. C. Scarborough was in command of the 12th Battalion. On April 2nd Lieut.-Colonel Osborne returned and resumed command of the Battalion. The Battalion lost 13 men (an entire working party) in a heavy raid launched by the enemy before dawn on the 13th April. The working party was engaged in digging out a piece of trench which had been filled in by the 30th Division who held the line before the 18th Division had taken it over. The men were hard at work when suddenly the enemy's artillery opened a heavy bombardment and, almost simultaneously, a large party of Germans who

5TH MARCH.

had laid up under cover of the dead ground just outside the Middlesex trenches rushed in and, having stunned most of the workmen, carried them off to their own trenches. A bombing party was immediately organised, but it was too late, the Germans having reached their own lines. On the 27th the Battalion raided the Germans, but it was not a success, though casualties were very small. The raiding party succeeded in reaching and bombing the German trenches, but nothing more. Almost the whole of May was spent out of the front line at Grove Town Camp, the Battalion celebrating Albuhera Day, on the 16th, in true Regimental fashion. On the 11th June the Middlesex entrained at Méricourt for Picquigny, where training on specially constructed trenches was to be carried out. This period of preparation was part of the training given to all Battalions, Brigades and Divisions who were to take part in the initial Battle of the Somme operations. The practice trenches were models of those which the units would be called upon to capture on "Zero" day. This training was very thorough. In addition, all specialist officers held classes for the training of specialist other ranks. Conferences were frequently held, lectures given and demonstrations carried out with Stokes mortars, and by the time the Battalion returned to Grove Town on the 26th June there was not one officer or man who did not know what was expected of him or what part he was to take in the coming operations.

13TH APRIL. 12TH BATTALION. 27TH APRIL. 16TH MAY. 11TH JUNE.

On the night of the 28th, at 8.15 p.m., the 12th Middlesex moved from Bray to Carnoy, taking over the front-line trenches north of the town from the 7th Bedfords. At 1 a.m. Lieut. Restall and his scouts went out and examined the wire in front of the enemy's trenches. They returned and reported the entanglements completely destroyed, and apparently there were no Germans in the front trench. The British barrage was then falling on the enemy's front line, so that Restall and his men had to return without entering it. On the 29th June, gas and smoke discharges by the divisions on the right and left of the 18th Division provoked a heavy hostile bombardment, but without doing much damage. That night a final raid was carried out by the Middlesex, and extracts are given from the Battalion Diary showing to what extent the terrible bombardment, to which the British guns subjected the German trenches, had affected the moral of the enemy.

28TH JUNE.

The raiding party was composed of 2nd Lieuts. Chase, Garstin, Card (bombing officer) and Restall (scout officer), the Battalion

29TH JUNE. 12TH BATTALION.

bombers, Battalion Scouts and two platoons of "D" Company; it was commanded by 2nd Lieut. Chase. The object of the raid was to find out to what extent the enemy's trenches had suffered from the bombardment, and whether they were being held. A hostile barrage was in progress as the party started. The party "went in columns through the German front and support-line trenches without encountering any opposition. They then extended and, dropping a blocking party under 2nd Lieut. Card, proceeded to extend and advance to the third-line trench, covered by the scouts under 2nd Lieut. Restall. Only four Germans were encountered in this trench, and three of these were disposed of satisfactorily, the fourth escaping up a communication trench. They appeared cowed by our artillery fire. The trenches were almost levelled and were completely destroyed. One German they tried to bring in as a prisoner seemed to be quite out of his mind and became unmanageable; he had to be abandoned, dead. 2nd Lieut. Card and his blocking party encountered a party of about twenty Germans in a communication trench between the front and support trenches. They bombed them heavily, and accounted for at least eight of this party. After examining about four hundred yards of the trench, the raiders returned in two parties. 2nd Lieut. Chase, who was returning with the left party, was unfortunately hit by machine-gun fire when crossing 'No Man's Land,' and severely wounded.* During the night there was another discharge of gas, which drew a heavy bombardment of our lines. The Company ('B') occupying the support trenches suffered heavy casualties in the two platoons occupying Glasgow Road. Casualties: 2nd Lieuts. Chase and Bennet wounded; other ranks, 10 killed, 38 wounded, 2 missing in raid."

30TH JUNE.

On the night of the 30th, at 10.30 p.m., the Battalion was relieved by the 11th Royal Fusiliers and returned to dug-outs in Carnoy, where, for the time being, they must be left.

13TH BATTALION. 4TH JANUARY.

The 13th Middlesex (Lieut.-Colonel L. G. Oliver) were still training at Hellebroucq on 1st January, 1916. On the 4th 2nd Lieut. C. B. Castle died in hospital of cerebro-meningitis. "He was," records the Battalion Diary, "a great loss to the Battalion."

On the 6th the tour out of the front line came to an end, the Middlesex men entraining at midnight, 6th–7th January, and

* Died of his wounds on 1st July, 1916.

reaching Poperinghe about 3.15 a.m. on the 7th. The Battalion detrained at 4 a.m. and set out on a dismal six and a-half miles' march to a camp about one and a-half miles N.E. of Reninghelst, which was reached about 8.30 a.m. The Battalion transport, however, did not reach camp until 2 p.m., having had a terrible time wallowing in thick mud along the narrow roads. 7TH JANUARY. 13TH BATTALION.

The 24th Division had orders to go into the line in the Hooge sector, and on the 14th January the 13th Middlesex (less the specialists, *i.e.*, machine-gunners, signallers and grenadiers who had gone into the line on the 13th) left camp at 10 a.m. for the trenches. On reaching Belgian Château a halt was made for three hours, then on through Kruisstraat to the Asylum at Ypres. Here "gum boots, thigh," were issued, and the march was continued through Ypres and along the Menin road until suddenly, branching off to the right, the Battalion reached Gordon House. From the latter place the Middlesex men, in small parties, moved up to the front line in Sanctuary Wood, relieving the 8th Queen's Regiment. "C" Company was in the firing line, "B" Company in support and "D" in reserve. "A" had been left behind at the camp to follow later.

The sector taken over by the Middlesex men was by no means a delectable spot. The British trenches ran from north to south in a very irregular line at the eastern end of Sanctuary Wood. The German trenches ran across the north-east corner of the Wood. In the centre of the sector "No Man's Land" was very much wider than on the northern and southern ends, where the opposing trenches were close together. At this stage "Wood" was something of a misnomer, for the trees had been shorn of almost all their branches and only blasted and torn stumps remained. The trenches were in poor condition, for the winter rains, with occasional frost and snow, played havoc with the defences, which were in constant need of repair. It was an ideal spot for sniping operations, and both sides took full advantages of the opportunities offered for carrying on their beastly work. The first victim appears to have been 2nd Lieut. T. W. O'Reilly, who was shot in the leg at Yeomanry Post on the 17th.

The first tour came to an end on the 18th; the Battalion moving back after relief to Belgian dug-outs. Back again in Sanctuary Wood on the 22nd and out on the 24th, then on the 31st to Camp "B," sums up the remainder of January. The next tour in the line was north of the Menin road, opposite Bellewaarde 31ST JANUARY.

7TH—8TH FEB. Farm in "H" trenches, the 13th Middlesex relieving the 9th East Surrey Regiment on the night 7th–8th February. On the 8th, although the enemy subjected the section to heavy shell-fire, as well as "whizz-banging" the front line and "Y" Wood, only 2 other ranks were killed. On the 9th 2nd Lieut. S. C. Saunders was wounded, and on the 15th Lieut. C. E. Morton was wounded by a sniper. The Hooge sector was always noisy and dangerous. The Battalion was relieved on the 29th: the casualties for the month were 2 officers wounded and 42 other ranks killed and wounded.

13TH BATTALION.

15TH FEBRUARY.

In March the 13th Middlesex went back into Sanctuary Wood, where, in a blinding snowstorm which lasted all night, the Battalion relieved the 8th Royal West Kents. Snowstorms, sniping and sapping were the chief features of the tour which followed. On the 14th, from 12 noon to 3 p.m., a particularly violent bombardment was opened by the enemy and 4 other ranks were killed and 18 wounded. At dusk on the 15th 2nd Lieut. M. E. King was shot dead by a sniper. The 16th was again signalised by a heavy hostile bombardment, though casualties were slight. Nevertheless, when the Battalion was relieved that night, the losses throughout the tour, 3 officers and 42 other ranks killed and wounded, were the heaviest since the Battle of Loos.

14TH MARCH.

In the third week in March the 24th Division relieved the 3rd Canadian Division west of Messines, but it was not until the 25th that the 13th Middlesex marched from Meteren, via Neuve Eglise, to Kortepyp Huts, where it was placed in Divisional Reserve. On the last day of the month the Battalion relieved the 9th Royal Sussex Regiment in the line opposite Messines, but this tour was uneventful. One officer, 2nd Lieut. Weldon Williams, was wounded. The Battalion had its first experience of gas on the night 29th–30th March. At 1 a.m. heavy hostile shell-fire broke out, and the enemy's machine guns swept the parapets of the trenches held by the Middlesex men in order to force the sentries to keep their heads down, also to drown the hissing noise from the gas as it was projected from the cylinders. No infantry attack followed this gas attack, but the Middlesex lost nine other ranks killed, one officer (2nd Lieut. R. M. Richford) and 20 other ranks wounded; 2 officers (2nd Lieuts. Weldon Williams and C. J. Romer*) and 40 other ranks were gassed. In addition, some 30 other ranks were slightly gassed but remained "at duty."

25TH MARCH.

* Died from gas poisoning on 3rd April.

When the Battalion marched out of the trenches on the night 31st March–1st April it had suffered casualties during the month of 4 officers and 163 other ranks. In May eight-day tours in the trenches were begun, but the month was bare of incident. . . . On the night of the 5th June between 11.30 p.m. and 12.30 a.m., Lieut.-Colonel Cunningham* was shot through both arms and body whilst walking along Sussex Trench, about twenty yards behind T. 140. Fortunately the wounds were not fatal. On the 7th the Brigade Major, 73rd Infantry Brigade—Major Howlett—assumed temporary command of the 13th Middlesex, but was succeeded on the 9th by Major Greene of the 7th Dragoon Guards. At the end of June the Battalion was out of the front line in Kemmel Shelters. 31ST MARCH. 13TH BATTALION. 5TH JUNE.

Between the 1st January and 25th February, 1916, on which date the Battalion was transferred to G.H.Q., there are few items of interest to relate concerning the 16th (Public Schools Battalion) Middlesex Regiment (Lieut.-Colonel J. Hamilton Hall). The Battalion, on the 2nd January, moved to Annequin North, taking over B.1 trenches on the 4th. Apparently this tour lasted until the 14th, when, on relief, the Battalion marched to Bethune. This tour cost the 16th Battalion 1 officer (2nd Lieut. H. J. Bowman) and 11 other ranks killed, and 24 other ranks wounded. The next tour in the line (2.0 sub-sector), from 27th January to 2nd February, was responsible for more serious casualties, for on the 28th the front-line and support trenches were heavily bombarded and Major G. C. Way, Captain S. Douglas and 2 other ranks were killed, whilst Captain G. H. Heslop and 15 other ranks were wounded. On the 29th January, at 11 a.m., the C.O. received a verbal order from the G.O.C., 100th Infantry Brigade, to make a bombing attack against the German line at Mad Point. That night, at 9 p.m., 3 officer patrols, under Lieut. Cleghorn, Lieut. James and Lieut. E. B. Samuel, went out to reconnoitre Mad Point. They returned about 1 a.m. on the 20th, having lost 1 other rank killed, 1 wounded and 1 missing; 2nd Lieut. E. B. Samuel was also reported "missing, believed killed."† The G.O.C.'s order for the bombing attack was subsequently cancelled. On the night of the 3rd February, while the Battalion was at Annequin Fosse in Brigade Reserve, an order was received at 10.45 p.m. from 1ST JANUARY. 16TH BATTALION. 3RD FEBRUARY.

* Lieut.-Colonel Cunningham was commanding the 13th Middlesex at this period, having succeeded Lieut.-Colonel L. G. Oliver on 30th March.

† Officially reported killed 30th January, 1916.

3RD FEBRUARY. 16TH BATTALION. the G.O.C., 100th Brigade, to make a bombing attack on three craters at Mine Point and to consolidate the western edge of the craters. "D" Company (strength 140) with 32 Battalion bombers under Lieut. Cleghorn, left Annequin Fosse to carry out this order, but owing to various reasons the attack was not a success, and on the approach of dawn (4th) the party returned, Lieut. Cleghorn and 3 other ranks having been wounded. At 10 a.m., however, the G.O.C. Brigade ordered another attack to be made on the craters and, at 6.30 p.m., "D" Company, with 2nd Lieut. James, 2nd Lieut. Tanqueray, 106 other ranks, plus 16 grenadiers under Lieut. Hopwood, the whole commanded by Capt. F. R. Hill, left Annequin Fosse for the front-line trenches. But again the attack was unsuccessful, and the casualties in this second attempt were killed: Lieut. R. H. Hopwood and 5 other ranks; wounded, 10 other ranks. No other incident of importance during February is related in the Battalion Diary. On the 25th the 16th Middlesex marched to Annezin, moving on the following day to Bethune, there entraining for St. Omer. At the latter place the Battalion detrained and marched to Quiestede, and the last phase in the Diary relates the conditions under which the Battalion found itself back at G.H.Q.: "Battalion is now withdrawn from 33rd Division, and forms part of G.H.Q. troops for the purpose of withdrawing men for temporary commissions."

For nearly two months the 16th Middlesex remained at Quiestede, training and supplying men for commissions, but on

24TH APRIL. the 24th April the Battalion marched to Aire and entrained for Doullens, having been ordered to join the 29th Division, then holding a front-line sector on the Somme. This famous Division, after several months of splendid fighting on the Gallipoli Peninsula, was transferred to France, and had a very distinguished career. The reason the 16th Middlesex were transferred to it is thus given in the Diary of the 86th Infantry Brigade (29th Division): "Orders received for 1/R.M.F. to withdraw to L. of C., they can get no drafts; their place will be taken by 16th Middlesex, Lieut.-Colonel Hall."

Late at night on the 24th the Battalion arrived at Mailly Maillet, went into billets, and on the following day took over front-line trenches in the Auchonvillers sector from a composite unit formed of one company of Lancashire Fusiliers and one company of Dublin Fusiliers. These two Battalions, with the 1st K.O.S. Borderers, were the three other units with which the

16th Middlesex were brigaded. For the remaining days of April and the whole of May there is nothing to record, and until the latter end of June, when preparations for the Somme Battles were in progress, there are no incidents of importance in the Battalion Diary. On the 23rd June the Battalion was relieved by the Lancashire Fusiliers in the northern section of the Auchonvillers trenches, and marched back to Acheux Wood. On the 24th the general artillery bombardment of the enemy's trenches began, and on the night of the 27th–28th a raid was carried out by the 16th Middlesex—one of many up and down the line—made for the purpose of finding out the condition of the enemy's wire entanglements and his trenches after the awful bombardment to which they had been subjected. The raid was carried out by twelve other ranks, under the command of Lieut. Cleghorn. This officer appears to have been an intrepid raider. The party left the trenches at 11.10 p.m., and, after getting through the wire, moved along the New Beaumont Road up to the enemy's trenches without being seen. They found the enemy's wire entanglements twisted and damaged, but with no clear passage through them. The raiders were, therefore, held up, and only Cleghorn and two of his men actually got through and entered the front German trenches. They were hardly in the trenches, however, before the enemy began to throw bombs from both flanks, not only into his front line but also into his wire entanglements. He also opened heavy machine-gun fire and placed a shrapnel barrage on the trenches of the Middlesex. The O.C. raid then gave the order to retire, and Lieut. Cleghorn and his men returned to their trenches, only two men being wounded. On the 28th instructions were received that the general assault would take place. On the 30th 9 officers and 75 other ranks were drawn from the Battalion as Reserves and proceeded, at 2.30 p.m., under Major A. N. G. Jones, to Mailly Woods. The Battalion (less the Reserves and bombing detachment), strength 22 officers and 689 other ranks, marched to Auchonvillers at 10.20 p.m., and there bivouacked for the night.

24th April. 16th Battalion. 23rd June. 27th—28th June.

The Battalion Diary of the 17th Middlesex (Colonel H. Fenwick) gives a very good idea of what was happening to that Battalion on the 1st January, 1916. "We are now back in Busnes for a divisional rest. The men were ordered to thoroughly cleanse themselves, change underclothing, etc. The billets were cleaned and disinfected. New Year's Day was celebrated as much

17th Battalion. 1st January.

17TH JANUARY. as the circumstances would allow." The " rest " period came to

17TH BATTALION. an end on the 17th January, when the Battalion marched to Gorre. All Companies had a tour in the front-line trenches at Givenchy before the month ended, but no untoward incidents

11TH FEBRUARY. happened. On the night of 11th February, the Battalion moved into sub-sector C.I. Festubert—a pestilential part of the line. Mud and water were everywhere, in fact the front line consisted of 16 " islands," each having a garrison of about ten men who could only be relieved at night.

Towards the end of February the 2nd Division relieved the 18th French Division in the Angres sector, south of Lens, the 17th Middlesex and the 1st King's Regiment taking over the Calonne sub-sector on the 26th of the month. The 6th Brigade was relieved on the 17th March, after a comparatively quiet tour, and all units of the Brigade moved back to Bruay, a twelve-mile march which severely tested the march discipline of all ranks. Weeks spent in the front-line trenches usually made a man " soft " for marching even a few miles. April and May were undisturbed by any attack on or by the enemy. On the 31st of the latter month Captain Dowsett was shot dead by a sniper.

Hitherto the 17th Middlesex had not been engaged in any

1ST JUNE. operations of importance, but on the 1st June their chance came. The Battalion was then in the Souchez sector, and, with the 1st King's Regiment, had received orders to make a bombing raid on the enemy. The attack was to be preceded by heavy artillery bombardment beginning at 4.5 p.m. and ending at 8.30 p.m. At the latter hour three mines were to be exploded, the guns lengthening their range to the enemy's support and second-line trenches. The explosion of the mines was the signal for the infantry attack to begin, when the raiding parties of Middlesex and King's men were to advance and occupy the craters and also enter the enemy's trenches.

The three mines were " blown," but immediately both Battalions were subjected to very heavy shell-fire, while from the volume of machine-gun and rifle fire coming from the German front line it was obvious that the hostile trenches were held in strength, despite the very heavy bombardment to which they had been subjected. Nevertheless, in the face of fierce opposition the 17th Middlesex made a very gallant attempt to carry out their orders, and Colonel Fenwick's report of the attack is given in full, as the account in the Battalion Diary conveys nothing of the nature of the operation :—

1ST JUNE. 17TH BATTALION.

"On mines being blown, the enemy raised a fierce burst of fire, which lasted till 9.40 p.m., at which time it began to slacken, and I ordered the arranged-for parties to start in the following order: (1) Raiding party under 2nd Lieut. E. C. Lee, (2) three covering parties under Lieut. Engleburtt, (3) consolidating parties consisting of forty men each of 'A' and 'B,' the rest of these two Companies resuming their places in the front line, whence they had been withdrawn shortly before 4 p.m. for the purpose of taking cover from shelling. The expectation was that on reaching the (enemy's) line it would be found that great damage had been done to the German front line by the explosion, and also by the five hours' continuous bombardment of our artillery. In fact, it was anticipated that the German front line would be practically non-existent. However, the reverse was the case. Our front-line and communication trenches suffered very severely from both the explosion and the German artillery, and the Germans were quite ready to meet the troops on their arrival with machine-gun fire.

"The right party, under 2nd Lieut. Lee, passed through Broadbridge Crater and Mildven Crater, when machine-gun fire was opened on them, and Lieut. Lee was killed. The remainder of this party, who were expert bombers, fell back and joined in with the covering parties under Lieut. Engleburtt.

"The covering parties were three groups of ten each, whose endeavour it was to seize the far lips of the new craters and hold them, while consolidating parties behind them built up and made tenable the near lips of the craters. It was first of all reported to me that these covering parties had succeeded in occupying the front lips as was their object, but this I found afterwards had not, and never could have been done. What they did was to establish themselves between the craters and on the sides of the craters, and by constant bombing keep off the enemy. In this they were greatly helped by the two Lewis guns which accompanied them, many of the teams of which were wounded. On learning the situation I sent an order to Lieut. Engleburtt to retire on the consolidating party and to guard the near lip of the crater while consolidation proceeded. This was done, and Lieut. Engleburtt got his men and guns back to our lines. All the time these parties were out continuous bombing contests kept taking place between

1st June. 17th Battalion.

small parties. Lieut. Engleburtt, though wounded in hand and arm, remained at his post and did real good work. I consider that these covering parties, though they did not achieve their purpose of occupying the further lip of the crater, nevertheless enabled the general objective to make progress satisfactorily, which was to occupy the near lip. As regards consolidation of the line of the near lip of the crater, this may be divided into two parts, as follows:—First, the left, led by 'B' Company under Captain Salter. Here a crater of considerable size was found on the left of Broadbridge. Explosions had only damaged our line in two places. The crater itself was of a favourable nature to consolidate. Much work was done here, and by daylight on the 2nd it was pretty safe. Second, as regards the crater on the right. This was a matter of much magnitude and difficulty, which difficulty was enhanced by the fact that two platoon leaders, 2nd Lieuts. L. A. Bradstreet and J. B. Skerry, were killed within five minutes of entering trenches by machine-gun fire. It took some time to send up two officers to replace them, and consequently work proceeded much slower. Also, Captain Rollason, who commanded this part of the line, did not have the advantage of any expert advice, the Engineer Officer who accompanied the consolidating parties confining his attention strictly to the crater on the left. Of two sappers who accompanied this party one was instantly killed by shell-fire before reaching the trench. Captain Rollason found himself without any technical advice and assistance, and had to do the best he could, which consisted in clearing and digging trench and sap to the crater to gain as much cover as possible. The front trench here was completely obliterated, and a dangerous position thus created."*

In this gallant attempt the 17th Battalion lost 3 officers killed and wounded, 7 other ranks killed and 51 wounded. The G.O.C., 2nd Division, in his report to IVth Corps Headquarters, stated: "This is the first occasion on which the 17th Middlesex have been engaged in serious fighting, but I consider they carried out the operation with steadiness and gallantry under very trying circumstances."

June was an unpleasant month. Periods of quietude were rudely broken by violent shelling. Lachrymatory shells made things uncomfortable, and constant mining and counter-mining was an increasing source of anxiety. The 17th Battalion made no

* "The History of the 2nd Division," Vol. I., by Everard Wyrall.

more raids or attempts on the enemy during the month, and on the 30th were holding support trenches in the Cabaret Rouge area. 30TH JUNE.

Of the 18th (1st Public Works Battalion) Middlesex (Lieut.-Colonel H. Storr), it is difficult to garner from the diaries any items of interest to the general reader. They were Pioneers, and these brave fellows led a most unselfish existence. They had no opportunities (or seldom had), such as fell to infantrymen in the front line, of engaging in exciting contests with the enemy; they could not retaliate when fired upon, though they worked almost always under shell fire, and frequently under machine-gun and rifle fire and the unpleasant attentions of German snipers. Yet they had not even the satisfaction of taking a shot at "Fritz." They just kept on with their work, repairing or making fresh defences, building machine-gun posts and emplacements, laying duck-boards in the trenches, digging communication trenches, wiring the front of trenches out in "No Man's Land." Once during January the Battalion was ordered to "stand to" as the enemy had made heavy attacks on the line and all available troops might be needed, but the Pioneers were not used though their machine-gun section was sent up into the line. Battalion Headquarters and billets were, at this period, at Le Préol, the 33rd Division holding a sector of the line in the La Bassée Canal area. For weeks and even months on end the Pioneers were engaged in this part of the line. On the 23rd April (it was Easter Day and the Battalion had been given a day's rest) they were paraded and addressed by the G.O.C., 33rd Division, and complimented on the work done during the past five months and on the spirit existing amongst all ranks. He also told them that they must keep in mind and train not only for defence of trenches but also for more open warfare. 18TH BATTALION. 23RD APRIL.

In June, in consequence of the 33rd Division having increased its frontage, taking over a part of the line north of the La Bassée Canal, the 18th Middlesex left their billets at Le Préol and moved to Annequin North. On the 22nd the Battalion had its first chance of taking a hand in a stiff fight. 22ND JUNE.

About 2 a.m. the enemy blew several large mines, making a huge crater and obliterating part of the front line near the Duck's Bill. Heavy shelling ensued and a raiding party of 150 Germans came across "No Man's Land." Two platoons of the Pioneers were at this time working in Coventry Street and the extension of

22ND JUNE. 18TH BATTALION. Cambridge Terrace to Piccadilly, and were involved, losing 5 men killed, 2nd Lieut. Latham and 12 men wounded and 1 man missing. "C" Company, also working in Cambridge Terrace, lost two men killed and 2nd Lieut. Chapman and seven men wounded. 2nd Lieut. Tollemache and No. 16 Platoon did good work and occupied a portion of the front line for one-and-a-half hours until reinforcements had been brought up and the enemy driven out. At 3 a.m. the enemy shelled Annequin North for 15 minutes with lachrymatory shells, but there were no casualties. The remaining platoons of "D" Company did good work during the day in clearing the damaged trenches and in re-establishing communication. No further incident of importance happened during June, 30TH JUNE. and the last day of the month found the 18th Battalion still carrying on their functions as Pioneers.

In May two more Battalions of the Regiment arrived in France. 19TH—23RD BATTALIONS. These were the 19th and 23rd. The 19th were Pioneers, *i.e.*, the 2nd Public Works Battalion, commanded by Lieut.-Colonel A. J. Irons. This Battalion, like the 18th, had been raised by Lieut.-Colonel John Ward, M.P., on the 15th April, 1915, who later was responsible for even a third—the 26th (3rd Public Works Battalion) Middlesex, whose war service must, for the present, be postponed, as they went out to Salonika, and eventually in 1919 to Russia.

23RD BATTALION. The 23rd (2nd Football) Battalion was raised by W. Joynson Hicks, Esq., M.P., on the 29th June, 1915; it was first commanded by Major A. Hicks, and subsequently by Lieut.-Colonel W. C. C. Ash. Both the 19th and 23rd Middlesex went out to France with the 41st Division, the latter Battalion forming part of the 123rd Brigade. In June the 19th and 23rd Middlesex were 20TH—21ST BATTALIONS. followed by two more Battalions, the 20th and 21st. The latter was known as the Islington Battalion, having been raised by the (then) Mayor of Islington on the 18th May, 1915. The first C.O. was Lieut.-Colonel W. S. Samuel. The 20th Battalion was commanded by Lieut.-Colonel F. P. Dunlop. Both Battalions formed part of the 121st Infantry Brigade of the 40th Division.

## CHAPTER XXIV.

# THE BATTLES OF THE SOMME, 1916.

1st July–18th November.

### INTRODUCTION.

IN no other series of battles fought on the Western Front were more Battalions of the Middlesex Regiment engaged than in the operations on the Somme in 1916. Nor alas! were the losses of the Regiment heavier. So far as officer casualties were concerned, the percentage was extraordinarily high; but a week or two from the first day of the Battles, and the common saying was that a subaltern's life was worth about a week's purchase. Fierce and bloody as were the operations of the first day of the Battles, the struggle abated not a whit until, for a while, the winter put a stop to the terrible sacrifice of human life: and it was mud, filth, slush and abominable conditions which beat the opposing forces in November of that year and forced them to stay their hands.

Controversy will continue to rage as to whether the Somme Battles of 1916 were justified: whether the objects of the Allied Commanders-in-Chief were sound tactics and strategy: whether the enormous expenditure of life was worth the relatively small gains of ground.

The objects of the offensive, which Sir Douglas Haig calls "the wearing-out battle," were briefly: (i) To relieve the pressure on Verdun, (ii) To assist the Allies in other theatres of the War by preventing any further transfer of German troops from the Western Front, (iii) To wear down the strength of the opposing forces. Such were the intentions of the Allied Commanders-in-Chief, and Regimental historians are not so much concerned with the tactics and strategies of the higher commands as with the endeavours of the gallant troops to carry out the orders given to them, and whether their brave efforts met with success or failure.

For months, preparations on a scale hitherto unknown had been going on in the Somme area and, as many Battalions of the Middlesex Regiment were engaged in preparing for the great offensive, it is as well to quote from the official despatches details of the work in which, between the intervals of maintaining the front line, they were employed, for it must not be forgotten that, in addition to the vast preparations, trench warfare of more or less intensity still went on.

"Vast stocks of ammunition and stores of every kind," said Sir Douglas Haig, "had to be accumulated beforehand within a convenient distance of our front. To deal with these, many miles of new railways, both standard and narrow gauge, and track tramways were laid. All available roads were improved, many others were made and long causeways were built over marshy valleys. Many additional dug-outs had to be provided as shelter for the troops, for use as dressing stations for the wounded and as magazines for storing ammunition, food, water and engineering material. Scores of miles of deep communication trenches had to be dug, as well as trenches for telephone wires, assembly and assault trenches, and numerous gun emplacements and observation posts. Important mining operations were undertaken, and charges were laid at various points beneath the enemy's lines. Except in the river valleys the existing supplies of water were hopelessly insufficient to meet the requirements of the numbers of men and horses to be concentrated in the area as the preparations for our offensive proceeded. To meet this difficulty many wells and borings were sunk, and over one hundred pumping plants were installed. More than one hundred and twenty miles of water mains were laid and everything was got ready to ensure an adequate water supply as our troops advanced.

"Much of this preparatory work had to be done under very trying conditions, and was liable to constant interruption from the enemy's fire. The weather, on the whole, was bad, and the local accommodation totally insufficient for housing the troops employed, who, consequently, had to content themselves with such rough shelter as could be provided in the circumstances. All this labour, too, had to be carried out in addition to fighting, and to the every-day work of maintaining existing defences. It threw a very heavy strain on the troops, which was borne by them with a cheerfulness beyond all praise."

The enemy's position on the Somme was of great strength: how great was not known until after the first day of the Battles, when the formidable nature of his defences and the extraordinary depth and security afforded by his dug-outs were indeed a revelation.

The following description of the Somme Battlefields-to-be is also from the official despatch, which cannot be paraphrased without loss: "The enemy's position to be attacked was of a very formidable character, situated on a high, undulating tract of ground which rises to more than 500 feet above sea-level, and forms the watershed between the Somme on the one side and the rivers of south-western Belgium on the other. On the southern face of this watershed, the general trend of which is from E.S.E. to W.N.W., the ground falls in a series of long, irregular spurs and deep depressions to the valley of the Somme. Well down the forward slopes of this face, the enemy's first system of defence, starting from the Somme, near Curlu, ran at first northwards for 3,000 yards, then westwards for 7,000 yards to near Fricourt, where it turned nearly due north, forming a great salient angle in the enemy's lines. Some 10,000 yards north of Fricourt the trenches crossed the River Ancre, a tributary of the Somme, and, still running northward, passed over the summit of the watershed about Hebuterne and Gommecourt, and then down its northern spurs to Arras. On the 20,000-yard front between the Somme and the Ancre the enemy had a strong second system of defence, sited generally on or near the southern crest of the highest part of the watershed, at an average distance of from 3,000 to 5,000 yards behind his first system.

"During nearly two years' preparation he had spared no pains to make these defences impregnable. The first and second systems each consisted of several lines of deep trenches, well provided with bomb-proof shelters and with numerous communication trenches connecting them. The front of the trenches of each system was protected by wire entanglements, many of them in two belts forty yards broad, built of iron stakes interlaced with barbed wire often about as thick as a man's finger.

"The numerous woods and villages in and between these systems of defence had been turned into veritable fortresses. The deep cellars, usually to be found in the villages, and the numerous pits and quarries common to a chalk country, were used to provide cover for machine guns and trench mortars. The existing cellars were supplemented by elaborate dug-outs, sometimes in two storeys, and these were connected up by passages as much as thirty feet below the surface of the ground. The salients in the enemy's line, from which he could bring enfilade fire across his front, were made into self-contained forts, and often protected by mine fields,* while strong redoubts and concrete machine-gun emplacements had been constructed in positions from which he could sweep his own trenches should these be taken. The ground lent itself to good artillery observation on the enemy's part, and he had skilfully arranged for cross-fire by his guns.

"These various systems of defences with the fortified localities and other supporting points between them were cunningly sited to afford each other material assistance and to admit of the utmost possible development of enfilade and flanking fire by machine guns and artillery. They formed, in short, not merely a series of successive lines, but one composite system of enormous depth and strength."

Sufficient has been said to show the formidable nature of the task before the British troops, and it is time to enumerate first those Divisions which were to carry out the initial attack, and then those Divisions in which Battalions of the Middlesex Regiment were contained.

From north of Maricourt (where the British right joined up with the left of the French) to Gommecourt, the Divisions holding the front line and ready to attack at Zero hour on 1st July were as follows: the 30th Division held the right of the line, *i.e.*, just north of Maricourt, having on its left the 18th Division, which, as already stated, occupied the Carnoy sector: the 12th Middlesex formed part of this Division. Next in line, south of Mametz and Fricourt, came the 7th Division, and to the N.W. of Fricourt the 21st Division: it will be remembered that the 4th Middlesex were now with this Division. On the left of the 21st Division the 34th lay opposite La Boisselle; south and north of this village were those two death-traps Sausage and Mash Valleys. The 8th Division was on the left of the 34th opposite Ovillers La Boisselle (known as "Ovillers" to distinguish it from the former

* The volume of enfilade machine-gun fire which swept Sausage and Mash Valleys, N. of Fricourt, with such fury on the morning of 1st July, 1916, will never be forgotten by all who crossed that terrible zone of death.

village of a similar name). The 2nd Middlesex formed part of the 8th Division, which had on its left the 32nd Division (opposite the Leipzic Salient) and the 36th Division (facing Thiepval). The line was here intersected by the Ancre River and the Albert-Arras Railway, but just north of the latter lay the 29th Division (the "Incomparable Division" of Gallipoli fame) opposite Beaumont Hamel, in which the 16th Middlesex were contained. The 4th Division (north of Beaumont Hamel) and the 31st (west of Serre) held the line on the left of the 29th. All these Divisions belonged to the Fourth Army: there were others in reserve, but they will be dealt with later. On the immediate left of the Fourth Army, however, holding the Hebuterne and Gommecourt sectors respectively, were the 56th (London) Division, commanded by an old 4th Middlesex officer—Major-General C. P. A. Hull—and the 46th Division: in the 56th Division were the 1/7th and 1/8th Battalions of the Middlesex.

Thus there were six Battalions of the Regiment in the front line at Zero hour, *i.e.*, from right to left, 12th, 4th, 2nd, 16th, 1/7th and 1/8th, either ready to go "over the top" as soon as the signal was given, or else lying close at hand in support or reserve. Of the Divisions in reserve to the Fourth Army, two only contained Middlesex men, *i.e.*, the 12th and 33rd. The 11th Battalion was in the 12th Division and the 1st Battalion and 18th Battalion (Pioneers) in the 33rd Division.

From the 24th June the British guns had hardly ceased pounding the enemy's front-line and support trenches and back areas. Guns of all calibre poured shell with unheard-of prodigality on to the enemy's positions. From 24th June to 1st July, in more than forty places along the line between Maricourt and Hebuterne, gas had been discharged with good effect on to the enemy's trenches; over seventy raids had taken place between Gommecourt and north of Ypres, and the results had given Sir Douglas Haig much information as to the enemy's dispositions. The final hour of this terrible bombardment, to which the enemy had been subjected since the 24th June, took place between 6.30 and 7.30 a.m. on 1st July. In fury and violence it far surpassed anything which had preceded it: thousands of guns were in action, and their fire was so accurate and murderous that later, when many Germans were taken prisoner, they were in a state of collapse bordering on insanity. Knowing that the destruction of the enemy's defences meant fewer casualties to them, the British troops watched with keen interest and satisfaction the work of their own guns.

## (1) THE BATTLE OF ALBERT.

1st July. Just before Zero hour, in many places along the whole front of attack from Maricourt to Serre, the ground beneath the enemy's trenches heaved and rocked and rumbled, clouds of smoke and tongues of flame, *débris* and the mangled bodies of Germans shot up into the air—the mines had been exploded. At intervals along the front, smoke had also been discharged, through which, as the synchronised watches announced 7.30 a.m., the troops advanced with great steadiness to the attack. The enemy's barrage had now fallen, but despite its heaviness and the loss of many men, the assaulting troops attacked with great *élan*. On the right (where the French were also attacking simultaneously on both sides of the Somme River) the attack met with immediate success, and before midday the 30th Division had carried Montauban. On the left of the 30th, the 18th Division* similarly made splendid progress, but the 12th Middlesex (Lieut.-Colonel F. Maxwell, V.C.) was the reserve Battalion of the 54th Brigade. The latter went into action with the 7th Bedfords on the right, the 11th Royal Fusiliers on the left, the 6th Northampton Regiment in support, and (as already stated) the 12th Middlesex in reserve. This Battalion on the first day of the Somme Battles had a strength of 21 officers and 820 other ranks. Major M. C. Scarborough was second-in-command, and the four Company commands were held as follows: "A" Company—Captain L. H. Methuen; "B" Company—Captain G. L. Harrison; "C" Company—Lieut. A. E. West; and "D" Company—Captain A. C. Davies. At Zero hour (7.30 a.m.), while the assaulting troops were going forward to the attack, the 12th Middlesex were kept in the dug-outs at Carnoy. At 8.30 p.m. Colonel Maxwell moved up to the Battalion Headquarters at Piccadilly in the old British front line. At 12.45 the Middlesex moved up into the forming-up trenches, shortly afterwards crossing No Man's Land to the old German front line, Companies taking up the following positions: "A" and "B" Companies each had two platoons

12th Battalion.

* Commanded by Major-General I. Maxse, now General Sir Ivor Maxse, K.C.B., C.V.O., D.S.O., Colonel of the Middlesex Regiment.

in Bund Trench, and " A " two in Emden Trench on the right of the Triangle, and " B " Company two in the same trench, but on the left of the Triangle ; " C " Company was in Austrian Support Trenches, and " D " in Austrian front line. The enemy's barrage was still falling, but it was weak and not very accurate. On Companies taking up the positions they began consolidating. The hostile trenches were much damaged and in places almost obliterated. Dead Germans were everywhere, and some prisoners taken from dug-outs were obviously much shaken and almost incoherent. At this period one officer—2nd Lieut. R. H. Hudlestone—had been killed, two other officers wounded, three other ranks killed, 27 wounded and four missing. Throughout the remainder of 1st and during the daylight hours of the 2nd July, the 12th Middlesex remained in the same positions, but at 8.30 p.m. on the latter date the Battalion was ordered to relieve the 11th Royal Fusiliers in the advanced trenches. Companies took over the following positions : " A " Company in White Trench, " B " and " C " Companies in Beetle Alley, " D " Company in Maple Trench from the junction of Black Alley to S.P. No. 5 inclusive. Colonel Maxwell's Headquarters were in Black Alley.

1st July. 12th Battalion.

2nd July.

The relief was completed by about 1.30 a.m. on 3rd. Casualties were one officer and four other ranks wounded. The Battalion was now south of Caterpillar and Mametz Woods.

3rd July.

To return to the 1st July.

1st July.

On the left of the 18th Division, the advance of the 7th Division is thus given in the official despatches : " Opposite Mametz part of our assembly trenches had been practically levelled by the enemy's artillery, making it necessary for our infantry (7th Division) to advance to the attack across four hundred yards of open ground. None the less, they forced their way into Mametz and reached their objective in the valley beyond, first throwing out a defensive flank towards Fricourt on their left."

The attack of the 21st Division (on the left of the 7th Division) is thus described, but all too briefly : " At the same time the enemy's trenches were entered by the 21st Division north of Fricourt, so that the enemy's garrison in that village was pressed on three sides." Neither do the official despatches state that a Brigade of the 17th Division—the 50th—was attached to the 21st Division for the purpose of covering the right flank of the latter, as will be seen later.

1st July. 4th Battalion.

The 4th Middlesex (Lieut.-Colonel H. P. F. Bicknell), of the 63rd Brigade, 21st Division, were in Divisional Reserve from 2nd to 10th June, but on the night 11th–12th, the Brigade relieved the 64th Brigade in the trenches, the Middlesex taking over the right and the 8th Somerset the left sub-sectors of the Divisional front line of the Fricourt sector. The Battalion went into the trenches with three companies in the firing line and one in support: the line was opposite the German Tambour, west of Fricourt. On the 14th, during patrol work, 2nd Lieut. St. John Jones was reported missing and later as killed. On the 16th the Battalion was relieved and moved back to Méaulte, and the whole of the 63rd Brigade came out of the front line on 20th.

The final period of preparation for the offensive now began, and the 4th Middlesex moved to La Neuville on 21st. "During the stay of the Battalion here," records the Diary, "men are to have as much rest as possible. In view of the coming offensive operations all ranks are to be kept as fit as possible. Sports were held, and Company Concerts and everything done to encourage and promote *esprit de corps*." On the 23rd, the Diary reports: "The men are looking very fit, and are quite eager to get to grips with the enemy."

Originally the operations were planned to begin on 29th June, and on 26th the 4th Middlesex and 8th Somerset moved up to their assembly area, but on 28th the date was altered to the 1st July, and the former Battalion withdrew to trenches in Queen's Redoubt, moving up again on the night of 30th.

The 21st Division was to attack with the 63rd Brigade on the right and the 64th Brigade on the left, the frontage of attack extending from the German trenches east of Guildford to the enemy's line west of Birch Tree Wood. The first objective of the Division was Fricourt Farm—Trench Junction X.28.C.8.7.—Crucifix Trench—Birch Tree Wood, the first objective of the 63rd Brigade being Fricourt Farm—X.28.C.8.7.—head of trench at X.28.a.5.0.—Crucifix Trench as far as X.27.b.7.4. Posts were to be pushed out to Railway Copse and the southern end of Shelter Copse.

The 4th Middlesex were to attack on the right and the 8th Somerset on the left. On the right of the 4th Middlesex, the 50th Infantry Brigade (17th Division) had been attached to the 21st Division for the initial attack, for while the left flank of the 7th Division was sufficiently protected by the lie of the ground, the right flank of the 21st Division was (or would be) dangerously exposed. To cover this flank was the first duty of the 50th Brigade. This done, its second task was to assault and clear Fricourt village and wood and ensure contact between the 7th and 21st Divisions. On the left of the 63rd Brigade, the 64th was to capture the northern portion of Crucifix Trench and Birch Tree Wood.

1st July. 4th Battalion.

The formation of the 4th Middlesex and 8th Somerset for the attack was two companies in the front line in lines of platoons, one hundred yards between platoons; a third company following in two lines (two-platoon frontage) and the fourth company following the three companies in similar formation. Of the Middlesex, "A" Company was on the right, "B" on the left, "C" in two lines behind "A" and "B" and "D" behind "C." The formation of the two supporting Battalions of the 63rd Brigade, *i.e.*, the 10th York and Lancaster Regiment and the 8th Lincolnshire Regiment, were similar when moving up in support and in advancing to the second objective, which these two Battalions were to capture. The second objective included Bottom Wood (where touch was to be gained with troops of the 7th Division), the high ground just east of the Wood and a line from the Wood north to Quadrangle Trench. One company of the 10th Y. & L. was to follow immediately behind the last platoon of the 4th Middlesex for clearing up the German trenches, and one company of 8th Lincolns was to carry out a similar duty for the 8th Somerset.

The method of advance is interesting. Five minutes before Zero hour the leading lines of the assaulting companies were to leave their trenches and creep forward as close to the German trenches as the British barrage would allow, having regard to the safety of the men. The second lines were also to leave their trenches and lie down close to the leading lines. Should the enemy's machine-gun and rifle fire prevent this method of advance, the assault was to begin direct from the front-line trenches. These orders were issued only to the first and second assaulting lines, all other lines were to attack from their assembly trenches.

Orders as to the dress of the attacking troops were brief. Packs were not to be carried: the haversack, waterbottle and waterproof were to be carried on the back: gas helmets were to be worn rolled up on the head: each man was to carry 220 rounds

1st July. 4th Battalion.

of ammunition, 2 sandbags and 2 grenades. In addition, each Battalion had to carry 150 picks and 150 shovels, and each Brigade was to have 500 flares.

Every possible contingency had been thought of, all but one, and that no one could foresee, for it was not until after the German front lines had been taken that the reasons for failure on many points along the front were discovered.

At 6.25 a.m. on 1st July the final hour of intense bombardment began. As the waiting troops saw great clods of earth, timber, trench boards, equipment and the mangled bodies of Germans flung up into the air, it seemed to them as if there could be no resistance whatever when the hour of assault—7.30 a.m.—came. Thousands of guns poured an unending stream of shells on to the hostile trenches and communications. The enemy's artillery replied at once with an accurate, but not heavy, bombardment of the front-line and close support trenches, and both "A" and "B" Companies of the 4th Middlesex suffered a good many casualties, "A's" losses being especially heavy.

At five minutes before Zero hour—7.30 a.m.—the leading platoons of "A" and "B," in accordance with instructions, attempted to leave their trenches and creep towards the German lines. But they were met by a violent machine-gun fire, the volume of which was an unpleasant reminder that the enemy was still full of fight, and had not lost heavily nor had become demoralised by the intense bombardment. The result was that the leading platoons, having again lost heavily, had to go back to their trenches as quickly as possible. At 7.28 a.m. there was a roar on the right of the Middlesex and two mines went up near the German Tambour. At 7.29 the attack began by the leading platoons, owing to the heavy casualties already suffered, advancing in one line instead of in two. The remainder of "A" and "B" Companies followed in lines of platoons at 100 yards distance, "C" Company coming on behind in two lines, and "D" Company following "C." The last line carried the Battalion reserves of ammunition and grenades. Colonel Bicknell, with the remainder of Battalion Headquarters, moved forward with the rear line of "C" Company.

At 7.30 a.m. the British barrage lifted off the German front line and the assault began, but again a murderous machine-gun and rifle fire swept No Man's Land. The Middlesex men, however, were not to be denied, and the leading companies reached, and passed over, the German front line. By this time all the officers of "A" and "B," with the exception of 2nd Lieut. Simpson, and most of the N.C.Os. had become casualties, but in small groups the survivors pushed on beyond the German support line to just west of the Sunken Road. Here, in spite of heavy attacks from the enemy, who advanced across the open on the right flank of the Brigade, the gallant survivors of "A" and "B" Companies of the Middlesex maintained themselves, for by this time their losses had become extremely heavy. They clung to this position, nothing daunted, until the supporting Battalion (8th Lincoln Regiment) came through, to which they attached themselves, and until they were brought back two days later by an intrepid N.C.O.—Sergeant Millwood. 1ST JULY. 4TH BATTALION

Meanwhile "C" and "D" Companies, with Battalion Headquarters, had similarly lost very heavily from machine-gun and rifle fire in crossing No Man's Land. Colonel Bicknell estimated that there were at least six guns firing on his Battalion, two in the open between Empress Support and Empress Trench, and the remainder from the German Tambour and Fricourt.

On reaching Empress Trench the C.O., 4th Middlesex, reported the situation as follows: The greater part of the survivors of the two leading companies had advanced towards the Sunken Road; the third company had reached Empress Trench, where it was shortly afterwards joined by the remainder of the fourth company. He thereupon decided that the only thing to be done was to hang on to Empress Trench and consolidate it. His available strength was then 3 officers, 100 other ranks and 3 Lewis gunners. The right of Empress Trench and the trenches leading to the Sunken Road were then blocked. Three attempts were made by the enemy to bomb his way up these trenches, but all were repulsed, the Battalion Diary recording that: "At this time most valuable services were rendered by Captain Willis and 2nd Lieuts. Lofts and Barnett, also by Sergeant Warboys, Sergeant Wright and Sergeant Millwood." On the right of the Middlesex, the 50th Brigade had been unable to hold the German trenches in front of Fricourt, and was forced to retire. This retirement exposed the right flank of the Middlesex and the 63rd Brigade, and parties of the enemy, from the direction of Fricourt, with machine guns, were able to work up between the remnants of the leading companies and the support companies. The situation of the 4th Middlesex was now critical, for on the left of the

1st July. 4th Battalion.

Battalion only scattered parties of the 8th Somerset had succeeded in reaching Lozenge Alley and the Sunken Road. As it was impossible to advance further owing to the severe losses and strong opposition, the C.O., 4th Middlesex, decided to hold the ground won, and, at 8.15 a.m., a message to this effect was sent back to Brigade Headquarters.

At about 9.15 a.m. the supporting Battalions began to arrive; the 10th York and Lancaster Regiment pushed through the left of the Middlesex and drove the enemy from his support trenches and occupied them; the 8th Lincolns went through the 8th Somerset and occupied Lozenge Alley, and eventually the Sunken Road.

About 11 a.m., Colonel Bicknell received orders from Brigade Headquarters to protect the right flank of the Brigade, as the York and Lancasters and Lincolns were going to make a further advance. The bombing posts which the Middlesex had established were therefore strengthened and Lewis guns mounted for their defence; all trenches leading to Fricourt were also blocked. But to form the defensive flank the whole Battalion was absorbed. The Lewis guns were able to bring a most effective fire on the enemy in Fricourt, and inflicted heavy casualties on parties of Germans moving about in the village.

At 4.35 p.m. further orders were received from 63rd Brigade Headquarters for all units of the Brigade to hold the trenches they were in and re-organise. This was done, and the positions held by the four Battalions were as follows: 4th Middlesex—Empress Trench from Ball Lane and Empress Support; 8th Somerset L.I.—in west end of Lozenge Wood, Sunken Road and Lozenge Alley; 10th Y. & L. Regiment—Dart Lane; 8th Lincolns from Dart Alley to Lozenge Wood. Throughout the night of 1st–2nd July the Battalions remained in these positions.

2nd July.

Early on the 2nd July, patrols of Lincolns went out towards Red Cottage and Fricourt Farm. One patrol got nearly as far as Red Cottage and found that Fricourt had been entered by British troops on the right of the 21st Division: another patrol entered Fricourt Farm and reported it clear of the Germans: the enemy had evacuated the Fricourt Salient during the night.

Soon after daybreak on the 2nd, also, Major Odling and the officers and N.C.Os. of the 4th Middlesex, who had been left behind as a reinforcement, joined the Battalion. Throughout the morning all available men were employed in carrying up ammunition and grenades to the 62nd Brigade, who had made urgent calls for supplies, that Brigade having attacked the enemy. The Middlesex continued to hold their positions and, though subjected at intervals to heavy hostile shelling by guns of large calibre, few casualties were suffered and little damage was done. Until after midday on the 3rd July, the 63rd Brigade remained in the same position. During the morning the bodies of officers and men who had been killed were collected and a grave was dug, but the hostile shell fire prevented the completion of this work. A heavy shell fell in the trench, killing 2nd Lieut. Barnett and Sergeants Millwood and Prosser, " all of whom had rendered most conspicuous good service during the action," besides killing and wounding about thirty other ranks.

2ND JULY. 4TH BATTALION.

3RD JULY.

At noon the Battalion received orders to move to Lozenge Alley and take up a position there in Brigade Reserve facing north; the three other Battalions of the Brigade were in the old German trenches further north covering the left flank of the Division. It was here that the worn-out remnants of the 4th Middlesex were relieved by a battalion of the 17th Division at 3 a.m. on the morning of the 4th and marched, in Brigade, back to Dernancourt, proceeding later by train to Vaux, north-west of Amiens.

4TH JULY.

In Vaux the 4th Battalion counted its losses: they were terrible indeed. No less than 14 officers had been killed, 1 wounded and died of wounds, and 4 wounded * ; in other ranks the casualties were 131 killed, 337 wounded, 15 missing, believed killed, and 38 missing. Total, 19 officers and 521 other ranks.

The unexpected opposition which had met the troops as soon as they set foot in No Man's Land on the 1st July was due to no fault on the part of the British Army, but to the foresight of the enemy. After the German first system of defences were captured and searched by the clearing-up parties (they had not then been termed " mopping-up " parties), great was the astonishment at the depth of the enemy's dug-outs. Some of these were at least 30 feet below the surface of the ground: they were of great strength, such as to defy the heaviest shell fire. Many were elaborately fitted, and formed a vast system of underground strongholds. When the British barrage was at its heaviest the enemy's troops

* Officers killed: Captain O. R. F. Johnston, Lieuts. A. Sapte and G. L. C. Ridpath, 2nd Lieuts. A. Branch, A. G. Chambers, A. A. H. Johnston, S. P. Churchfield, A. H. Winn-Simpson, W. J. Wood, E. Peyton, E. V. Whitby, A. F. C. Panton, G. R. Money and P. Barnett. Officers wounded: Captain D. C. L. Rowley (died of wounds, 2nd July), and 2nd Lieuts. P. Leigh-Pemberton, A. J. Marvin, F. E. Coumbe and R. T. C. Cory.

betook themselves to these dug-outs, and, waiting until the storm had abated, were able to man their trenches and meet the advance of the British infantry with heavy rifle and machine-gun fire, for the barrage had passed beyond the German front-line trenches. This was found to be the case all up and down the line on the first day of the Somme Battles, 1916, and it is hardly to be wondered at that in places the attack was held up.*

1ST JULY. Continuing the story of the first day of the Battle, the official despatches state that: "Further north (of Fricourt), though the villages of La Boisselle and Ovillers for the time being resisted our attack, our troops (34th and 8th Divisions) drove deeply into the German lines on the flanks of these strongholds and so paved the way for their capture later."

But many gallant soldiers gave their lives before that way was "paved," and none gave them more valiantly or unselfishly than the officers and men of the 2nd Middlesex Regiment of the 8th Division.

2ND BATTALION.

Between Maricourt and Hebuterne there were not two more powerfully defended sectors of the enemy's trenches than those at La Boisselle and Ovillers La Boisselle. Sited upon a hill, both villages commanded No Man's Land and every approach from the British trenches. La Boisselle formed a pronounced salient in the enemy's line: on the right and left of the village (respectively) were Sausage and Mash valleys, and any attempt to advance up these two depressions would be open not only to heavy frontal fire, but a murderous enfilade fire from both flanks. At Ovillers the salient was much less pronounced, nevertheless the defences of the village looked down upon Mash valley, dominating it just as La Boisselle dominated Sausage valley. To add to the difficulties of any attack from the British front between the two villages, No Man's Land in this part of the line was broader than in any other sector along the whole front: the attack would have to cross about 1,000 yards of ground swept by machine-gun and rifle fire. So that no easy task lay before the attacking troops of the 23rd Brigade, 8th Division.

The 2nd Middlesex had spent the whole of June between Millencourt, Albert, the trenches east of Aveluy, Hénencourt Wood and the Long Valley. Apparently little happened of outstanding importance during the month, for the Battalion Diary

* It might be said with a certain amount of truth that until 1st July, 1916, we did not know how to build dug-outs.—*Author.*

1st July. 2nd Battalion.

is bare of any item of interest. Like other battalions when out of the line, the Middlesex men were kept hard at work, either in training or on the defences, and when parades were over, games and other amusements claimed their attention, for the order of the day was " work hard and play hard."

Towards the end of the month the 2nd Battalion (in Brigade) moved to the Long Valley, and, on the night of 30th, to assembly positions in the front and support lines. The IIIrd Corps (to which the 8th Division belonged) was to attack on a two-division front, 34th Division on the right, 8th Division on the left. The 8th Division was to attack with all three Brigades in the front line, *i.e.*, 23rd on the right, 25th in the centre and 70th on the left. The Divisional front line ran approximately from Dorset Street to the Nab. Each Brigade was to have two Battalions in the front line, one in support and one in reserve. Of the 23rd Brigade the 2nd Middlesex were to be on the right of the front line, the 2nd Devons on the left, the 2nd West Yorkshires in support, and the 2nd Scottish Rifles in reserve. Inasmuch as there are no orders with the Battalion Diary of the 2nd Middlesex, nor any appendices with the Diary of the 23rd Brigade Headquarters, it is impossible to give details of the forming-up plans and objectives allotted to the various units, but apparently the 2nd Battalion attacked from about Dorset Street to George Street. The formation of the attack was in four waves, the leading wave consisting of two platoons of " B " Company on the right and two platoons of " A " Company. The second wave, which was to follow at 50 yards distance, consisted of the remaining platoons of " B " and " A " Companies. The third and fourth waves were similarly formed of " D " and " C " Companies, a like distance being kept between the waves.

At 6.25 a.m., when the final hour of bombardment began, the 2nd Battalion, with the 2nd Devons on the left and a Tyneside Battalion of the 34th Division on the right, stood ready to " go over " when ordered. Each man carried 220 rounds of small arm ammunition, two Mills grenades and two sandbags: every third man carried either a pick or a shovel. Packs had been left behind and haversacks were carried on the shoulders. The strength of the 2nd Middlesex (Lieut.-Colonel E. T. F. Sandys) was 23 officers and 650 N.C.Os. and men.

The effects of that final and terrible hour of " intense " shell fire could hardly be observed, for, added to the distance across

1st July. 2nd Battalion.

No Man's Land, there was a ground mist. Nevertheless, the waiting troops and their officers were confident that from that awful avalanche of shell little could emerge unscathed. Disillusion was to come quickly. Shortly before Zero hour (7.30 a.m.) the leading waves of the Middlesex and Devons left their trenches and began to crawl towards the German front line. During this manœuvre they were subjected to a heavy fire from rifles and machine guns, and suffered many casualties. And this ere ever the attack had been launched. At 7.27 and 7.28 respectively two mines " went up " under the La Boisselle salient, the objective of the 102nd Brigade, 34th Division.

As the watches touched Zero hour the waiting waves of Middlesex and Devons rose to their feet and charged towards the German trenches. For many of those brave fellows it was nothing but rising and falling almost immediately, for with the fury of a Norwegian maelstrom, German machine-gun and rifle bullets now swept No Man's Land, sweeping away also the first, second and third waves of the attacking troops. It was a ghastly sight, heart-breaking to the observers, who could do nothing to help the gallant fellows out of their terrible situation. The artillery barrage had by now lifted from the German front line, and the enemy was free to man it and resist the oncoming troops. For of the final waves of the Middlesex Regiment only about 200 succeeded in reaching the enemy's front line, where, after killing and bayoneting every living soul they found, they passed on quickly to the second line. Here another stiff fight, much of it of a hand-to-hand nature, with an enemy superior in numbers and well entrenched, took place. It did not last long, for in a little while yet another 100 gallant Die-Hards had gone down, and the survivors were forced to retire to the German front line. Here, under the leadership of Major H. B. W. Savile, Captain and Adjutant R. J. Young, and 2nd Lieuts. P. M. Elliott, W. Spatz and H. C. Hunt, they proceeded to consolidate their position. But gradually the little band of survivors grew less and less, until at 9.15 a.m. only a mere handful of unwounded men, numbering perhaps a dozen, were forced to leave the German front line and retire to shell holes in No Man's Land. In this position they remained all day, and when darkness had fallen crawled back to their own lines.

The Devons had shared a similar fate, and, on the right of the Middlesex, the Tynesiders of the 34th Division had been annihilated before they reached their objective. On the left of the 23rd Brigade, the 25th Brigade had failed to capture the German front line, excepting at one spot on their left front. 1ST JULY. 2ND BATTALION.

Of the gallant Die-Hards, only one officer (2nd Lieut. H. C. Hunt) of the 23 who had taken part in the assault in the morning, crawled back at night to the British trenches, unwounded. Of the 650 N.C.Os. and men who had rushed bravely to their doom at Zero hour, a bare 50 answered to their names when, in the early hours of 2nd July, the roll was called.

The following officers were amongst the casualties: Killed—Captains C. S. Hilton and W. S. Meeke; 2nd Lieuts. P. M. Elliott, R. E. Grundy, W. Spatz, J. Wilson, C. S. Davis, W. F. Forge, G. Scott, F. Van-den-Bok, H. D. Wood and A. I. Frost. Wounded—Lieut.-Colonel E. T. F. Sandys; Major H. B. W. Savile; Captain and Adjutant R. J.Young; Captain G. Johnson; Lieuts. W. J. Clachan, R. McD. Yorston and H. Peckham; 2nd Lieuts. C. H. Rawson and O. N. S. Dobbs. Wounded and Missing—2nd Lieut. J. S. McManus. Total—22 officers.

Of the attack on La Boisselle and Ovillers La Boisselle on 1st July the official despatches said: "Further north, though the villages of La Boisselle and Ovillers for the time being resisted our attack, our troops (34th and 8th Divisions) drove deeply into the *flanks* of these strongholds, and so paved a way for their capture later."

During the night of 1st–2nd July, the 12th Division began the relief of the 8th Division, and by 6 a.m. on the latter date the 23rd Brigade had been relieved by the 35th Brigade and was on the road back to bivouacs near Millencourt. Only a four hours' rest was allowed in the latter place, and at 4 p.m. the Brigade entrained at Méricourt for Ailly-sur-Somme and, on reaching the village, detrained and marched to billets in Yzeux and La Chaussée: it was 2 a.m. on 3rd July before all units were settled in. The 2nd Middlesex billeted in La Chaussée. 3RD JULY.

Continuing the quotation from the official despatches describing the first day of the Somme Battles, Sir Douglas Haig said: "On the spur running south from Thiepval the work known as the Leipzig Salient was stormed by the 32nd Division, and severe fighting took place for the possession of the village and its defences. Here and north of the valley of the Ancre as far as Serre on the left flank of our attack, our initial successes were not sustained. Striking progress was made at many points, and parties of troops

1st July. penetrated the enemy's positions to the outer defences of Grandcourt (36th Division) and also to Pendant Copse (4th Division) and Serre (31st Division), but the enemy's continued resistance at Thiepval and Beaumont Hamel (29th Division) made it impossible to forward reinforcements and ammunition, and, in spite of their gallant efforts, our troops were forced to withdraw during the night to our own lines."

It is to the struggle at Beaumont Hamel by the 29th Division that the story now turns, a struggle so fierce and bloody that yet another Battalion of the Middlesex Regiment (the 16th), though in support, numbered at the close of the 1st July but a mere handful.

16th Battalion. In the early hours of the 1st July, the 16th Middlesex (Lieut.-Colonel J. Hamilton Hall) moved up from Auchonvillers to their assembly positions, Cripp's Cut and Cardiff Street. The 86th Brigade, to which the 16th Battalion belonged, was to attack with two Battalions in the front line, 2nd Royal Fusiliers on the right (from Bridge End, inclusive, to the Southern Boundary, exclusive of Cripp's Cut), the 1st Lancashire Fusiliers on the left, from the fire and support trenches (but not including Cripp's Cut), north of Bridge End. The 1st Royal Dublin Fusiliers was the right supporting Battalion and had been allotted Essex Street and 88 Trench, the 16th Middlesex were on the left and were to move forward from Cripp's Cut and Cardiff Street. The Brigade was to assault the German trenches from a point about 100 yards west of Hawthorn Redoubt to the northern edge of Beaumont Hamel.

Owing to the subsequent results of the attack, it is unnecessary to go further into such details as objectives, but there are many interesting points in the Battalion Orders* issued by Colonel Hall, though it is only possible to record a few of them. The distribution of the Battalion at the moment of attack was to be—in Cripp's Cut "C" Company on the right, Battalion Headquarters in the centre, "D" Company on the left: "C" and "D" Companies were each to have one Stokes gun with them. In Cardiff Street—"A" Company on the right, "B" Company on the left, with two sections of 1/2nd Monmouthshire Regiment on the right of "A" Company. Each Company was to advance on a frontage of 100 yards, "C" (right) and "D" (left) leading:

* This Battalion Order is a model of completeness: it is rare to find every detail of an impending attack laid down with such clarity.

"A" Company behind and to the right of "C," "B" following "A." Companies were to move in platoon columns, sections moving in single file and extending when necessary. Battalion Headquarters, with the two sections Monmouthshire Regiment, were to follow behind "B" Company. Details of the formation for any attack are always interesting, for they are instructive. Other items in the Battalion Order are concerned with communications, medical arrangements, discipline (in which the men are warned that looting is a Court-Martial offence, for which the punishment is "to be shot"), equipment, reinforcements and many others.

1st July. 16th Battalion.

The attack was to be preceded by the final hour of intense bombardment, and just before Zero a mine under Hawthorn Redoubt was to be fired.

All units of the 86th Brigade appear to have reached their assembly positions by 3 a.m.: at 3.30 a.m. the 1st Lancashire Fusiliers reported that they had occupied the Sunken Road (in front of Jacob's Ladder ?): at 6.25 a.m., the artillery bombardment became intense, and at 7.20 a.m. the mine beneath Hawthorn Redoubt went up with a roar, the near lip of the crater being at once occupied by troops of the 2nd Royal Fusiliers.

At 7.30 a.m., the attack "went over," but from this time onwards, just when the narrative of the battle should be most interesting, it ends. The Battalion Diary of the 16th Middlesex Regiment thus describes that day of terrible happenings: "Battalion in action 7.30 a.m. from support trenches. Casualties—Officers, killed, 3; wounded, 10; missing, believed killed, 6; missing, 5. Other ranks: killed, 19; wounded, 306; missing, believed killed, 37; missing, 138,* 10.30 a.m. Balance of Battalion took over front-line trenches Auchonvillers sector." That is all. Twenty-four officers and 500 other ranks casualties and yet no word of what happened. The Diary of 86th Brigade Headquarters is hardly more illuminating. As the leading lines

* From the Battalion Diary the following is the complete corrected list of officer casualties: Killed—Captains T. H. Watts, G. H. Heslop; Lieuts. H. J. Heath, H. D. Goodwin; H. W. Barker, 2nd Lieuts. H. E. Asser, R. F. Michelmore (d-of-w., 7/7/16), J. K. Orr, H. C. Hertslett, F. B. Tanqueray, E. V. Whitby and C. J. J. K. Deakin (d-of-w., 2/7/16); 12 officers missing—Captains E. Hall, F. S. Cockram; 2nd Lieuts. D. B. Tuck, T. Shearstone, F. E. Bennet, E. A. Cuff-Adams, C. H. F. Lushington. Total, 6. Total officers killed, wounded and missing, 22. The Battalion Diary gives the total number as 24, but no names are given: the above list is taken from the Casualty Return in the 86th Brigade Diary, and corrected by "Officers died in the Great War, 1914–1919," issued by the War Office.

1st July. 16th Battalion. of the attack left the trenches they came under a terrific machine-gun fire: the enemy's guns also placed a very heavy barrage on the British front and support trenches, causing enormous casualties. It was, however, the machine-gun fire which, the Brigade Diary records, "crumpled up our attack, not the artillery fire." By 12 noon the attack had failed all along the line of the 86th Brigade: "We had lost 79 officers out of 100 engaged," states the Brigade Diary in another paragraph, and this sad record ends at "20.10" (8 p.m.) with the entry: "Bombardment on both sides dwindled down to very occasional desultory fire."

Again the enemy's deep dug-outs had served him well. Securely sheltered from that final hour of intense bombardment, which immediately preceded the attack, he had sufficient time to man his trenches and meet the advancing troops with a murderous machine-gun fire, not only frontal but in enfilade. It is probable, however, that Colonel Hall's Battalion lost more heavily from the enemy's artillery fire than from his machine-gun fire, for the Brigade Diary makes no mention of the 16th Middlesex getting as far as No Man's Land, only the Royal and the Lancashire Fusiliers are mentioned. Be that as it may, that splendid Battalion of Public School Men was reduced to a mere handful when night fell on 1st July. There is no entry for the 2nd July in the Battalion Diary, though the Brigade Diary records that the day was spent in "collecting wounded and burying the dead." The slaughter had been so terrible that search parties of both British and Germans were out in No Man's Land, and neither side fired at the other. 3rd July. At noon on 3rd the remnants of the 16th Middlesex were relieved in the trenches and moved back to 88 Trench and Auchonvillers; on 4th the survivors of the 86th Brigade were withdrawn from the line and proceeded to Englebelmer and Mailly Woods.

This narrative of one section of the Battle north of the Ancre as far as Serre on 1st July ends for the time being the story of the opening of the main operations. But north of Serre grim fighting had taken place at Gommecourt, where VIIth Corps troops, *i.e.*, 56th (London) and 46th Divisions, had stormed the German trenches. "The subsidiary attack at Gommecourt," records the official despatches, "also forced its way into the enemy's positions, but there met with such vigorous opposition that as soon as it was considered that the attack had fulfilled its object our troops were withdrawn."

The 56th (London) Division was commanded by Major-General C. P. A. Hull, who, as Lieut.-Colonel Hull, at the Battle of Mons in 1914, had so ably handled his Battalion—the 4th Middlesex—on 23rd August of that year. 1st July.

At this period Gommecourt formed a powerful salient in the enemy's trench system north of Hebuterne. The village itself was not only protected by a powerful system of trenches, but west of it was Gommecourt Park, similarly protected by strong defences which completely enclosed the salient. In the British trench system were Hebuterne, south of Gommecourt, and Fonquevillers, north of it. The attack by the VIIth Corps (Lieut.-General Sir T. D'O. Snow) was to be made from south of the salient by the 56th (London) Division, and north of it by the 46th Division, the attacks converging. The objects of the attack were to distract attention from the main operations farther south, to draw the enemy's artillery fire and, if possible, his infantry reinforcements to the salient.

The attack of the 56th Division was to be made by the 168th and 169th Brigades, the 167th Brigade remaining in Divisional Reserve. The 7th and 8th Middlesex were, therefore, not assaulting Battalions; nevertheless the part they took in the operations is of interest from a regimental point of view.

1/7th & 1/8th Battalion.

On the night of 21st June, the 1/7th (Lieut.-Colonel E. J. King) and 1/8th (Lieut.-Colonel P. L. Ingpen) Battalions had taken over front-line trenches in the Hebuterne sector. The period spent by both Battalions in Divisional Reserve had been of a strenuous nature, for all troops in support and reserve were engaged nightly on digging and improving the trenches or communications, or in other ways completing the preparations for the Somme Battles.

The 1/7th were in "Y" sector, having relieved the London Rifle Brigade: two companies in the front line and two in reserve: Battalion Headquarters were in the village. The 1/8th had relieved the 13th London Regiment in "W" sector in front of Hebuterne, having the 1/7th on their left and 1/4th Royal Berkshires on their right.

On the night of 23rd June a violent thunderstorm broke over the whole front and the trenches were, in places, knee-deep in water, dumps were flooded, and work for a while was completely hindered.

The next day (24th) the first day of preliminary bombardment began. The enemy's reply was very slight, and casualties were

1/7TH & 1/8TH BATTALION.

slight. On the second day of the bombardment, hostile shell fire was more intense, and, although the 1/7th had only four men wounded, the 1/8th lost seven other ranks killed and 25 wounded. The third day of the bombardment drew very severe retaliation from the German guns, especially during the simulated smoke attacks—the 1/7th lost six other ranks killed, 30 wounded, including two officers—2nd Lieuts. Price and Sherlock: the casualties of the 1/8th were five other ranks killed and 25 wounded. The trenches were severely damaged not only by the hostile guns, but by a further heavy fall of rain. The men were now standing in water up to their knees and their physical condition began to be serious: on the 24th they had been soaked to the skin; there were no means of furnishing hot food or hot drinks, and the hostile shell fire made sleep impossible. The fourth day of the bombardment (27th) again drew heavy retaliation from the enemy which, with constant rain, produced appalling conditions in the front-line trenches. The 1/8th were withdrawn from the line at night, many men suffering from "trench feet," and went into billets at Hénu and Souastre. But the 1/7th had another day of purgatory before relief. On the 27th the Diary of the latter Battalion records: "Our men to-day in so exhausted a condition that a report was rendered to the General that the Battalion was not fit for action and that a complete rest of at least twenty-four hours was essential." On the 28th, the 2nd London Regiment relieved the 1/7th Middlesex, who were taken back to Souastre. The men, on relief, were so utterly exhausted that large numbers of them collapsed as they came out of the trenches, and had to be carried back in vehicles sent forward by the Division in anticipation of their condition.

From the 21st to 27th the losses of both Battalions were: 1/7th—101 killed and wounded and 49 sent to hospital; 1/8th—killed, other ranks, 16; wounded, officers, 3; other ranks, 116; missing, 11; evacuated sick with trench feet, 63.

Colonel King (1/7th) speaks in eulogistic terms of one of his officers and two men, whose devotion to duty during that terrible time was a splendid example to their comrades: "Amongst the many gallant men conspicuous for their example and self-sacrifice during those trying days, none were more conspicuous than Lieut. W. G. Woodroffe, commanding 'A' Company, Lance-Corporal C. L. Jones, a signaller, and Private J. H. Ward, a stretcher-bearer, all of whom received 'immediate' awards.

Upon Lieut. Woodroffe* a French decoration was conferred—the Croix de Guerre with Palms—and of him it was said: 'it was almost entirely due to his conduct, cheerfulness, indefatigable energy and gallant personal bearing, that his Company remained an efficient fighting unit under the exceptionally trying circumstances that prevailed: what he did may have been only his ordinary duty, but it was done in so exceptionally brilliant a manner as to be worthy of immediate award.' Lance-Corporal Jones, who received the Military Medal, had, on the 25th, kept his signal station, in an important but exposed part of the line, open throughout the day although exposed to constant shell fire, whilst Private J. H. Ward, the stretcher-bearer, had carried no less than thirty wounded men of different units, in most cases under heavy shell fire. This Private Ward was one of the bravest men who ever served in the Battalion: he afterwards gained a bar to his Military Medal and also the Distinguished Conduct Medal, and finally died of wounds only five days before the Armistice." 1/7TH & 1/8TH BATTALION.

After a day's rest at Souastre the 1/7th Middlesex moved forward at midnight, 30th June, to the trenches west of the Keep at Hebuterne, in readiness for the Battle on 1st July. The Battalion reached its position of assembly at 2 a.m., and, having been issued with S.A.A. and other stores, awaited orders, the 1/7th being in Divisional Reserve. Similarly, the 1/8th Battalion paraded at 5 a.m. on 1st July, in fighting order, and marched to Souastre, also in Divisional Reserve. For, as already explained, the 167th Brigade was in reserve, the 168th and 169th Brigades of the 56th Division launching the right (or southern) attack on the Gommecourt Salient. Of the savage and awful struggle which took place between the latter Brigades and the enemy after the attacking troops had "gone over" at Zero hour, of how the Division north of the Salient failed in its attack, which left the enemy free to concentrate his guns and reserves against the 56th Division, how, when the gallant troops had gone forward to the attack, a barrage fire, so continuous and heavy that no supports of any sort or description were able to pass through it, during which the enemy by savage bombing attacks proceeded to destroy the attacking Battalions by a series of terrible bombing attacks, which the reserve troops were compelled to witness from the 1ST JULY.

* This gallant young officer gained his Captaincy, but was killed on 9th September, 1916.

1st July.
1/7th & 1/8th Battalion.

opposite slopes at Hebuterne in helpless impotence—all these things should be read in the "History of the 56th (London) Division," for it is impossible in a Regimental History to do more than refer briefly to the actions of other Battalions and units.

Throughout the day the 1/7th remained in trenches at "The Keep," in close touch with the 169th Brigade, at whose disposal the Battalion had been placed. At night they sent out two raiding parties, one into Gommecourt Park and the other to the German trenches south of it; but the enemy was on the alert, and several casualties were suffered by the Battalion.

At 2.30 p.m., the 1/8th had marched up from Souastre to the Corps line of trenches immediately east of Sailly, reaching their position at 5.15 p.m. But just over an hour later the Battalion was again on the move, having been ordered to take over and hold "W" sector of the front line, the scene of its discomfort between 21st and 27th June. On reaching the front line, however, it was found that the enemy's bombardment had been so terrific as to fill in two lines of trenches; two Companies ("B" and "C") were therefore put into the reserve trenches: "D" occupied a line in close support, and "A" was in a trench immediately west of Hebuterne.

2nd July.

The 2nd July was uneventful for both Battalions, though in front of 1/8th, during the afternoon, the enemy displayed a white flag and left his trenches to attend the wounded in "No Man's Land." This unofficial truce lasted two hours, and the Battalion M.O. of the 1/8th took advantage of it to go out and bring in wounded men of the Battalions which had made the original attack on the 1st July. On the 3rd July there was constant heavy shelling by both sides, and again towards evening, after showing a white flag, the Germans left their trenches to look for their wounded, the British following suit.

3rd July.

With the close of the attack on the Gommecourt Salient ends the story of the initial stages of the Battles of the Somme, 1916. Terrible losses had been suffered by the Middlesex Regiment, who, with their gallant comrades of other units, fought splendidly in the face of fierce opposition, the intensity of which had not been foreseen. Of the many lessons learned by the Allies on that first day of the struggles on the Somme, one—the value of deep dug-outs—was never forgotten.

# (1) THE BATTLE OF ALBERT.

## II.

At the close of the first day of the operations Sir Douglas Haig decided that it was necessary to limit the area of the Battle. He therefore, gave orders that the attack was to continue from the junction of the French and British line (just north of Curlu, on the Somme) to a point about half-way between La Boisselle and Contalmaison, limiting the offensive to a slow and methodical advance. North of the Ancre the enemy was to be held to his ground, so that the attack could be resumed if desirable.

Of the six Battalions of the Middlesex Regiment which took part in the fierce fighting on the 1st July, only one—the 12th—had escaped with slight loss, and at 1.30 a.m. on 3rd July was just south of Caterpillar and Mametz Woods: the 4th, 2nd and 16th Battalions had been withdrawn from the line, but the 1/7th and 1/8th were still in the trenches at Hebuterne.

1ST JULY. 11TH BATTALION. Meanwhile several reserve Divisions had been moved up into the front line, and amongst them was the 12th, which contained the 11th Middlesex (commanded by Lieut.-Colonel G. L. Oliver, Lieut.-Colonel Ingle having been sent down to the base ill). On the 1st July the 11th Battalion (in Brigade) had moved to Baizieux Wood, and there bivouacked until 6.30 p.m., when the 9th Royal Fusiliers moved up into the front line from Mersey Street to Longridge Street; the 11th Middlesex, with the remaining units of the 36th Brigade, were in Divisional Reserve in the Intermediate Line (Albert–Bouzencourt). 2ND JULY. The 2nd July was uneventful. At 3.15 a.m. on the 3rd the Battalion moved to the railway cutting north of Marmont Bridge, Albert. Early that morning the 35th Brigade of the 12th Division had been ordered to attack Ovillers, and at 4.30 a.m. "A" and "B" Companies of the 11th Middlesex were moved up in support to Ribble Street. Four hours later Battalion Headquarters, with "C" and "D" Companies, moved to a field north of Crucifix Corner to support the 37th Brigade, also attacking Ovillers. Apparently, however, the Battalion was not called upon, for at 8 p.m. Companies collected at Crucifix Corner and marched back to reserve trenches and dug-outs on the south-east side of Authuille Wood, where the Middlesex men were in support of the 9th Royal Fusiliers. 4TH JULY. On the 4th, at 5 p.m., the 11th Battalion took over

4TH JULY. 11TH BATTALION.

the front line from the Fusiliers, "A" Company from Longridge to Quarry Brae, "C" from Quarry Brae, Nab Salient to Mersey Trench, "D" Company in support, Quarry Brae and Nab Trench, "B" Company in reserve in Glasgow Street.

The Battalion now had its first sight of No Man's Land, and it was truly a horrible spectacle. Dead bodies were everywhere, and many poor fellows, who had been lying out wounded in that terrible space of dead ground between the opposing trenches, were brought in. At intervals the guns on both sides were active. One officer—2nd Lieut. D. G. Gilfillan—and six other ranks were wounded during the day.

All along the line from east of Maricourt to Thiepval the "slow and methodical advance," which Sir Douglas Haig had ordered, was in progress, and continued until the night of 13th July, when the first phase of the Battles ended, by which date Montauban, Mametz, Fricourt, Contalmaison, and La Boisselle had fallen into the hands of the British.

2ND-3RD JULY. 12TH BATTALION.

On the night of 2nd–3rd July the 12th Middlesex (18th Division) had relieved the 11th Royal Fusiliers in the front line, the Battalion taking over White Trench ("A" Company), Beetle Alley ("B" and "C" Companies), Maple Trench from junction of Black Alley to Strong Point No. 5 ("D" Company). Throughout the 3rd the Battalion remained in the same positions, all Companies consolidating the line. In the evening "B" and "C" Companies set to work to dig a communication trench between White Trench and Beetle Alley. The enemy shelled both the latter trenches during the day, but his shell fire was weak and not very effective: 2nd Lieut. Souster and two other ranks were wounded. At night, "D" Company was withdrawn from Maple Trench and took over Strong Points from the 6th Northants. The 4th was also without incident, but during the evening the dispositions of the Companies were again slightly altered: "A" remained in White Trench, "B" was in Montauban Alley, between Caterpillar Trench and Pommiers Redoubt, with four strong points in the Caterpillar Trench, one at the junction of Loop Trench and Montauban Alley and one at White Trench. These posts were garrisoned with one Vickers gun and section. "C" Company was in Caterpillar Wood with two sections and one Vickers gun as a detached post in Marlborough Wood. "D" Company was in Pommiers Trench with a strong point at the Loop. The 12th Middlesex now held part of the 53rd Brigade front as well as the front line of their own Brigade, the 54th. 5TH JULY. The 5th was similarly a day of comparative quietude, though 12TH BATTALION. hostile shelling was at times heavy. Patrol work was carried out each night. During the afternoon of 6th, " B " and " D " Companies were relieved by the 7th Bedfords, and " A " Company in the early hours of the 8th. The Battalion marched back and bivouacked west of Bonfray Wood, putting up what shelter they could from pieces of corrugated iron. On the 7th a violent thunderstorm broke over the camp, making everything muddy and wet, so that later two Companies were sent back to Carnoy. On the 8th the Battalion was ordered to move to the east side of Bonfray Wood, the two Companies in Carnoy having been recalled. At 9.30 p.m. the Battalion was again on the move, on this occasion to huts in Bois des Tailles. But the camp was in such a filthy state that, on the 9th, Colonel Maxwell moved his men to some cleaner ground.

The 12th Battalion remained at Bois des Tailles until the morning of 13th, when a move was made to Maricourt. On 13TH JULY. arrival Companies occupied the old British line, " B " and " C " in the front-line trenches on the western side of the Montauban Road, " A " Company on the eastern side, and " D " Company the support trenches on the western side of the road.

It was from these positions that the Battalion was moved forward by Companies to take up preliminary positions which ended in the now-famous attack on Trônes Wood.

About 4 p.m. orders were received to send a company forward to support the 55th Brigade which was going to attack Trônes Wood : " C " Company was detailed and took up a line of trenches on the west face of Bernafay Wood. Two hours later " D " Company was ordered to take over Dublin Trench from the East Surreys : at 8 p.m., " B " Company was moved up to the Sunken Road.* Thus when, during the night of 13th–14th July, Colonel Maxwell was sent for and told that his Battalion and the Northants were to capture and hold Trônes Wood, his Companies were already scattered. For a little while, however, it is necessary to leave them in their positions and turn to other portions of the battlefield where the " slow " advance had also been in progress.

The 2nd and 4th Battalions of the Regiment, of the 8th and 21st Divisions respectively, had, as already described, been withdrawn from the battlefield. The latter had reached Vaux with

* Presumably the Sunken Road south of Montauban.

other units of the 63rd Brigade on 4th July. The losses of the Brigade had been so severe that it was now transferred from the 21st to the 37th Division, so that very shortly the 4th Middlesex again found themselves with new comrades.

On the 7th July a footing was gained in the outer defences of Ovillers by the 25th and 12th Divisions. The latter was one of the reserve Divisions, and had been moved up after the first day of the operations.

4TH JULY. 11TH BATTALION. The 11th Middlesex, of the 36th Brigade, 12th Division, on the night of 4th July, occupied the front line from Longridge to Mersey Trench, which included the Nab, north-west of Ovillers. The Battalion was, however, relieved on the 5th, and moved back to billets in Albert. Their stay in this town was short, for on the 6th they were again moved up to the trenches in Ribble Street, where they were in Brigade Reserve to the front-line units of the 36th Brigade.

On the night of 6th–7th the Battalion furnished carrying parties for the R.E. as the three front-line Battalions of the Brigade which were to make the attack on Ovillers on the morning of 7th. At 1 a.m. on 7th, Lieut. Eden, with a party of "D" Company, tried to establish a new bomb store in the Sunken Road which crossed No Man's Land in a south-westerly direction, but the trenches were in such a congested state with troops that he could not get through. Moreover, he was wounded with a bullet through his left forearm.

7TH JULY. At 6.45 a.m., on 7th, the artillery bombardment began, and continued until 8.30 a.m., when the three front-line Battalions of the 36th Brigade, *i.e.*, 8th and 9th Royal Fusiliers and 7th Royal Sussex, went forward to the assault. The 11th Middlesex at once moved up into the line vacated by the assaulting Battalions, "C" Company from Rivington Street to Ryecroft, "B" Company thence to Argyll Street, "A" Company thence to Dorset Street. By 10 a.m. the attacking troops, in the face of fierce oppositions and a very heavy enfilade rifle and machine-gun fire, had carried the first and second German lines and part of the third line. The enemy's shell fire was now intense, and "C" Company of the Middlesex suffered numerous casualties. Lieut. Redford, though wounded in the foot as he was getting over the parapet, succeeded in taking the wireless apparatus across No Man's Land to the captured trenches, but on arrival there found that the accumulators had been damaged by fire and were useless.

At 2.30 p.m., six volunteers of "A" Company tried to cross No Man's Land with a fresh supply of bombs for the attacking Battalions who were in desperate need of them, but with the exception of two lance-corporals of the party, all were shot down and brought in wounded. At 3 p.m., "A" Company (under Captain Lewis and Lieut. Moore), which consisted of sixty other ranks only, with one platoon of 7th Royal Sussex and details of 8th Royal Fusiliers, crossed over to the captured trenches, each man carrying twenty bombs. They obtained touch with troops about the Sunken Road and began bombing their way south of this road. About 4 p.m., Captain G. S. Lewis, who had just shot a German with his rifle, was himself killed by a rifle shot. Lieut. Moore then took charge and established a bombing and Lewis-gun post on his right, being in touch with the Sussex in the front line. Later, at 7.45 p.m., "B" Company (50 other ranks) under Captain Crombie, Lieut. Shaw and 2nd Lieut. Tatham, crossed to the captured trenches. The enemy had now been definitely beaten back, and this Company got across without being fired on. Throughout the remainder of the night 7th–8th, and throughout the latter date, the Middlesex, with other troops of the Brigade, held on to the captured positions, and, though under shell fire and exposed to counter-attacks, no ground was lost. About 10 p.m. on 8th, the 11th Battalion was relieved and marched back to billets in Albert. On 7th, the casualties suffered by the 11th Middlesex were 3 other ranks killed, 54 wounded, 7 shell shock, 3 missing, and 2 missing, believed killed: on 8th, 1 other ranks was killed, 31 were wounded, 10 suffered from shell shock, and 3 were missing. The total casualties suffered by the Battalion, according to the Brigade Diary, were 1 officer killed, 3 officers wounded, and 128 other ranks killed, wounded and missing. 7TH JULY. 11TH BATTALION.

On 9th July the Battalion moved to Senlis, on 10th to Forceville, and on the 11th to Bus, where re-organisation and training were carried on until the 20th.* Thus, the 11th Middlesex were not in action when the first phase of the operations closed, nor were they in the opening of the second phase, which began on 14th July. 9TH JULY.

Early in July, the 33rd Division left the Bethune area and entrained for the Somme. Moving by stages via Gonnehem, Rainneville, Corbie and Ville, the 98th Brigade, in which the

* On the 17th Lieut.-Colonel Oliver was invalided to the Base, and Major L. L. Pargiter took over command of the Battalion.

1st Battalion. 1st Middlesex were contained, reached Méaulte on 14th July, just as the first stage of the Battle ended. Since the 1st June the 1st Battalion had passed a comparatively quiet existence in the Cuinchy sub-sector, or in billets in Bethune. On the 10th, Lieut.-Colonel Rowley, who had served continuously with the Battalion since its arrival in France in August, 1914, left to take over command of the 56th Infantry Brigade to which he had been appointed. His departure was felt keenly by all ranks of the 1st Battalion. Major Bagley assumed temporary command. On the 17th, Lieut. C. F. N. Draper was severely wounded in the leg, and died the same night in hospital in Bethune. Lieut.-Colonel H. Lloyd arrived at Battalion Headquarters on 24th and took over command from Major Bagley.

14th July. With other units of the Brigade, the 1st Middlesex had arrived at Méaulte on the night of 13th July, but at 11 a.m. on 14th the Battalion moved to Bécordel and bivouacked for some two or three hours. The 33rd Division had been ordered to attack between High Wood and the railway, and later the 1st Battalion moved forward and, after various halts and stops, reached the southern edge of Mametz Wood, finally bivouacking on the western lip of the valley just north of Fricourt. Orders to the 98th Brigade to attack Switch Trench had been cancelled.

18th Battalion. The 18th Middlesex (Pioneers) of the 33rd Division had also arrived at Méaulte on 14th, and billeted for the night north-west of the village.

## (II) THE BATTLE OF BAZENTIN RIDGE.

### 14th–17th July.

### I.—The Capture of Trônes Wood.

---

" Arrangements were . . . made for an attack to be delivered at daybreak on the morning of 14th July against a front extending from Longueval to Bazentin-le-Petit Wood, both inclusive. Contalmaison Villa, on a spur 1,000 yards west of Bazentin-le-Petit Wood, had already been captured to secure the left flank of the attack, and advantage had been taken of the progress made by our infantry to move our artillery forward into new positions.

The preliminary bombardment had opened on the 11th July. The opportunities offered by the ground for enfilading the enemy's lines were fully utilised, and did much to secure the success of our attack."—*Official Despatches.*

---

The Battle opened very early in the morning of the 14th (3.25 a.m.); indeed, there was only just sufficient light in which to distinguish friend from foe at short ranges. Just before Zero hour, the Divisions, from right to left, as they stood in line ready to go forward to the attack were: 18th at the Briqueterie and west of Trônes Wood, the 9th north of Montauban, 3rd north of Caterpillar Wood, 7th between the latter wood and Mametz Wood, 21st on the north-west edge of Mametz Wood, 1st north-east of Contalmaison, and the 34th north-west of the latter village: the 33rd Division (98th Brigade) lay between Mametz village and Mametz Wood.

Three Battalions of the Regiment, *i.e.*, 1st, 12th and 18th, were therefore engaged in the Battle, for although the 21st Division took part in the operations, the 4th Middlesex, with that Division on 1st July, had already been transferred with other units of the 63rd Brigade and Brigade Headquarters to the 37th Division. 1ST, 12TH & 18TH BATTALIONS.

The capture of Trônes Wood has now an official place amongst the "Tactical Incidents" of the Battle of Bazentin Ridge; for the Middlesex Regiment it was not only an exceedingly difficult operation, but one of the most successful actions of the Battles of the Somme, 1916, and ranks high on the lists of achievements of the 18th Division, to which the 12th Middlesex Regiment belonged.

It will be remembered that on the night 13th–14th July the four companies of the 12th Middlesex (Lieut.-Colonel F. Maxwell, V.C.) were not concentrated but were split up, three having been placed under the command of the G.O.C., 55th Brigade, and only one remaining with its own Brigade, *i.e.*, the 54th. "C" Company had been sent off to Bernafay Wood, "D" Company was in Dublin Trench with Battalion Headquarters, "B" Company was in Trônes Wood supporting the Royal West Kent Regiment. These three Companies were under the orders of the 55th Brigade, and only "A" Company remained under the G.O.C., 54th Brigade, back in the Maricourt Defences. 12TH BATTALION.

Such was the disposition of his Battalion when very early on the morning of 14th July Colonel Maxwell received verbal 14TH JULY.

14TH JULY. 12TH BATTALION.

instructions, first from the G.O.C., 55th Brigade at 55th Brigade Headquarters, and later from the G.O.C., 54th Brigade, that, with the 12th Middlesex and 6th Northants,* he was to attack and capture Trônes Wood (already partly held by the West Kent Regiment, 55th Brigade). The attack was to be made before dawn. Having made good the whole of the wood, the Middlesex and Northants were to hold the eastern edge as a defensive flank to the attack of the 9th Division on Longueval. The establishment of this defensive flank was essential, and upon it rested the success of the whole Battle. The 30th Division had failed to capture it, and the 18th Division had been put into the line to accomplish what the former Division had failed to do.

After giving Colonel Maxwell these orders, the G.O.C., 55th Brigade, then explained the situation in the wood as was then known to him: the Royal West Kent Regiment held the southern apex of the wood, also the railway line and a considerable section of the southern edge of the wood. The G.O.C. also undertook to direct the Northants to rendezvous at the Sunken Road, also the three Companies of Middlesex "not in Trônes Wood."

It was 2.30 a.m. on 14th before Colonel Maxwell left 54th Brigade Headquarters, the G.O.C. of the latter Brigade having taken over command of the operations from the G.O.C., 55th Brigade, about half-an-hour earlier. On leaving Brigade Headquarters, the C.O. of the 12th Middlesex made his way to the Sunken Road, which lay about 1,000 yards south-west of Trônes Wood, and there found the 6th Northants already concentrated under Major Clark: one company of the Middlesex was also with the Northants, and another on its way up from the Maricourt defences. (The company in Bernafay Wood did not rejoin Colonel Maxwell until 15th.)

Dawn was now breaking and every second was priceless: to wait for his own Battalion to concentrate would mean loss of time. Colonel Maxwell therefore decided to send the Northants into the front line,to be followed by the 12th Middlesex in support. The important thing was to get the men across that deadly 1,000 yards of open space between the Sunken Road and Trônes Wood before daylight in order to rob the enemy's machine-gunners and riflemen of their human targets. The enemy's artillery had already placed a very heavy barrage on that terrible

* Colonel Maxwell was to have under him for the operation the 6th Northants Regiment as well as his own Battalion.

open space, and his shells were falling thick and fast on the ground over which the attack would have to go forward. 14TH JULY. 12TH BATTALION.

To Major Clark, who was in temporary command of the Northants, Colonel Maxwell explained the situation in the wood as given to him by the G.O.C., 55th Brigade, and first directed him on arriving in the wood to push on to the line across it held by the West Kent Regiment, and there to halt as a starting point for an advance in line northwards through the wood, with the Middlesex in support. The strong point ("A") which was known to exist on the eastern exits of the wood was also to be captured. A little later, probably feeling none too sure of the line held by the Royal West Kents, Colonel Maxwell modified these orders, and directed Major Clark to halt his Battalion when it reached the inside edge of the wood. These orders, which had to be given verbally, were coupled with instructions to move immediately across the open space in order to minimise loss. Shortly after giving Major Clark these orders, Major Charrington arrived to assume command of the Northants, but Colonel Maxwell states in his report that "I think his Battalion had already begun to move before he found Major Clark."

With great steadiness the Northants crossed from the Sunken Road and disappeared into Trônes Wood through the heavy barrage: they were followed by the two companies of 12th Middlesex. A little later, accompanied by Major Charrington, Colonel Maxwell followed the Northants to the southern edge of the wood.

"Disappeared" is the only adequate term which could be applied to the vanished Northants, for Trônes Wood at this period was in an appalling condition. When the Somme Battles opened, the trees in the wood were in full leaf and the ground beneath was covered by a thick undergrowth. But the guns of both sides had played havoc with its beauty: many of the trees had been shorn of their branches, which lay in hopeless confusion on the ground: others had been torn off almost to the roots, the upper parts toppling down to add still further to the wreckage: some had been completely uprooted by the explosions of huge shells. Amidst all this hopeless mess the enemy had endeavoured to dig trenches, but they mostly consisted of holes scraped wherever there was a clearing, or where a clearing could be made.

"Never," said Colonel Maxwell, "was anything so perfectly dreadful to look at, at least I could not dream of anything worse,

14TH JULY. 12TH BATTALION.

particularly with its dreadful addition of corpses and wounded men, many lying there for days and days. (Our doctor found one to-day (15th) who had had no food or water for five days: I am afraid there are more like him.) But so dense is the tangle that even if one finds a man, gets someone to bandage him, and then leave him, you have lost him probably, simply because you can't find your way back to him. Talk of the City of Dreadful Night, it must be incomparable to (this) Wood of Dreadful Night, or Day." The killed and wounded in the wood were casualties from the previous unsuccessful attempt to capture the wood.

Finding the Northants had apparently advanced, the C.O. of the Middlesex asked Major Charrington why his Battalion had gone right in instead of halting inside the edge. The latter replied that Major Clark had not mentioned that part of Colonel Maxwell's orders, but said he was going on to the line held by the West Kents.

Having seen the two companies of Middlesex halted inside the edge of the wood, the C.O. of the Middlesex went to the south-west part of the wood, where the C.O., Royal West Kent Regiment, had his Headquarters. The latter gave Colonel Maxwell the same appreciation of the situation as that given by the G.O.C., 55th Brigade, but with this addition, that the Company of 12th Middlesex already in the wood occupied a sector of the trench C.1—C.2, running roughly parallel with the south-west edge. "In this connection," states Colonel Maxwell in his report, "I am inclined to believe that the O.C., Royal West Kent Regiment, may have thought that the Company was holding the trench BX, and possibly a continuation of it to eastern edge of the wood. The Company Commander himself thought he was in BX instead of C.1—C.2, and only a portion of it at that, as shown in sketch* . . ., and this idea would perhaps account for O.C., West Kents', belief that he held a considerable portion of the southern part of the wood."

Having finished his interview with the O.C., Royal West Kent Regiment, the O.C., 12th Middlesex, fixed his Battalion Headquarters at a point about midway along C.1—C.2, and there waited for reports from the Northants, which he assumed had pushed on in search of the line believed to be held by the West Kents further in the wood ("but which in reality did not exist").

The first reports (two) received by Colonel Maxwell were

* *Not* shown on sketch.

urgent requests for bombs, as the enemy was holding up the sender of the message. The Middlesex bombers were at once sent forward to assist, and a little later, on receiving a further call, all the bombs which could be found were sent up, the men who took them being ordered to bring back news of the situation; but no news was received. Next, a messenger arrived from the O.C., "A" Company Northants, stating that he had only eight men of his company left, most of whom really belonged to "C" Company. Although the situation appeared unsatisfactory, the O.C., Middlesex, sent up "D" Company (Captain Dennis) of his Battalion as promised to the O.C., Northants, for the purpose of finding and dealing with Strong Point "A." Two Companies of Middlesex were now left in C.1—C.2.

14TH JULY. 12TH BATTALION.

Receiving no further reports from the Northants and nothing from Captain Dennis, Colonel Maxwell determined to find out something of the situation for himself. He accordingly set out in the direction of the Strong Point "A," and on reaching point "D," near the south-eastern edge of the wood, came upon a conglomeration of units, principally Royal West Kents, intermingled with Northants and Middlesex. "No one knew anything nor was doing anything." Working still further up the edge of the wood, he was met by Captain Dennis, who said he was as yet unable to get near the Strong Point owing to the activities of a hostile machine-gun firing from the Point, nor could he get north of it by working inside the wood, as there appeared to be another hostile machine gun in the centre of the wood which opposed any effort of his to move. Colonel Maxwell then pushed westwards in order to ascertain whether there was any prolongation of troops in that direction, but all he found was a party of Northants at about "F." These men told him that they were held up in the trench near that point ("F") by the enemy: apparently each side was holding the other up.

The C.O., 12th Middlesex, thus sums up the situation at this period in the following terms: "With the exception of two Companies Middlesex in or near C.1—C.2, one Company Middlesex attempting to take Strong Point 'A' and a group of Northants near 'E' there were no formed units anywhere: that the disorganised groups of units near 'D' had no cohesion and no purpose. Of the Northants as a whole, I could neither hear nor see anything. In the trench east of the wood running into Strong Point 'A' the Buffs had men, but so far as I could see, they were

14TH JULY.
12TH BATTALION.

inactive.* It appeared to me, therefore, that it was necessary to start afresh, and I decided to collect every man within reach, and with them form a line east to west right across the wood and then advance northwards. With this in view, I sent back to C.1—C.2 trenches for one of the two companies there, and in the meantime collected as many men of the Northants as I could, plus a platoon from the company detailed for the attack against Strong Point 'A.' I had also hoped to include the Royal West Kent officers and men (3 officers and about 50 men, I think), but they were already on the move out—on relief by the 54th Brigade, it was explained—and I was too late to order them to remain."

It is interesting to note that apparently Colonel Maxwell now had under him only the Middlesex and Northants, which he originally commanded, the Northants being placed under him at the beginning of the operations by the G.O.C. Brigade.

The C.O., Middlesex, then digresses in his report in order to describe the "topographical illusion" of Trônes Wood, and his arguments are so potent that they are given in full: "The topography of Trônes Wood was known to nobody, for up to a few minutes of the attack it had no personal or tactical interest for anyone. Maps had, therefore, not been studied. I had not yet met an officer who knew even that there was a railway in the wood (let alone two). Probably the only feature that anyone's eye retained was the triangular shape of the wood with its apex north of the base. But the base of the triangle does not run east and west, as a cursory glance at the map would lead one to suppose, but south-east, so that on entering the wood and making for an apex believed to be straight ahead, the direction would not be, and was not north, but north-east or east-north-east. On reaching the eastern edge, therefore, in most cases towards the Strong Point 'A,' the angle of the wood there (which was more defined on the ground than on the map) was unquestionably taken to be the northern apex. To a few the false apex may have appeared further north on the point where the lower railway entered the wood through a widish clearing. Captain Podmore of the Northants, for instance, seems to have fallen into the error at this point, for in a report of his which I have seen he wrote:

*** In a pencilled note to his report, Colonel Maxwell says: "I learnt subsequently that Captain Podmore (of the Northants) was at this time on the 'E' edge of the wood between Southern Railway Line and Strong Point "A."**

'I have secured *all* Trônes Wood (the italics are mine) except a small "T" head containing about six men at Strong Point (A) on Guillemont road and about forty Germans in a trench outside wood just south of same strong point. Buffs are attacking with a Stokes gun, and we must have a Stokes gun if we are to take these two places and consolidate eastern edge of Trônes Wood.' It is known that Captain Podmore wrote this somewhere south of the railway, beyond which none of the Northants advanced (except with the line or behind it). I believed, therefore, that he considered that the apex of the wood was formed, not by the junction of western and eastern edges some seven hundred yards further north, but by the northern edge of the railway clearing and the eastern edge of the wood south of it. Major Charrington is in agreement with me that this was so. The great difference in the distance between the south-west edge of the wood and the supposed apex and the real apex is, of course, accounted for, first, by no one probably having measured the length of the wood beforehand, and, secondly, to the fact that all sense of distance was lost in such a wood as Trônes, the density of which was trebled and quadrupled by the top of the forest being shot down into the undergrowth below, making it almost impenetrable to passage or vision. I have my own personal experience to add to this conviction, for, though I had happened to study my map the previous morning and knew much about the wood, I found myself when following this line (to be mentioned hereafter) doing so in a north-easterly direction. Subsequently, when I got the line facing north, the moment it got into motion it swung its left shoulder up, and every officer and man made instinctively and unconsciously for the light showing on each side of any small angle in the wood to the east, and it was only by constant use of the compass and halting to readjust direction that the advance was kept on the true line. If this error occurred with the two battalions under me, I think that the same mistake must have occurred to the Royal West Kents. So far as I saw for myself, and from information received from anyone else, the only men of the Regiment, either grouped or singly, met with were at 'D,' and I believe, though I did not ask, they considered themselves to be at the apex.* If they did not, I cannot account

14TH JULY. 12TH BATTALION.

* Lieut.-Colonel Maxwell added the following remark to this paragraph: "Captain Meares states that he saw another party of this Battalion at or near the copse north of Strong Point 'A,' so this paragraph is modified accordingly."

14TH JULY.
12TH BATTALION.

for Colonel Fiennes'* definite belief that he was in possession of it. As to the Royal West Kents holding the railway, possibly some had been there, but none were seen by the Northants,† and none were on it when my line passed over it. As to the rest of the wood, north of the railway, I doubt if anyone had been there since one of the first attacks: in any case, there were practically no killed or wounded (British) there. Outside the wire near the apex I found three men of the Queen's who had been confined in their hiding place for 48 hours; they said they had had a Lewis gun at the apex and they had lost it when driven out by the enemy."

The story of the formation of the line and the drive northwards through the wood, which led to the capture of the whole of it, is also better told in the words of the C.O. of the 12th Middlesex: "Reverting now to the formation of the line across the wood," he said, "this was effected on the arrival of the Middlesex Company. It was a mixed line of Northants and Middlesex, the majority of the latter on the right. To get the line into position, I sent an officer on a compass bearing due west, followed in single file by the men, and when he had nearly reached the western edge the whole turned right into line and advanced north. Then, as already indicated, there persisted the continual tendency to drift north-east, as also the extreme unwillingness of the men to advance in any sort of line. They would bunch, and then follow in single file any man bold enough to lead them. Nerves were very highly strung, and, indeed, under the conditions seen or endured by the men since dawn, nerves of the best type of old Regular regiments would have been strained. To counteract this nerve trouble, so destructive to the line formation, I ordered every man to fire as he advanced: fire into anything in front of him—at two crossed twigs if necessary. This almost immediately had the desired effect, and the advance continued much more steadily and in better order. Little opposition was met and casualties were few till the advance approached the south line of the railway, where near the eastern (western ?)‡ edge of the wood a machine gun opened. Ordering the whole line to halt,

* Commanding Royal West Kents.

† To this sentence Colonel Maxwell added the following comments: "This again may not be correct, for it is possible that some of the Royal West Kents may have been on the line a second time, though none appear to have been seen there."

‡ This is obviously a mistake in the typescript report, and should read "western."

I took about seventy men on the left to deal with it. This was done after some delay, the enemy detachment destroyed and the gun captured. Then, the line re-forming, the advance was continued. By the time the railway was crossed all the Northants that were not with me were, I think, lining the eastern edge of the wood from the railway entry point down to Strong Point 'A,' which had meanwhile been taken by the Middlesex Company and Buffs. After crossing the second line of railway there was a new development, for, though we hardly saw a man in the dense wood ahead of us, the enemy began to break close ahead of the line out of the wood to the east. Some possibly had moved up from the centre of the wood ahead of the line: some may have left the machine-gun company previous to our finding it: others were no doubt occupying the trenches and dug-outs in the area north of the railway, but wherever they came from, they seemed to think that the advancing line left them no chance, and they cleared its front. Lewis guns on the eastern edge of the wood and men dropped along it also accounted for a large number of the enemy as they left the wood. More could have been killed had I allowed the men to go out to the shell holes in which they sheltered, but I had to forbid this: first, because I wanted to make good the whole of the wood, of which there was still a long stretch in front (it seemed interminable), and then to secure its eastern edge against counter-attack; secondly, because I was anxious not to show the enemy the extent of our progress, and so bring upon us his artillery fire, which so far was kept with great intensity on the southern portions of the wood. Finally the apex was reached, the enemy breaking out till the very end: from twenty to forty bolted from the apex itself. Though temporarily many managed to avoid the fire from the wood edge, the majority were subsequently picked up when the process of organising the defences of the edge was completed. Having arranged for the holding of the apex and roughly disposed the scattered units and Lewis guns along the edge down to Strong Point 'A,' I returned to Battalion Headquarters to report. On arrival there, I sent Major Scarborough and Major Charrington to reorganise the intermingled groups of Northants and Middlesex and to superintend the preparation of strong points at apex and Strong Point 'A.' "

14TH JULY. 12TH BATTALION.

The above full description of the capture of Trônes Wood is followed by several points which Colonel Maxwell brought

14TH JULY.
12TH BATTALION.

to the notice of the Higher Command: they are also given word for word.

The first deals with the Northants, placed temporarily under his command, and to whom the C.O. of the Middlesex pays great tribute: "Thus the leading Battalion (Northants) entered the wood in small columns, hoping to halt and form up on a line supposed to be held inside the wood by the Royal West Kents. That finding none where expected, and, moreover, coming under fire very soon after entry, it continued to advance in small units without any definite object except to push through to the northern extremity; but, losing its direction, it worked north-east, and finally found itself with its left on or near the railway line and its right down the eastern edge of the wood towards Strong Point 'A.' That any portion got so far as it did is, in my opinion, no small feat. A less efficient unit, starting under the circumstances it did—*i.e.*, no halt inside the wood in order to reform, take up direction or even to issue orders—could not have done it." His next point deals with the deceptive nature of the bottom edge of the wood and the false apex, which need not be repeated. The third point discusses the "line on line" across the wood, which needs no justification, seeing that it was eminently successful, and the last point the method of advance, each man firing as he went. The adoption of this method clearly showed how great an understanding Colonel Maxwell had of "nerves" and of his men.*

Finally he said: "I have not touched on the subsequent holding of the wood from the afternoon of 14th to morning of 17th. Nor do I intend to, for there is nothing in that except 'sticking it out' under artillery fire, which I am glad to be able to report was done staunchly by the Battalion (12th Middlesex) in spite of considerable losses (about 40 per cent.)."

With the capture of Trônes Wood the right flank of the advance was secured, and General Maxse was able to report that his Division (18th) had carried out the task allotted to it, so that a little later, when the Division left the Fourth Army, the Army Commander, General Sir Henry Rawlinson, wrote: "The part

* But of his own part—the splendid leadership and indomitable pluck he had displayed—there is naturally no mention. Neither is there any mention—because at that period it was impossible to appreciate it—of the great feat performed by his Battalion, of which Sir Ivor Maxse afterwards said: "I doubt if any other Battalion of the Regiment performed a more important or more essential piece of fighting throughout the war."

Map IX.

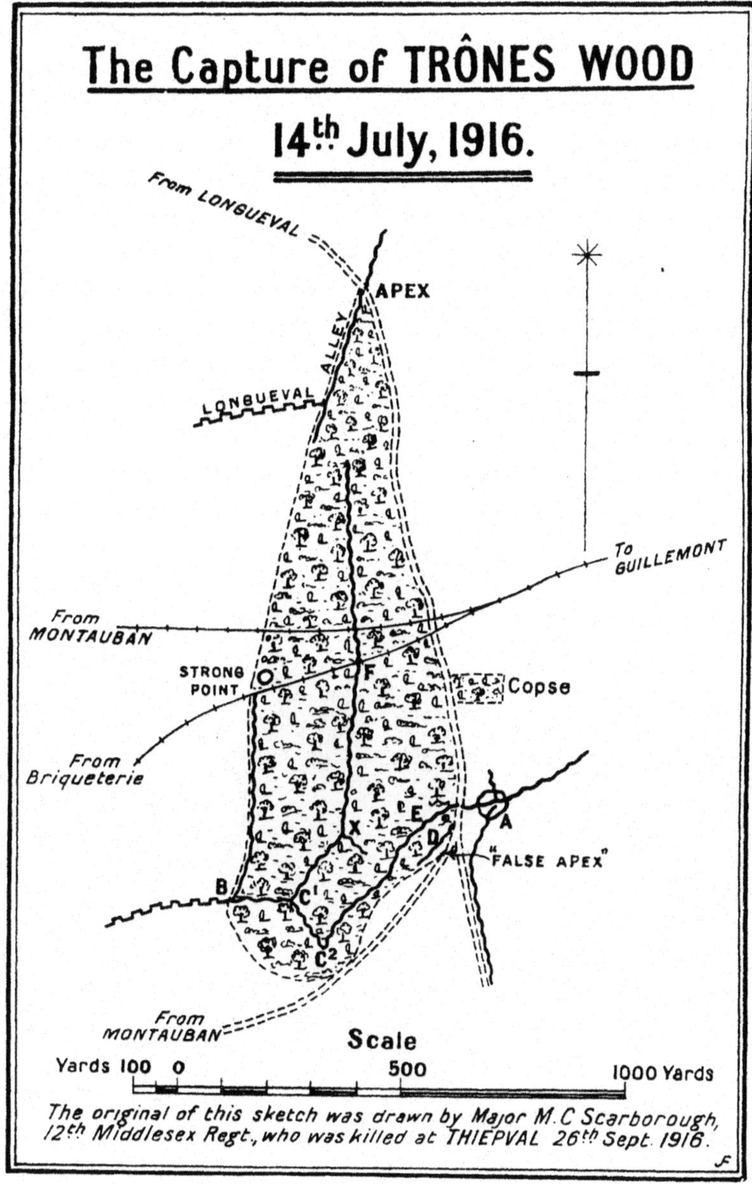


[To face p. 282.

which the 18th Division has taken in the Battles of the Somme reflects the highest credit on every officer, non-commissioned officer and man, and I desire to tender to one and all my gratitude and congratulations."

The losses sustained by the 12th Middlesex in the operations between the 14th and 17th July, 1916, were 1 officer (2nd Lieut. A. J. Keith) killed, 6 officers wounded,* 32 other ranks killed, 215 wounded, 29 missing. Total, 7 officers and 276.

## II.

Whilst the 12th Battalion at Trônes Wood was adding another glorious page to its war history, two other Battalions of the Regiment, the 1st (33rd Division) and 18th (Pioneers, 33rd Division), were also engaged on the right in the Battle of Bazentin Ridge. 1ST & 18TH BATTALION

In accordance with orders from 33rd Divisional Headquarters, the 98th Brigade (of which the 1st Middlesex formed part) moved to Bécordel on 14th July, arriving at that place about 12.30 p.m. At 5 p.m. further orders were received stating that the Brigade was to attack Switch Trench between High Wood and the railway, but before units reached their assembly positions these orders were cancelled and the Brigade bivouacked. The Middlesex in their advance had reached the southern edge of Mametz Wood, but here the Battalion turned about and bivouacked on the western edge of the valley just north of Fricourt. 14TH JULY. 1ST BATTALION

At 3 a.m. the next morning the Brigade was again ordered to attack, and the 1st Middlesex (Lieut.-Colonel H. Lloyd) set out at about 6.30 a.m. for Bazentin-le-Petit, from which village the assault of the enemy's position was to be made. The advance was made through a gas cloud, which made everyone feel most uncomfortable, though apparently none of the troops were actually "gassed." On reaching the church at Bazentin-le-Petit, "B" and "C" Companies worked round the northern side of the village, whilst "A" and "D" Companies went straight through it. Just beyond the eastern edge of the village there was a road running north and south; here the Companies deployed for the attack. "B" and "D" formed the front line, with "C" and 15TH JULY

* Capt. Harrison, Capt. Parsons, Capt. Methuen and Capt. A. C. Dennis (died of wounds 17th July, 1917); 2nd Lieuts. Stubbs and Fish.

15TH JULY.
1ST BATTALION.

"A" in support. The Battalion attacked on a frontage of 800 yards. The 1st Queen's of the 100th Brigade (33rd Division) were on the right of the Middlesex, and 2nd Welch Regiment (1st Division) was on the left. Supporting the 1st Middlesex of the 98th Brigade were the 1/4th Suffolks, while the 2nd Argyll and Sutherland Highlanders and the 4th King's Regiment were in reserve.

The first objective allotted to the Battalion was the German Switch Trench.

The Battalion had scarcely deployed for action when a party of the enemy in the northern corner of Bazentin-le-Petit Wood* fired into the left flank of the advancing Middlesex men, with machine gun and rifle. Moreover, the enemy sent up red and white flares, and soon the hostile field guns and howitzers had placed a heavy barrage on the line of advance. Machine-gun fire "principally (from) High Wood, which we had been informed was in our possession,"† now began to take heavy toll of the advancing Companies, which were finally brought to a standstill on the crest of a slight ridge east of the village. Shelled unmercifully and machine-gunned from both flanks, the gallant Middlesex, attempting to "dig in" on the position gained, were eventually compelled to fall back to the road running north and south on the eastern outskirts of Bazentin-le-Petit from which they had started. The flanking units apparently fared no better, and the Suffolks, in support of the 1st Middlesex, were likewise brought to a standstill.

The day's fighting had cost the 1st Battalion many brave lives. Of the officers, 6 had been killed and 7 wounded; in other ranks the losses were 44 killed, 201 wounded, and 63 missing. The total casualties on 15th were 13 officers and 308 other ranks. The C.O. (Lieut.-Colonel H. Lloyd) and the second-in-command (Major G. O. T. Bagley) were amongst the wounded.

On reaching the original "jumping-off" positions Captain G. E. Bucknall assumed temporary command, and every effort was made to reorganise the Battalion. One Company of the 2nd Argylls was brought up to strengthen the left flank of the Battalion, for opposite this flank the party of Germans who had caused so many casualties by their flanking fire had not been

* The diarist here, apparently, means High Wood, for Bazentin-le-Petit Wood was west of the village through which the Battalion had just passed.

† From the Battalion Diary, 1st Middlesex.

dislodged. The road was held until about 10 p.m., when the 4th King's Regiment arrived to relieve the Middlesex. The latter (under Major Potter, who had arrived from the Transport lines shortly before the relief and assumed command) then marched back to the valley just north-east of Mametz Wood, and there bivouacked for the night. The 16th was spent in cleaning up and reorganising. On the 17th, at 9.30 a.m., the German guns shelled the valley heavily, and continued to do so until 4.30 in the afternoon. But as soon as the hostile artillery opened fire, orders were given for the Battalion to "scatter," and very few casualties were suffered. About 6 p.m., after the shelling had died down, the Battalion re-assembled, and two hours later moved up into the line, again taking over Bazentin-le-Petit Wood. The relief was completed about 4 a.m. on 18th.* 15TH JULY. 1ST BATTALION. 18TH JULY.

Of the Pioneer Battalion (the 18th, commanded by Lieut.-Colonel H. Storr) in this Battle there is little to record. The gallant fellows worked continually under shell fire, for they had moved up to Bécordel–Bécourt at 6 a.m. on 15th July, thence to repair the road just east of Mametz Wood and the road crossing the old German second-line trenches. Nine men were wounded. Again on the 16th, work in Mametz Wood (on the repair of the trolley line) was carried out amidst heavy shell fire, though no one was hit. The programme of 17th was similar to those carried out on 15th and 16th, save for a removal of the Battalion bivouacs to the south-east corner of Fricourt Wood. Three more men were wounded on this date. 18TH BATTALION. 17TH JULY.

## The Attack on High Wood,

### 20th–25th July, 1916.

Only the 18th Battalion (Pioneers) of the Regiment was involved in the several attacks on High Wood, which took place between the 20th and 25th July. 18TH BATTALION.

From their bivouacs in the south-east corner of Fricourt Wood the Battalion had moved out to work on the repair of roads on 18th. On this day Captain Jones and eight men were wounded. On the 19th similar work was allotted all companies. At 6 p.m., 19TH JULY.

* It is strange that no mention is made in the official despatches of the part taken by the 33rd Division in the Battle of Bazentin Ridge, though the other Divisions are mentioned.

18TH BATTALION. however, word was received that the 33rd Division was going to attack High Wood on the morning of 20th, and two companies of Pioneers were ordered to be placed at the disposal of the G.O.C., 19th Infantry Brigade, the remainder of the Battalion being in Divisional Reserve and remaining in Fricourt Wood. "B" and "D" Companies were the two selected, the company commanders interviewing the Brigadier of 19th Infantry Brigade, who gave them their orders.

21ST JULY. At 12.20 a.m. on 21st "B" and "D" paraded and marched off to the position of assembly assigned to them, in the rear of the 20th Royal Welch Fusiliers. They were to dig a communication trench from High Wood back to the low ground as soon as the assault had been made. The advance began, the Pioneers following the Royal Fusiliers as directed, but some 300 yards south-west of High Wood the latter Battalion halted, while the remainder of the Brigade went into it. Just as the Fusiliers were moving into the wood the enemy put down a heavy barrage round the southern end of it, which effectively prevented the Pioneers from digging a trench, as it was impossible to work in the midst of a perfect inferno of falling and bursting shells. But at 3.45 a.m. they began work on a trench from just west of the south-west corner of High Wood back to the Longueval–Bazentin-le-Grand road, just north of the latter village. For no less than seven hours these gallant Pioneers worked hard on this trench, digging for all they were worth; but at last, about 10.45 a.m., men began to fall dead asleep; they could do no more—their strength was spent and they were utterly exhausted. The two companies were then ordered back to Fricourt Wood. How they got there, seeing that they had to march nearly 5,000 yards back across very difficult country, it is impossible to say, but about 12.30 p.m. they reached the wood, dead beat. During the time they were up in the line they had suffered some 35 casualties.

It was now the turn of the two remaining Companies, "A" and "C." Under Major Best they were paraded at 7 p.m. and marched up to carry on the work, and by 8 p.m. "A" was digging hard, and "C" half an hour later was similarly engaged.

About 9 p.m. a Sapper officer came out of High Wood and told Major Best that the Germans were counter-attacking and that, as only some two hundred British troops were in the wood, reinforcements were urgently needed. He then asked Major Best if he would line the south-west edge of the wood. The

Major undertook to do this and gave orders accordingly, going off to the Headquarters of the 2nd Royal Welch Fusiliers, which were in the Longueval–High Wood Road, south-west of the wood, to report to the O.C. of the Battalion. While he was there an orderly brought a message from the Royal Welch Fusiliers in the wood which stated that the 20th Royal Welch Fusiliers had been forced out of the front line. This orderly was followed immediately by a Major of the Royal Welch Fusiliers, who not only confirmed the message brought by the orderly, but stated that the Germans were advancing. He asked for a party of men to advance through the wood without firing and meet the enemy with the bayonet. Hastily collecting the two leading platoons of "C" Company, Major Best took them into the wood guided by the Major of the Royal Welch Fusiliers. One platoon was sent off to the eastern part of the wood and there became engaged with the enemy. No reports exist (alas !) concerning this bayonet-fighting episode, but it is certain the Pioneers gave a good account of themselves. The other platoons went off to support a party of the 20th Royal Welch Fusiliers who were holding the second line in the centre of the wood. Major Best then returned to bring up the remaining one and a-half platoons of "C" Company and sent them also to the eastern part of the wood. He once more returned to Headquarters, Royal Welch Fusiliers, reported what he had done, and asked if he should take "A" Company up also. He was on his way back to fetch up the last company when he met Captain Hill, who stated that the message had been passed back for "A" to go forward, and that he had sent up one platoon, but before bringing up the remainder of the company he had come to ascertain what was required. A heavy hostile barrage was now falling, and these two officers went back to the Headquarters, 2nd Gordon Highlanders (just north of Bazentin-le-Grand), where they met a staff officer of the 7th Division, who advised the resumption of work on the trench. Eventually "A" Company resumed work on the trenches. About 12.30 a.m. on 21st July Major Best returned to High Wood, by which time the garrison was being relieved by fresh troops. He therefore collected the men of "C" Company and marched back to Fricourt Wood : about 5 a.m. "A" Company also returned to the bivouacs in the wood. At 7 a.m. "B" and "D" Companies again went up to work, and in the afternoon "A" Company was sent forward, to be followed at 9.30 p.m. by "C." Relief, however,

21ST JULY.
18TH BATTALION.

22ND JULY. 18TH BATTALION.

came that night, and, utterly weary and worn out from constant digging and little sleep, the 18th Middlesex eventually reached billets at Ridemont at 9.15 a.m. on 22nd.

The Battalion had played its part well in the attacks on High Wood, and the records show how these brave Pioneers, whose ordinary functions were to dig trenches and repair roads, etc., did so under extraordinary difficulties and with indomitable pluck.

## (III) THE BATTLE OF DELVILLE WOOD,

15th July–3rd September.

Delville Wood had been captured from the enemy on 15th July, but on 18th the expected German counter-attack was launched and, by sheer weight of numbers, hostile troops forced their way through the northern and south-eastern portions of the Wood and into the northern half of Longueval. In the south-eastern corner of the Wood, however, the enemy was held up by a gallant defence (9th and 18th Divisions), and his attack on Waterlot Farm failed. On 24th another powerful hostile attack was made from the north-west of Delville Wood, but was completely broken up. The recapture of the whole of the Wood was necessary to Sir Douglas Haig's plan, and for this purpose the 2nd Division was brought up to relieve the 3rd Division, which then held the south-eastern portion of the Delville Wood sector. At the time the enemy's counter-attack of 18th July was made the 2nd Division was still resting and training near Diéval, but two days later entrained for the Somme battlefields. By the

17TH BATTALION.

23rd the Division was located in the reserve area of the Fourth Army, Happy Valley–Sand Pit Valley–Bois des Tailles, the 6th Infantry Brigade (of which the 17th Middlesex formed part)

24TH & 25TH JULY.

being in trenches in the latter place. On the night of 24th–25th July the 99th Brigade took over that portion of Delville Wood still held (the south-eastern corner) from the 3rd Division, and on the night of 25th–26th July the 5th Brigade relieved other units of the 3rd Division in the Waterlot Farm sector. The 6th Brigade remained in Divisional Reserve, and on 25th moved up to the old German trenches on either side of the Carnoy–Montauban road. The hostile guns were very active, and a huge shell fell on the trenches occupied by the Middlesex men, killing four other ranks and wounding four more. Early on the morning of

27th July the 99th Brigade of the 2nd Division attacked the northern portion of Delville Wood, capturing practically the whole of it. The 5th Division, on the left of the 2nd Division, attacked Longueval simultaneously. It was not, however, until 11 a.m. that Colonel Fenwick (commanding 17th Middlesex) received sudden orders to reinforce the 99th Brigade, which, having forced the enemy almost out of the Wood, was being heavily counter-attacked and needed assistance, the Brigade having suffered very heavy casualties. The Battalion moved at once by Montauban, Bernafay Wood and Trônes Wood, a furious artillery bombardment going on the whole time. From 2.45 p.m. until darkness fell the enemy's shell fire was terrific, and no reinforcements could get into the Wood to support the hard-pressed troops of the 99th Brigade. But about 5.15 p.m. two companies of the 17th Middlesex and two of the 17th Royal Fusiliers (5th Brigade) managed to get through, though suffering heavily on the way up. By 11 p.m. that night three and a-half companies of the Middlesex had reached the Wood, and, with one company of the 1st King's Royal Rifles, held the line from Regent Street eastwards to south of Princes Street. 27TH JULY. 17TH BATTALION.

No description of the conditions of Delville Wood at this period exists in the official diaries, but it was even worse than Trônes Wood when the latter was captured by the 12th Battalion of the Regiment. The trees, torn and blasted by the awful avalanche of shells which fell on them continuously, were even now in many places but naked stumps, beneath which the ground lay covered with thick undergrowth and fallen branches. Gaping shell holes were everywhere evident; the trenches in many places were shallow, mere excavations, insufficient to protect the troops crouching in them from the lurking snipers who, hidden by the horrible debris thrown about in all directions, crawled to within 20 yards in the hope of finding a target in some incautious officer or man. In parts of the Wood, patrols, and even single men, of the opposing forces were hunted or stalked, one by the other. The air was thick with a horrible stench from dead bodies and the pungent odour of gas. The "Devil's Wood" was indeed a terrible place.

Early on the morning of 28th all troops, with the exception of the 2nd South Staffords and 17th Middlesex, were withdrawn from Delville Wood, which was now occupied solely by these two Battalions. Throughout the day the enemy's shell fire was heavy, 28TH JULY.

28TH JULY. 17TH BATTALION.

but at night, about 9 p.m., it suddenly became "intense," and soon portions of the trenches held in the Wood were completely obliterated. A fierce counter-attack was then launched by the Germans, but, with magnificent tenacity, the garrison of the Wood (South Staffords and Middlesex) held on to the line and beat off all attempts. "We beat him off with great loss and held our line," records the Diary of the 17th Battalion. The 29th was another day of trial and "sticking it out," for again the enemy's guns poured a merciless stream of shell on to the Wood. At 9 p.m. the 13th Essex moved into the Wood and relieved the tired-out Middlesex men, who took over the support line in Montauban Alley. The casualties of the 17th Battalion during the tour in Delville Wood were: 2nd Lieut. J. A. Guest and 35 other ranks killed; Lieut.-Colonel Fenwick, Major F. S. Buckley, Captain and Adjutant E. J. Bell, Lieut. Elliott, 2nd Lieut. Englebürtt, Lieut. R. Felton, R.A.M.C. (Battalion M.O.), 2nd Lieuts. C. M. W. Robertson, L. F. Beaumont, and 192 other ranks wounded. The Battalion Diary ends on 29th July with these words: "All ranks behaved with great gallantry. The devotion to duty was magnificent. The Division has been thanked by G.H.Q. for capturing the Wood." Major W. H. Carter now commanded the Battalion.

## (IV) THE BATTLE OF POZIÈRES RIDGE:

### 23rd July—3rd September.

A close study of the official diaries describing the fighting of 1916 will reveal at once the fact that many of the operations classified under the general heading of the Somme Battles, 1916, overlapped. As an instance, the Battle of Delville Wood was in progress simultaneously with the struggle for the possession of Pozières Ridge, the latter involving much bloody fighting about Moquet Farm.

The battle opened on the morning of 23rd July, and by the morning of 25th the village of Pozières had fallen to the 1st Australian Division. But it was not until the 27th that the 11th Middlesex (Lieut.-Colonel L. L. Pargiter), of the 36th Infantry Brigade, 12th Division, moved up into front-line trenches north-west of the village and about half-way between the latter

27TH JULY. 11TH BATTALION.

and Moquet Farm: the latter was still in possession of the enemy. 11TH BATTALION.

After the attack on Ovillers on 7th July, the 11th Middlesex, in Brigade, had moved back to billets in Senlis, Forceville, Bus, Mailly-Maillet, and Warnimont Wood. From the latter place the Battalion (in Brigade) moved back to the line, spending the nights of 25th and 26th July in bivouacs in Hédauville. On the 27th, at 9 a.m., the Battalion marched to Martinsart Wood, thence to trenches north-west of Pozières, taking over from a battalion of the Royal Warwickshire Regiment: "D," "B" and "C" Companies in the front line, "A" in reserve. The three forward companies were in an unenviable position, "D" especially, seeing that the enemy were both east and west of the trench, which lay about 100 yards west of the Cemetery, north-west of Pozières. Indeed, the Company was hardly settled in its new position when the enemy (about fifty in number) launched a bombing attack from both flanks. The attack was repulsed by means of a bomb and rifle barrage, but Lieuts. Maynard and Scott were wounded. On the 28th the dispositions of "B" and "C" Companies 28TH JULY. were altered slightly. "B" now held a line resembling two sides of a triangle, just south-west of "D": "C" was south-west of "B," with its left joining up with "B" on right. But just west of "B's" left, and immediately north of "C," there was a German bombing post of some strength. This post was destined to be the scene of considerable trouble. "B" Company made the first attempt to clear the Germans out, Lieut. E. M. Shaw taking 20 men across for the purpose, but the attempt failed owing to a steady hostile bomb barrage. A second attack also failed, the enemy being very much on the alert. Lieut. Shaw was seriously wounded in this attempt, and died of his wounds on 30th. At about 1.30 a.m. (on 29th) "D" Company made a similar attack on a German 29TH JULY. bombing stop, on the left of that Company and in the same trench held by the Middlesex men. 2nd Lieut. Wright and 20 men of "D" succeeded in getting inside the enemy's wire, but were then driven back by bombs, and Lieut. Wright was wounded. The casualties in other ranks are not given, but they were apparently heavy. On 30th, whilst erecting distinguish- 30TH JULY. ing marks on the parados of his trench, Captain I. O. Crombie was killed. At 11 p.m. that night about forty men of "A" Company, under Lieuts. Moore and Newton, again attacked

30TH JULY. 11TH BATTALION. the enemy's trench, which ran south-west of the hostile bombing post, but in the darkness there was loss of direction and the attack failed. This attempt was repeated on the night of 31st, when 48 men under Lieut. Moore and 2nd Lieut. Tatham again made a gallant effort to capture the enemy's position. The enemy was, however, prepared, and from the time the party left the trench it was under heavy machine-gun and rifle fire. Despite the opposition the German trench was reached, but the enemy now put down a strong bomb barrage which the Middlesex men could not penetrate and the order to retire was given. Lieut. Moore was wounded and 2nd Lieut. Tatham collapsed. After the Middlesex attempt had failed, a party of Royal Sussex succeeded in capturing the bombing stop and bombing their way about fifty yards up the enemy trench, but were then held up by machine-gun fire. A very gallant effort was now made by Sergeant May, of the 11th Middlesex, to knock out the machine gun which was doing so much mischief. Taking with him the survivors of the first attempt to capture the stop, he "went over" again from the original "jumping-off" point. The fire from the gun was, however, still murderous, and, though May and his men made a great effort to reach, and indeed got within ten yards of, their objective, the enterprise had to be abandoned, the men being by this time so thoroughly exhausted that they were unable to charge. The total casualties in this affair were 26, and throughout the whole operation Lieut.-Colonel Pargiter (the C.O.) was personally in charge. These various small attempts to capture hostile positions were practically the only fighting the 11th Middlesex saw in the Battle of Pozières Ridge, though, indeed, after the initial stages the operations consisted mostly in "nibbling off"
7TH AUGUST. portions of the enemy's line. On 7th August the Battalion was relieved and moved back to Bouzincourt. On the 11th a move was made by route march to Varennes, on the 12th to Puchevillers, thence to Vauchelles, Ivergny, and Manin. From the latter place, on 19th, the C.O. and Company Commanders reconnoitred front-line trenches south of Arras, and when the month closed the Battalion, having already served a tour in the front line, was in reserve at Agny.

## Guillemont.

It is difficult to understand why the Battles Nomenclature Committee fixed the date of this battle as from 3rd to 6th

September, 1916, for, as the following account will show, there was heavy fighting for the possession of the ruined village on 30th July and the 8th August, though those attacks, carried out with great gallantry, were unsuccessful. The Battle of Guillemont is therefore not amongst the Battle Honours granted to the Middlesex Regiment, and although the 17th Battalion, with other units of the 2nd Division, fought hard for the village, the Division having made two attacks, they were not "in at the death," Guillemont finally falling to troops of another division. 17TH BATTALION.

On the 29th July the 17th Battalion (Major W. H. Carter commanding) was holding the support line in Montauban Alley, where for a day or two the men were given as much rest as possible, for, as the Battalion Diary records, they "needed it badly." On the night of 5th–6th August, however, the 6th Brigade relieved the 5th Brigade in the Waterlot Farm sector, the 17th Middlesex relieving the 13th Essex in the front line: the 1st King's Regiment (6th Brigade) was on the right of the Middlesex and the 5th Brigade held the sector on the left. 5TH–6TH AUGUST.

On the 6th August orders were received for an attack by the 55th and 2nd Divisions on Guillemont (55th Division) and the enemy defences between Waterlot Farm and Guillemont (2nd Division). The attack by the 2nd Division was to be carried out by the 6th Infantry Brigade (with Sappers and Pioneers attached) with two Battalions, 1st King's Regiment on the right and 17th Middlesex Regiment on the left. The latter Battalion had been ordered to capture the northern portion of Z–Z Trench, whilst the King's were to capture the southern portion and the enemy's defences north of Brompton Road, which ran practically along the northern exits of Guillemont Village. From aeroplane photographs the northern portion of Z–Z Trench appeared to be linked up by a communication trench running into the trench system west of Ginchy: the Middlesex men were also to block this communication trench.

As soon as the Middlesex had seized their portion of Z–Z Trench they were to establish a defensive flank from a sap which ran eastwards from an enemy trench parallel with High Holborn. They were then to open covering fire in a south-easterly direction in order to assist the 1st King's Regiment. This fire was to be maintained until Zero+20 minutes unless men of the King's Regiment could be clearly seen. A series of posts were to be established along the remainder of Z–Z Trench, which were

17TH BATTALION.

to be held as a strong outpost line so as not to offer too large a target for the enemy's guns. Intermediate posts between Z–Z Trench and Waterlot Farm, as a support line to Z–Z Trench, were to be formed, and joined up later into a continuous line and carried eventually across to Delville Wood. Such, briefly, were the objects of the attack and the orders given to the 17th Middlesex.

After the Delville Wood operations the Battalion, tired and worn out, had been given a day or two in support, where existence was not quite as strenuous as in the front line, but the losses sustained in the "Devil's Wood" had not been made good.

Between the 27th July and 2nd August the 17th Battalion had lost 10 officers and 280 other ranks, and only 47 other ranks were "advised" as reinforcements; they had not yet joined.

Every battalion of the 6th Infantry Brigade had, indeed, suffered heavily, so that on 2nd August the Brigadier felt it his duty to call the attention of Divisional Headquarters to the serious depletion and exhaustion of his Brigade, though he added: "The fighting spirit of the Brigade is entirely undiminished, and the heat and general conditions cause a good deal of physical exhaustion. . . . All ranks are determined that any attack they are called upon to undertake shall be a success if such is humanly possible."

Zero hour for the attack was to be 4.20 a.m. on 8th August. An artillery bombardment, lasting 17 hours, was to precede the attack.

The preliminary bombardment began at 9 a.m. on 7th and at 9 p.m. lifted, and between the latter hour and 12 midnight the assaulting troops moved into their assembly positions. But there are no records of the disposition of the four Companies of the 17th Middlesex, nor is it possible from the confused mass of information dealing with the attack to gather exactly what happened on the Battalion's front.

8TH AUGUST.

Apparently at 4 a.m. the assaulting party left the "jumping-off" trench in the neighbourhood of Waterlot Farm and lay down in No Man's Land until the barrage lifted at 4.20 a.m. About 4.24 a.m. the C.O., Middlesex, saw a Véry light soar up into the sky from the German lines towards Waterlot Farm. This was the pre-arranged signal signifying that the assaulting party was in Z–Z Trench. But other lights were going up and bursting, and the C.O. deemed it advisable to await confirmation by runner before taking action. At 4.35 a.m. Major Carter issued orders to one platoon, in close support, to work along a sap on the left and the German sap to reinforce. A runner from Z–Z Trench arrived at 5 a.m. with a message that the assaulting party on the right had been bombed out of the trench. "A" Company was therefore ordered to send six bombers and 13 bayonet men along the old German trench running south-east from the end of the Loop, close up to Machine-gun House, thence to the left of Z–Z Trench, with orders to consolidate. The bombing party moved along the old German trench, and by 5.35 a.m. had reached the corner near Machine-gun House: the party was then held up, though making great efforts to get on. At 5.35 a.m. the C.O. received a message that only one Lewis gun had reached Z–Z Trench and was in position on the northern end. A machine gun was therefore sent after the bombing party then engaged in fighting its way along the German trench running south-east towards Machine-gun House. 8TH AUGUST. 17TH BATTALION.

Despite the gallant efforts of the bombers to get on, at 6.10 a.m. a message reached Battalion Headquarters that they were being forced back along the trench running from Machine-gun House. A little later orders were issued for machine-gun and Stokes-mortar fire to be concentrated on this spot. Just after 7 a.m. Major Carter received word that practically the whole of the party who had entered the German trench (Z–Z Trench?) were either killed, wounded or captured. A patrol was then sent up the German sap leading back to the northern end of Z–Z Trench to gather any information possible. All efforts to get into touch with the 1st King's on the right of the Middlesex, had failed: three companies of the gallant King's men had been swallowed up in Guillemont and with their C.O. were never seen again.

The first attack was a failure, though the Middlesex succeeded in taking and holding the German strong point west of Machine-gun House and in consolidating their gains in the neighbourhood of the latter: Z–Z Trench had been taken and lost again.

Late in the day, when the failure became known at Brigade Headquarters, Major Carter was ordered to organise a strong bombing party to isolate Machine-gun House from the German system of defences. At 2.30 a.m. on 9th the attack began, but by half an hour later it had failed—the position was too strong. A second attempt was then organised and launched at 4.20 a.m. A strong bombing party, with Lewis guns, made a determined 9TH AUGUST.

9TH AUGUST. 17TH BATTALION. demonstration towards Point 66, the right flank of Z–Z Trench. The enemy immediately retaliated and put down a very heavy artillery barrage. The C.O., deciding that the demonstration had drawn fire and thinking the enemy had concentrated at that point, ordered a bombing party, consisting of 20 brigade bombers and 50 bayonet men of the 17th Middlesex (all under Captain Fluke, 2nd South Staffords), to occupy a trench south-east of Machine-gun House. Captain Fluke was then to block the main German trench, along which he proceeded 100 yards past and south-east of his objective; also to block the sap leading from Z–Z Trench to Machine-gun House. The latter was reached, but here the party came under very heavy enfilade fire from south-east, and bombs were coming from practically all directions. Eight Germans had been killed, but of the bombing party all the leading bombers and bayonet men had either been killed or wounded, and, seeing that he was in danger of being cut off and surrounded, Captain Fluke gave the order to retire, which order was duly carried out slowly in small parties in succession, by short distances at a time, the remainder keeping up a covering fire. In this way the party regained their trenches without very severe casualties. A third attack was then organised, but, as Machine-gun House was being shelled both by the German and British artillery, the attack was abandoned.

The 17th Middlesex were later relieved and marched back to Breslau Trench, proceeding on 10th to a tented camp in Happy Valley.

The attempts to capture Z–Z Trench had caused the Battalion further heavy losses: Captain W. Salter and 2nd Lieuts. E. L. Cocks and W. F. Henderson, first reported missing, were later numbered amongst the killed; 2nd Lieuts. Clark and Banks were wounded. In other ranks the losses were 29 killed, 9 died of wounds, 115 wounded, and 45 missing. After resting one day in the Happy Valley, the Battalion (in Brigade) marched to Méaulte on 12th, and on the 13th to Méricourt l'Abbé, where the Battalion entrained and proceeded to Saleux. From the latter place buses carried the troops to La Chaussée. Good billets were found near the river and were much appreciated. Here, 15TH AUGUST. on 15th, a draft of 716 men had arrived, and it is interesting to note that these men came from the 1st, 2nd, 4th, 6th, 7th, 8th, 10th, 11th, 12th, 13th, 14th, 15th, 16th, 20th, 21st, 23rd, 24th, 27th and 28th Battalions of the Regiment.

## (VI) THE BATTLE OF GINCHY:

### 9th September.

Guillemont was finally stormed and consolidated on the 3rd September, and the attacking troops pushed on unchecked to Ginchy: " For three days the tide of attack and counter-attack swayed backwards and forwards amongst the ruined houses of the village till, in the end, for three days more the greater part of it remained in the enemy's hands." Such, briefly, is the story of the early attempts to capture Ginchy. It fell, finally, on 9th September in an attack launched at 4.45 p.m. by three Divisions —16th, 56th, and 55th—two Territorial Battalions of the Middlesex Regiment, the 1/7th and 1/8th of the 167th Brigade, 56th Division, being in the area of the Battle. 1/7TH & 1/8TH BATTALIONS.

6TH SEPT. On the night of the 6th September, just as the Battle of Guillemont was drawing to a close, the 56th (London) Division relieved the 5th Division in the line between Guillemont and the left of the 1st French Division.

Apart from the subsidiary operations in the Gommecourt Salient on 1st July, the 1/7th and 1/8th Middlesex had hitherto taken no part in the great battles which had followed the Battle of Albert (1st–13th July). Trench warfare of a more or less vigorous nature had succeeded the gallant, but unsuccessful, attempt of the 1st July to gain a permanent footing in the enemy's trenches at Gommecourt. Raids and patrol work were almost continuous when in the front line, these dangerous and exciting enterprises furnishing both officers and men with many opportunities in which to display their initiative and daring. But the weeks which intervened between the beginning of July and the third week in August were bare of attacks on or by the enemy. On the 18th August the relief of the 167th Brigade (56th Division) by the 52nd Brigade (17th Division) began, and by the end of the month all units of the former were training in the Gapennes area, the 1/7th being billeted in the village and the 1/8th at Maison-en-Ponthieu. Early in September the 56th Division began to move towards the battle front again, and on the 4th the 167th Brigade left in two tactical trains for Combles, moving thence to huts and tents in Bois des Tailles. The next day (5th) orders for the move up to the front were received, and, as already stated, the 56th Division relieved the 5th Division in the

1/7TH & 1/8TH BATTALIONS.

line between Guillemont and the left of the 1st French Division during the night of 6th September. The 168th and 169th Brigades were first into the front line, whilst the 167th was placed in Divisional Reserve, west of Billon Copse, where all units of the Brigade bivouacked. In these bivouacs the 7th and 8th were spent, and they were days not likely to be forgotten. The scene was extraordinary even to those who had by now become accustomed to the sight of large numbers of soldiers. Everywhere as far as the eye could see there were thousands and thousands of troops, great masses of them, still in reserve—infantry, guns and cavalry—they spread over the whole country, whilst away to the right were the French reserves. Turcos from Morocco and the Black Senegalese, interspersed with the blue-coated troops of European France.

9TH SEPT.

In the Battle on 9th September the 169th was to attack the German trenches south-east of Leuze Wood and there form a strong defensive flank against any attack from Combles, whilst the 168th Brigade was to carry the hostile trench system north of the Ginchy–Combles road. The 167th Brigade was to be in reserve, and, although the 1/7th Middlesex (Lieut.-Colonel E. J. King) and the 1/8th Middlesex (Lieut.-Colonel P. L. Ingpen) were subsequently placed at the disposal of the 169th Brigade, the 1/7th moving up to Falfemont Farm, south of Leuze Wood, to support the right flank of the Brigade and maintain touch with the French, and the 1/8th to Casement Trench, neither of these two Battalions actually took part in the fighting which resulted in the capture of Ginchy. They, nevertheless, fulfilled their duties, acting as supports, the 1/8th Middlesex as carriers for the 168th Brigade on the night of 9th.*

11TH SEPT. 1/8TH BATTALION.

On 11th September Colonel Ingpen's Battalion (1/8th) was engaged in a small attack which should properly be included in the operations described as the Battle of Ginchy, though the official date of the latter was the 9th. On the Ginchy–Morval road there was a small salient strongly held by the enemy, which prevented a junction of the left of the 56th Division and the 3rd Guards Brigade. It was with the intention of cutting off this salient, killing or capturing the Germans in it, and gaining touch with the Guards, that the attack was to be made; the Guards were to co-operate.

* Up to (and including) the 9th September (from the time when they went into the line) no casualties are reported in the Battalion Diaries of the 1/7th and 1/8th Middlesex.

The 1/8th Battalion, which on the 9th had been in support in Casement Trench during the attacks made by the 168th and 169th Brigades north of Leuze Wood, took over trenches in front of the latter and west of Bouleaux Wood from the two Brigades on the night of 10th September: Battalion Headquarters were in a quarry on the eastern side of Maltz Horn Ridge. 11TH SEPT. 1/8TH BATTALION.

At 4.50 p.m. on the 11th the 1/8th Battalion received orders for the attack. Two companies of the 1/7th Middlesex were lent to the 1/8th to hold the latter's trenches during the operation. The assaulting troops consisted of "B" Company (Captain T. O. White), followed by "A" Company (Captain G. W. Tremlett); "C" and "D" Companies were to hold the front line and support the attack on the flank with Lewis guns and bombers. Between 4 p.m. and 7 p.m., however, the enemy placed a very heavy barrage on and behind Leuze Wood, so that it was only with great difficulty that the troops were assembled for the attack. The Division cancelled the first Zero hour and postponed it until 12 midnight.

At midnight, supported by artillery and trench-mortar barrages and bombers, the 1/8th made their attack. The objective was reached, but the Guards on the left did not co-operate as was expected, with the result that when the Germans launched a heavy bombing counter-attack the position could not be held and the attacking companies of Middlesex men were bombed back a certain distance. The net result of this small operation was that the 1/8th had gained about fifty yards of trench and established a new block. Many Germans were killed and seven prisoners were taken, but the casualties of the 1/8th were heavy: 2nd Lieuts. E. H. Calcott and W. J. Macdonnagh were killed; Captains J. D. White, W. S. Tennent and C. W. Tremlett, Lieuts. E. R. Reynolds and 2nd Lieuts. R. H. Cleverley, W. G. S. Simpson, W. G. Barney, and W. Roughsedge were wounded. In other ranks, killed, wounded and missing, the losses were 155. On the 17th the Battalion was relieved, and went back to bivouacs near German Wood. 17TH SEPT.

The 1/7th Battalion made no attack in this small operation, but the two Companies ("B" and "D") which had been lent to the 1/8th suffered heavily from the enemy's barrage. Captain C. F. Challen and 2nd Lieut. Macintyre and fifty other ranks being wounded. On the 12th the 1/7th Battalion returned to bivouacs in Billon Copse. 1/7TH BATTALION. 12TH SEPT.

## (VII) THE BATTLE OF FLERS–COURCELETTE:

15th–22nd September.

The Third Phase of the Somme Battles of 1916 was now about to begin. The centre of the British line was well placed, but on the flanks there was still difficult ground to be won. Briefly, the general scheme of the Allied attack which was to begin on the 15th September was as follows: To pivot on the high ground south of the Ancre and north of the Albert–Bapaume road, while the Fourth Army devoted the whole of its efforts to the rearmost of the enemy's original defence system between Morval and Le Sars. If sufficiently successful to warrant it, the attack was to include the villages of Martinpuich and Courcelette. Then, as soon as the advance on this front reached the Morval line, the left of the British front would be advanced across the Thiepval Ridge. In close co-operation with the British, the French had arranged to continue the line of advance from the Somme to the slopes above Combles, their main efforts being directed against Rancourt and Frégicourt, thus isolating Combles and opening the way for their attack on Sailly–Saillisel.

The attack of the Fourth Army between the Combles Ravine and Martinpuich had as its object the capture of Morval, Les Bœufs, Gueudecourt, and Flers. Nine British divisions were to attack the enemy's defences on the above front, but with two only —56th and 41st—is this narrative concerned, for both Divisions contained battalions of the Middlesex Regiment, *i.e.*, 1/7th and 1/8th in the first named and the 23rd and 19th (Pioneers) in the latter Division.

1/7TH & 1/8TH 23RD & 19TH BATTALIONS.

The 56th Division was on the extreme right of the line, with orders to clear Bouleaux Wood and form a protective flank covering all lines of advance from Combles, whilst the 6th and Guards Divisions (on the left of the 56th) were to capture Morval and Les Bœufs respectively.

The 41st Division, with the 14th Division on its right and New Zealand Division on its left, was to attack the Flers line and capture the village.

Of the four Battalions of the Middlesex Regiment in the battle area, however, only one—the 1/7th—took part in the initial attack, though the 1/8th and 23rd were put in a few hours later, about midday.

The operation orders of the 56th Division are full of intricacies, and therefore it is probably more interesting to give briefly the objectives of each Brigade (all three were to attack), with such other information as will assist the reader in understanding the operations.

West of Combles, the right of the British line was still very irregular. Leuze Wood could hardly be called our own, since the German trenches ran right up to its eastern exits; only the western and northern exits were consolidated, though a British trench ran through the centre, roughly, on a north and south line. Of Bouleaux Wood only a very small portion of the southern end was held by us, though from the western exits of that portion the line ran right away in a north-westerly direction to the Ginchy–Morval road, where it bent back due west, following the line of the road to the eastern exits of Ginchy. Thus the right flank faced east, north-east, and direct north.

The 56th Division had been ordered to protect this flank and also seize and clear the remainder of Bouleaux Wood: the ultimate intention was to "squeeze out" Combles. To establish a strong protective flank, the 169th Brigade was to hold the line facing Combles and to capture the German trenches covering the town. On the left of the 169th Brigade the 167th was to clear the hostile trenches running through Bouleaux Wood as far as a small clump of trees west of the wood, afterwards known as Middle Copse: the 168th Brigade was then to pass through the 167th in order to secure the right flank of the 6th Division in its attack on Morval. Such, briefly, was the scheme of attack as issued by Divisional Headquarters to Brigades, and by the latter to Battalions.

The objectives allotted to the 167th Brigade (in closer detail) were: (*a*) the front-line German trench astride Bouleaux Wood, and also Middle Copse; (*b*) on the left, the line of the railway from the point where it crossed the road north-west of the northern corner of Bouleaux Wood on the right, thence along a line running 100 yards south-east of the Wood to the point of junction with the 169th Brigade, just north of the Combles–Ginchy road.

1/7TH BATTALION.

The first objective (*a*) was to be captured by the 1st London Regiment, which was to form up in trenches at the northern end of Leuze Wood and the southern end of Bouleaux Wood; the 1/7th Middlesex were to capture the second objective (*b*). Advancing from its assembly trenches in Leuze Wood, the 1/8th Middlesex were to form up in the valley between the southern end of Leuze

1/8TH BATTALION.

Wood and Wedge Wood: the 3rd London Regiment was to assemble in trenches from Wedge Wood to Falfemont Farm (exclusive).

The Battle of Flers-Courcelette is noteworthy in that Tanks were used by the British for the first time in the War, three being allotted to the 56th Division: the "creeping barrage" was also introduced for the first time in these operations.

13TH SEPT. 1/7TH BATTALION. Until 6 p.m. on the 13th the 1/7th Middlesex (Lieut.-Colonel E. J. King) remained resting at Billon Farm, but at that hour moved forward to a position between Falfemont Farm and Wedge Wood in support of the troops holding Leuze Wood. The scheme of attack for the operations of the 15th was received on this date, and when the Battalion moved up into support on the night of the 13th September all Company commanders had been informed of the rôle allotted to their respective companies.

The scene as the 1/7th moved up to the support trenches on the night of the 13th is thus described by Lieut.-Colonel King: "There was something indescribably eerie in that march forward in the dim light of the closing day. The country was desolate to a degree that baffles either description or imagination. Farms and villages had been blotted out of existence, and the sites of many could be traced only by the heaps of brickdust discolouring the soil. All roads had disappeared. And the fields, torn and rent, into a mass of shell craters, could be compared only to a barren landscape. Even the positions of woods and forests, blasted and burnt and shattered, were traceable only by the few scattered stumps of charred trees. And the whole land was a charnel-house, foul with the debris of many battles, poisoning the very atmosphere. Yet the scene was not without a certain wild beauty of its own—the heavens lighted up by the red flash of guns, the long lines of 'fairy lights' dancing upwards, here and there the coloured rockets calling loudly for help, the glare of the searchlights, and always the never-ending rumbling roar of countless guns."

14TH SEPT. On the night of the 14th September the troops of the 167th Brigade took up their battle positions, the 1/7th Middlesex moving up from support to their assembly trenches in Leuze Wood. Two companies of the Battalion, "A" on the right (Captain Woodroffe) and "C" on the left (Captain Tully), each with two platoons in the first line and two in the second, were to make the initial assault, "B" and "D" Companies remaining in reserve. The 1st Londons were in front of the 1/7th Middlesex.

At 6.20 a.m. on the 15th the Battle opened, the British bombardment becoming "intense." The 1st Londons succeeded in carrying that portion of the German front line that lay astride and to the left of Bouleaux Wood, but suffered very heavy losses and were brought to a standstill. At 8.20 a.m. the 1/7th Middlesex were ordered to push forward two companies to pass through the 1st Londons and clear Bouleaux Wood. They advanced gallantly. Arriving on the line held by the Londoners, they carried the survivors of that Battalion with them for a short distance, but were then also brought to a standstill. The Wood was full of German riflemen, and from the road leading into Combles a murderous enfilade machine-gun fire tore gaps in the ranks of the 1/7th. On the right, "A" Company (Hampstead and Highgate) were practically annihilated, only 25 men being left. Captain W. G. Woodroffe, who had so gallantly distinguished himself at Hebuterne, fell dead, shot through the head, and of the three subalterns of his Company, 2nd Lieut. H. C. B. Taylor was killed and 2nd Lieuts. P. H. Rowe* and C. Smith were desperately wounded. The left Company, "C" (Hornsey), slightly sheltered from the enfilade fire, suffered a little less severely, but Captain Tully lay mortally wounded† and his three subalterns were also among the casualties, 2nd Lieut. H. L. Cooper having been killed and 2nd Lieuts. Jones and Tucker badly wounded. 15TH SEPT. 1/7TH BATTALION.

The reserves ("B" and "D" Companies) were then ordered to be thrown in and the attack driven home "at all costs"; the 1/8th Middlesex (Lieut.-Colonel P. L. Ingpen) were moving up to assist the 1/7th Battalion. 1/8TH BATTALION.

The desperate nature of the task before the two reserve companies was terribly evident to all ranks. The infernal din of machine-gun and rifle fire, the cries of the wounded, the sight of dead and mangled corpses on every side, did not deter the gallant men of Tottenham, Barnet, and Enfield from rushing forward into the bullet-swept zone. "D" Company was on the right under Capt. D. W. Hurd; "B," on the left, was led by Capt. H. G. Hanbury. By now the conditions were clearer, and it was possible for the two reserve companies to press their attack with more definite knowledge of the difficulties ahead of them. The murderous enfilade machine-gun fire from the right had first to be dealt with, and Captain Hurd, of the Tottenham

* Died of wounds on the 17th September, 1916.

† Died of wounds on the 19th September, 1916.

15TH SEPT. 1/7TH BATTALION. Company (" D "), brought up his Lewis gunners for this purpose. He was directing their fire when he fell, shot through the head.* It was about this time that Colonel King's orderly officer—2nd Lieut. W. A. Whyman—was also killed. On the left of " D " Company the Barnet and Enfield men (" B " Company) made a dash at the German riflemen concealed in the Wood; but they were checked by a withering fire and pinned to their ground. Rallying his men, the Company Commander (Capt. Hanbury) led them forward a second time, but he too fell dead at the edge of the German trenches, 2nd Lieut. J. E. Whitehead being killed by his side. No progress had been made by the two reserve companies. The whole attack had now been brought to a standstill. The gallant 1/7th Middlesex had lost all four company commanders and nine other officers besides.

1/8TH BATTALION. At 1.30 p.m. the 1/8th Battalion was ordered to advance, and moved to the attack down the north-west side of Bouleaux Wood, but half an hour later the Battalion was ordered to dig in.

Throughout the remainder of the 15th fighting was desultory all along the front. Here and there small parties of men of the Middlesex attacked the enemy and got home with the bayonet, while sniping and bomb-throwing were practically unending. On the left of the line the enemy's resistance was less obstinate, and there was continual working by troops of the 167th Brigade towards that flank. By the evening men were beginning to establish themselves along the edge of Middle Copse. During the afternoon another officer of the 1/7th, 2nd Lieut. W. D. Westory, attached to the Machine-gun Company, was killed. At night the 1/7th took over the old front-line trenches running through the southern end of Bouleaux Wood; the 1/8th Battalion was in support in Leuze Wood. The 1/7th had gone into action in the morning at a strength of just under 500 rifles; by evening 300 casualties, including 12 officers, had been incurred, 10 officers and 113 other ranks being killed. The day's operations had, indeed, resulted practically in the end of the original 1/7th Middlesex.†

(Margin beside "noon another officer of the 1/7th": 1/7TH BATTALION.)

1/8TH BATTALION. The 1/8th Battalion had the following casualties amongst officers: Lieut. A. S. Carey killed and Captains C. M. Hughman

* Died of wounds on the 17th September, 1916.

† It was in memory of this fatal day that the village of Guillemont, close to the assembly positions of the 1/7th Middlesex the night before the battle, was afterwards " adopted " by the Borough of Hornsey.

and T. M. Peake and 2nd Lieut. R. P. Burn wounded. The Battalion's losses in other ranks are not given in the diaries, though on the 19th the casualties of the 1/8th, from the 15th to 18th, are recorded as 245 other ranks.* 15TH SEPT.

On the 19th the 167th Brigade was relieved and moved back to Maltzhorn Trenches, but again went into the line on the 22nd September (the day on which the battle closed), the 1/7th Middlesex on the left and the 1/8th in support. Both battalions had received large drafts of reinforcements when out of the line, without which neither could have gone into the forward trenches, being too weak. 19TH SEPT. 1/7TH & 1/8TH BATTALIONS.

In the meantime, the 19th and 23rd Middlesex (of the 41st Division) had also taken their part in the Battle. Both battalions had arrived in France during May and had gone into the line in the Le Touquet area, where they received their initiation into trench warfare. At the end of August the 41st Division moved south towards the Somme to take part in the operations, the 123rd Brigade, of which the 23rd Battalion formed part, reaching Gorenflos, where active preparations and training began immediately. On the 6th September the Brigade moved to Bécordel Camp, marching thence to Fricourt Camp on the 9th, preparatory to going into the front line in the Delville Wood sector. 19TH & 23RD BATTALIONS. 6TH SEPT.

On the 10th the 123rd Brigade began the relief of troops holding the line in front (north) of Delville Wood, the 23rd Middlesex relieving the Liverpool Scottish. At this period the line was being gradually pushed forward towards Flers by means of sapping, so as to provide suitable positions from which, on the 15th September, the assault was to be made. The enemy's shell fire was heavy, and on the 11th the 23rd lost two other ranks killed and 15 wounded. On the 12th "B" and "D" Companies were sent back to Montauban, casualties for the day numbering eight other ranks killed, 22 wounded, and 2 missing. All companies were back in Montauban, from which place, at 11 p.m. on the night of the 14th, the Battalion moved forward again to take up assembly positions in Carlton and Savoy Trenches, for the operations to begin on the next day. 10TH SEPT. 23RD BATTALION. 14TH SEPT.

* The Diary of the 167th Brigade gives the following casualties of the two Battalions of the Middlesex Regiment during the operations from the 15th to 19th:—1/7th: officers, 7 killed, 10 wounded; other ranks, 60 killed, 100 missing, 235 wounded; total, 17 officers and 395 other ranks. 1/8th: officers, 3 killed, 13 wounded, 1 missing; other ranks, 57 killed, 53 missing, 311 wounded; total, 17 officers and 421 other ranks.

23RD BATTALION. The 41st Division was to attack with the 124th Brigade on the right and 122nd Brigade on the left, the 123rd Brigade being in reserve, but the 23rd Middlesex became actively involved in the operations during the day, with disastrous results to the Battalion, though it fought gallantly and gained ground.

15TH SEPT. By 1 a.m. on the 15th the 23rd were in their assembly trenches—Carlton and Savoy. The attack began at 6.20 a.m., led by tanks. At 10 a.m. the Middlesex men were sent forward to the left of Flers road, on the left of previous positions held in Delville Wood. In moving, the Battalion had taken shelter on several occasions from the enemy's barrage, then falling heavily. About midday Divisional Headquarters ordered the 41st Brigade to move battalions forward to Flers Trench, Scimitar Trench, the old British first line and Carlton and Savoy Trenches. The Middlesex were then ordered up to Scimitar Trench. The Battalion set off up the Flers road, "B" and "D" Companies on the right, "C" and "A" Companies on the left. They had not gone far before the Adjutant (Capt. H. W. R. Warneford) was wounded. A little later the Battalion was ordered by the G.O.C., 124th Brigade, to push on beyond Flers Trench, along the right of Flers Wood, and assist the 124th Brigade. Flers had been captured, but the position north and north-east of the village was still obscure.

The Battalion was then formed up for the attack, "B" and "D" Companies (personally led by the C.O., Lieut.-Colonel W. C. C. Ash) leading, with "A" and "C" Companies in support. At 5 p.m. Lieut.-Colonel Ash fell severely wounded.* A little later the O.C., "A" Company, was told by the G.O.C., 124th Brigade, that the strong point north of Flers Wood, known as the "Hog's Head,"† must be held at all costs, but as the Middlesex men reached the north-east corner of Flers village about 250 survivors of units of the 124th Brigade, who had taken part in the attack, were met streaming back from the front line. These men were rallied, and "A" Company, with the help of "B" and "D" Companies, re-occupied the strong point. Just before 7 p.m., as the enemy was making a flank attack on the right, the Middlesex were ordered by the O.C., 10th Queen's Own, to retire to the line east of Flers village at nightfall. The retirement was carried out at 7.30 p.m. O.C., "A" Company, 23rd Middlesex, who had taken command of the Battalion after Colonel Ash

* Died of wounds on the 29th September, 1916.

† As given on the map: the Battalion Diary gives it as "Hog's Back."

had become a casualty, handed over command to Major Beatty, of the 10th Queen's Own. 23RD BATTALION.

In the position they held east of Flers village the Middlesex hung on all night. From dawn on the 16th until midday, thence at intervals until the evening, the Battalion was exposed to heavy enfilade shell fire. At 6 p.m. the situation was reported to Brigade Headquarters and instructions and rations asked for. The Brigade then ordered the Battalion to retire to Switch Trench, and the worn-out Middlesex, now numbering only 3 officers and 110 other ranks, fell back at nightfall. On the 17th the Battalion moved back first to Carlton Trench and then to Green Dump, where reorganisation was carried out. But the Battle was over so far as the 123rd Brigade was concerned, for on 18th all units marched back to Bécordel Camp, where they rested in reserve until the 27th September. 16TH SEPT. 17TH SEPT.

The first Battle in which the 23rd Middlesex was engaged resulted in its losing quite half of the original Battalion.

2nd Lieut. H. Wilson and N. P. Nixon had been killed, whilst besides the C.O. and the Adjutant, Major F. Knapp Captain A. V. Gayer, Lieut. F. W. Brown,* and 2nd Lieuts. H. V. Brent, H. R. Odling, S. Wallis Smith and S. F. Rogers were wounded. The Battalion M.O.—Lieut. H. Farnescombe, R.A.M.C.—was also wounded. In other ranks the losses were 22 killed, 129 wounded, and 32 missing.

Of the 19th Middlesex (Pioneers), commanded by Lieut.-Colonel A. I. Irons, little can be told excepting that the Battalion was at work on the roads or digging cable trenches in the neighbourhood of Delville Wood, returning to Fricourt Camp on the 22nd for rest. 19TH BATTALION.

## (VIII) THE BATTLE OF MORVAL:

### 25th–28th September.

Seeing that they were in reality one operation, it is difficult to understand why the Battles Nomenclature Committee divided the attacks between Combles and Thiepval into two battles, giving one the title of the Battle of Morval, 25th–28th September, and the other the Battle of Thiepval, 26th–28th September;

* Died of wounds on the 16th September, 1916.

for the former took place on the right and the latter on the left of the Albert–Bapaume road.

The Battle of Morval, which began at 12.35 p.m. on 25th September, resulted in the capture of Combles (56th Division), Les Bœufs (Guards and 6th Divisions), and Gueudecourt (21st Division). The 168th Brigade of the 56th Division (whose task was again to form a defensive flank to the 5th, 6th, and Guards Divisions attacking Morval and Les Bœufs) was, however, the attacking Brigade, the 167th being relieved on the night of the 24th–25th in the left sub-sector of the line. Patrols from the 1st Londons (who were holding from Leuze Wood to Middle Copse whilst the attack was in progress), were pushed into Combles on the 26th, where touch was obtained with French troops.

1/7TH & 1/8TH BATTALIONS.

But neither the 1/7th nor the 1/8th Middlesex appear to have been engaged in the battle, the first-named Battalion remaining in Maltzhorn throughout the operations, and the latter first in Casement Trench, then in support trenches south-east of Leuze Wood, and finally, on the 27th, moving back to sandpits at Méaulte, where the 167th Brigade Headquarters were established. On the 26th Lieut.-Colonel E. J. King was evacuated sick to hospital, and temporary command of the 1/7th Battalion was taken over by Major L. R. King.

The 23rd Middlesex, to whom this Battle Honour was also granted, remained in reserve on the 25th and 26th, moving up between Pommiers Redoubt and Montauban on the 27th, and to Flers Avenue Trench on the 28th.

## (IX) BATTLE OF THIEPVAL RIDGE:

### 26th–28th September, 1916.

12TH BATTALION.

Thiepval—" Bloody Thiepval," as it was so often called in those days—was the next battle in which the Middlesex Regiment was engaged—the 12th, Colonel Frank Maxwell's Battalion, again covering itself with glory and adding still further to its laurels by winning two Victoria Crosses.

After the splendid capture of, but desperate fighting in, Trônes Wood, the 12th Middlesex (in Brigade and Division) was withdrawn from the line and moved north to the Second Army area, all units going into billets in villages west of Hazebrouck.

A short stay in the latter place and then a move was made to the Armentières sector, where until the end of August the Battalion spent periodical tours in the front line, which at this period may be written down as "quiet." About the end of the month, however, the 18th Division began to move south again. The 54th Brigade entrained at Bailleul on the 25th for the St. Pol area, the 12th Middlesex going into billets in Marquay. Here until 9th September the Battalion remained, but on the latter day began, by march, to move towards the battle area once more. By the 12th of the month the Middlesex had reached Arquéves, where a final period of training began before front-line trenches south of Thiepval were taken over. 12TH BATTALION.

At 9 a.m. on the 23rd September the 12th Middlesex paraded in the main street of Arquéves and then marched off to Hédauville, where the Battalion billeted. Orders were then received that the Battalion would relieve the 4th West Ridings in the Leipzic Salient on the 24th, and the line to be taken over was reconnoitred by Major Scarborough and Company Commanders. On the 24th, at 8 a.m., "B" and "C" Companies left Hédauville and took over the reserve trenches; "A" and "D" Companies followed at 1.30 p.m. and took over the front line. Eleven officers and a proportion of N.C.Os. and Specialists were left behind as reserve in Hédauville. 23RD SEPT.

On the 25th Operation Orders for the attack on Thiepval were issued, and, briefly, were as follows: The 18th Division was to attack Thiepval from south to north* with two brigades in line—53rd on the right, 54th on the left. Of the latter Brigade, the 12th Middlesex were to be on the right and the 11th Royal Fusiliers on the left. The 11th Division was to be on the right of the 18th and 49th on the left. The Middlesex were to attack with "C" Company on the right, "B" Company on the left, "D" Company in support, and "A" Company in reserve. The 18th Division had three objectives: (i) the road running north-west and south-east through Thiepval, (ii) the trenches on the northern outskirts of Thiepval, (iii) the Schwaben Redoubt and the trenches south-east and south-west of it. 25TH SEPT.

Into all the intricate details of the Operation Orders it is impossible to go (they occupy 11 pages of the Battalion Diary), but, roughly, the task allotted to the 54th Brigade was the capture

* Not from west to east as may be inferred from the sketch map published in Colonel Boraston's edition of Sir Douglas Haig's despatches.

25TH SEPT. 12TH BATTALION.

of the whole of the enemy's front-line system covering Thiepval from attack from the west. This system included an extraordinary number of dug-outs in the first and support lines, so constructed as to afford practically absolute protection from shell fire. Within the Brigade boundary, south of the second objective, there were 144 alone, not including those round the Château. This system also included several strong points and the Château Redoubt: the Schwaben Redoubt was the final objective. The Brigade had to advance 1,800 yards to its final objective on a front which continually varied from 300 to 450, then from 200 to 900 yards. Serious opposition was expected throughout the whole of the advance owing to the splendid cover at the enemy's disposal. It was necessary to provide strong dug-out clearing parties with definite objectives, but these parties were found by the 11th Royal Fusiliers. Thus the honour of capturing practically the whole of Thiepval (the western half, which was by far the strongest portion) was to fall to the 12th Middlesex, the assaulting Battalion. The 12th Middlesex Operation Orders close with a message from Colonel Maxwell to his Battalion: The Die-Hards are having a *great* chance to-day, viz., to take Thiepval, which has defied the efforts of all other regiments, brigades, and divisions for three months. We must do it, and will do it, 'on our heads,' as the enemy is demoralised. We have enormous superiority of guns, and all of us are out to kill and reach our objective. Yesterday we had a big success all along our right,* and the attack there is being pushed forward with ours to-day. It may be an easy job, but if it is tough we can carry it through if we keep going: don't stop and don't retire a yard. Be out to kill and get Thiepval on our Colours."

"Zero" hour had been fixed for 12.35 p.m. on the 26th, an unusual hour as attacks invariably took place at dawn. For three days the guns had bombarded Thiepval and the enemy's defences surrounding it, the IInd Corps Artillery alone firing over 100,000 rounds, and on one night the village was heavily gassed.

25TH–26TH SEPT.

The night of the 25th–26th was spent in final preparations. Bombs and flares were issued, special equipment drawn, and in the 12th Middlesex all ranks were filled with some such thoughts as those contained in a letter which their C.O. wrote to his wife just Before the battle opened: "If we do it, it will be something for the Regiment, as all efforts have so far failed."

* The Battle of Morval, which began on the 25th September.

At "Zero" hour on the 26th the British barrage began—a row so deafening that it was impossible for one man to hear another speak. Under the storm of shell, howling and screeching over the enemy's front line, the first waves of the assaulting troops moved out and forward across No Man's Land, the distance to the German front-line trenches being, on an average, 250 yards. The whole of the Middlesex had cleared their forming-up trenches and were on the move before the German guns replied, and their barrage fell practically on empty trenches. One company of 11th Fusiliers, however, which followed the last Company of the Middlesex, was caught in the hostile barrage, a whole platoon being buried. On the left of the Middlesex the 11th Royal Fusiliers had been ordered to capture the enemy's front-line trenches and then advance with the object of protecting the flank of the former Battalion as it attacked northwards up to the line of the first objective. This entailed hard fighting by the Fusiliers, though they gallantly performed their task, which finally helped the Middlesex to achieve their objectives.

26TH SEPT. 12TH BATTALION.

The Fusiliers were, indeed, the first to gain contact with the enemy, at a German strong point where Brawn Trench joined the old German front line going west. The left flank of the Middlesex was, however, held up until after some stiff hand-to-hand fighting, in which many Germans were killed and 25 taken prisoner, the Fusiliers captured the strong point. The attack then proceeded slowly northwards, practically every yard of ground having to be fought for. The Germans in their trenches waited for the attackers, and received them with showers of bombs of the "jam-pot" and "egg" type. From dug-outs, as the assaulting troops passed, bombs were thrown and even machine-gun fire opened on them, but by means of Lewis guns the defenders were either shot down or captured, and if they refused to come out of their dug-outs and surrender, the dug-outs were set on fire, many Germans perishing in this way.

From the old German front-line trenches and from the Château machine-gun fire swept the waves of Middlesex men as they advanced, and many casualties were suffered ere the line of the first objective was reached. The Battalion was checked for some time on the right until the arrival of a tank, which effectively dealt with the enemy's machine guns round the Château. Indeed, but for the timely arrival of this tank it is doubtful whether the advance would have progressed beyond the Château. The action

26TH SEPT. 12TH BATTALION.

of the tank, however, cleared the way for the Middlesex, who passed right and left of the Château.

About 1 p.m. the position was roughly as follows: The right of the 12th Middlesex was getting on well, but the left was making only slow progress, due to a devastating fire from German machine guns in the enemy's old front-line trenches; some of the Royal Fusiliers, who attempted to clear the defenders from this trench, were still engaged in fighting for it on the 27th. But soon after 1 p.m. the first objective (the road running from north-west to south-east through Thiepval) appears to have been captured and the advance begun towards the second objective. General progress now became slow again, and practically every inch of ground had to be covered, as, in addition to their organised defences, trenches, dug-outs, etc., the Germans had posted snipers in every other shellhole. About 2.30 p.m. Colonel Maxwell was able to report that his right company had reached the line of the second objective, but that his left was held up about the junction of the road through Thiepval and the old German front line (in co-ordinates given as R.25 central): he also reported that he had had heavy casualties. From now onwards until about 5.30 p.m. the position appears to have been somewhat obscure, but at that hour the 54th Brigade reported that, as far as could be ascertained, the Brigade was on the line of the second objective, though the enemy was still holding out at R.25 central.

The position of companies, closer details of the fighting and other interesting information concerning the attack are lacking from the documents, which are full of "generalities." It is, therefore, impossible to give more details of the two gallant men of the 12th Middlesex who won Victoria Crosses on the 26th than those contained in the official citations which appeared in the *London Gazette* of 25th March, 1916. Of Private F. J. Edwards the official account said: "His part of the line was held up by machine-gun fire and all officers had become casualties. There was confusion and indications of retirement. Private Edwards, grasping the situation, on his own initiative dashed out alone towards the gun, which he knocked out with bombs. This very gallant act, coupled with great presence of mind and a total disregard of personal danger, made further advance possible and cleared up a dangerous situation." Of Private Robert Ryder the citation said: "His company was held up by heavy rifle fire and all his officers had become casualties. For want of leadership

Map X.

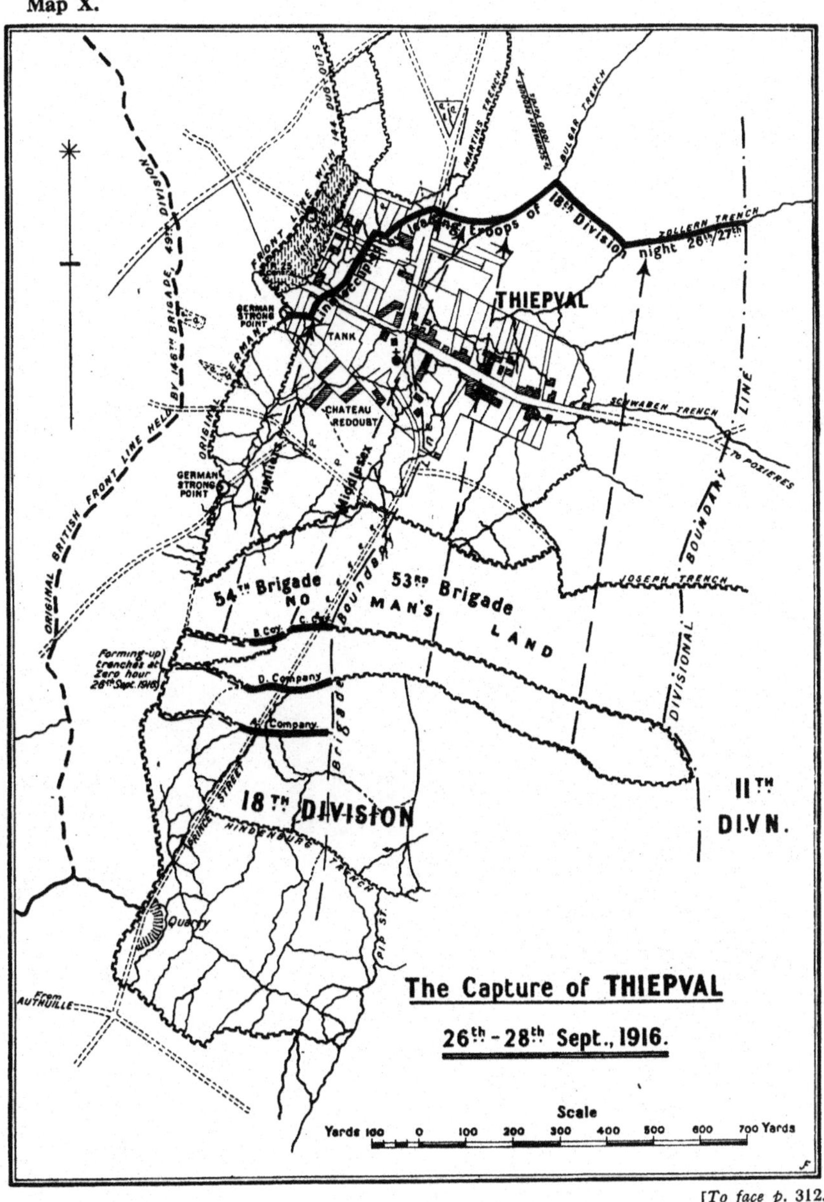


[To face p. 312.

the attack was flagging. Private Ryder, realising the situation, without a moment's thought for his own safety, dashed absolutely alone at the enemy trench and, by skilful manipulation of his Lewis gun, succeeded in clearing the trench. This very gallant act not only made possible, but also greatly inspired, the subsequent advance of his comrades and turned a possible failure into success." 26TH SEPT. 12TH BATTALION.

Colonel Maxwell said in his report of the action of the 26th that practically every German seen by Middlesex men was killed, an exception being made in the case of a small party which had no arms. The majority were killed at or in the neighbourhood of their dug-outs. Some fought well, chiefly with bombs, but others put their hands up and surrendered. At two dug-outs (as an instance) there was close fighting, the Middlesex men using the bayonet. Two brothers (named Stubbs), one a sergeant and the other a private, fought splendidly side by side. The private had his leg shattered by a bomb, but, picking up a revolver, continued to fight on until he collapsed and died from his terrible wound. His brother, the sergeant, was also killed. A German officer, with his revolver pointed at their backs, was seen urging his men on to stand up on the parapet and fire. At certain moments of the fight the air was thick with bombs, of which the Germans had large quantities.

About 4 p.m. orders were received from Divisional Headquarters to the effect that it was not proposed to go any further that night and that all troops were to consolidate on a line from Zollern Trench, just east of Thiepval, thence westwards (and northwards of the village) to a point in the old German front line, *i.e.*, R.25.b.3.4. Thus the whole of Thiepval had fallen to the 18th Division, though there were one or two strong points which still held out and were being attacked.

But the Middlesex men were spared any further fighting during the Battle of Thiepval, for on the 27th they proceeded to Aveluy Wood, where the Battalion re-formed and had time to count its losses. The latter were severe. Ten officers had been killed* and six wounded of the 20 engaged, while another on Brigade duty and the Battalion "Padre" were also wounded.† In other ranks 60 were reported killed, 233 wounded, and 121 missing. 27TH SEPT.

* Majors M. C. Scarborough and E. Whinney; Lieuts. E. C. McDonnell and A. G. Rogers; 2nd Lieuts. K. Restall, L. Hughes, W. S. Scruby, A. Brewerton, A. J. Wilkinson, and A. H. Card.

† Captains R. M. Gould, W. J. Parsons, and L. H. Methuen; Lieut. R. P. Walker; 2nd Lieuts. E. J. L. Garstin, L. N. B. Odgers and G. I. Price, and the Rev. C. H. Weller.

28TH SEPT. 12TH BATTALION.

Late in the afternoon of the 27th the Battalion marched to Martinsart Wood and there bivouacked; the 28th was spent in cleaning up.

Great praise was bestowed on the 18th Division for the splendid capture of Thiepval, and General Sir Ivor Maxse (the Divisional Commander) had good reason to be proud of his officers and men, for they had wrested from the best German troops the village and all its defences, which the garrison had been pledged to hold to the death.

## (X) THE BATTLE OF LE TRANSLOY RIDGES:

1st–18th October.

In this Battle, which had for its object the exploitation of the successes gained at Morval and Flers-Courcelette, four Battalions of the Middlesex Regiment took part, though only one was actually engaged with the enemy, the remaining three being either in support or reserve. These four Battalions were the 1/7th and 1/8th of the 167th Brigade, 56th Division, the 11th of the 36th Brigade, 12th Division, and the 23rd of the 120th Brigade, 41st Division.

1/7TH & 1/8TH 11TH & 23RD BATTALIONS.

The 1/7th and 1/8th Battalions (in Brigade) had moved back to Méaulte on 27th September with anticipations of a rest in billets, as (so rumour said) the 56th Division was to be withdrawn from the Somme Battles. But two days later the Division was again ordered up to the front line, and on the 30th of the month the 36th Brigade held the Guillemont sector with 1st Londons on the right, 1/7th Middlesex on the left, 1/8th Middlesex in support in the Flers Line, and the 3rd Londons in support in Trônes Wood.

1ST OCTOBER. 1/7TH BATTALION.

When the Battle opened on 1st October the 167th and 169th Brigades were ordered to establish a line of posts over the crest of the ridge along the divisional front. The 1/7th Middlesex, which then had "A" and "B" Companies in the front line with "C" and "D" in support, pushed forward an officer and 20 men from each Company under cover of a shrapnel barrage, and established four posts 700 yards in front; in the evening a fifth post was established to cover the exposed left flank of the Battalion, touch with the 20th Division on the left of the 56th not having been obtained. After darkness had fallen the posts were linked up by a trench and wired. These posts were not, however, established without loss, for seven other ranks were killed and 2/Lieuts. Moxon and T. T. Harris* and 13 other ranks wounded. 1/7TH BATTALION.

In order that the 1/7th might have a short rest before the general attack, which had been ordered to take place on 5th October, the Battalion was relieved by the 1/8th on the night of 3rd. The posts also were in due course relieved by the 1/8th. 3RD OCTOBER. One of these posts—No. 6—had been held by Lieut. F. Prockter 1/8TH BATTALION. and 17 other ranks, all Hornsey men, who on relief marched out to rejoin the Battalion. In the inky blackness of the night Lieut. Prockter lost his way and, after moving about apparently in a circle, walked into the German trenches. Although surrounded by the enemy, this little party refused to surrender and stiff hand-to-hand fighting took place, and it was not until every man had either been killed or wounded that the survivors gave themselves up. In this little affair Lieut. Prockter and 12 of his men were killed, and the remaining 5, all wounded, were taken prisoners. This was the first occasion in the war that men of the 1/7th Middlesex became prisoners in the hands of the enemy.

Abominable weather forced a postponement of the attack until the morning of 7th. Heavy rain had fallen, turning the trenches and the ground into masses of thick, sticky mud in which men stuck fast and had to be pulled out by their comrades. The attack, so far as weather conditions were concerned, was not going to be easy.

The 56th Division was on the extreme left of the British line, joining up (curiously enough) with the 56th French Division.†

The objectives allotted to the Division were: (1) the capture and consolidation of the enemy trenches known as Hazy, Dewdrop Spectrum and part of Rainbow (*i.e.*, the Green Line), (2) the establishment of a line on the forward slopes of the ridge from which Le Transloy trench system could be seen (*i.e.*, the Brown Line). The 168th Brigade was to attack on the right and the 167th Brigade on the left

Of the 167th Brigade the 1st Londons were to be on the right and the 1/7th Middlesex on the left, these two Battalions capturing 1/7TH BATTALION. both objectives. The attack was to be made in four waves: the first two waves attacking the first objective, the third wave the second objective, and the fourth wave in reserve.

* Died of wounds 4th October, 1916.

† Another remarkable coincidence was that the 56th French Division was also to attack with the 168th Brigade on the right, the 167th on the left and the 169th in reserve.

5TH OCTOBER. 1/7TH BATTALION.

Throughout the 5th October the 1/7th remained in Trônes Wood resting, but at 6 p.m. on the 6th moved up to assembly positions, " C " and " D " Companies taking over the freshly-dug trenches linking up the posts, " A " Company in rear of " D," and " B " in reserve on the Sunken Road in rear of " C."

The Battalion's objective was Spectrum Trench and the formation of a line of posts beyond. " C " and " D " Companies had been allotted the first objective, " A " Company the second. By 11.30 p.m. the 1/7th were in their assembly positions ready for the attack next day, which had been fixed for 1.45 p.m. All ranks were in the best of spirits and were determined to avenge the loss of many gallant comrades who had been killed in the attack on Bouleaux Wood. The Battalion was weak in officers and five were lent from the 10th London Regiment.*

7TH OCTOBER.

Just before " Zero " on 7th a creeping barrage of shrapnel was placed on the enemy's trenches which were some 400 yards from the Middlesex men. On the barrage lifting the advance began. " D " Company, on the right, went forward under Lieut. Groser; " C," on the left, was under 2/Lieut. Moss; " A," in support, was commanded by 2/Lieut. Williams; " B " was under Lieut. G. A. King.

The Companies advanced with great steadiness and, indeed, they might have been moving forward on parade, so well did they keep their formation. A Staff Officer, who saw the 1/7th go forward, was so impressed that he wrote a special report on this advance.

The fight was sharp but decisive. Hornsey and Tottenham, on reaching the German front line, carried it almost at once. Some of the men jumped into the trenches and, with bomb and bayonet, fought the enemy and overpowered him. Other men remained on the parapet shooting down on the enemy whenever a target offered itself. The arrival, a few minutes later, of the Hampstead and Highgate men completed the discomfiture of the enemy and the line was cleared and consolidated. Heavy losses were inflicted on the enemy: 77 unwounded Germans, including 4 officers, were sent back as prisoners, as well as many who were wounded. Numbers of the enemy were killed.

It had been intended that the Hampstead and Highgate should pass through the line and establish a line of posts beyond, but this

* These five officers fought most gallantly, and only one (2/Lieut. Evans) was left 24 hours later.

was found to be impossible. At 8.30 p.m. a strong counter-attack was made against the right of the 168th Brigade, most of the latter being driven back to its original position, leaving the 1/7th Middlesex almost isolated in the German lines. 7TH OCTOBER. 1/7TH BATTALION.

This attack was the most brilliant hitherto carried out by the 1/7th, but, alas! the cost was heavy. Lieut. A. G. Groser (O.C., "D" Company), 2/Lieut. H. A. Moss (O.C., "C" Company) and 2/Lieuts. W. B. Hawke and E. D. Binns were killed. The wounded included 2/Lieuts. V. S. M. Williams and H. R. Hewlett. Of the 5 officers lent by the 10th Londons, 2 were killed and 2 wounded. The total losses of the Battalion were 63 killed (including 7 officers), 130 wounded (including three officers); the 1/7th had gone into action 450 strong. Major L. R. King, who was in command during the operation, was severely injured by the burst of a H.E. shell, but "carried on" for four days.

No further attacks were made by the 1/7th in this Battle, though on the 8th the 3rd Londons made an unsuccessful attempt to capture the remainder of Spectrum Trench. During the bombardment which preceded this attack the 1/7th lost some 30 men from the fire of their own guns, for the Battalion was holding a portion of the German line that was being shelled, but the Middlesex men hung on grimly until relieved, when they marched back to the Flers line, and on the 9th moved back to the Citadel. 9TH OCTOBER. On this day 2/Lieut. T. J. Webster was killed by a bullet from a hostile aeroplane.

The 1/8th Middlesex, although in support of 1/7th and 1st London Regiment, did not attack the enemy, and when the former was relieved in the front line both Battalions moved back, first to reserve positions and then to the Citadel, as the whole of the 56th Division had been withdrawn from the line on 9th October and, so far as the Somme Battles of 1916 were concerned, the Division was not again engaged in them. The Division moved to the Flesselles area, 8 miles from Amiens. 1/8TH BATTALION.

The 12th and 41st Divisions (of XVth Corps), the former on the right and the latter on the left, were on the left of the 56th Division in the attack which took place on 7th October.

Of the 12th Division the 37th Brigade, right, and 36th Brigade, left, attacked Bayonet Trench, which ran from the Factory Corner —Ligny Thilloy road to just north-east of Gueudecourt. The 11th Middlesex (Lieut.-Colonel L. L. Pargiter) were, however, in reserve during the attack of the 36th Brigade, moving up at 11TH BATTALION.

7TH OCTOBER. 11TH BATTALION.

5.30 a.m. to support trenches, and at 9 p.m. relieving troops in the front line, who had been engaged during the day. For several days the Battalion had to endure heavy shelling, during which wounded were collected, trenches dug or repaired, and much work carried out. Both on 8th and 9th casualties were heavy, 10 other ranks killed and 48 wounded on the former date, and 2 killed and 30 wounded on the latter. Relief came on 10th and the Battalion moved back to camp in Bernafay Wood. On 19th the Battalion moved to Fricourt Camp, on 21st to Buire, and by the end of the month was back again in Agny.

10TH OCTOBER.

21ST OCTOBER.

1ST OCTOBER. 23RD BATTALION.

The 123rd Brigade of the 41st Division was in reserve during the attack of 7th October, and the 23rd Middlesex (Lieut.-Colonel A. R. Haig-Brown) were located in Mametz Wood. The Battalion had, however, on 1st October, when the New Zealanders, on the left of the 123rd Brigade, attacked eastwards towards Eaucourt l'Abbaye, sent out three patrols in conjunction with the 20th Durham Light Infantry (on the left of the 23rd Middlesex) to keep touch with the attack by the Colonials. Second-Lieutenant Gear took the Middlesex patrols out, but no sooner had the parties started than they were met with decided opposition. The enemy placed a heavy barrage on the front line immediately. A hundred yards from the Battalion front line Lieut. Gear was wounded and the patrols became disorganised, though the right party succeeded in digging itself in about two hundred yards from the enemy. Eventually the patrols were withdrawn and search parties were sent out to collect the remnants of the parties and bring in wounded. At night the 23rd Middlesex were relieved by the 9th Royal Fusiliers and moved back to Montauban. Casualties on 1st October were 18 other ranks killed, 29 wounded and 11 missing.

8TH OCTOBER.

On 8th October the Battalion moved up to Carlton Trench as reserve, and on 9th went into the front line north-east of Eaucourt l'Abbaye. On relief, two days later, the 23rd Middlesex again moved back to Mametz Wood and then to Dernancourt. From the latter village the Battalion (on 17th) marched to Edge Hill and entrained for Oisemont.

## (XI) THE BATTLE OF THE ANCRE HEIGHTS:

1st October–11th November.

### Capture of the Schwaben and Stuff Redoubts and Regina Trench.

After the successful operations at Thiepval, the 12th Middlesex had arrived at Martinsart Wood about 6.30 p.m. on 27th September, where the following day was spent in cleaning up and compiling casualty returns. At about 2 p.m. on 29th the Battalion was ordered to "stand by" and later marched to hutments in Mailly Wood. On 2nd October the 12th moved by motor buses to Prouville, where, until 15th, training and practising the attack were carried out. A ten-mile march, begun on the morning of 15th, saw the Battalion in Beauval. Another march of 13 miles (in Brigade) on 16th to hutments in Vadencourt Wood was followed by a third, on 17th, to Bouzincourt, a distance of 6½ miles. 27TH SEPT. 12TH BATTALION. 15TH OCTOBER.

From Bouzincourt, on 18th, the C.O., Second-in-Command, Company Commanders and Adjutant went up to the front-line trenches in front of Courcelette to make themselves acquainted with the ground in view of forthcoming operations. The Schwaben Redoubt had already been captured by the 18th Division (28th September–5th October), and an assault was to be launched against Regina Trench on 21st October. But the 12th Middlesex were not engaged in this attack, the Battalion on that date being at Albert, where at 11 a.m., in the Iron Factory, Brigadier-General F. A. Maxwell, V.C., in a farewell speech, addressed the Battalion. He had been appointed to command the 27th Infantry Brigade, 9th Division. 21ST OCTOBER.

Some may think that the speech made by this gallant soldier to the officers and men who had served under him bloodthirsty and callous, but it was according to the spirit of the times. During the Somme Battles of 1916 everyone was "out to kill," both sides had lost heavily, both were animated by an intense desire for revenge—it was war at its bloodiest, and the cry of "kill, kill," was everywhere and on everyone's lips. And, be it remembered, that the 12th Middlesex was a very gallant Battalion.

Before leaving the Battalion Brigadier-General Maxwell published this message: "Although I have personally said 'Good-bye' to the Battalion this morning, I would like to leave

12TH BATTALION. it on record in my last Battalion Orders the deep regret with which I leave the 'Die Hards.'

"I have spent nearly six months in this happy family, and these have been amongst the happiest, saddest and proudest of my life. Happy, because I believe no man could be anything but happy in this Battalion: sad, because of the good men and true we have lost in action since July: proud, because of the Battalion's achievements, particularly in Trônes Wood and at Thiepval. No failure has spoiled our record since real business began nearly four months ago, and none is going to. In that period we have begun to learn that the only way to treat the Germans is to kill them, but that lesson is only half-learned, for we either do not want to kill them enough, or we forget to use that best of weapons, our rifles, to 'down them.' We shout for bombs, instead of shooting with our guns.

"Discipline has a knack in this Battalion of looking after itself, and as a C.O. I hardly know what a prisoner looks like, and one of the reasons of this is that the Battalion knows how to look after its thirsty souls. Its turn-out is gradually approaching the stage when we shall look like what we are—first-class, but we can still achieve something in this respect.

"Finally, remember that the 12th Die-Hards *do* kill; don't get taken prisoner unless wounded, and don't retire. And with these one 'do' and two 'don'ts' I wish all ranks 'Good-bye' and 'God speed.'"

25TH OCTOBER. On 25th October the 12th Middlesex moved up to the front line, taking over from the 11th Royal Fusiliers that part of the Regina Trench held by them. This relief was difficult, bad weather and heavy mud in the trenches made the "going" very slow, and it was 8.30 p.m. before the line had been taken over. The enemy's artillery was fairly active all the while, with the result that three other ranks were killed, seven wounded and five missing. Until the 29th the Battalion remained in the front line, fighting hard against the terrible conditions of the trenches, and worried continually by the enemy's shell fire which harassed the relief on the 29th. By midnight the 12th Middlesex were back in billets in Albert. This tour had cost the Battalion one officer (2/Lieut. A. E. Morgan) killed during the relief, one officer wounded and 18 other ranks killed, 30 wounded and 2 missing. 31ST OCTOBER. On 31st October the Battalion moved to Warloy.

## The Attack on Zenith Trench.

### 23rd–26th October.

During the Battle of the Ancre Heights the 2nd Middlesex (in Brigade and Division) had returned to the Somme area. The Battle of Le Transloy Ridges (1st–18th October) was followed by a series of local attempts to push the line forward as soon as the 8th Division was settled in the line. An attack was launched on 23rd October against the salient, west of Le Transloy, formed by Eclipse and Zenith Trenches. 2ND BATTALION.

After the terrible losses sustained by the 8th Division on 1st July the Division was transferred to the First Army and reached Bruay on the 6th and 7th, the 23rd Infantry Brigade being billeted in the Barlin area.

On the 14th July the 23rd Brigade took over the Cuinchy sector just south of the La Bassée Canal, the 2nd Middlesex relieving troops of the 118th Infantry Brigade immediately south of the Canal. With the exception of the normal activity of trench warfare the tour was uneventful from a regimental point of view, and on 30th the 23rd Brigade was relieved and moved back to billets in divisional reserve, the 2nd Middlesex to Beuvry. On 7th August the Battalion paraded at 6 a.m. and marched to the Hohenzollern sector, taking over reserve trenches in the village line. On 8th Lieut.-Colonel R. H. Hayes left for England, his tenure of command having expired, and on 9th Lieut.-Colonel H. W. E. Finch joined the Battalion and assumed command. Front-line trenches were taken over on 15th August, but after an uneventful week the Battalion was withdrawn to reserve billets in Labourse. The next tour in the front line was in the Quarries sector (from 1st–9th September) and the final tour (29th September–7th October) in front of Hulluch. The relief of 7th October was the last in this part of the line, for the 8th Division had received orders to move back to the Somme area, and on 15th October the 2nd Middlesex marched to Chocques and entrained for Pont Remy, and by 17th had reached Méaulte, where the 23rd Brigade had been allotted billets. 14TH JULY. 7TH AUGUST. 7TH OCTOBER. 17TH OCTOBER.

By the night of 19th/20th October the 24th and 25th Brigades of the 8th Division had relieved the 16th and 71st Brigades of the 6th Division in the line north of Les Bœufs, the 23rd Brigade occupying reserve positions about Montauban and Bernafay and Trônes Wood on the morning of the 20th. In the evening the

2ND BATTALION.

23rd Brigade relieved the 12th Brigade of the 4th Division on the right of the 8th Divisional Area. All three brigades of the latter were now in the front line, 23rd right, 25th centre and 24th left.

The front line taken over by the 23rd Brigade was Spectrum Trench, the 2nd Scottish Rifles holding the right sub-sector and the 2nd Middlesex the left. Brigade Operation Orders were issued on 22nd. In conjunction with the attack by the 4th Division on the right of the 8th, and by the 25th and 24th Brigades on the left, the 23rd Brigade was to attack Zenith Trench, and if the attack was successful dig a fresh line beyond. The 4th Division, on the right, was attacking Dewdrop Trench, and the 25th Brigade the remaining section of Zenith Trench and a portion of Eclipse Trench on the left.

On arrival in Spectrum Trench the 2nd Middlesex were disposed as follows: "A" Company right, "B" left, "C" and "D" right and left supporting Companies respectively.

Zero hour was finally fixed at 2.30 p.m. on 23rd October.

From 21st the German trenches had been subjected to a very heavy bombardment by guns of all calibre, and at Zero hour on 23rd the hostile front lines were covered by a creeping barrage.

23RD OCTOBER.

At 2.30 p.m., following close on the heels of the barrage, the 2nd Scottish Rifles and 2nd Middlesex attacked the enemy. The former Battalion, though momentarily checked by machine-gun fire, eventually carried the first objective, taking 25 prisoners.

On the left of the Scotsmen, the Middlesex, advancing with great steadiness, carried the German front line, inflicting heavy losses on the enemy in a stiff hand-to-hand fight. By 3.45 p.m. the Scottish Rifles and Middlesex were both reported on the line of the second objective. Two weak counter-attacks, one at 3.15 p.m. and the other at 4.15 p.m., were easily repulsed. Owing to the failure of the right battalion of the 25th Brigade, the left flank of the Middlesex was exposed and a defensive flank had to be thrown back to the junction of Gusty and Spectrum Trenches. On the Middlesex front Zenith Trench had been cleared and captured, and a new line established some 200 yards beyond the old hostile front line. On the right of the 23rd Brigade the 4th Division had captured Dewdrop Trench, but could get no further; the Scottish Rifles therefore had to throw back their right flank to gain touch with the left flanking troops of the 4th Division. Consolidation had begun immediately.

The brilliant manner in which the 2nd Middlesex had carried out the task allotted to them drew congratulations from the Brigadier. But, again, the gallant Die-Hards had suffered heavily. 2/Lieuts. F. O. Kemp, L. W. Smith and G. Hall and 62 other ranks had been killed, and Captain H. C. Hunt and 2/Lieuts. K. L. N. McCulloch and A. L. St. John-Jones and 117 other ranks were wounded ; 47 other ranks were missing. Total, 6 officers and 226 other ranks.

23RD OCTOBER. 2ND BATTALION

From 26th to 27th (inclusive) the position gained was strengthened and consolidated, though constantly under heavy shell fire. On 26th the Battalion M.O.—Captain T. C. Kidner, R.A.M.C.—was killed, and on 27th, before the relief of the Battalion took place, two more officers—2/Lieuts. H. Hess and E. Evans—were wounded.

On the night of 27th the Battalion was withdrawn from the line and, tired and worn out, reached a camp near Montauban in the early hours of 28th. The latter date was spent in resting and cleaning up, and at noon on 29th the Battalion paraded and marched to Mansell Camp ; thence, on 30th, to Méaulte.

27TH OCTOBER.

## (XII) THE BATTLE OF THE ANCRE, 1916.

### 13th–18th November.

On the 9th November the bad weather, which had dogged the gallant efforts of the troops throughout the greater part of October, took a turn for the better, and for some days thereafter remained dry and cold, with frosty nights and misty mornings—both of great advantage during the preparations for further operations on the Ancre. Nevertheless, the ground in places still resembled a quagmire, which compelled a limitation of the attack planned by Sir Douglas Haig.

From east of Schwaben Redoubt to north of Serre the enemy had spent the four months succeeding the initial assault on 1st July in improving, and adding to, the already formidable defences in this area. He evidently intended that the hamlet of St. Pierre Divion and the villages of Beaucourt and Beaumont Hamel, like other villages which had formed part of his original front line, should form a permanent line of fortifications whilst he developed his offensive elsewhere. But, realising that his position had become dangerous, he had multiplied the number of his guns covering this part of his line, and towards the end of October had reinforced his troops between Grandcourt and Hebuterne.

Between a point due west of St. Pierre Divion and northwards to opposite John Copse, the 63rd, 51st, 2nd and 3rd Divisions of the Vth Corps (in the order given from right to left) were to carry out the attack north of the Ancre; the 37th Division was in reserve. On the right of the Vth Corps the IInd Corps was attacking St. Pierre Divion and towards Grandcourt; the 18th Division formed part of the IInd Corps. Thus, three

17TH, 4TH & 12TH BATTALIONS.

battalions of the Middlesex Regiment, 17th, 4th and 12th, were in the battle area, though only one—the 17th—saw heavy fighting.

17TH BATTALION.

Previously, the 17th Middlesex had seen fighting in the Somme area, in the Delville Wood and Guillemont sectors only, after which the Battalion (in Brigade and Division) was relieved on 9th August,

14TH AUGUST.

and by the 14th August the 2nd Division was concentrated in the Belloy–Picquigny–Vaux–en–Amienois area. From this area the 2nd Division moved again into the front line just south of Hebuterne, relieving the Guards Division on 19th/20th and 20th/21st August, all three Brigades of the former Division going into the line, which was divided into three sub-sectors. The right of these sub-sectors was held by the 6th Infantry Brigade, and on 22nd the 17th Middlesex relieved the South Staffords east of La Signy Farm. The remainder of August and the early days of September were comparatively quiet and no untoward incidents are reported

17TH SEPT.

in the Battalion Diaries. On the 17th September, however, the enemy became aggressive, and at 9.10 p.m. suddenly opened a terrific minenwerfer bombardment of the trenches held by the Middlesex men. The air literally whistled with mortar bombs, as many as eight being seen at once. Between Grey and Warloy as many as 750 of these objectionable bombs fell on the trenches, flattening them completely. The enemy seemed to be concentrating his fire on the Bleneau Sap. As a result of this bombardment 2/Lieut. J. R. Stagg and three other ranks were killed, 2/Lieuts. Templeman and Fowler were gassed and 14 other ranks were wounded. An S.O.S. signal to the divisional artillery brought no response and so the Battalion was forced to undergo the " strafe," which lasted half an hour. On the following afternoon, at about 4 p.m., the enemy again sent over trench-mortar bombs, and blew a mine near Grey Sap. The results of this second " strafe " were 14 other ranks killed, 5 missing, 6 wounded and 2 died of wounds.

A retaliation "stunt" was carried out by the divisional artillery, trench mortars and Stokes guns on 19th. 17TH BATTALION.

The 2nd Division was relieved by the 39th Division on 19th/20th September, and it was not until 22nd October that the 17th Middlesex moved back into the front line, into the Redan Sector (south of Serre), taking over trenches from the 1st Royal Berks, of the 5th Brigade. The period out of the line had been spent largely in training for the operations which were to begin as soon as the weather permitted. The march back to the trenches was an uncomfortable business, for the guns of both sides were very active; they had been indulging in "retaliation shoots," which always meant more casualties among the infantry. On this day, in Mailly Wood East alone, the Battalion had 23 casualties, and as the troops got nearer the front line two more N.C.Os. were lost—Sergeant W. J. Baker being killed and C.S.M. McFadden severely wounded. 22ND OCTOBER.

The trenches were in a truly shocking condition and mud was deep and water lying about everywhere. Constant work was necessary repairing and clearing the defences, though probably immediately afterwards they were again thrown into confusion by the enemy's shells or trench-mortar bombs. But the work of preparation went on, the "jumping-off" trenches were cleared, ladders and bridges carried up, and Bangalore torpedoes, with which to blow gaps in the enemy's wire, got ready.

The 12th November was "Y" day—that is to say, the day before the attack—and all ranks were busy making final preparations.

The 2nd Division was attacking the enemy from about the centre of Hunter Street, due east of the White City to Board Street, with the 5th Brigade on the right, the 6th Brigade on the left, and the 99th Brigade in reserve. The 6th Brigade was to attack from Dog Street (exclusive) to Board Street, the 13th Essex Regiment on the right, 2nd South Staffords on the left, the 1st King's Regiment right support and the 17th Middlesex left support. The Essex and South Staffords were to capture the first objective and the King's and Middlesex were to go through and capture the second objective.

During the night 12th/13th all troops took up their assembly positions. The 17th Middlesex (Lieut.-Colonel H. Fenwick) left Mailly at 11.15 p.m. and arrived in their allotted positions at about 12.20 a.m. on 13th. The Battalion then took up its correct 12/13TH NOV.

17TH BATTALION.

dispositions "on top." The hostile guns were inactive and caused very little disturbance, the Middlesex suffering no casualties whilst in their forming-up places.

13TH NOV.

At 5 a.m. on 13th, in order to trick the enemy into thinking that he was merely about to receive his usual morning "strafe," the siege batteries opened fire and during this bombardment dawn broke. A thick fog hung over the battlefield-to-be. No Man's Land and the opposing trenches were not to be seen and visibility was impossible for more than 30 yards ahead. The advent of fog had been foreseen, and all officers had been instructed to advance by compass-bearing if the fog obscured the objectives. For three-quarters of an hour the "strafe" continued, the enemy's reply being feeble—he was getting used to these morning displays of "hate"—and this particular morning, he evidently thought, was like the others. But at 5.45 a.m. the field guns and howitzers joined in the bombardment and a very heavy barrage was placed on the German front-line trenches. Six minutes later the infantry attack was launched.

The 17th Middlesex, following in rear of the 2nd South Staffords, "went over" in four waves. The objective of the former Battalion was Pendant Copse, but from No Man's Land it was invisible, the thick fog obscuring everything beyond a distance of from 25 to 30 yards. But all ranks were extraordinarily cheerful, and two Companies of the 17th Middlesex ("B" and "D") actually went "over the top" playing mouth-organs. What, indeed, will coming generations say of these men? They were then in the midst of all the dirt and mud of the front-line trenches, with the possibility of a horrible death or mutilation facing them; they would soon be in the very throes of war at its worst; they would in places have to flounder through thick, sticky, stinking mud, to get to grips with the enemy, and yet they "went over the top" playing mouth-organs. In truth, they were men prepared to taste of death but once.

Success seemed inevitable as the troops disappeared over the parapet into No Man's Land, and indeed all along the right and centre of the Vth Corps front the attacking infantry swept all before them. Both the 63rd and 51st Divisions were soon fighting their way eastwards, with the tumbled ruins of Beaumont Hamel at their backs. But along the front of the 2nd and 3rd Divisions things went not so well. The right of the 2nd Division got well into the enemy's line, but the left flank was held up.

13TH NOV. 17TH BATTALION.

At Battalion Headquarters of the Middlesex nothing was heard of the results of the attack until 7.20 a.m., when Captain L. J. Horniman (O.C. "D" Company) returned wounded. He reported that across No Man's Land, in front of the enemy's trenches, there was confusion, units were mixed up in No Man's Land and hostile machine-gun fire was causing a lot of trouble, though the enemy's artillery retaliation was only slight. Ten minutes later 2/Lieut. Barnfather, who had been sent out to select a site for Battalion Headquarters in the German trenches (so certain seemed success), returned, and stated that the South Staffords had not even penetrated the German trenches; they were in a terrible position, lying under the enemy's wire, unable to get on, as the thick wire entanglements had not been cut by the artillery. To make matters worse the right Brigade of the 3rd Division had come across No Man's Land into the attacking troops of the 6th Brigade, with the result that a mixed crowd of 2nd and 3rd Division troops, unable to make progress, came under the fire of the enemy's machine guns from front and flank, and casualties soon became very heavy. Seeing the impossibility of getting on, the Company and Platoon Commanders of the Middlesex withdrew the remnants of their men back to the "jumping-off" line—a wise precaution—for to advance was impracticable and the only alternative was death. Soon after 9 a.m. a message was received from the Brigadier ordering all men collected to Legend Trench, which was to be held strongly. When this order had been carried out there were only 79 Middlesex men, with 2/Lieut. E. Parfitt in command. A little later a message was received stating that the 5th Brigade, on the right of the 6th, had been successful and had taken the enemy's front line. But nothing more could be done by the 6th Brigade, and at 2.15 p.m. orders were received to hold the front line by forming strong machine-gun posts. So far as the Middlesex were concerned the situation remained the same during the remainder of the day, though Legend and Bow were heavily shelled by the enemy. The trenches by now were in such a shocking condition that all ranks had to move about "on the top."

14TH NOV.

The morning of 14th was also misty, and although further attacks were made by troops of the 2nd Division on the right of the Middlesex, the latter remained in the same positions occupied on the 13th. On 15th, at 10.15 a.m., the Battalion was relieved by the 4th Royal Fusiliers and moved back to support trenches

15TH NOV.

17TH BATTALION. in the neighbourhood of Ellis Square. From the latter position the Battalion set out for Mailly, arriving there at 2.30 p.m. On the 16th motor lorries carried the Battalion to billets in Louvencourt, where, after a "clean up," the roll was called and a count taken of the losses sustained in the battle. Captain J. O'C. Kissack, Lieut. E. B. D. Brunton, and 2/Lieuts. G. Swade, P. G. Fall, W. H. Austen, L. F. Christmas, S. E. O. Rothe and 15 other ranks had been killed; Lieut. E. W. Marchant and 2/Lieuts. A. M. Murray, C. Koop and C. W. Flint, and 133 other ranks were missing, and Captain L. J. Horniman and 2/Lieut. F. N. Stansfeld and 145 other ranks were wounded. Total, 13 officers and 293 other ranks.

During the 16th and 17th November the whole of the 2nd Division was being relieved and withdrawn from the line for rest and training, and to the close of the year there is little of further interest in the Diary of the 17th Middlesex Regiment. On the
31ST DEC. 31st December the Battalion was in billets in Argenvillers.

The 37th Division, the reserve division of the Vth Corps, did not take part in the initial attack on the 13th November, and the 63rd Brigade* remained in Léavillers and Acheux Wood until the 14th, when the Brigade moved to Hedauville, with orders to take over the front-line trenches of the 189th Brigade (63rd Division) that night.

4TH BATTALION. The 4th Middlesex (Lieut.-Colonel H. P. F. Bicknell) arrived at Hedauville at about 3 p.m. and, after dinners had been eaten, marched again to positions of assembly one mile south-east of Englebelmer. The Battalion had been detailed to act as Brigade Reserve, and after arrival at Englebelmer moved up to Station
15TH NOV. Road, east of Hamel, arriving about 2 a.m. on 15th. The position of the 63rd Brigade was then as follows: the 10th Yorks and Lancs and 8th Lincolns were holding the right and left front line of the Brigade sector: the 8th Somerset Light Infantry were in support just east of Station Road, and the 4th Middlesex in reserve. In Station Trench and the Valley the 4th Middlesex
18TH NOV. remained in reserve until the morning of 18th November, furnishing carrying and working parties for the Battalions in the front line. The Valley and Station Trench were heavily shelled at intervals and the Battalion had 40 casualties.

* The 63rd Brigade was transferred from the 21st Division to the 37th Division after the terrible losses suffered at the beginning of the Somme Battles on 1st July. The Brigade was withdrawn from the line on 4th July.

At 8.45 a.m. on 18th a message was received stating that the IInd Corps, south of the Ancre, was going to attack Grandcourt at 8.10 a.m., and the 37th Division was to be prepared to capture Puisieux and River Trenches, north of the River. The 8th Somerset, supported by the 4th Middlesex, were to attack these trenches up to their junction with Miraumont Alley. At 10.20 a.m. a message was received that the attack would begin at 11 a.m. The Middlesex, therefore, left immediately for Beaucourt, to be in position to support the attack. Knee-deep in mud, along a road heavily shelled, the Battalion eventually reached the Headquarters of the 8th Somerset, about six hundred yards east of Beaucourt, at 11.15 a.m. On arrival, however, the O.C. 8th Somerset stated that owing to non-receipt of orders his Battalion was not yet assembled, and he was therefore not ready to begin the attack. 18TH NOV. 4TH BATTALION.

Apparently this attack took place, "C" Company of the 4th Middlesex moving up to support one Company and patrols of the Somerset. In going forward Lieut. R. Underhill was killed and 2/Lieuts. Burch and Macleod were wounded, whilst there were numerous casualties in other ranks. "D" Company, sent up to reinforce "C" Company, suffered similarly, 2/Lieut. Lofts being amongst the wounded. About 3 p.m. the 4th Middlesex relieved the Somerset, who withdrew, leaving "C" and "D" Companies of the former Battalion holding that portion of Puisieux Trench between the Ancre and the Miraumont Road, the enemy holding the remainder—an unenviable situation which continued until the 19th November when, the attack on Grandcourt having failed, it was decided to withdraw from Puisieux Trench. As soon as it was dark "A" Company of the Middlesex began to dig a new line from Bois d'Hollande to the Ancre, and when the trench was ready "C" and "D" Companies, after demolishing the portion of Puisieux Trench held by them, withdrew without a single casualty, carrying back all the stores. On 20th the Battalion was relieved, moving back to the Old German Third Line till 25th, when the relief of the 37th Division was begun. On the 26th the relief was completed, and the 4th Middlesex, in Brigade, moved back to billets in Mailly Maillet. Apart from the officer casualties already given, the Battalion lost about 140 other ranks during the operations. 19TH NOV. 26TH NOV.

The 12th Middlesex (53rd Brigade, 18th Division) remained in reserve during the whole course of the battle—*i.e.*, from 12TH BATTALION.

12TH BATTALION.

18TH NOV.

13th to 18th November, the 55th Brigade of the Division making the attack from the divisional front. The Middlesex were at Ovillers Huts until 18th, but moved up closer to the battle front on that date. They did not, however, take part in the operations.

Map XI.

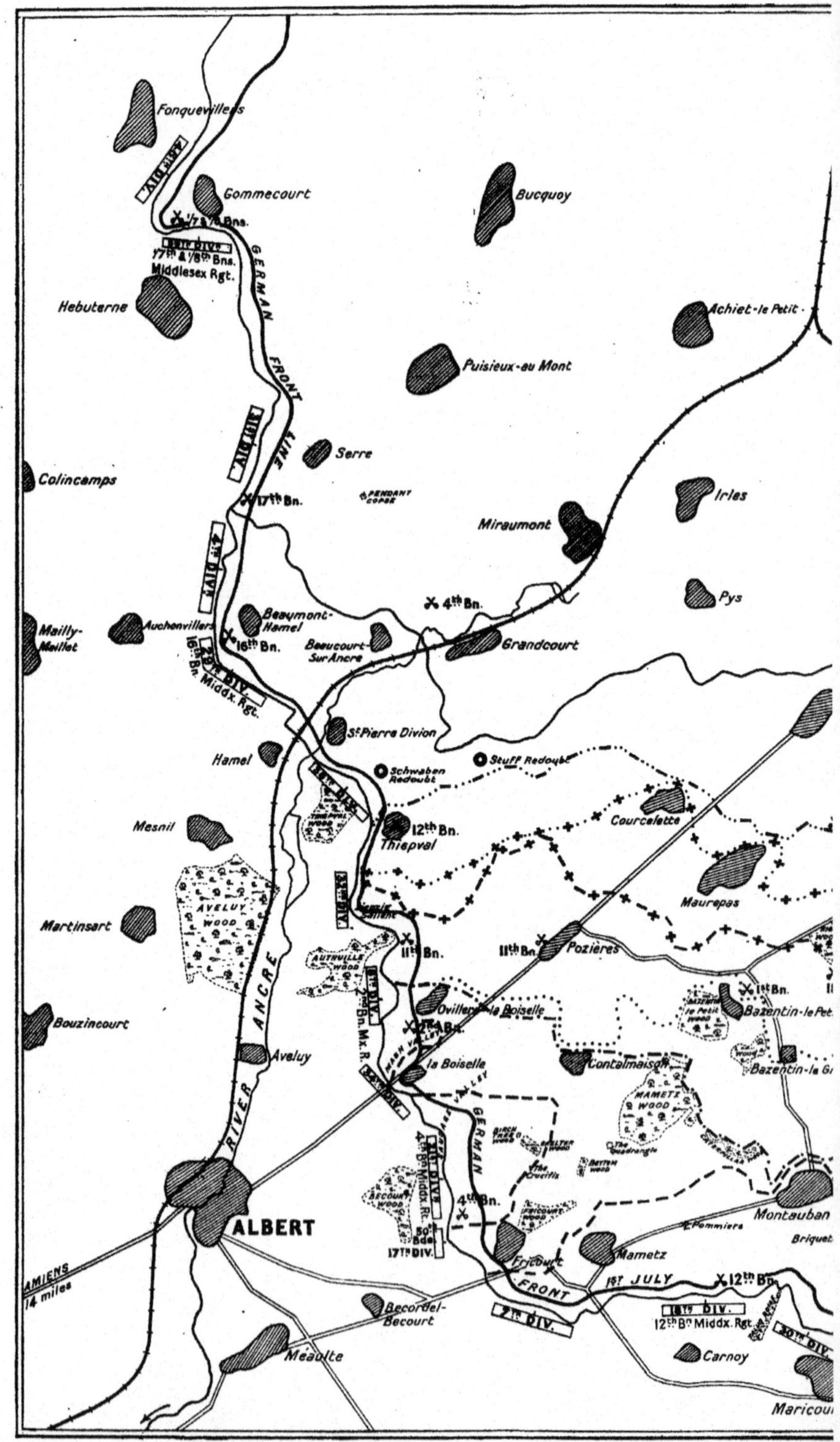
Fonquevillers
46th DIV
Gommecourt
Bucquoy
1/7th & 1/8th Bns.
56th DIV
1/7th & 1/8th Bns.
Middlesex Rgt.
GERMAN FRONT LINE
Hebuterne
Achiet-le Petit
Puisieux-au Mont
Serre
31st DIV
Colincamps
17th Bn.
Pendant Copse
Irles
Miraumont
4th DIV
4th Bn.
Pys
Mailly-Maillet
Auchonvillers
Beaumont-Hamel
16th Bn.
Beaucourt-Sur Ancre
Grandcourt
29th DIV
16th Bn. Middx. Rgt.
St Pierre Divion
Hamel
Schwaben Redoubt
Stuff Redoubt
36th DIV
Courcelette
Mesnil
12th Bn.
Thiepval
Aveluy Wood
Maurepas
32nd DIV
Martinsart
11th Bn.
11th Bn.
Pozières
Authuille Wood
8th DIV
2nd Bn. Mx. R.
1st Bn.
Ovillers la Boiselle
Bazentin-le Petit
Bouzincourt
Aveluy
la Boiselle
Contalmaison
Bazentin-le Gr
RIVER ANCRE
Mametz Wood
GERMAN
21st DIV
4th Bn. Middx. Rt.
Becourt Wood
4th Bn.
Montauban
ALBERT
50th Bde
17th DIV
Fricourt
Mametz
Briquet
AMIENS
14 miles
FRONT
1st JULY
12th Bn.
7th DIV.
18th DIV.
12th Bn. Middx. Rgt.
30th DIV
Becordel-Becourt
Carnoy
Meaulte
Maricou

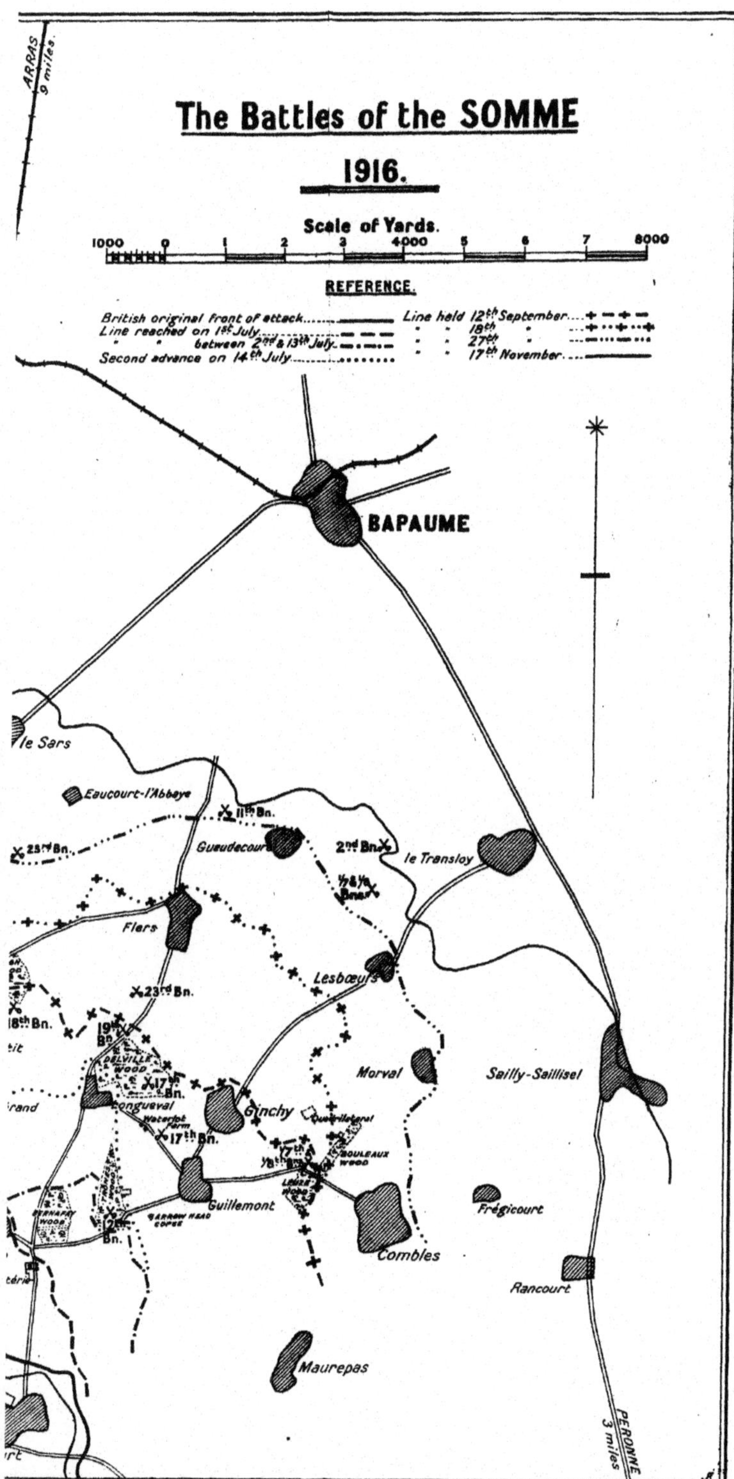
The Battles of the SOMME
1916.
Scale of Yards.
1000 0 1 2 3 4000 5 6 7 8000
REFERENCE.
British original front of attack
Line reached on 1st July
" " between 2nd & 13th July
Second advance on 14th July
Line held 12th September
" " 18th "
" " 27th "
" " 17th November
ARRAS 9 miles
BAPAUME
le Sars
Eaucourt-l'Abbaye
11th Bn.
25th Bn.
Gueudecourt
2nd Bn.
le Transloy
Flers
Lesbœufs
23rd Bn.
18th Bn.
19th Bn.
DELVILLE WOOD
17th Bn.
Longueval
Waterlot Farm
17th Bn.
Ginchy
Quadrilateral
Morval
Sailly-Saillisel
BOULEAUX WOOD
LEUZE WOOD
Guillemont
ARROW HEAD COPSE
BERNAFAY WOOD
Bn.
Combles
Frégicourt
Rancourt
Maurepas
PERONNE 3 miles

[To face p. 330.

## CHAPTER XXV.

# EGYPT AND PALESTINE.

## Western Frontier.

### THE AFFAIR OF HALAZIN.

23rd January, 1916.

NEW YEAR'S DAY, 1916, still found the 2/7th and 2/8th Middlesex at Matruh in Western Egypt. The early days of January were marked by bad weather, which made active operations impossible. On the first of the month a collection of 80 tents was observed by aeroplanes at Gebel Howimil, and a column was formed to clear up the situation in that neighbourhood; but it was not until the evening of the 9th that the weather improved, and it was the 12th before the roads were sufficiently passable to warrant a start being made. 1ST JANUARY. 2/7TH & 2/8TH BATTALIONS. 12TH JANUARY.

The column, which included the 2/7th Battalion (Lieut.-Colonel J. S. Drew), reached Baggush on 13th, and on the 14th the march was continued to Gebel Howimil, where several Senussi camps were destroyed, a quantity of stores burnt and some camels and livestock taken, but nowhere was hostile opposition encountered. The column returned to Baggush the same evening, having covered during the day close on 50 miles. These operations involved much hard marching for the 2/7th Middlesex, but they had the satisfaction of burning a Senussi Zowiat (or monastery), a centre of enemy activity. 2/7TH BATTALION. 14TH JANUARY.

For the next few weeks little excitement came the way of the 2/7th Middlesex, the Battalion being engaged in the reconstruction of the Matruh defences.

Meanwhile the 2/8th Battalion took part in an expedition against a considerable enemy force which, on 12th January, had been discovered by aerial reconnaissance located at Hazalin, 25 miles south-west of Matruh. This camp comprised at least 2/8TH BATTALION. 12TH JANUARY.

2/8TH BATTALION. 100 European and 250 Bedouin tents, including that of the Grand Senussi.

The force, under General Wallace, consisted of some six squadrons of cavalry, five battalions of infantry, artillery, signal section, Field Ambulance and a detachment of the R.N. Armoured Car Division.

23RD JANUARY. The force moved off at 6 a.m. on 23rd January in two columns, right and left. The 2/8th Middlesex (less two Companies—"C" and "D") belonged to the left column, but "A" and "B" Companies formed part of the reserve, and as such remained parked at Bir Shola during the operations. The attack on the Senussi was successful, some 200 of the enemy being killed and about 500 wounded. On the 25th the force returned to Mersa Matruh.

22ND FEB. 2/7TH BATTALION. On the 22nd February "C" and "D" Companies of the 2/7th Middlesex arrived from Alexandria—the Battalion was at last reunited.

By the end of March the Senussi army had broken up, and the bulk of the Western Force returned to Alexandria, but the 2/7th and 2/8th Middlesex remained at Mersa Matruh. Elements of the enemy's army, however, still roamed about the country, and a force, consisting of the 2/7th Middlesex, 1/6th Royal Scots, Camel Corps, mountain artillery and armoured cars, was ordered to assemble at Sollum to deal with them. Lieut.-Colonel Drew, of the 2/7th, was in command, Major Whinney assuming temporary command of the 2/7th Battalion.

The situation at Sollum at the time was interesting. The enemy in his retreat had hidden in wells and caves great stores of arms and ammunition. A systematic search over many miles of country was made for them and considerable quantities were recovered. The Turks, at this period, were endeavouring to rally the Senussi forces and organise another invasion of Egypt further south. Turkish officers, ammunition and equipment were being landed from German submarines in a lonely little bay, some 25 miles from Sollum, thence conveyed by land to the scattered Senussi.

On the 7th April a detachment of four armoured cars, accompanied by the machine-gun section of the 2/7th Middlesex, conducted a raid from Sollum on Dur es Sahel, 60 miles west of Sollum. The Middlesex machine guns were put into Ford cars. The raid was a complete surprise: a number of the enemy were killed, a Turkish captain captured, much ammunition was destroyed and the village burnt. Tarek Bey, the Turkish commander, clad in night attire, escaped by galloping away into the desert. 2/7TH BATTALION.

This was the last action of importance in which the 2/7th Middlesex took part in Egypt. Early in May orders were received for both Battalions to prepare for France. On the 5th May the 2/7th and 2/8th moved to Alexandria, embarked on the "Saxonia" on 8th and reached Marseilles on 15th. But there had been a case of typhus on board and the two Battalions were therefore ordered in quarantine, to a camp at La Valentie, 10 miles out of Marseilles.

After disembarkation the 2/7th and 2/8th Battalions marched through Marseilles, where they had a wonderful ovation from the French: "The route lay through the crowded streets of the city," said Colonel Drew. "The band responded by playing the 'Marseillaise' and the cheering doubled. It was a very pleasant welcome to France. In the pink of health, bronzed with the Egyptian sun and hardened by nearly two years' soldiering, the Battalions presented a very fine appearance and fully justified the compliments one heard on all sides." Three tedious weeks were spent at La Valentie, but on 10th and 11th June the two Battalions entrained for Rouen. 2/7TH & 2/8TH BATTALION.

But, alas! here ends the history of the 2/7th and 2/8th Middlesex, for, in common with other Battalions from Gallipoli and Egypt which had arrived in France, they were to be broken up and disbanded, and the officers and men transferred to other units. The fatal day was the 13th June, the officers of the 2/7th going to different Divisions, but the other ranks to various Battalions of the 56th (London) Division. The 2/8th sent a large draft of men to the 1/8th Battalion of the 56th Division, but where the others went it is impossible to say. It is, however, worthy of record that the C.O. of a Battalion reinforced by men from the disbanded 2/7th said: "My Battalion was decimated. We didn't know which way to turn. Then came your chaps. They were the best lot we ever had and were the salvation of our Battalion." 13TH JUNE.

# CHAPTER XXVI.

# THE EASTERN FRONTIER AND PALESTINE.

## The Defence of Egypt.

### THE BATTLE OF RUMANI.

4th–5th August, 1916.

20/19TH BATTALION.

1ST JANUARY.

THE evacuation of Gallipoli was followed by the transfer of the 53rd Division to the Egyptian Expeditionary Force, and on 1st January the 2/10th Middlesex (Lieut.-Colonel C. H. Pank) was located at Beni Salim Camp, Wardan, Egypt, engaged in training. On

15TH FEB.

the 15th February the 160th Brigade (53rd Division), to which the 2/10th belonged, moved by rail to Medinet el Fayoom, one Company—"C"—under Captain A. O. Dick, establishing a post at Kafr Mahfuz on 22nd. On the same date Nos. 1 and 2 platoons of "A" Company were sent out to establish posts at Kom She Sha and Kom Abu Radi respectively. All these posts

12TH MARCH.

were relieved between 12th and 15th March and returned to the Battalion which was then located in Flazab Camp, Fayoum.

30TH MAY.

On the 30th May, the 2/10th took over trenches about 12 miles east of Ismalia from the 55th and 53rd Australian Battalions. These trenches extended from Gazelle Heights (exclusive), on the south, to the Plateau, on the north (inclusive). June and

6TH JULY.

July were months of work and training. On the 6th of the latter month Lieut.-Colonel C. H. Pank vacated command of the Battalion and returned to England: he was succeeded on 24th by Lieut.-Colonel V. L. N. Pearson.

4TH AUGUST.

In the Battle of Rumani, which took place on 4th and 5th August, the 2/10th Middlesex were not engaged, but the Battalion was in the area east of the Suez Canal and is therefore entitled to that Battle Honour.

From August to the end of 1916 there is little of interest in

31ST DEC.

the Diary of the 2/10th Battalion, and the last day of the year found the Middlesex men at Mazar, carrying out Company training.

# The Duke of Cambridge's (Own Middlesex Regiment).*

(57th and 77th Foot.)

## Allocations of Battalions to Brigades and Divisions, 1914–1918.

1st Battalion. Went out to WESTERN FRONT as Lines of Communication Troops August, 1914, and posted to 19th Infantry Brigade, 21st August, 1914; Brigade under IIIrd Corps till end of September, 1914; then joined 6th Division till 28th May, 1915; then transferred to 27th Division, transferred to 2nd Division, 19th July, 1915, to 33rd Division 25th November, 1915. Battalion transferred to 98th Infantry Brigade 27th November, 1915.

2nd " Went out to WESTERN FRONT with 23rd Infantry Brigade, 8th Division, November, 1914.

3rd " Went out to WESTERN FRONT with 85th Infantry Brigade, 28th Division, January, 1915; Brigade transferred to 3rd Division, 19th February, 1915; rejoining 28th Division, 6th April, 1915. Division removed to SALONIKA, November, 1915.

4th " Went out to WESTERN FRONT with 8th Infantry Brigade, 3rd Division, August, 1914; transferred to 63rd Infantry Brigade, 21st Division, 14th November, 1915. Brigade transferred to 37th Division, 7th July, 1916.

* The pre-war and war-time title of the Regiment.

7th (T.F.) Bn. Went out to GIBRALTAR September, 1914; moved to WESTERN FRONT, February, 1915, and posted to 23rd Infantry Brigade, 8th Division, 15th March, 1915, temporarily amalgamated with 8th Battalion, 21st June, 1915; resumed independent formation, 2nd August, 1915; transferred to 167th Infantry Brigade, 56th Division, on formation of latter, 5th February, 1916.

2/7th „ Went to GIBRALTAR, February, 1915; moved to EGYPT September, 1915, part of Egyptian Garrison till July, 1916, then moved to WESTERN FRONT and disbanded.

8th „ Went to GIBRALTAR, September, 1914; moved to WESTERN FRONT, March, 1915; and posted to 85th Infantry Brigade, then in 3rd Division. Joining 11th March, 1915; Brigade rejoined 28th Division, 6th April, 1915. Battalion transferred to 23rd Infantry Brigade, 8th Division, 21st June, 1915. Amalgamated temporarily with 7th Battalion same day. Resumed independent formation 2nd August, 1915, and transferred to 25th Infantry Brigade, 8th Division. Transferred to 70th Infantry Brigade, 23rd Division (attached to 8th Division), 23rd October, 1915; transferred to 167th Infantry Brigade, 56th Division, 5th February, 1916.

2/8th „ As 2/7th Battalion (q.v.).

9th „ Went out to INDIA with 44th Division, October, 1914. Moved to MESOPOTAMIA November, 1917, and posted to 53rd Indian Infantry Brigade, 18th Indian Division.

10th „ Went out to INDIA with 44th Division, October, 1914.

2/10th „ Went out to GALLIPOLI with 160th Infantry Brigade, 53rd Division, July, 1915; Division moved to EGYPT, December, 1915. Disbanded 20th August, 1918.

| | |
|---|---|
| 3/10th Bn. | Went out to WESTERN FRONT, June, 1917; attached temporarily to South African Brigade, 9th Division, 6th June–20th July, 1917, then posted to 10th Infantry Brigade, 4th Division. Disbanded 8th February, 1918. |
| 11th (S.) „ | Went out to WESTERN FRONT with 36th Infantry Brigade, 12th Division, May, 1915. Disbanded 7th February, 1918. |
| 12th „ | Went out to WESTERN FRONT with 54th Infantry Brigade, 18th Division, July, 1915. Disbanded 12th February, 1918, and became 18th Entrenching Battalion. |
| 13th „ | Went out to WESTERN FRONT with 73rd Infantry Brigade, 24th Division, September, 1915. |
| 16th „ | Went out to WESTERN FRONT with 100th Infantry Brigade, 33rd Division, November, 1915; transferred to General Headquarters 25th February, 1916, to 86th Infantry Brigade, 29th Division, 25th April, 1916. Disbanded 7th February, 1917. |
| 17th „ | Went out to WESTERN FRONT with 100th Infantry Brigade, 33rd Division, November, 1915; transferred to 6th Infantry Brigade, 2nd Division, 8th December, 1915. Disbanded 10th February, 1918. |
| 18th „ | Went out to WESTERN FRONT with 33rd Division as Pioneers, November, 1915. |
| 19th „ | Went out to WESTERN FRONT with 41st Division as Pioneers May, 1916; Division moved to ITALY, November, 1917; returned to WESTERN FRONT, March, 1918. |
| 20th „ | Went out to WESTERN FRONT with 121st Infantry Brigade, 40th Division, June, 1916; reduced to Training Cadre 16th May, 1918, and transferred to 16th Division 31st May, 1918, to 14th Division 16th June, 1918; returning to UNITED KINGDOM 16th June, 1918. Re-formed and returned to WESTERN FRONT 1st July, 1918, with 43rd Infantry Brigade, 14th Division. |

| | |
|---|---|
| 21st Battalion. | Went out to WESTERN FRONT with 121st Infantry Brigade, 40th Division, June, 1916; transferred to 119th Infantry Brigade, same Division, February, 1918; reduced to Training Cadre 5th May, 1918, transferred to 34th Division, 3rd June, 1918, to 39th, 17th June, 1918, to 25th Division 29th June, 1918; returned to UNITED KINGDOM, 30th June, 1918. Left in UNITED KINGDOM when Divisional Headquarters returned to WESTERN FRONT, September, 1918. |
| 23rd " | Went out to WESTERN FRONT with 123rd Infantry Brigade, 41st Division, May, 1916. Division moved to ITALY, November, 1917; returned to WESTERN FRONT, March, 1918. |
| 25th " (Garrison.) | Went out to INDIA; moved to HONG KONG; sent to VLADIVOSTOCK August, 1918, in SIBERIA. |
| 26th Battalion (S.) | Went out to SALONIKA, 1916; joined the 27th Division as Pioneers 28th August, 1916. |
| No. 1 Special Company. | Formed at Mill Hill Barracks, April, 1919. Went out to N.R.E.F., April, 1919; returned to England 17th October, 1919, and was broken up. |

# INDEX.

Lightning Source UK Ltd.
Milton Keynes UK
UKOW06f0719311217
315211UK00015B/1568/P

9 781847 345745